The Concise
CHILDREN'S
ENCYCLOPEDIA

Contributors

David Lambert M.A.
Brian Murphy M.A.
Brian Williams B.A.
Keith Lye B.A. F.R.G.S.
Christopher Maynard B.A. M.Sc.
Anita Townsend B.A.
Jenny Vaughan B.A.
Catherine Dell L. es L.

Educational Advisers

Harry le Comte
Headteacher
St Martin of Porres School,
London
Joan Jacobs
Headteacher
The Holy Family Primary School,
Hertfordshire

Editorial

John Grisewood B.A.
Leslie Firth B.A.
Jennifer Justice B.Sc.
Vivian Croot B.A.
Jane Olliver B.A.
Simon Franklin B.Sc.

Michael Dempsey M.A.
Markie Robson-Scott M.A.
Hilary Bunce B.A.
Belinda Hollyer B.A.
Caroline Royds B.A.
Denise Gardner

The Concise
CHILDREN'S
ENCYCLOPEDIA

Edited by

John Paton

KINGFISHER BOOKS

This edition (revised) published in 1984 by
Kingfisher Books Limited, Elsley Court,
20–22 Great Titchfield Street, London W1P 7AD.
A Grisewood & Dempsey Company

© Grisewood & Dempsey Limited 1982

First published in 1982 by Ward Lock Limited
Abridged from Finding Out Children's Encyclopedia

BRITISH LIBRARY CATALOGUING IN PUBLICATION DATA
    The Concise children's encyclopedia
    1. Children's encyclopedias and dictionaries
    I. Paton, John
    032   AG5

ISBN 0 86272 100 8

Printed and bound in Portugal

About Your Encyclopedia

The entries in THE CONCISE CHILDREN'S ENCYC-LOPEDIA are arranged in alphabetical order. You should therefore find most of the information you want by first looking up the main entry word. If the subject you are looking for does not have an entry to itself, look in the Index at the back of the book. Usually you will find some information about your subject in another article.

Throughout the encyclopedia you will find words printed in small capitals, like this: ALLIGATORS. These words are *cross-references*, and when you meet one you will know that there is a separate entry on that subject in the encyclopedia. That entry may have more information about the subject you are looking up.

In addition to the main Index, you will find a Subject Index at the end of the book. This will also help you to find articles that have further information on the subject in which you are interested. The Subject Index is also a study guide for any of your projects.

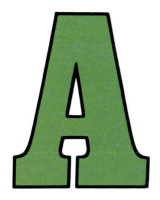

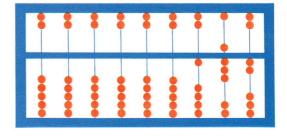

The abacus can be used to add, subtract, multiply and divide.

ABACUS

The abacus is a simple counting machine first used by the ancient Greeks and Romans. It consists of rows of beads strung on wires; those on the first wire count as ones, those on the second wire count as tens, on the third wire they count as hundreds, and so on. The abacus is still used in Eastern countries such as China and Japan, and experts on the abacus can calculate more quickly than most westerners can do with pencil and paper. The Romans sometimes used small stones as counters. They called these counters *calculi* and it is from this that we get our word 'calculate'.

AARDVARK

The aardvark is an animal that eats termites. When it has broken open a termites' nest with its powerful claws, it pokes in its long, sticky tongue and pulls it out covered with the insects. The aardvark lives in central and southern Africa. It has large ears like a donkey and is an expert burrower. If caught away from its home it can dig a hole for itself at astonishing speed. The word 'aardvark' is Dutch for 'earth pig'. These shy animals can be 2 metres (over 6 ft) long and nearly a metre high.

The aardvark is a strange-looking animal that lives in the dry parts of Africa. It spends the day in holes which it digs in the ground with its long, strong claws.

ABBEY

An abbey is a monastery or convent, the home of monks or nuns, headed by an abbot or abbess. During the MIDDLE AGES many abbeys were built all over Europe. Some of them had beautiful churches attached to them. Westminster Abbey in London, for example, is part of an abbey begun by EDWARD the Confessor, though most of the other abbey buildings have been destroyed.

The abbey often included an open space, or great court; cloisters where the monks walked, studied and thought; and a dormitory where they slept. There were also kitchens, stables, storehouses, a guest-house and vegetable gardens within the abbey walls. The monks ate their meals in a refectory, or dining hall.

They did all the work in the abbey, including cleaning, cooking, carpentry, farming and beekeeping. Some abbeys became famous for making wine and spirits. Others are well known for their honey, their medicines and their cheeses. Monks were one of the few groups of educated people, and their beautiful hand-written and illustrated books were famous.

Between 1524 and 1540 all the abbeys in England were closed down by HENRY VIII and their lands and possessions taken away.

A medieval abbey included the abbey church (1), cloisters (2), refectory (3), kitchens (4), dormitory (5), Chapter House (6), main gate (7), guest-house (8), stables (9) and brew and bakehouse (10). Old or sick monks were housed in the infirmary (11).

ABORIGINES

The word 'aborigine' really means the first people who lived in any country. But it is now used when we talk about the natives of AUSTRALIA. These are slim black people with broad noses and black wavy hair. They came to Australia thousands of years ago from south-eastern Asia. In Australia they had no permanent homes but wandered about the desert hunting or gathering their food. Their chief weapons were the BOOMERANG and the throwing spear.

The Aborigines were very badly treated by the white men who came to Australia. Today Aborigines have rights as Australian citizens. Their numbers are increasing.

This Aborigine still follows a primitive way of life. Many others now live and work alongside white Australians.

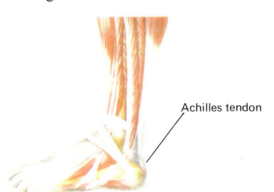

Achilles' heel was his only vulnerable spot. The Achilles tendon is the name given to the hard tendon connecting the calf muscles to the heel.

Vinegar (1) contains acetic acid. Its sharp flavour makes salads more appetizing. Lemon juice's sharp tang (2) is actually citric acid.

ACHILLES

Achilles was the Greek hero of the siege of Troy in HOMER's poem the *Iliad*. Achilles' father was human but his mother was a goddess. She tried to make him immortal like herself by dipping him in the River Styx. Unfortunately the heel she held him by stayed dry and unprotected. After killing the Trojan hero Hector, and just as Troy was about to fall, Achilles was killed by an arrow which hit him in the heel.

ACID

An acid is a liquid chemical COMPOUND that has a sour taste. Some acids, such as sulphuric acid, nitric acid and hydrochloric acid, are very strong and can *corrode*, or eat away, even the strongest metals. Other acids are harmless. These include the citric acid that gives lemons and oranges their sharp taste, and the acetic acid in vinegar. Lactic acid is produced when milk goes sour. All acids turn a special sort of paper called *litmus* from blue to red.

AFRICA

Africa is the world's second largest continent. It covers an area of 30,319,000 square km (11,706,000 square miles), one-fifth of the world's land. Africa stretches from the Mediterranean Sea in the north to the Cape of Good Hope at its tip in the south. Large parts of Africa are empty wasteland. The burning SAHARA Desert spreads over much of the northern part of the continent. Near the equator, which runs through the centre of Africa, are thick rain forests. There the trees grow so close together that their leaves blot out the sunlight.

More than a third of Africa is a high, flat plain, or plateau. Grassland called *savanna* covers much of the plateau region. Great herds of grazing animals roam the savanna. They include zebras, giraffes, wildebeest and impala. Other animals, like lions, cheetahs and hyenas, prey upon the grazing animals. In the past, many animals were killed by hunters, but today special reserves have been set up to protect them.

This beautifully carved ivory mask was worn as an ornament by the king of the West African kingdom of Benin. Great empires grew up in Africa before the white men came. Another of these was the civilization of Zimbabwe, built in the 800s where Zimbabwe-Rhodesia lies today.

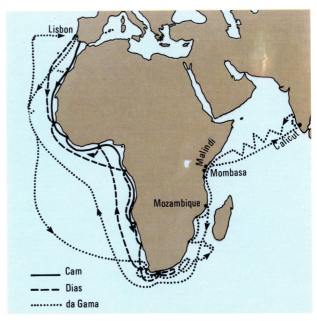

The routes followed by Diogo Cam, Bartholomeu Dias and Vasco da Gama, the Portuguese explorers who first charted the African coast.

Mt Kilimanjaro, the highest mountain in Africa, rises 5895 metres (19,340 feet) in Tanzania. Africa's largest lake, Lake Victoria, lies between Kenya and Tanzania. The continent's great rivers are the NILE, CONGO, (now called Zaire), Niger and Zambezi.

Many different types of people live in Africa. In North Africa are ARABS and Berbers, who mostly follow the Moslem religion. So-called 'black Africa' lies south of the Sahara Desert. The Negroid peoples who live there make up three-quarters of Africa's population. People with European and Asian ancestors make up the rest of the population.

Most Africans are farmers, growing crops such as cocoa, coffee, cotton, sisal and tea. Africa produces nearly three-quarters of the world's palm oil and palm kernels, which are used to make things like soap and margarine. The continent has valuable mineral resources, too, including gold and diamonds, copper, tin and bauxite for making aluminium. ▷

Arab dhows like this one filled the busy East African harbours at Mozambique and Mombasa when the Portuguese explorer da Gama visited them. These lateen-rigged boats have changed little in design over the centuries.

5

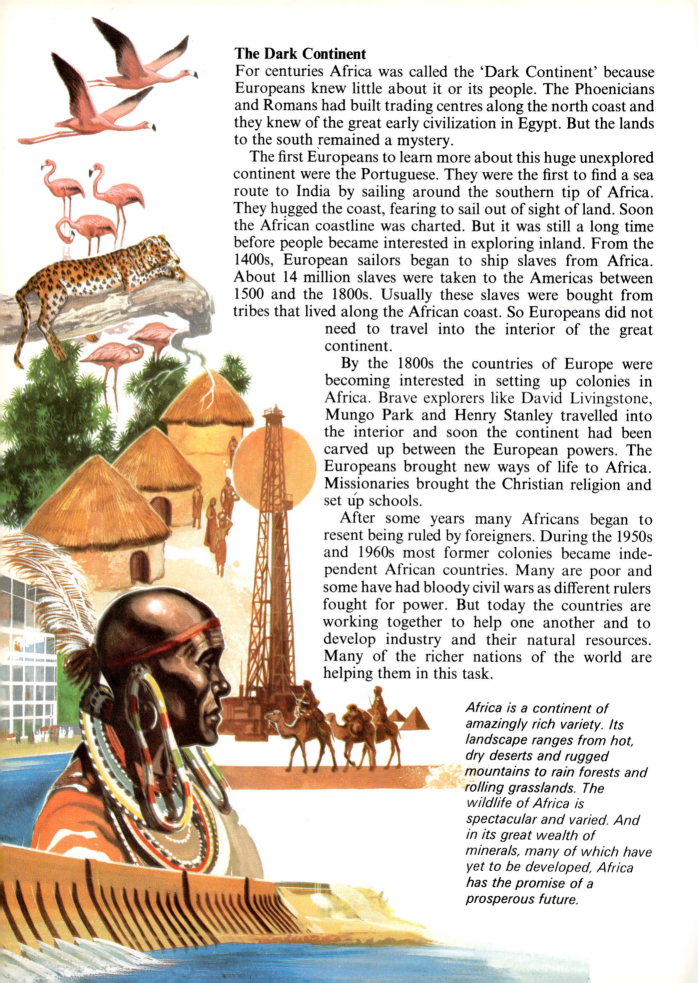

The Dark Continent

For centuries Africa was called the 'Dark Continent' because Europeans knew little about it or its people. The Phoenicians and Romans had built trading centres along the north coast and they knew of the great early civilization in Egypt. But the lands to the south remained a mystery.

The first Europeans to learn more about this huge unexplored continent were the Portuguese. They were the first to find a sea route to India by sailing around the southern tip of Africa. They hugged the coast, fearing to sail out of sight of land. Soon the African coastline was charted. But it was still a long time before people became interested in exploring inland. From the 1400s, European sailors began to ship slaves from Africa. About 14 million slaves were taken to the Americas between 1500 and the 1800s. Usually these slaves were bought from tribes that lived along the African coast. So Europeans did not need to travel into the interior of the great continent.

By the 1800s the countries of Europe were becoming interested in setting up colonies in Africa. Brave explorers like David Livingstone, Mungo Park and Henry Stanley travelled into the interior and soon the continent had been carved up between the European powers. The Europeans brought new ways of life to Africa. Missionaries brought the Christian religion and set up schools.

After some years many Africans began to resent being ruled by foreigners. During the 1950s and 1960s most former colonies became independent African countries. Many are poor and some have had bloody civil wars as different rulers fought for power. But today the countries are working together to help one another and to develop industry and their natural resources. Many of the richer nations of the world are helping them in this task.

Africa is a continent of amazingly rich variety. Its landscape ranges from hot, dry deserts and rugged mountains to rain forests and rolling grasslands. The wildlife of Africa is spectacular and varied. And in its great wealth of minerals, many of which have yet to be developed, Africa has the promise of a prosperous future.

AIR

Air is all around us—it surrounds the Earth in a layer we call the *atmosphere*. All living things must have air in order to live. Air is colourless and has no smell. Yet it is really a mixture of a number of different gases. We can feel air when the wind blows, and we know air has weight. Air carries sounds—without it we would not be able to hear, because sounds cannot travel in a VACUUM.

The chief gas in air is nitrogen, which makes up nearly four-fifths of the air. About one-fifth of the air is made up of OXYGEN. Air also holds some water in very fine particles called *vapour*. When we talk about the degree of HUMIDITY in the air, it is the amount of water in the air we are measuring.

The air that surrounds the Earth gets thinner the higher you go. All high-flying aircraft have to keep the air in their cabins at ground-level pressure so that passengers can breathe normally. In the same way mountaineers carry their own air supply because the air at the top of high mountains is too thin to breathe properly.

When air is heated it expands and becomes lighter. In a hot-air balloon, air is heated by a jet of burning gas. The balloon rises when the weight of the gas plus the balloon is lighter than the surrounding air.

Air presses on everything. To show this, take a glass of water and place a card over the top (left). Turn the glass upside down (centre). When you take your hand away (right) the card stays in place. This shows that the air pressure beneath is greater than the weight of the water.

AIRCRAFT

Men have always dreamed of being able to fly like birds. At first, they attached artificial 'wings' to their arms and tried to flap them. They failed, because their muscles were not strong enough to keep them in the air.

In the 1800s, the British scientist Sir George Cayley suggested that a vehicle could be built that was designed like a bird but with fixed wings. Many people tried to build such a machine, and some built gliders. But these could only fly short distances and were difficult to control.

In 1903 two American brothers, Orville and Wilbur WRIGHT, built the *Flyer*, a flimsy-looking machine with a petrol engine at the back. They were successful. The first powered flight in the world took place at Kitty Hawk, North Carolina, on December 17, 1903. The new means of transport did not catch on straight away. But by 1908, after the Wright Brothers had demonstrated their planes all over Europe, many others had caught the flying 'bug', and the development of aircraft was rapid. In 1909 Louis BLERIOT flew the English Channel. During WORLD WAR I, aircraft were used both for watching enemy movements (called *reconnaissance*), and later for fighting.

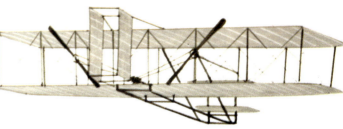

Wilbur and Orville Wright's flying machine, the Flyer, *was powered by a petrol engine. The engine was attached to two propellers by bicycle chains. The Air Age began on December 17, 1903, when Orville flew the* Flyer *for 37 metres and landed safely.*

A cross-section through an aircraft's wing shows its aerofoil *shape. It is curved on top and flat on the bottom. When air passes over and under the wing a difference in air pressure is created because of the curved shape. This lifts the wing, and the aircraft flies.*

Hawker Hurricane

Messerschmitt Bf 109

Two famous fighters of World War II, the Messerschmitt Bf 109 and the Hawker Hurricane.

Spad

The Spad was a favourite fighter plane of World War I. Nearly 15,000 were flown by the Allies. The Fokker D-VII was the best German fighter of the war.

Fokker D-VII

The great Boeing 747 'jumbo-jet' can carry almost 500 passengers on journeys of up to 9000 km (5600 miles). It flies at a speed of 950 km/h (600 mph).

The war proved that aircraft were not only useful, but a necessity. In 1919 John Alcock and Arthur Whitten Brown made the first Atlantic crossing; Charles LIND-BERGH made the first solo crossing in 1927. In 1936 the Douglas DC-3, or Dakota, went into service, and proved itself the most successful airliner ever built. WORLD WAR II saw the development of fast fighter aircraft and heavy bombers, and by the end of the war jet aircraft had appeared.

The first aircraft to fly faster than the speed of sound (*supersonic* speed) was tested in 1947. Today, military fighter aircraft and some airliners such as *Concorde* are de-signed for supersonic speeds. Others, like the 'jumbo' jets, can carry almost 500 people and big freight loads.

Getting off the Ground

To fly, an aircraft must have *lift* to raise it against the pull of the Earth's GRAVITY. This lift is produced by the movement of air over the aircraft's wings, which have a special shape called an *aerofoil*. The force (*thrust*) needed to push the aircraft forward comes either from propellers or from a jet engine. The tail on the aircraft steadies it and helps to control its flight. The *rudder* and *elevators* on the tail and the *ailerons* on the wings all help the pilot to control the craft. A modern airliner also has a wide variety of controls to help the pilot keep a check on all the aircraft's systems and to navigate on course.

Concorde, *the supersonic airliner, has wide swept-back wings designed in what is called a* delta *shape. This shape is best for high-speed control of the aircraft. Concorde can cruise at a speed of over 2000 km/hr (1200 mph) for almost three hours. The nose of the aircraft can be moved down to give the pilot a better view of the runway at take-off and landing. Concorde carries up to 140 passengers.*

9

ALBANIA

Albania is a small, rugged country that lies between Yugoslavia and Greece on the eastern shore of the Adriatic Sea. Most Albanians live in small, remote mountain villages. Albanian farmers grow wheat, barley, tobacco and cotton. Beneath the ground there are deposits of chrome, copper, iron, oil and natural gas. Albania was ruled by Turkey for over 400 years. After World War II it became a communist state.

ALEXANDER THE GREAT

Alexander the Great (356–323 BC) was a ruler of GREECE and one of the greatest generals that ever lived. The son of Philip of Macedon, Alexander conquered the Greek city-states after he became king when Philip died in 336 BC. He then marched east to conquer Persia, which was at that time the greatest empire in the world. By 327 Alexander's empire stretched from Greece to India. When his armies reached India they were worn out from marching and fighting. Alexander had to turn back.

Alexander the Great, who conquered an empire that stretched from Greece to India.

ALBATROSS

The albatross is a large seabird that spends most of its time in the air over the oceans. The wandering albatross has a wingspan of 3·5 metres (11 feet), the largest span of any bird. Most albatrosses live in regions south of the Equator, where they soar gracefully over the waves. They come ashore only to breed or in stormy weather. Albatrosses will follow ships for hundreds of kilometres, picking up scraps of food thrown overboard.

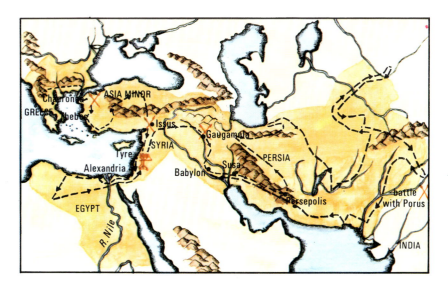

The route Alexander followed into Asia. By the time he was 25 he had conquered all the land from Greece to India.

Alfred the Great was a scholar as well as a warrior. He translated many Latin books into English so that his people could read them.

When he reached BABYLON he became ill with a fever and died. He was still only 33. Alexander's body was carried back to Alexandria, the great city he had founded in EGYPT. There it was placed in a magnificent tomb.

ALFRED THE GREAT

Alfred the Great (849–899) was a wise and able ruler who saved England from being conquered by the Danes. He formed an army and a navy to defend his Kingdom of Wessex from the invaders, and drove out the Danes in 896. When peace returned, Alfred did much to bring justice and education to his people. Under his direction the Anglo-Saxon Chronicle was begun. It was a record of the events of each year, and much of our knowledge of King Alfred's time comes from this record.

ALLIGATORS

The alligator is a large reptile that belongs to the same family as the CROCODILE. There are two species: one is the American alligator of the south-eastern USA; the other is the smaller Chinese alligator that lives in the YANGTZE RIVER. Alligators look very like crocodiles, but have broader, flatter heads with rounded snouts.

The alligator lays its eggs in a mud nest. When the young hatch, she helps them down to the water, carrying them gently in her huge jaws.

11

AMAZON, RIVER

The Amazon is the mightiest river in South America, and, at a length of 6448 km (4000 miles) is the second longest in the world, after the Nile.

This fly, trapped in resin that fossilized millions of years ago to become amber, is beautifully preserved.

AMBER

Amber looks like stone, but it is in fact the fossilized, or hardened, resin that oozed from pine trees millions of years ago. It is often used to make jewellery.

AMERICA

The word 'America' is often used to mean the United States, but it originally covered a much larger area that today is more properly called the Americas. The Americas include North America, Central America and South America, and the islands of the Caribbean and northern Canada. The Americas were named after the Italian navigator Amerigo Vespucci, who explored part of the South American coast in the 1400s, about the same time as COLUMBUS.

AMERICAN INDIANS

American Indians are the native peoples of the Americas—that is, the first people to live there. They are known as Indians because when Christopher Columbus reached America in 1492 he thought he had arrived in India.

The Indians of the Americas are thought to have crossed to the North American continent from Asia about 20,000 years ago. Very gradually, over the centuries, they spread through North America and down into what is now Central and South America. They developed different ways of life according to where they lived. 'American Indians' now usually refers to the Indians of North America.

There, in the eastern woodlands, the Iroquois and Algonquin tribes built domed WIGWAMS of wood and bark and hunted deer and other game. On the Great Plains, tribes like the Sioux and Cheyenne lived off the huge herds of bison which they hunted, first on foot, and then on horses brought to the New World by the Spaniards.

When Europeans began to settle in America, conflict broke out as they invaded the Indians' hunting grounds. Many Indians were killed or forced to move farther west. By the late 1800s almost all the tribes had been given land on special reservations by the US government. Today many Indians are working to gain equal opportunities for themselves as American citizens.

AMPHIBIANS

Amphibians are animals such as FROGS, TOADS, salamanders and newts. They can live in water or on land, but most of them start their lives in water. Amphibians are cold-blooded creatures. They do not drink like other animals but absorb water directly through their skins. For this reason they must keep their skins moist. Amphibians were one of the earliest groups of animals on Earth. They crawled out of the water and on to the land about 400 million years ago.

All amphibians have backbones. Nearly all of them lay their eggs in water, in a layer of jelly which protects them. When the young amphibians hatch, they feed on algae (tiny water plants). A young frog at this stage is called a tadpole. It breathes the oxygen dissolved in water through GILLS. After two or three months the tadpole begins to change into an adult. Its tail gradually disappears, and its gills turn into LUNGS. Hind legs and then front legs appear. The little frog leaves the water and spends the rest of its life as an air-breathing adult. But it must return to the water to mate and lay its eggs.

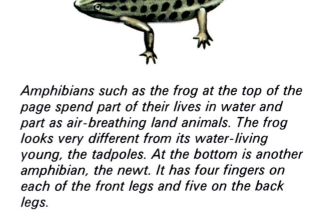

Amphibians such as the frog at the top of the page spend part of their lives in water and part as air-breathing land animals. The frog looks very different from its water-living young, the tadpoles. At the bottom is another amphibian, the newt. It has four fingers on each of the front legs and five on the back legs.

ANDERSEN, HANS CHRISTIAN

Hans Christian Andersen (1805–1875) was a Danish storyteller, whose fairy tales, such as *The Little Mermaid* and *The Ugly Duckling*, are still popular all over the world.

ANGLE

An angle is formed when two straight lines meet. The size of all angles is measured in degrees. The angle that forms the corner of a square is called a 'right' angle and has 90 degrees. An *acute* angle is less than 90 degrees; an *obtuse* angle is between 90 and 180 degrees.

ANGLO-SAXONS

Anglo-Saxon is the name given to the group of Germanic tribes who settled in Britain during the AD 400s and 500s. These tribes were the Angles, Saxons and Jutes. They gradually occupied all of England, driving the original Celtic people of Britain into Wales and Cornwall. By the 700s there were seven main Anglo-Saxon kingdoms— Wessex, Sussex, Kent, Essex, East Anglia, Mercia and Northumbria. The Anglo-Saxon language is one of the two main ingredients of modern English.

During 1938–1939 an Anglo-Saxon chieftain's funeral ship with many beautiful treasures was excavated at Sutton Hoo in Suffolk (right). The Anglo-Saxons were fond of highly decorated jewellery like the solid gold brooch below.

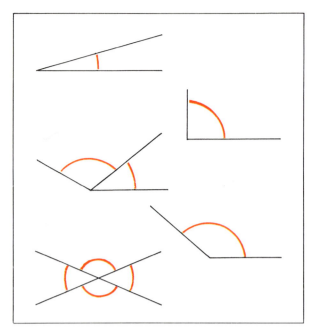

Above: The top angle is acute; that on the right is a right angle; the one below the right angle is an obtuse angle. The two angles below the acute are called adjacent angles. Those at the bottom are opposed angles.

Few animals can live in the harsh Antarctic. But penguins huddle together in large colonies. Nowadays husky dogs have been replaced by motor tractors.

ANTARCTIC

The Antarctic is the continent that surrounds the South Pole. It is a vast region of cold waste, with very little animal or plant life. Nearly all of the Antarctic is covered by an ice cap, broken only by a few mountain ranges. This ice cap averages 2500 metres (8200 feet) in thickness, but is as much as 4700 metres (15,400 feet) thick in places.

ANTEATERS

The anteater of South America is a curious creature with a long, tapering snout. This snout is specially shaped to winkle ants, termites and grubs from their nests. It catches the insects with its long, whip-like tongue. An anteater may measure over 2 metres (7 feet) from the tip of its tail to its snout. It uses its strong front claws to tear open ant and termite nests.

The claws on the front feet of the anteater are so long that the animal has to walk on the sides of its feet instead of the soles.

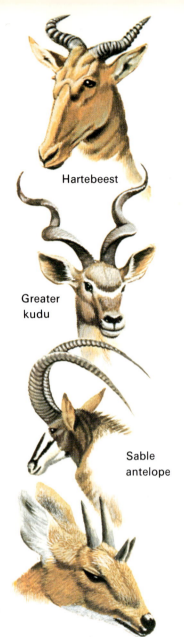

Hartebeest

Greater
kudu

Sable
antelope

Four-horned antelope

ANTELOPES

Antelopes are a family of grazing animals with horns and hoofs. They look rather like DEER, but are actually related to the goat and the ox. Most antelopes live on the African plains. They are fast runners and often live in large herds, fleeing suddenly at any hint of danger. Some of the best known are the impala, the waterbuck, the hartebeest, the gnu, the eland and the little dik-dik, hardly bigger than a rabbit.

The hartebeest has short, screw horns. More handsome are the long corkscrew horns of the greater kudu. Longest of all are the splendid curving horns of the sable antelope. Most antelopes have only two horns, unlike the curious four-horned antelope.

ANTS

Ants are 'social' insects—they live together in colonies. Some colonies are in heaps of twigs; others are in chambers deep in the ground. Still others are hills of earth or sand. There are three types of ant: males, queens which lay eggs, and workers or females that do not mate or lay eggs.

The Legionary or Army ants march across country in a great horde that may have as many as 100,000 ants. If they reach a house they will strip it of anything that can be eaten, even tied up animals.

The life-cycle of the ant begins when the queen lays her eggs (1). Worker ants carry the eggs to the nursery where they hatch into larvae (2). The larvae are fed by worker ants (3). The larvae then spin cocoons, in which they turn into pupae (4). In the hatching chamber the young ants come out of the cocoons (5). Waste material is taken away and stored in a refuse chamber (6).

APES

Apes are man's closest animal relatives. We share the same kind of skeleton and have the same kind and number of teeth. We also have the same kind of blood and catch many similar diseases. Apes have large brains, but even the gorilla's brain is only half the size of a man's. Unlike monkeys, apes have no tails. There are four kinds of ape: the GORILLA and CHIMPANZEE are African; ORANG-UTANS live in Borneo and Sumatra; gibbons live in south-east Asia.

From top to bottom: a gibbon, orang-utan, gorilla and chimpanzee. All apes have highly developed hands and fingers.

APOLLO

After ZEUS, Apollo was the most important god in Greek mythology. He was always pictured as young, strong and handsome and was a symbol of wisdom, truth and justice. Apollo was also the god of prophecy, of shepherds, of music and of healing, and later he became the Sun god.

Apollo, god of youth and beauty, was a favourite subject for Greek sculptors. This head is cast in bronze.

17

ARABS

Arabs were originally those people who lived in Arabia. But from the AD 600s Arabian Arabs, inspired by their new faith, ISLAM, swept through western Asia and North Africa, conquering and settling a huge area. They taught the inhabitants the Arabic language and their Islamic religion. Today, Arabs are those people whose mother tongue is Arabic and who share a common history and religion. This includes Arabic-speaking peoples from countries such as Algeria, Syria, Iraq and Libya. Moslems in Iran, India and Pakistan pray in Arabic, but do not use it in everyday speech, so they are not considered Arabs.

The Arabs ruled North Africa and southwest Asia for 900 years, until they were defeated by the Turks in the 1500s. They lived under Turkish rule until World War I. After World War II many Arab countries became extremely rich from the production of huge quantities of valuable OIL. There have been several attempts to unify the Arab nations, though in recent years conflict with the state of Israel has caused a split in the Arab ranks. The oil-producing countries hold great political power in the world because of their control of important oil resources.

A Bedouin Arab of the desert stands outside his tent home. Many Arabs still lead a wandering, or nomadic, life, herding sheep and goats.

Before oil was discovered in the Middle East, many of the Arab peoples were poor herdsmen. But today this region produces over a third of the world's oil Below, a pipeline is laid from the oil wells to a coastal port.

ARCHAEOLOGY

Archaeology is the study of history through the things that men have made and built. These may include tools, pottery, houses, temples, or graves. Even a garbage pit can help to reveal how people lived. Archaeologists study all these things, from the greatest of monuments to the tiniest pin. Modern archaeology began during the RENAISSANCE, when people became interested in the culture of ancient GREECE and ROME. At first archaeological sites were ransacked for the treasures they contained. But by the early 1800s archaeologists had begun to uncover sites carefully, noting all they found and where they found it. Many exciting and important discoveries were

Many archaeological sites are excavated by using the grid system. Workers dig squares separated by strips of undug earth. This method divides the site into clear areas and makes all parts easy to get at.

made, including the remains of ancient Troy (1871); the early Greek civilization at Mycenae (1876); and the tomb of the pharaoh Tutankhamen in Egypt (1922).

Today, science helps the archaeologist in his work. Radiocarbon dating and *dendrochronology* (dating by tree rings) help tell us when particular objects were made. Infrared and X-RAY photography can show up designs under the rotted surface of a bronze bowl. Archaeology has even gone under the sea. With modern diving equipment, archaeologists can explore sunken wrecks and other long-lost remains of the past.

ARCHIMEDES

Archimedes (282–212 BC) was a famous Greek scientist who lived in Sicily. Among many other things he discovered Archimedes' Principle which tells us that if we weigh an object in the air and then weigh it again submerged in a liquid, it will lose weight equal to the weight of the liquid it displaces. Archimedes is supposed to have discovered this when he stepped into a bath full to the brim, and water spilled on to the floor.

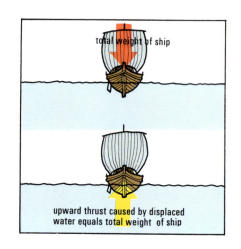

total weight of ship

upward thrust caused by displaced water equals total weight of ship

Archimedes showed that a floating ship weighs the same as the water it displaces.

ARCHITECTURE

Architecture is the art of designing buildings. If we look at old buildings still standing we can learn a great deal about the people who built them.

Architecture as we know it began about 7000 years ago in ancient EGYPT. The Egyptians built huge pyramids as tombs for their kings, and many of these pyramids still stand.

Greek architecture began to take shape about 600 BC and developed into the beautiful styles we can see today on the Acropolis at Athens.

When the Romans conquered GREECE they copied Greek architecture. But they soon discovered how to make an arch, so they could build larger, stronger buildings. They also began to make domes for the first time.

About AD 800 the Romanesque period of architecture began. Romanesque architecture at first imitated the style of ancient Rome, but soon took on a style of its own—a style that was strong and heavy. This style was followed by the Gothic. Most of the fine old cathedrals are in the Gothic style. They have graceful pointed arches over doors, windows, and often in the roof as well. The roof of a Gothic cathedral is usually made of a series of criss-cross arches which take the weight of the ceiling. Roofs like this are called *vaulted* roofs. ▷

In Medieval times builders used cranes and wooden scaffolding, much like those used in Roman times. They had winches and pulleys for lifting small loads. They also had the wheelbarrow which appeared in Europe about 1200. It has remained almost unchanged ever since.

In about 1400 a new style of architecture began in Italy. This was called the *Renaissance* (the word means re-birth) and it spread all over Europe. Renaissance architects paid almost as much attention to public buildings and people's houses as they did to building churches.

Later, many famous architects changed the building styles to fit the times in which they lived. Christopher Wren (1632–1723) designed buildings such as St Paul's Cathedral in London and Hampton Court.

Today people still build with brick and stone, but they also have new materials which have changed the way in which buildings are constructed. Concrete and steel, glass and plastic are shaping the new world in which we live. Architects are designing offices, factories and sports arenas so as to make the best use of these new materials. They even have the opportunity sometimes to design whole new cities.

Three inventions made the skyscraper possible. They were steel, concrete, and a safe system of lifts. The skyscraper's steel frame is sunk deep into concrete foundations.

The Egyptians below had no lifting tackle when they were building the pyramids. The huge blocks of stone had to be hauled up ramps on sledges. The set square and plumb line were used by the stone masons.

ARCTIC

The Arctic is the region round the North Pole. At the very North Pole there is no land, only a huge area of frozen sea. The land in the Arctic region is frozen solid for most of the year. In the short summer the surface soil thaws and some plants can grow, even brightly coloured flowers. There are now more people in the Arctic than there used to be. This is because valuable minerals and oil have been found there.

It is cold near the North Pole because the Sun never rises high in the sky. In winter there are days when it does not rise at all. In summer there are days when it can be seen all day and night.

Top, right: The Lapps live in the Arctic.
Some of them herd reindeer. Right: Eskimos
go fishing in kayaks made from sealskin.

Below: The polar bear usually has two cubs
which are born in the middle of winter.
The seal is looking for fish to eat while the
arctic fox chases birds. The colourful bird
in the foreground is a king eider.

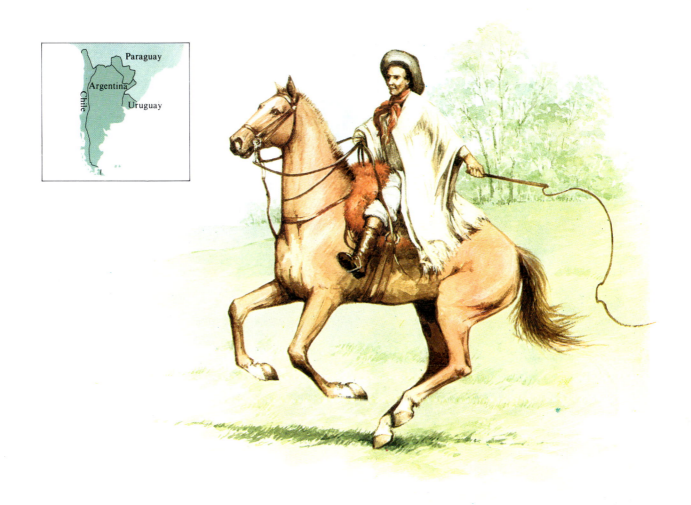

ARGENTINA

Argentina is the second largest country in SOUTH AMERICA. Most of the country's 27,796,000 people are farmers and ranchers, for much of Argentina's wealth comes from livestock and crops. Argentina is one of the world's top producers of beef and veal, fruit, wheat, millet and sorghum, and wool. The chief farming region is on the *pampas*, a Spanish word meaning 'plains'. The pampas lie to the north-west and south of Argentina's capital, Buenos Aires. Here, vast farms raise millions of cattle and sheep, which graze on the rich pasture. Northern Argentina is an area of tropical forests, and is little developed. In the far south, near the tip of South America, is Patagonia, a desert waste. The western part of the country is dry, and the land rises to the Andes Mountains, including Aconcagua, at 6960 metres (22,834 feet) the highest peak

Gauchos are the cowboys of Argentina. They tend the great herds of cattle on the pampas. Their colourful dress includes wide trousers tucked into their boots, a poncho, and a felt sombrero.

in South America. Argentina was ruled by Spain from 1535 to 1810. Today most Argentinians are descended from Europeans, though there are still about 20,000 native Indians.

ARISTOTLE

Aristotle (384–322 BC) was a Greek philosopher and a student of another famous Greek philosopher, Plato. At the age of 17 Aristotle went to Athens to become Plato's pupil. He worked there for 20 years and then became tutor to ALEXANDER THE GREAT. Aristotle invented the method of thinking called *logic*. His writings cover many areas, including nature and politics.

23

ARITHMETIC

Arithmetic is the branch of MATHEMATICS that deals with counting and calculating, using numbers. The four operations in arithmetic are addition, subtraction, multiplication and division.

ARKWRIGHT, RICHARD

Richard Arkwright (1732–1792) was an English inventor best known for his spinning frame, which made factory production of cotton cloth possible. Arkwright patented his spinning machine in 1769, after which he built his first spinning mill. He became the pioneer of the modern factory system. His great success laid the groundwork for the INDUSTRIAL REVOLUTION.

ARM

An arm is the fore limb of a human being, extending from the shoulder. The upper arm contains one large bone, the *humerus*. Two smaller bones, the *ulna* and *radius*, make up the forearm. Nineteen muscles attached to these bones move the hand and fingers.

ARMADA

Armada is a Spanish word for a great fleet of armed ships. The most famous armada was the Spanish fleet that tried to invade England in 1588. The 130 Spanish ships were large, clumsy and heavily armed. The English ships were faster and easier to manoeuvre, and were manned by more skilful seamen. The English sent fire ships towards the Spanish fleet, which retreated out to sea. Later, several Spanish ships were sunk and many damaged in battle. The Armada was forced to flee around the northern tip of Britain. Only 67 of the original 130 ships reached Spain.

Elizabeth I reviews her troops at Tilbury before the arrival of the Spanish Armada. The defeat of the Armada made England a greater sea power than ever before.

ARMADILLO

Armadillos are strange animals that live in Central and South America. Their backs are covered with an armour of bony plates. Some kinds of armadillo can roll themselves into a ball when attacked, giving them complete protection. They have strong claws which they use for digging burrows and tearing open termite nests to find food. There are ten different kinds of armadillo, the biggest being about 1·2 metres (4 feet) long.

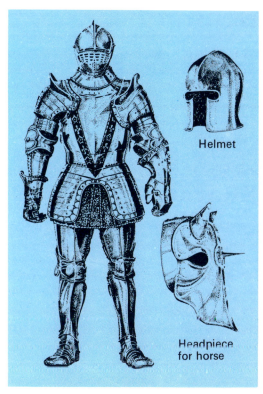

Helmet

Headpiece for horse

ARMOUR

Armour is covering used to protect the body in battle. It goes back at least 5000 years and was originally made of tough leather. Then men made metal breast-plates, helmets and shields. But the rest of the body was still protected by leather or chain mail, many small iron rings linked together to form a flexible metal coat. In the Middle Ages, knights rode into battle encased from head to toe in plate armour which weighed up to 30 kg (70 pounds). When firearms were invented, armour was no longer worn, except for the helmet. The weight of metal needed to stop a bullet was too great.

Today, tough light metals and plastics are being used in armoured jackets worn by soldiers and the police.

Knights armed for jousting were a splendid sight. They wore full armour that was even heavier than that used in war. Colours streamed from their helmets and on each knight's shield was his coat of arms. The horses also had armoured headpieces.

ART

Since the very earliest times men have painted and made sculptured objects. We can still admire cave paintings that were drawn over 20,000 years ago. Beautiful wall paintings and sculptures from ancient EGYPT, GREECE and ROME still survive.

The Christian religion had a great influence on art. During the MIDDLE AGES painters worked on religious scenes, often in a rather stiff way. But when the Renaissance came in the 1300s art began to flower and artists became famous for their work. Painters such as LEONARDO DA VINCI and MICHELANGELO began to make their subjects more life-like. Great Dutch painters like Rembrandt painted everyday scenes. In the 1700s and 1800s many artists went back to making their work look something like early Greek and Roman art.

Later, painting became more real looking, but by the 1870s a new style called Impressionism was starting. Artists such as Monet (1840–1926) and Renoir (1841–1919) painted with little dabs of colour, making soft, misty outlines. Painting in the 1900s

Above: Among the earliest paintings ever made are these bison, painted on the walls of a cave at Lascaux, France, about 20,000 BC. Below, left: A watercolour painting of a hare by the German Albrecht Dürer (1471–1528). Below: A miniature portrait by Nicholas Hilliard (1547–1619). It was meant to be worn in a locket, like the one the man in the picture is wearing.

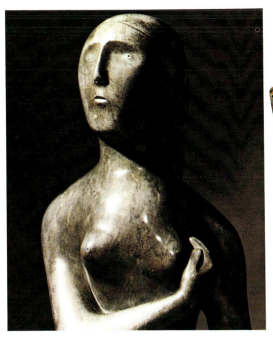

became even freer. Styles included Abstract Art and Cubism, with famous painters such as Cézanne (1839–1906) and PICASSO.

The oldest pieces of sculpture we know were made by STONE AGE men about 30,000 years ago. The ancient Egyptians made very fine sculptures between 2000 and 4000 years ago. Many of them were huge statues of kings and queens. Some of the world's most beautiful carving was done by the sculptors of ancient Greece and Rome, in what is known as the Classical period. During the RENAISSANCE, especially in Italy, the art of sculpture advanced by leaps and bounds. MICHELANGELO carved superb statues such as his *David*, which can be seen in Florence.

Modern sculptors often carve sculptures in which the general shape is more important than showing the likeness of a figure.

Above: A figure by the great modern sculptor Henry Moore. It is in the Tate Gallery, London. Above, right: An ancient Chinese bronze elephant. Far right: A beautiful porcelain vase made at Sèvres in France about 1785. Sèvres porcelain is famous for its rich colours. Right: A tiny Easter egg of gold, enamel and precious stones made by the Russian goldsmith Fabergé (1846–1920).

ASIA

Asia is the largest of all the continents. It also has more people (2,693,000,000) than any other continent. Places such as the Ganges-Brahmaputra delta, the river valleys of CHINA and the island of Java are among the most thickly-populated places in the world.

Northern Asia is a cold, desolate tundra region. In contrast, the islands of INDONESIA are in the steamy tropics. The world's highest mountain range, the HIMALAYAS, is in Asia, and so is the lowest point on land, the shores of the Dead Sea. Asia's people belong to the three main races of man: Caucasoids live in the south-west and northern INDIA; Mongoloids, including the Chinese and Japanese, live in the east. A few Negroids are found in the south-east. And all the world's great religions began in Asia—Judaism, CHRISTIANITY, ISLAM, Buddhism, Confucianism and Shinto.

Most Asians are farmers, and many are very poor. The chief food crops are wheat and rice. Other crops are exported: they include tea, cotton, jute, rubber, citrus fruits and tobacco. Many nations such as China are developing their industries, but JAPAN is the only truly industrialized nation.

Asia was the birthplace of civilization, and was the home

Civilization began in Asia about 5000 years ago, before it began in the West. The pure gold Buddha (centre left) is in a temple in Bangkok, the capital of Thailand.

of many great civilizations, including those of Mesopotamia, Babylon, CHINA and the Indus Valley in what is now Pakistan. Europeans began to visit Asia in the 1400s and trade quickly grew up between the two continents. Later, for several centuries, China and Japan closed their doors to trade with Europe. By the late 1800s most of the rest of Asia was ruled by European powers. But after World War II, during which Japan occupied parts of east Asia, most European colonies became independent. In 1949 the Chinese Communists took control of mainland China. In 1975 Communists took over VIETNAM, Laos and Cambodia after a seven-year war for control, fought mainly in Vietnam.

Asia is a continent of contrasts, from the dry plains of southern India to the fertile river valleys and terraced rice paddies of China (below).

ASTRONOMY

Astronomy is the scientific study of the heavenly bodies, and is the oldest science in existence. Early observations of the heavens enabled men to divide the year into months, weeks, and days, based on the movements of the Sun, Earth and Moon. The development of the CALENDAR helped early astronomers to forecast the appearance of COMETS and the dates of ECLIPSES. For many centuries people believed that the Earth was the centre of the UNIVERSE, until, in the 1540s, Nicolaus COPERNICUS revived the idea that the Sun was at the centre of the SOLAR SYSTEM. In 1608 Hans Lippershey invented the TELESCOPE, an important new tool for astronomers. Today, big telescopes are aided by radio telescopes, which collect radio waves emitted by objects in space, such as pulsars and quasars.

Below left, a huge transit*, a platform that was used in the East to observe the stars. Below, big telescopes collect light from stars.*

ATOMIC ENERGY

An atomic bomb produces an enormous amount of heat in a fraction of a second. Atomic energy is produced in an *atomic reactor* in a similar way, but the energy is controlled. Heat is produced much more slowly and safely.

To make useful power from the atom, scientists use a special kind of a metal called URANIUM. The atoms in uranium are always breaking up and making heat. To control

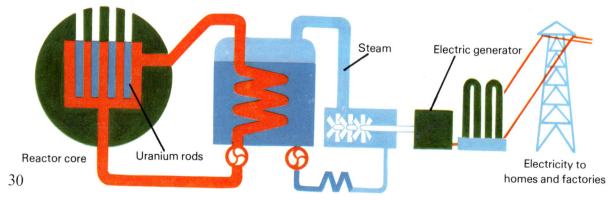

Reactor core

Uranium rods

Hot water

Steam

Electric generator

Electricity to homes and factories

the amount of heat, the uranium is made into long rods. The rods are put into a *reactor core* and are separated by other rods made of CARBON. With the right number of uranium rods and carbon rods, the reactor goes on making a lot of safe heat.

Water flows around inside the reactor. This water boils and the steam is made to drive turbines. The turbines drive generators which make ELECTRICITY. This electricity is fed into the ordinary grid system, just like electricity from power stations which run on oil or coal. The diagram below shows how the energy gets from the uranium rods to the power points in your home.

ATOMS

Everything is made of atoms. Things you can see, like the wood in a table; things you cannot see, like the air, are all made of atoms. You are made of atoms, too. If the atoms in something are packed closely together, that something is a solid. If the atoms in something are not so tightly packed—if they move about more—that something is a liquid, like water. And if the atoms move about a great deal, we have a gas, like air.

It is very difficult to imagine how small an atom is. We cannot see them—they are far too small. Look at the full stop at the end of this sentence. It has in it about 250,000 *million* atoms! But even atoms are made up of smaller pieces. The simplest atom is that of the light gas HYDROGEN. We can show the hydrogen atom something like this:

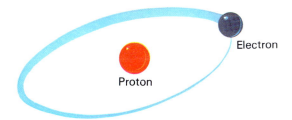

The centre is a tiny body called a *proton*. Around it spins an *electron*. Other atoms are much more complicated than the hydrogen atom. The carbon atom, for example, has at its centre 6 protons and 6 other things called *neutrons*. Round these spin 6 electrons.

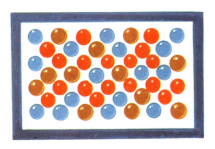

In a solid, atoms pack tightly.

In a liquid, atoms can move about.

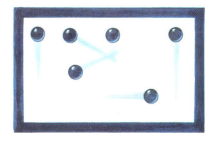

In a gas, atoms move about a lot.

AUSTRALIA

Australia is one of the world's seven CONTINENTS. It is a huge island about three-quarters the size of the whole of Europe, but the population is only about 15 million compared to Europe's 695 million. The heart of Australia is a region of forbidding desert, with very few people. Ringing the coasts on the east of the country are a long chain of low-lying mountains. But Australia is a flat land with few high mountains. Off the north-east coast is the world's longest underwater CORAL reef, the Great Barrier Reef. It is over 2000 km (1250 miles) long. ▷

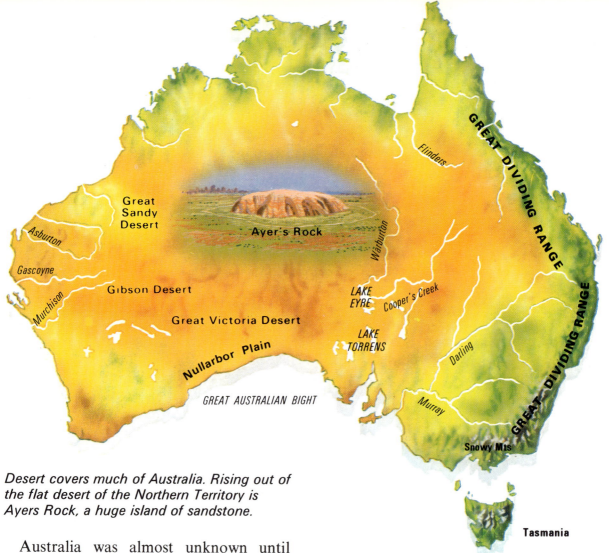

Great Sandy Desert

Asburton

Gascoyne

Murchison

Gibson Desert

Great Victoria Desert

Nullarbor Plain

GREAT AUSTRALIAN BIGHT

Ayer's Rock

Warburton

Flinders

GREAT DIVIDING RANGE

LAKE EYRE

Cooper's Creek

LAKE TORRENS

Darling

Murray

GREAT DIVIDING RANGE

Snowy Mts

Tasmania

Desert covers much of Australia. Rising out of the flat desert of the Northern Territory is Ayers Rock, a huge island of sandstone.

Australia was almost unknown until 1770, when the explorer Captain James Cook landed in Botany Bay, on the south-eastern coast, and claimed the great land for Britain. The only people living there were the Aborigines who had arrived on the continent about 30,000 years before. At first the British used Australia as a penal settlement—a place to send criminals—but a few other immigrants arrived to raise sheep. Then, in 1851, gold was discovered and in 10 years Australia's population doubled. But at the start of this century the population was still little more than $3\frac{1}{2}$ million.

Now Australia is one of the world's richest lands, with great wealth in minerals and farmland. The country exports large quantities of wool, meat and wheat.

Australia has only a few kinds of animals of its own. Among them are the famous MARSUPIALS—animals that carry their young in pouches. These are the KANGAROOS, the wallabies, the wombats and the KOALAS. The duck-billed platypus is a strange mammal that lays eggs.

Australia has a federal form of government, something like that of the United States of America. Each of the Australian states—New South Wales, Queensland, Tasmania, Victoria, South Australia, and Western Australia—has its own parliament. But they all come under the central government, together with two territories— Northern Australia and Australian Capital Territory, a small area around CANBERRA, the federal capital.

Australia is a member of the COMMONWEALTH.

AUSTRIA

Today, this small country is hardly much bigger than Ireland. But once it was one of the largest and most powerful nations in Europe.

For more than 700 years, from 1278 to 1918, Austria was ruled by a dynasty of kings and queens called the Hapsburgs. Their lands covered most of Central Europe. They included Hungary, Czechoslovakia, large parts of Italy, Yugoslavia, Poland, Germany, Spain and the Netherlands.

The Austrian Empire collapsed after World War I. But there are many relics of the rich court life of the Hapsburg emperors. Vienna, the capital city where over $1\frac{1}{2}$ million Austrians live, is filled with castles, beautiful buildings and churches, statues and royal parks.

AZTECS

The empire of the Aztecs was a great Indian civilization in Mexico and Central America when Spanish soldiers discovered it. A Spanish commander by the name of Hernando Cortés landed with 600 men on their shores in 1519. Within two years he had smashed the Aztec empire for ever.

Emperor Montezuma, was the last ruler of the Aztecs. He was captured by Spanish soldiers soon after a small army of them arrived in his capital city. By holding him hostage, they were able to control his subjects even though they were greatly outnumbered.

The Aztecs were famous for their grim religious practices. One of their gods regularly had human beings sacrificed to him in front of his temple.

Baboons are fast runners because their front and hind legs are about the same length. They travel in bands called troops.

BABOONS

Baboons are the largest members of the MONKEY family. A fully grown male can reach the size of a large Alsatian dog. Their coats are short-haired, usually yellow-brown in colour, and their rumps are marked a bright red-pink. They have long snouts that give their faces a doglike look.

Baboons spend most of their time on the ground and can run quickly on all fours. However, they can also climb well and often escape from their enemies, such as lions, by running up tall trees.

Baboons live in Africa and Arabia. They move about in troops of 10 to more than 100 animals. Their homes are in high, rocky places that are easy to guard. They are very aggressive and will bark loudly and bare their great dagger-like teeth at intruders. A group of angry baboons are so fierce that they can even discourage a prowling leopard.

33

BACH, JOHANN SEBASTIAN

Johann Sebastian Bach (1685–1750) was one of the greatest composers of all time. He was born at Eisenach in Germany, and all his family were musical. In fact, there were more than sixty musical Bachs before the family died out in the 1800s. From an early age Bach played the violin and the viola. He studied music passionately, often creeping out of bed to copy music from his brother's collection.

At the age of 38 Bach moved to Leipzig, where he lived for the rest of his life. Here he wrote some of his greatest pieces of music—mostly music for singing and for the organ.

When Bach died, his music was almost at once forgotten. No one even put up a monument to him. Almost a hundred years passed by before people began to realize what a genius Johann Sebastian Bach had been.

Johann Sebastian Bach was one of the greatest composers of all time.

BADGER

Badgers are big, weasel-like animals. They are common in North America, Europe and Asia.

Badgers are MAMMALS. They have thickset bodies, long blunt claws used for digging, sharp teeth and powerful jaws. A fully-grown adult badger measures about 75 cm (29 inches) from nose to tail and stands almost 30 cm (12 inches) high.

People rarely see badgers during the day. They are night creatures. After sunset they emerge from their underground dens to begin feeding. They browse on plant roots and hunt mice, rats and voles, insects, frogs and other small animals.

Badgers build elaborate underground burrows which are called *sets*. A set has several entrances, a system of long tunnels and a number of rooms. Here, a badger couple makes its home and raises from two to four young at a time. Badgers are quite peaceful animals. However, they can fight fiercely if they are attacked.

BAKING POWDER

Baking powder is used in cooking to make cakes puff up so that they are light and fluffy. It is a mixture of bicarbonate of soda and some weak ACID. When baking powder is added to a cake mixture, or batter, the liquid in the batter makes the baking powder produce thousands of tiny bubbles like those in a fizzy drink. In the oven these bubbles grow bigger and spread all through the cake. There are different kinds of baking powders. Some of them act quickly, others act more slowly.

BALKANS

The Balkan peninsula is a mountainous region of south-eastern EUROPE. It includes GREECE, ALBANIA, and parts of TURKEY, YUGOSLAVIA, BULGARIA and Romania.

The Turks ruled much of this region for 500 years, from the 1300s to the 1800s. In the 1800s the Balkan countries were in great turmoil. They fought the Turks for their independence and threw them out.

It was in the Balkans that Archduke Ferdinand of Austria was assassinated in 1914. This event triggered off WORLD WAR I.

BALLET

Ballet is a precise and beautiful form of dancing that is performed in a theatre. A kind of ballet first appeared in Italy in the 1400s, but ballet as it is danced today began in France. During the reign of King Louis XIV, in the 1600s, it was officially recognized as a form of art. The French Royal Academy of Dance was founded in 1661 to promote ballet.

Traditional, or *classical*, ballet follows strict rules and traditions. There are standard positions for the arms, legs and hands, and special movements that make the dance flow smoothly.

Classical ballet uses orchestras, elaborate scenery and splendid costumes. Many ballets tell a story. But the dancers do not speak any words. They mime (act out) the story, using their bodies. The person who arranges the dance movements is called the *choreographer*.

Some ballets are very famous. They have been danced for many years. *Giselle*, a story of a tragic young village girl who dies in love-stricken grief, was first performed in 1841. Two other long-time favourites are *Swan Lake* and *Sleeping Beauty*. These two ballets are as famous for their music as for their dancing.

Modern ballets often look very different from classical ones. They include freer, more modern dance steps. Sometimes, instead of telling a story, they dwell on certain moods or themes. Special effects may be produced with lighting, rather than scenery.

Ballet dancers perform a number of exercises. Assemblés *are jumping steps. The dancer springs from one foot, brings both feet together, and lands.*

Below: Louis XIV's dance master, Pierre Beauchamp, devised the five basic ballet positions over 300 years ago. Each foot position has an arm position to go with it.

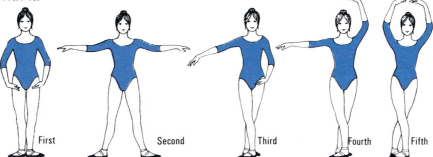

First   Second   Third   Fourth   Fifth

The first air balloon to carry people was built by the Montgolfier brothers in 1783.

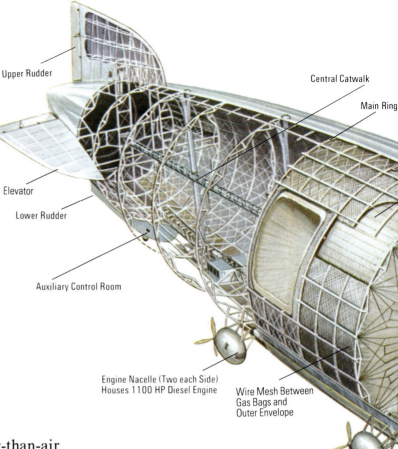

Upper Rudder

Central Catwalk

Main Ring

Elevator

Lower Rudder

Auxiliary Control Room

Engine Nacelle (Two each Side) Houses 1100 HP Diesel Engine

Wire Mesh Between Gas Bags and Outer Envelope

Four-Bladed Wooden Propeller

Cargo Area

Cargo Area

Engineer's room

BALLOONS AND AIRSHIPS

Balloons and airships use lighter-than-air gases to fly. Balloons can only drift in the wind, but airships can be flown and steered.

The first manned balloon was a hot-air craft launched in 1783. It was built by two French brothers, the Montgolfiers. Their balloon was an open-ended bag. A fire burned under the opening to keep it filled with hot air. The biggest problem the Montgolfiers had was to keep the balloon from bursting into flames. It had to be drenched with water throughout the flight.

In the same year, the first gas-filled balloon took to the air. The gas used was HYDROGEN, and it was a simpler craft to fly. To go down, one simply opened a valve and let some gas out.

In the 1800s, manned balloons were used by the military for observations. Today, most balloons are used to study the weather.

Airships

Most airships are much bigger than regular passenger use. Today, new, safe helium-filled airships are being built.

cabin and the engines. More advanced kinds of airships have a rigid skeleton covered with fabric. Inside the skeleton are a number of large gas bags that give the airship its lift.

The first successful airship flew in 1852. It was powered by a steam engine and could manage a speed of 8 km/hr (5 mph). During World War I, airships were used to bomb cities. In 1919, the British-built R34 made the first Atlantic crossing. In 1929 the famous *Graf Zeppelin* of Germany flew round the world. But a series of disasters brought the building of airships to an end. They were simply not safe enough for regular passenger use. Today airships are used for special purposes such as advertising.

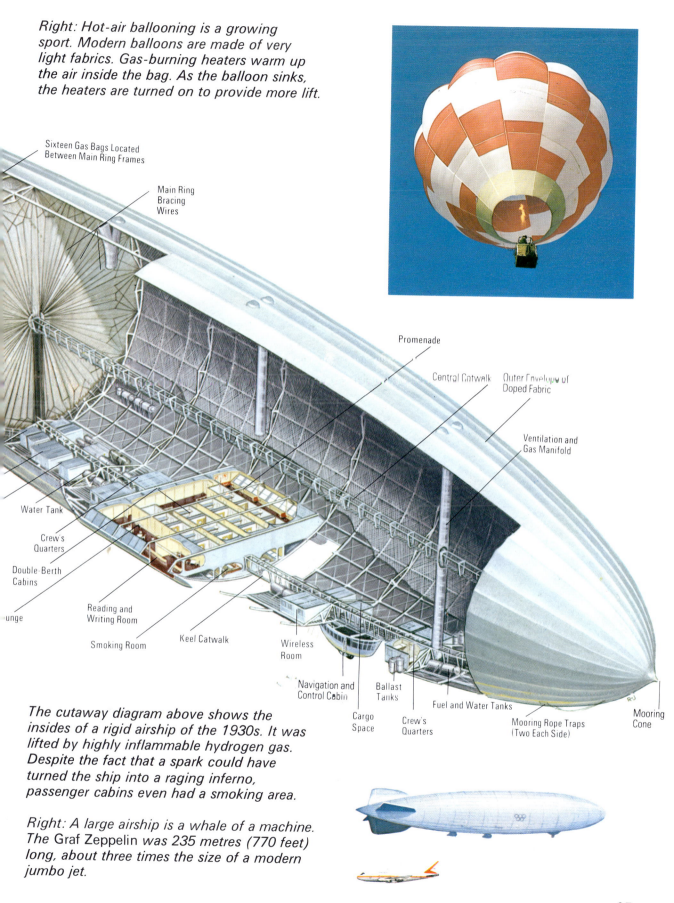

Right: Hot-air ballooning is a growing sport. Modern balloons are made of very light fabrics. Gas-burning heaters warm up the air inside the bag. As the balloon sinks, the heaters are turned on to provide more lift.

Sixteen Gas Bags Located Between Main Ring Frames

Main Ring Bracing Wires

Promenade

Central Catwalk

Outer Envelope of Doped Fabric

Ventilation and Gas Manifold

Water Tank

Crew's Quarters

Double-Berth Cabins

Lounge

Reading and Writing Room

Smoking Room

Keel Catwalk

Wireless Room

Navigation and Control Cabin

Cargo Space

Ballast Tanks

Crew's Quarters

Fuel and Water Tanks

Mooring Rope Traps (Two Each Side)

Mooring Cone

The cutaway diagram above shows the insides of a rigid airship of the 1930s. It was lifted by highly inflammable hydrogen gas. Despite the fact that a spark could have turned the ship into a raging inferno, passenger cabins even had a smoking area.

Right: A large airship is a whale of a machine. The Graf Zeppelin was 235 metres (770 feet) long, about three times the size of a modern jumbo jet.

BAMBOO

Bamboo is a GRASS, but it often grows so tall that it looks more like a tree. Over 200 different kinds of bamboo grow in tropical regions all over the world. Bamboo grows in such thick clumps that a forest of bamboo is almost impossible to walk through.

Bamboo stems are woody. They are very long and thin, and are hollow on the inside, and smooth to touch. The stems of the giant bamboos may grow as high as 36 metres (120 feet) above the forest floor and measure anything up to one metre (3 feet) around in the steaming monsoon jungles of southern Asia.

Bamboo has hundreds of uses. Young shoots are tender enough to be eaten. Even slightly larger plants are soft enough to weave into mats and baskets, and to make fences and thatched roofs. Larger bamboo trunks may be sawn up to make furniture, water pipes, or planks for building. In the Far East, bamboo is also used in preparing certain kinds of medicine. These are made from a fluid found in the stem joints.

Bamboo grows very quickly, sometimes at a rate of 40 cm (16 inches) a day. The huge stems may reach a height of 36 metres (120 feet) and be as much as a metre (3 feet) around.

BALLOT

Voting by ballot is popular in many countries because each voter can make his choice in secret. When the voter has marked his ballot paper, he drops it into a box. After the voting has been completed, the box is opened and the ballots are counted.

Voting by secret ballot is quite a recent way of holding ELECTIONS. Ballots of this type were not used in Britain until 1872. Before then, voting took place at open meetings, often by a show of hands.

BANANAS

The banana is a tropical FRUIT. It is grown on plantations in many places, though the largest ones are in Central and South America. The original home of the banana, however, is the East Indies and Malaya.

Banana plants grow into 'trees' that are as much as 6 metres (20 feet) tall. A single bunch of fruit forms at the crown of each plant. When the bunch is four months old it is ready to be cut. At this time it weighs anything from 20 to 65 kg (45 to 143 lb). There may be as many as 150 individual bananas on it. Each banana is known as a 'finger'. The fingers grow in clusters of 10 to 20, each of which is called a 'hand'.

Bananas are always harvested while they are still green and not quite ripe. They are transported to other countries in fast refrigerator ships, so that they do not ripen too quickly.

BARK

The outer layer of WOOD on the trunk and branches of a TREE is the bark. Bark is dead wood. It is tough and waterproof and protects the living wood underneath. In this way it has the same purpose as the outer layers of skin on our bodies.

As trees grow, they form layers, or rings, of new wood and become thicker. When this new wood is formed inside a tree it pushes against the dead bark and makes it crack and peel off.

The most useful bark is probably CORK, which comes from the cork oak, a tree found in southern Europe. The cork is carefully removed from the tree and used for many different purposes. Other types of bark are used for tanning and dyeing and in making medicines.

Bark

Cross-section of a tree trunk

Living wood

Growth rings

BAROMETER

Put simply, high air pressure is a sign of good weather. Low air pressure is a sign of changing and bad weather. The barometer is used to measure such changes.

There are two kinds of barometer, the aneroid and the mercury. The aneroid is more widely used. Inside it is a flat metal box. The air inside the box is at very low pressure. The metal walls of the box are so thin they will bend very easily. They do not collapse because a spring keeps them apart.

As air pressure drops, the spring pushes the sides of the box apart. As it rises, the sides of the box are squeezed together. These movements are picked up by levers and gears that move a pointer around.

Aneroid barometer

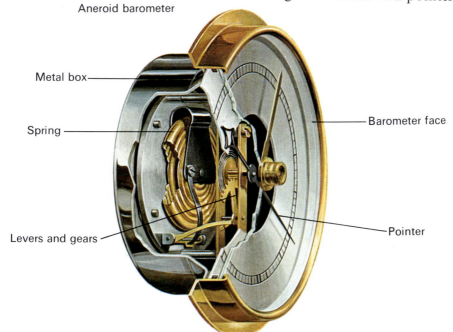

Metal box

Spring

Levers and gears

Barometer face

Pointer

BATS

Bats fly like birds, yet in fact they are MAMMALS. They are the only mammals that can truly be said to fly. Their wings do not have feathers. They are made of a thin sheet of skin stretched between the long 'finger' bones. In most bats the wings are also joined to the legs and tail.

There are more than 2000 different kinds of bat. Most live in the tropics and warm parts of the world.

The biggest of all bats are the fruit-eaters or flying foxes. One, the kalong, has a wing-span of 1·5 metres (5 feet). The insect-eaters are usually smaller. Their wing-span is rarely as much as 30 cm (12 inches). They live in most parts of the world. Where winters are cold, they HIBERNATE.

The vampire bat of South America has a very unusual way of feeding. It bites animals with its teeth and drinks their blood. However, vampires do not suck blood, they merely lap it up as it flows.

Most bats are nocturnal—they sleep in the day and fly at night. Scientists have shown in experiments that bats do not need good eyesight for flying. They find their way in the dark by using a 'sonar' system. They make high-pitched shrieks that no human ear can hear, and use the echoes bouncing off objects to tell where they are.

Sloth bear

BEARS

Bears are found in most parts of the world except for Australia and Africa. They are some of the biggest meat-eaters on Earth.

The largest of all bears are the brown bears of Alaska. These can reach a weight of over 750 kg (1653 lb). Other giants include the polar bear of the Arctic and the grizzly of western North America.

The only bear that lives in South America is the small spectacled bear. Its name comes from the ring-like markings around its eyes.

The smallest bear in the world is the sun bear of the jungles of South East Asia. It weighs no more than 65 kg (143 lb). Sloth bears, found in India and Sri Lanka, have enormously long tongues for lapping up insects which are an important part of their diet.

Bears are slow, lumbering beasts. They have short, powerful limbs and heavy, broad heads with powerful jaws. They also have long, dangerous claws for digging and tearing.

Bears normally live alone except during the mating season. Young bears live with their mother. In cold places many bears spend the winter asleep in dens made in caves and quiet places.

Sun bear

Spectacled bear

BEAVERS

Beavers are big RODENTS more than a metre (1 yd) long, including the tail, and weigh more than 25 kg (55 lb). They live in woods by the side of lakes and rivers and are good swimmers. Beavers are able to stay under water for up to 15 minutes. They have a broad, flat tail covered in scaly skin. This is used for steering when they swim.

Beavers need pools to build their homes in, and often block up, or dam, streams with mud and sticks to make one. They cut down small trees with their sharp teeth and drag them to the pool to strengthen the dam.

They build a home of mud and sticks by the side of the pool. This home has an underwater entrance and an escape hole. Inside, there is a nest above water for the young beavers.

Beavers eat bark, mainly from alder and willow trees. They store twigs in their homes to feed on during the winter.

Beavers have thick FUR which keeps them warm in the water. They live in many parts of North America where, for hundreds of years, hunters have trapped them for their fur. The hunters killed so many beavers that they are now protected by law and can only be hunted during a particular season.

Beavers were once common in Asia and Europe too, but they were also over-hunted and are now found only in some places. There have been no beavers in England for a thousand years but they lived in Scotland until the 1500s.

BEES

There are many different kinds of bee, but the best known kind is the honey bee. Honey bees live in hives or colonies of about 50,000 worker bees. Worker bees are female but they do not breed. Each colony also has a queen bee which breeds, and a few hundred stingless drones which are male.

Right: A worker bee gathers pollen. It stuffs the pollen into a sac on its hind legs to carry it back to the hive.

The worker bee's life is very short, usually about four weeks, so the queen has to lay many eggs to provide enough bees. She can lay up to 1500 eggs in one day. From time to time a new queen is born. The old queen then leaves the hive with a *swarm* of about half the workers to seek another home.

The workers collect POLLEN and nectar from flowers. The nectar is made into honey. It is stored in the hive to feed the bees in winter. Beekeepers carefully remove the honey from the hive. They give the bees sugar-syrup to replace the honey they take.

There are other types of bee which do not live in large colonies. These are called solitary bees. They produce a small family of a few hundred bees which die each winter.

Below: Only the queen and workers have stings. These have barbs so that when a bee stings you the sting is left behind.

Worker

Drone

Queen

BEETHOVEN, LUDWIG VAN

Ludwig van Beethoven (1770–1827) was a German musician who composed some of the greatest music ever known. This included symphonies, concertos, choral and chamber music. When he was young, Beethoven was well-known as a pianist and was admired by many famous people. He began to go deaf at the age of 30 but continued to compose music even when he was totally deaf.

When Beethoven was young he studied with Mozart and Haydn. Beethoven's music is dramatic and full of feeling.

BEETLES

Beetles are INSECTS. There are over 300,000 species of beetle known.

Some beetles are as small as a pinhead. Others are very large. The giant African goliath beetle measures up to 10 cm (4 inches) long and can weigh 100 grams (3·5 oz).

In prehistoric times all beetles had two pairs of wings. But over millions of years the front pair changed, or *evolved*, into hard, close-fitting coverings for the second pair underneath. All beetles used to be flying insects but now many of them live on the ground.

Beetles start their lives as eggs which hatch into grubs, or larvae. The larvae then turn into chrysalises, or pupae, before the adult beetles emerge.

Many beetles and their larvae are destructive pests. Woodworms, weevils, wireworms, cockroaches, Colorado and flea beetles do great damage to crops, trees and buildings.

Some beetles can be very useful. Ladybirds are small beetles which eat harmful insects such as greenflies. Dung beetles and burying beetles clear away dung and dead animals.

The shape and size of beetles vary, but all have six legs and a pair of hard wing covers. They also have a pair of feelers, or antennae.

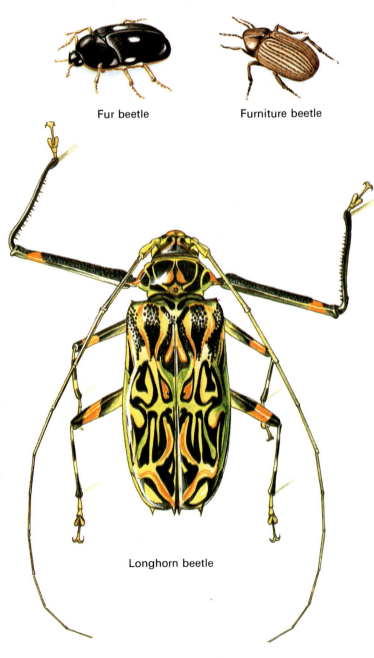

Fur beetle   Furniture beetle

Longhorn beetle

The main square in Antwerp, Belgium's chief seaport.

BELGIUM

Belgium is a small country sandwiched between France, Germany and Holland. Its capital is Brussels. Belgium's population of 10,048,000 is made up of two main groups: the Germanic Flemings of the north, and the French-speaking Walloons of the south. Because of its central and strategic position, Belgium has been invaded and fought over throughout the course of European history. Today Belgium is an international centre. The headquarters of the European Economic Community (EEC) and NATO are both in Brussels.

BELL, ALEXANDER GRAHAM

Alexander Graham Bell (1847–1922) is remembered as the inventor of the TELEPHONE. Bell was the son of a Scottish teacher who went to Canada with his family in 1870. Two years later Alexander set up a school for teachers of the deaf in Boston, Massachusetts. Through his work with devices to help the deaf, Bell became interested in sending voices over long distances. On March 10, 1876, the first sentence was transmitted by telephone. The historic words were spoken by Bell to his assistant: 'Mr Watson, come here; I want you'.

In 1876 Alexander Graham Bell demonstrated the first practical telephone. In 1892 he personally opened the telephone link between New York and Chicago (below). Below right, an early Bell telephone.

BETHLEHEM

Bethlehem is a small town on a hillside about 8 km (5 miles) south of Jerusalem. It is famous as the birthplace of JESUS. In Old Testament times it was also the birthplace of King David. Although Bethlehem was largely destroyed by the Roman Emperor Hadrian, its fame as the birthplace of Jesus grew. Today thousands of Christian pilgrims visit it every year.

BIBLE

The Bible is the sacred book of the Christian religion. It is in two parts. The first is called the Old Testament and records the history of the Jewish people and the teachings of their prophets before the birth of JESUS. The second part, the New Testament, records the life and sayings of Jesus and his disciples.

Right: The first printed Bibles were produced by Johannes Gutenberg in the 1400s.

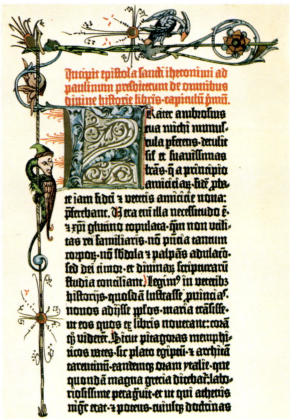

BICYCLE

The bicycle is a two-wheeled vehicle powered by its rider, who turns two pedals with his feet. The earliest bicycles, called 'dandy-horses', were invented in the 1700s. They were simply two wheels joined by a rod, with a seat on top and the rider pushed it along the ground with his feet.

The first bicycle with pedals did not appear until 1865. These machines were known as 'bone-shakers' because the seats had no springs. The next important development was the 'penny farthing', which had an enormous front wheel and a tiny rear wheel. The modern style of bicycle appeared in the 1880s. It had a chain-driven rear wheel and air-filled tyres, and this basic style has changed very little since then.

The most famous bicycle race in the world is the Tour de France. The bicycles used have lightweight frames, no mudguards and special racing tyres.

BIRDS

Birds come in all shapes and sizes, but they all have wings and FEATHERS. Some birds can fly thousands of kilometres. Others, such as the OSTRICH and the PENGUIN, cannot fly at all. The ostrich is the largest bird. It can weigh more than 150 kg (330 lb). The smallest bird, a HUMMING-BIRD, weighs less than 2 grams (0·07 oz).

Birds developed from scaly REPTILES that lived about 180,000,000 years ago. Their scales changed over millions of years into feathers, and their front legs became wings. Birds have hollow bones for lightness in the air and strong breast muscles for working their wings. Large birds can flap their wings slowly and float, or hover, on air currents. Small birds need to flap their wings fast to stay in the air.

All birds lay EGGS. Most birds are busy parents who work hard to rear their young. Some, like the CUCKOO, lay their eggs in other birds' nests for foster parents to rear. Other birds bury their eggs in warm places and leave them. Most birds are wild but some, such as chickens, PIGEONS and canaries, have been tamed or *domesticated*. Many birds are bred on farms for their eggs and meat.

There are many different kinds of bird. Tropical birds such as the toucan, bird of paradise and the lorikeet, are often brightly coloured. The wood-pecker and the treecreeper build nests inside trees. The hobby hunts other birds and animals.

Above: The bones of a bird are strong but not heavy.

Great spotted woodpecker

Hobby

Rainbow lorikeet

Treecreeper

Tailorbird

Toucan

Wood pigeon

Bird of paradise

BLÉRIOT, LOUIS

Louis Blériot (1872–1936) was a famous French airman. He was a pioneer of aviation and designed and built a number of early aeroplanes. On July 25, 1909, he took off from Calais in one of his own AIRCRAFT. Twenty-seven minutes later he touched down at Dover, becoming the first man to cross the English Channel by air. In doing so he won a prize of £1000 offered by the London *Daily Mail* newspaper. Blériot went on to design other aircraft and became the owner of a large aircraft company.

Louis Blériot takes off near Calais in his Type XI monoplane on July 25, 1909. Blériot became the first person to fly across the Channel in a heavier-than-air craft.

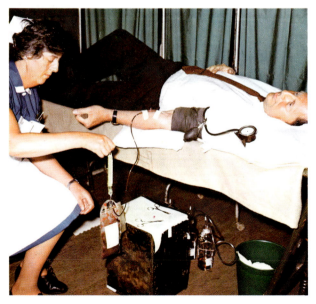

BLOOD

Blood is the fluid that nourishes our bodies and removes waste products. It takes in food from the DIGESTIVE SYSTEM, and oxygen from the LUNGS, and carries them to all the CELLS in the body. Each cell takes exactly what it needs from the blood and the blood carries away cell waste, including water and carbon dioxide. Blood also carries special body chemicals to where they are needed. And it kills germs and keeps the body at the right temperature.

Blood is made in the marrow of the bones. The adult human body contains about five litres (eight pints) of blood. This blood is made up of a pale liquid called *plasma*, and millions of cells, or *corpuscles*. Corpuscles are tiny red discs that give the blood its colour. The blood also contains white corpuscles. There are about 5 million red corpuscles and between 5000 and 10,000 white corpuscles in every tiny cubic millimetre of blood.

Fighting Disease

White corpuscles attack GERMS that enter the body by absorbing them. Often many white corpuscles are killed in the fight against disease or infection. Large numbers of dead white corpuscles collect as *pus*. Other blood particles, called *platelets*, help our blood to clot when we bleed. This helps scratches and other wounds to heal more quickly.

We can all be classified into blood groups A, B, AB, or O, according to the type of blood we have. Blood groups are important when patients are given blood transfusions. Transfusions are given either to replace diseased blood, or blood that has been lost through an injury. The blood a person is given is generally the same blood type as their own.

Left: Many lives are saved because donors like this one give blood for transfusions. Blood taken from donors is stored at a temperature of 4·5°C (40°F).

BOER WAR

The Boer War (1899–1902) was fought in SOUTH AFRICA between the Boers—settlers of Dutch descent—and the British. The slow and badly-led British troops were no match for the fast and lightly-armed Boers in the early days of the war. But in the end Britain's overwhelming strength won. There were about 450,000 soldiers in the British armies during the Boer War, and only about 60,000 Boers.

Right: British troops during the Boer War, sometimes called the South African War. The British victory brought South Africa into the Empire as a British colony.

BOLIVIA

Bolivia is a land-locked country in central SOUTH AMERICA, west of Brazil. Most of Bolivia is an enormous plain stretching from the Brazilian border to the eastern foothills of the Andes Mountains. High in the Andes lies the great Bolivian plateau, over 4000 metres (13,000 feet) high. Two-thirds of Bolivia's people live here. The capital is La Paz, the highest capital in the world, and Lake Titicaca, at 3812 metres (12,507 feet) above sea level, is one of the highest lakes in the world.

Spain ruled Bolivia from 1532 until 1825. It gained freedom from Spain with the help of Simón Bolívar, a Venezuelan general, after whom Bolivia is named. More than half the people are Indians, a third are *mestizos* (people who are part European, part Indian) and the rest are direct descendants of Europeans. Bolivia is the world's second largest producer of tin, and mining is the country's most valuable industry.

Above: A market in La Paz, Bolivia. La Paz is Bolivia's capital and seat of government, but the city of Sucre is also called the capital.

Right: Simón Bolívar was a great leader who helped six South American republics to become independent. He became the first president of Colombia and Peru.

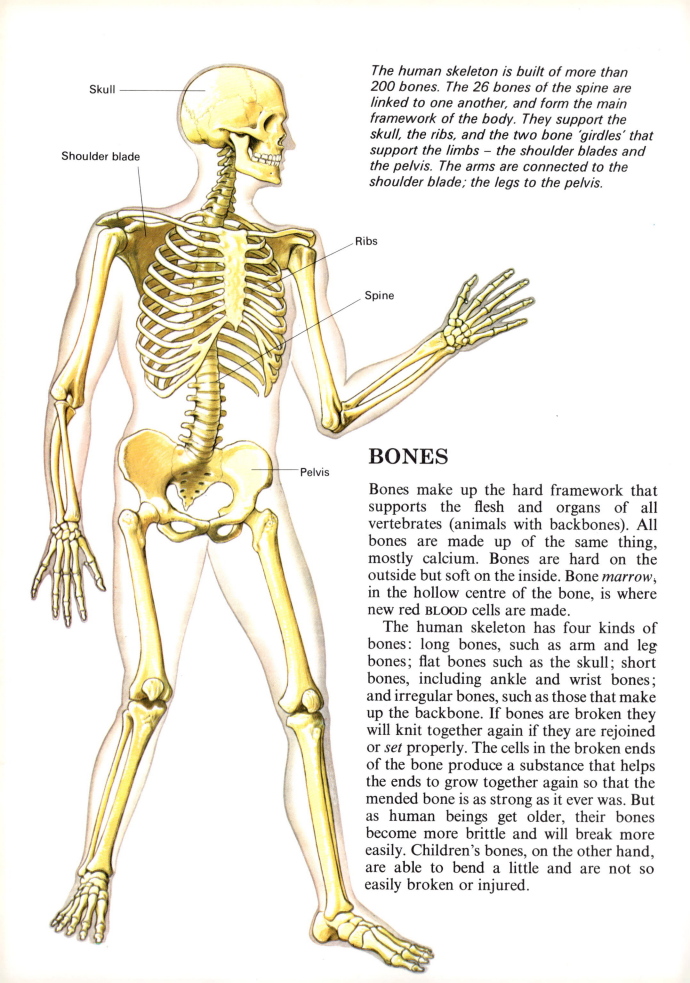

Skull

Shoulder blade

Ribs

Spine

Pelvis

The human skeleton is built of more than 200 bones. The 26 bones of the spine are linked to one another, and form the main framework of the body. They support the skull, the ribs, and the two bone 'girdles' that support the limbs – the shoulder blades and the pelvis. The arms are connected to the shoulder blade; the legs to the pelvis.

BONES

Bones make up the hard framework that supports the flesh and organs of all vertebrates (animals with backbones). All bones are made up of the same thing, mostly calcium. Bones are hard on the outside but soft on the inside. Bone *marrow*, in the hollow centre of the bone, is where new red BLOOD cells are made.

The human skeleton has four kinds of bones: long bones, such as arm and leg bones; flat bones such as the skull; short bones, including ankle and wrist bones; and irregular bones, such as those that make up the backbone. If bones are broken they will knit together again if they are rejoined or *set* properly. The cells in the broken ends of the bone produce a substance that helps the ends to grow together again so that the mended bone is as strong as it ever was. But as human beings get older, their bones become more brittle and will break more easily. Children's bones, on the other hand, are able to bend a little and are not so easily broken or injured.

BOOKS

Books are used for storing and passing on all kinds of knowledge, ideas and stories. Some of the earliest books were made by the ancient Egyptians. These were written by hand on rolls of paper made from the papyrus plant.

By the time of the Roman Empire many books were hand written on parchment or *vellum*. This material was made from animal skin. It was cut into sheets which were fastened together to look much the same as a modern book.

During the Middle Ages monks made many beautiful books. They were decorated, or *illuminated*, by hand with bright colours and sometimes gold and silver.

In the 1400s PRINTING on paper was introduced to Europe. At first this was very slow because much of the work still had to be done by hand. Then Johann GUTENBERG invented a machine with movable type which could print books quickly. Today, many thousands of books are produced every year, in all the languages of the world.

BOOMERANG

The boomerang is a wooden throwing stick used mainly by the Australian ABORIGINES. There are two kinds. One is very heavy and is thrown straight at the target. The other is lighter. It is shaped in a special way so that when it is skilfully thrown it is possible to make it return to the thrower.

The curved boomerang, seen here, with an Aborigine shield, is used for sport, not hunting.

A big modern printing press can print thousands of books an hour, but the earliest books were written by hand on long strips of paper (above). The book was rolled round a stick when not in use. In the Middle Ages books, like the one shown below, had to be printed one at a time by hand. Before this they were written and illustrated by hand, usually by monks.

BOY SCOUTS

The Boy Scouts is a world-wide organization for boys that was founded in Britain in 1908 by Robert Baden-Powell. Today it has over 10 million members in 100 countries.

BRAILLE

Braille is an alphabet for the blind. It is made up of raised dots which the reader can feel with his fingertips. Many books have been translated into braille for blind readers. Special braille typewriters make it easy to write braille. The system was invented by a Frenchman, Louis Braille, in the 1800s.

BRAIN

The brain controls all the other parts of the body. In some tiny insects it is no bigger than a speck of dust. Even in some mighty dinosaurs it was no bigger than a walnut. But MAMMALS have big brains in relation to their size, and man has the biggest brain of all. The human brain is largely made up of grey and white matter. Grey matter is NERVE cells, and white matter is the nerve fibres that carry messages from the nerve cells to the body. These nerve fibres leave the brain in large bundles like telephone cables and reach out to all parts of the body. Messages from the body are travelling back along the fibres to the brain all the time.

Different parts of the brain control different parts of the body. For example, most thinking is done in the front part. But sight, on the other hand, is controlled from the back of the brain.

Left: A braille reader scans a page with his fingertips. Louis Braille also worked out a system for writing music in braille.

Below: The main parts of the brain. The cortex makes up 80 percent of the brain.

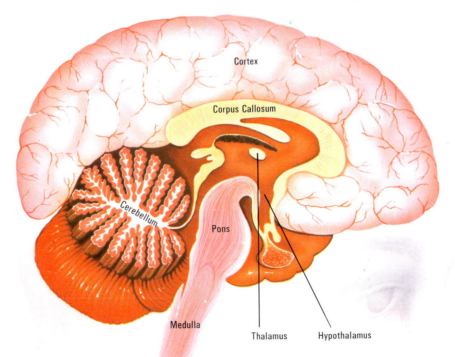

BRASS

Brass is an alloy of ZINC and COPPER. Small amounts of other metals may sometimes be added for special uses. Brass is often used for plumbing and electrical fixtures and for making delicate instruments.

The amount of copper in brass may vary from 50 percent to more than 95 percent. Brass with a large amount of copper in it is quite soft and is a reddish-yellow colour. Brass with a small amount of tin added is used for many of the fittings on boats and ships, as it does not rust.

BRAZIL

Brazil is by far the largest country in SOUTH AMERICA and the fifth largest country in the world. Much of Brazil is low-lying, and contains the huge basin of the AMAZON river and the world's largest rain forest. Until recently, only tribes of Indians lived here. Today, the government is trying to open up the Amazon region.

Over half of Brazil's 133,882,000 people live in cities that include Rio de Janeiro, São Paulo, Belo Horizonte and Recife. Brasilia, a specially built modern city, has been the capital of Brazil since 1960.

Brazil was ruled by Portugal from the early 1500s until 1822, and most people still speak Portuguese. About three-quarters of the people are descended from Europeans; most of the rest are of mixed European, Indian and African ancestry. There are some pure Indians and Negroes. Most Brazilians work on farms. The country leads the world in producing coffee, and oil is becoming more and more important. Brazil is also one of the biggest producers of beef, cocoa, cotton, maize, sugar cane and tobacco. Most of Brazil's great mineral wealth is still undeveloped.

Rio de Janeiro is Brazil's second largest city. It was once the country's capital. Rio de Janeiro's population is increasing quickly.
A Brazilian cowboy, called a gaucho, rounding up sheep.

BREAD

Bread is one of man's oldest foods, dating back to at least 2000 BC. It may be made from wheat, maize, oats, barley, or rye FLOUR. At first bread was flat, but the Egyptians added YEAST to make the dough rise. Today most bread is baked with yeast.

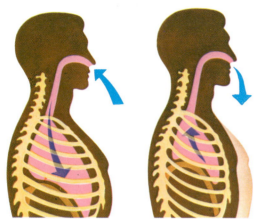

Above: Oxygen reaches the body through the lungs. When our chest expands, air rushes in through the nose. When our chest muscles relax, the lungs are squeezed and air is pushed out.

BREATHING

Breathing is something we rarely have to think about. As soon as a baby is born, it starts to breathe, and we go on breathing all our lives. It is the OXYGEN in the air that we need. Like all other animals, we must have oxygen to stay alive. This oxygen is used with the food we eat to give us energy to move about and keep our bodies going.

We draw air into our LUNGS. From there it goes through tiny tubes which allow the oxygen to pass into the BLOOD vessels. So oxygen goes all round our bodies in the blood. We breathe out another type of gas called carbon dioxide.

An adult normally breathes in and out about 20 times a minute (children usually breathe faster than this).

BRICKS

A brick is a building-block of hardened clay. Bricks have been used for more than 5000 years and are the oldest man-made building material. Some of the earliest types of bricks that were made can still be seen today.

Ancient brickmakers discovered that rectangular bricks were the easiest to build with. Today, bricks are still rectangular in shape. The first bricks were left to dry in the sun and the clay had to be mixed with straw to stop them crumbling. Later on it was discovered that if bricks were heated in a furnace they became much harder and the straw was not needed. Modern bricks are shaped by machine rather than by hand.

Good bricklaying is very skilled work. Often ornamental designs are worked into brick walls.

Below: In ancient Mesopotamia houses were built with bricks. The bricks were made with mud and straw and dried in the sun.

BRIDGES

Bridges are used to take roads, paths and railways over rivers, valleys or other obstacles. People have been building bridges for thousands of years.

The first simple bridges were probably fallen tree trunks placed across a river or small valley. Later, they may have been supported underneath by stones or logs. Another kind of simple bridge is the rope bridge made from long pieces of rope slung across a river.

The Romans were among the first great bridge builders. Some of their stone bridges are still standing today. In the Middle Ages bridges in towns often had shops and houses built on top of them.

Today there is a great variety of bridges. They have to be carefully planned and built. The weight of the bridge must be balanced so that it does not fall down. It must also be strong enough to carry traffic and stand up to the force of the wind.

There are three main kinds of bridge. These are the *beam*, the *arch* and the *suspension* bridge. Some are fixed and others can be moved.

Above: The Golden Gate suspension bridge in San Francisco, USA, was finished in 1937. It has a span of 1280 metres (4200 feet). Each cable is 92 cm (over 3 ft) thick, and is made up of 25,570 separate wires.
Right: The Romans were expert bridge builders. They built many arched bridges all over their empire. A number of these bridges still remain. This bridge has three arches and is built of stone. It crosses a river in Syria.

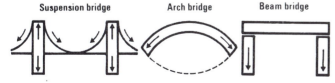

Suspension bridge   Arch bridge   Beam bridge

BRITISH ISLES

The British Isles are made up of two main islands, Britain and IRELAND, and more than 5000 smaller ones. These range from large islands such as the Isle of Man, Shetland, the Orkneys and the Channel Islands, to bare rocks sticking out of the sea.

Britain is divided into ENGLAND, SCOTLAND and WALES. Ireland is divided into Eire (the Republic of Ireland) and Northern Ireland.

The British Isles are part of EUROPE. They are on the European CONTINENTAL SHELF. During the last ICE AGE Britain was joined to Europe by a wide land bridge across what is now the English Channel.

The climate of the British Isles is mild and quite wet. Most of the country is low-lying. There are some mountains and high ground in Scotland, Wales, the north of England and parts of Ireland. Much of the country used to be covered in forests or bog but most of this has been cleared or drained.

The British Isles are part of north-west Europe. During the last Ice Age Britain was joined to Europe.

BRONTOSAURUS

The brontosaurus was a giant DINOSAUR which lived 150,000,000 years ago. It is also known as apatosaurus. It was one of the largest animals that ever lived. Fully grown it was more than 20 metres (65 feet) long and weighed more than 35 tonnes.

Brontosaurus fed on plants. It had a long neck with a small head and a very long tail.

Skeleton of brontosaurus

Length: 20 metres (65 feet)
Height: 9 metres (29 feet)
Weight: 35 tonnes (34 tons)

BRONZE

Bronze is an alloy of COPPER and TIN. Sometimes small amounts of other metals such as lead and zinc are added to make it harder or more easy to mould. It is a reddish-yellow metal.

Bronze can be hammered or shaped into many things. Early craftsmen of the BRONZE AGE used it to make swords and tools. These were much sharper and stronger than the flints they replaced.

Left: This is a bronze head of Aphrodite, the Greek goddess of love. It was made by the sculptor Praxiteles in the 400s BC.

Top: A bronze axe from China, made about 1500 BC.

Bronze Age people also made pots, armour and jewellery from bronze.

Because bronze is so hard and long-lasting it is also used to make coins. The Greeks and Romans were among the first people to make bronze coins thousands of years ago.

Bronze is also used to make statues. It may be beaten into shape or *cast* by heating it until it melts and pouring it into a mould. Bronze statues which are kept in the open air often become green. This coating stops the bronze from rusting and the statues may last a long time.

Bells are usually cast from bronze. They have a much better sound than bells made from other metals. Guns used to be made from gun metal, which is bronze with zinc added.

BUDDHA

The word Buddha means 'Enlightened One'. This name is given to great teachers of the Buddhist religion.

The first Buddha was Siddhartha Gautama. He was born about 563 BC in northern India. For most of his life he travelled round India teaching people. Buddha taught his followers that the only way to true happiness was to be peaceful and kind to other people and animals, and to avoid evil.

Like the HINDUS, Buddhists believe that after they die they are born again as an animal or human being. If they are very good, they are not born again but live in a kind of heaven called *Nirvana*.

The picture below shows a big statue of Buddha lying down. The Buddhist monks next to it have saffron (yellow) robes. Other statues of Buddha (right) show him sitting with his legs crossed.

The Romans were great builders. Their stone-masons cut and carved blocks of stone with many tools that we still use today.

BUILDING

Early man built with the materials he found around him—stones, branches, mud and turf. In Europe, poor people usually lived in houses made of wattle and daub. Wattle was a wickerwork of branches, and this was plastered over with a 'daub' of wet mud. When this hardened it made quite a strong wall.

Because in some areas certain materials were easily available, buildings look quite different in different places. Where there was plenty of clay, people built with BRICKS; where there was plenty of limestone or sandstone, people built their houses with those.

Today, houses being built everywhere look very much the same. Large buildings have a framework of steel girders or reinforced concrete which takes all the weight of the building. The walls can be light and there can be plenty of windows.

All buildings especially high ones, have to be built on firm foundations. If they are not they may collapse or sink into the ground like the Leaning Tower of Pisa.

BULB

Many PLANTS, such as tulips, daffodils and onions, grow from bulbs. The bulb is the underground part of the plant where food is stored during the winter months. When the plant has finished flowering, the bulb begins to grow under the ground. Then the leaves above the ground wither away, leaving only the bulb. It is made up of fleshy scales packed tightly together. The scales feed the bud as it grows.

This bulb has been sliced in half to show the fleshy layers surrounding the bud. If a bud forms between the scales, it splits off to make a new bulb.

BULGARIA

Bulgaria is a country in Eastern EUROPE. It belongs to a group of countries which are all communist, that is, their governments practise the beliefs of COMMUNISM. In these countries much of the land and most industries are owned by the government.

Bulgaria has 8,990,000 people and covers 110,912 sq km (42,823 sq miles). Its capital city is Sofia.

In the north are the Balkan Mountains. To the east is the Black Sea where many people spend their holidays. In the centre of Bulgaria is a big valley with many farms. The farmers grow fruit, flowers, vegetables, grain and tobacco. There are also many factories and mines in Bulgaria.

The Bulgarians grow much tobacco. This woman is threading tobacco leaves together before they go to the factory.

BURMA

Burma is a country in South-East ASIA. It has mountains, forests and rivers. The biggest river is the Irrawaddy which is 2080 km (1290 miles) long.

Burma has 35,211,000 people and covers 676,552 sq km (261,218 sq miles). The capital city is Rangoon. Most of the people are farmers. They grow rice, teak, rubber and jute. Most Burmese follow the Buddhist religion.

BUSHMEN

Bushmen are the ABORIGINES or native people of the southern African deserts. Long ago they lived in many parts of Africa. They were pushed into the deserts when other Africans and Europeans spread into southern Africa.

Bushmen are small, gentle people. They live together in groups, or bands, of families. These bands travel round the desert looking for food and water. Often they stop and camp. Then they build small houses of branches and grass.

Bushmen live by hunting and by picking wild vegetables, nuts and fruit.

BUTTER

Butter is a FAT made from cream. Cream from MILK is first cooled and then the germs are killed by *pasteurizing* it (see PASTEUR). The cream is then put into a machine called a churn. This moves the cream about until it turns into butter. In some countries such as India the butter is nearly liquid. Indian butter is called *ghee*.

BUTTERFLIES

Butterflies are flying INSECTS. There are about 12,000 kinds of butterfly. They are related to MOTHS. They live in most parts of the world, even as far north as the Arctic circle.

Butterflies have many colours and sizes. One of the smallest, the dwarf blue of South Africa, has a wing-span of only 14 mm (0.5 inches). The largest, the Queen Alexandra birdwing, has a wing-span of 28 cm (11 inches).

You can tell butterflies from moths because they keep their wings up when resting. Moths fold their wings. Butterflies are also usually more brightly coloured and fly in the daytime. Butterflies often have different colours or patterns on each side of their wings.

Green-veined white

Brimstone

Peacock

Wall brown

White admiral

Underside of wing

All butterflies begin their lives as CATERPILLARS which hatch from eggs. The caterpillars spend their lives eating the plant they were hatched on. They change their skins several times as they grow. When a caterpillar is fully grown it changes into a chrysalis with a hard skin. Inside this the chrysalis changes into an adult butterfly. When it is ready, the butterfly breaks out and flies away to find a mate and lay eggs of its own.

CABBAGE

Cabbages are round, leafy VEGETABLES. The leaves can be eaten raw, pickled or cooked. There are many varieties, and they may be green, white or red. They grow in cool moist climates. Some ripen in spring and summer. Others are only ready to be eaten in winter.

CACTUS

Although there are dozens of different cacti, they all have one thing in common. They are able to grow in hot DESERT climates. Cacti can do this because they store water in their fleshy stems. They are covered with prickly spines instead of leaves. The spines protect the plant's store of water from the desert animals.

Below: Barrel cacti swell up with water when it rains. During droughts they lose water and shrink in size.

CAESAR, JULIUS

Julius Caesar (*c*.100–44 BC) was a great leader of the Roman Empire. He is most famous for his part in turning the Roman Republic into an empire ruled by one man.

He first became powerful when he commanded an army that conquered what is today France, the Netherlands and Germany. In 55 BC, he crossed the Channel and invaded Britain. He rebelled against the Roman Senate (the government), when he led his victorious armies into Italy itself. He captured Rome without a struggle, and in 48 BC he defeated Pompey, his main rival for power. Caesar then became the sole ruler of Rome.

Caesar made many enemies who hated what he was doing to the Republic. A group of them plotted to kill him. On the 'Ides of March' (the 15th of the month), 44 BC, they stabbed him to death in the Roman forum.

In 46 BC during the reign of Julius Caesar, a new calendar was worked out to replace the older, less accurate one. The month of July was named after Caesar in his honour.

CALENDAR

Calendars were first used in ancient Babylon. There have been many different ways of keeping track of the days, months and seasons of the year. The one we use today is called the Gregorian calendar, named after Pope Gregory XIII who introduced it in 1582. It divides the year into 365 days, with every fourth year (the 'leap year') having 366 days.

CAMELS

With their wide splayed feet, gangly legs, humped body and long thick neck, camels

The single-humped camel on the left is an Arabian. The two-humped one on the right is the Bactrian camel of Asia. The humps do not contain water but are filled with stores of fat that enable camels to go for up to a week without eating or drinking.

look as if they have been made up from the parts of half a dozen other animals. But if it were not for these beasts of burden, life in some desert regions would have been almost impossible.

Camels are one of the few creatures that can stand up to extreme heat and still do

60

work carrying heavy loads. They are ideally suited for the job of making long journeys across deserts. Their wide padded feet grip well on loose sandy ground. They are powerful and swift and can go for days without eating or drinking, living off the fat stored in their humps. Camels will eat almost anything. As well as the thorny shrubs and thistles found in the desert, they will chew their way through tent cloth, mats and even baskets.

CAMERA

Modern cameras work in much the same way as the box cameras of a hundred years ago. A shutter opens for a fraction of a second—just long enough to let light from the scene being photographed pass through the glass LENS to fall on the film. The light forms an upside-down image of the scene on the film. The film is then treated with chemicals (developed). The image on the piece of developed film is printed onto a special type of paper. The result is a photograph.

Today, most cameras have a lot of different parts to help us to take photographs in many kinds of light, and from close up or from far away.

CANADA

The second biggest country in the world, Canada covers an area of some ten million sq km (almost four million sq miles).

In the ARCTIC, Canada reaches almost as far north as Greenland. To the south, it extends to the same LATITUDE as southern France. The distance from the Pacific coast in the west to the Atlantic in the east is further than from North America to Europe. But in spite of its size, two-thirds of the population of Canada lives in a narrow belt of land no more than 200 km (about 120 miles) from the United States' border. Most Canadians speak English, but many speak French.

Canada is a country of many different kinds of land. The great central plains are given over to pasture land and wheat farming. Further east are the GREAT LAKES, five huge inland seas that empty into the St Lawrence river. Many people live along its fertile valley, and the great cities of Toronto and Montreal are found here. The capital of Canada is Ottawa.

Above: The Niagara Falls sits on the border between Canada and the United States. Here, waters from the Great Lakes tumble into the St Lawrence valley.

CANALS

Any man-made waterway could be called a canal, but we usually mean one that is built to carry water traffic.

Canals have been in use for thousands of years. In ancient Egypt and Babylon they were used to irrigate farmland.

Until the 1500s, canals could only be built across flat country. With the invention of canal locks, however, they could be built across high ground too. The locks allowed boats to sail over hills by lifting them in a series of steps from one level to another.

Early canals could only be used by narrow, shallow-bottomed boats. These boats were pulled along by horses that walked on tow paths running alongside the canal. Modern canals like the SUEZ CANAL and the PANAMA CANAL, are big enough to let ocean liners pass through them.

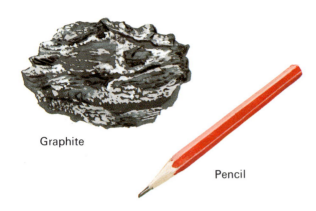
Graphite

Pencil

Above: One form of carbon is graphite. The name 'graphite' comes from a Greek word meaning 'to write'. What we call the 'lead' in our pencils is actually graphite.

CARBON

Carbon is an important ELEMENT, which is found in every living thing—both plant and animal. Many of the things we use every day have carbon in them, such as sugar and paper. Forms of carbon also exist as COAL, OIL, graphite (the 'lead' in our pencils is graphite) and DIAMONDS.

CARNIVORES

Carnivores are a group of MAMMALS that feed mainly on the flesh of other animals. They do not include birds of prey or people.

Although carnivores mostly live on meat, they will sometimes eat insects and plants. But what they all have in common is a set of very powerful jaws for chopping up their food, deadly curved claws for tearing, and long sharp teeth for seizing, stabbing and killing their victims.

Carnivores include CATS, DOGS, BEARS, RACCOONS, weasels and hyenas. All have good eyesight, smell and hearing and are fast, intelligent and skilled at hunting down other animals. Some carnivores, like wild dogs and HYENAS, hunt in packs. In this way they can kill animals much larger than themselves. Other carnivores, like the LEOPARD and the JAGUAR hunt alone.

Jaguar

CARPETS

As long as 2000 years ago, hand-woven woollen carpets were being made in Turkey and the Middle East. But until the 1500s, they were very rare in Europe. In those days, people put their carpets on walls and over tables rather than on the floors.

Today, most carpets are machine-made of wool, cotton or synthetic fibres. One type of carpet WEAVING is called Wilton—the pattern is woven separately with loops of wool onto the main weave of the carpet. Another type is Tufted—the pile is sewn into a woven backing. The loops are then cut to make a soft pile.

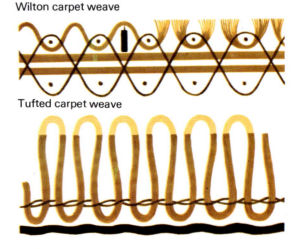
Wilton carpet weave

Tufted carpet weave

CARTOONS

Most people think of short, funny films with talking creatures and plants when they speak of cartoons. But originally, cartoons were rough sketches of the design for a PAINTING or a TAPESTRY. These sketches were drawn to the same size as the finished thing. Comic strips in newspapers are called strip cartoons.

Cartoon films are made by joining together a series of drawings. Each drawing is a little different from the one before. When they are shown one after another at a very fast speed it looks as if the scene is moving.

The films of Walt Disney are some of the most famous of all cartoons. Here, pieces of a film can be seen frame by frame. Each frame used to be drawn by hand, now computers help speed up the process.

CASTLES

One of the few places where kings and lords in the Middle Ages could feel safe was behind the thick stone walls of their castles. There, they and their men could fight off attacks by roving bandits and sit out long sieges by invading armies. ▷

The keep of a castle is its strongest point. Around the keep is the walled inner bailey. Around that, the outer bailey, walls and moat.

Keep

Inner bailey

Outer bailey

As castles developed they became larger and more comfortable. Instead of having all the living quarters crowded into the main keep, small 'villages' of huts and buildings sprang up inside the castle walls.

Castles had high, thick stone walls. A wall-walk ran right around the top, and through each tower. Soldiers could run from one point of attack to another without ever showing themselves to their enemies.

The rounded towers could stand up to battering rams and hurled rocks much better than square ones. The towers also jutted out from the main wall. This let the defenders fire on the attackers from three sides and stopped them from reaching the foot of the castle walls.

CAT

A cat belongs to a group of MAMMALS called the feline family. Although the cat family range in size from domestic breeds to TIGERS, they all have many things in common. Cats have short, rounded heads, long face whiskers, sharp teeth that serve as deadly weapons for grabbing and biting their prey to death, and powerful claws. All cats except the cheetah can pull their claws back into a sheath of skin when they are not in use. Their long tails help them balance and make them superb at jumping and climbing. LIONS and cheetahs live in families. All other cats live mostly alone.

CATERPILLARS

The middle or 'adolescent' stage in the lives of BUTTERFLIES and MOTHS is when they are called caterpillars.

Butterflies and moths usually lay their eggs on plants. After they hatch, small, soft, worm-like creatures—the caterpillars—emerge. Some are smooth-skinned. Others are spiny or hairy.

Caterpillars spend their whole time feeding. Their only purpose in life is to eat and grow and prepare for the change into adulthood. For this reason they have powerful jaws for chewing up plants. Many feed on crops and can cause great damage.

As caterpillars grow, they become too big for their skins. After a while the skin stretches and splits and they emerge with a new one. This happens several times. The last 'skin' is quite different from the others. It forms a hard layer which makes it impossible for the caterpillar to move. In this state it is called a *chrysalis*. Inside the chrysalis, the caterpillar changes into a butterfly. A moth caterpillar will spin a cocoon around itself before turning into a chrysalis. Caterpillars take almost a year to grow to full size.

Below: Caterpillars crawl with a set of fleshy hind legs. There are usually five pairs. The front three pairs are for grasping food. The thorn moth caterpillar shown here, has only two pairs of hind legs. It moves these back legs first, forming a loop, then its front legs move forward to straighten out again.

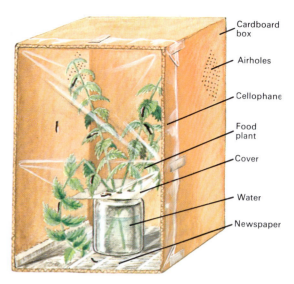

Cardboard box
Airholes
Cellophane
Food plant
Cover
Water
Newspaper

Many moth caterpillars live in hedges and fields. Some are easy to find, but camouflaged ones may be hard to see. Nibbled leaves will give you a clue. You can keep caterpillars in a simple, well-aired box (above). Give them fresh leaves to eat regularly—make sure they are the right kind. Put some peat and moss into the cage. The caterpillars will burrow into it when they are ready to turn into chrysalises. Some may take up to a year to emerge as adult moths.

Below: The caterpillar of the puss moth protects itself by squirting acid.

CAVEMEN

Anybody who lives in a cave could be called a caveman. But what we usually mean are people who were the ancestors of modern man. Caves are natural places to shelter from the weather and from wild animals. They were some of the first dwelling places used by human beings.

The mouth of a cave is often dry and it is possible to build a fire inside when the weather is cold. In hot weather, caves give shelter from the sun. Also, with walls all around them, the cavemen could fight off dangerous animals from the cave mouth. The remains of ancient cave dwellers have been found in sites all around the world— in China, southern Asia, Europe and Africa. Here, bits and pieces of their tools and weapons have been dug up along with bones of the animals they hunted. Remains of their fires have also been found.

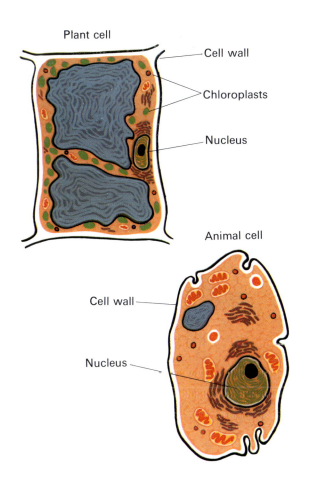

Plant cell

Cell wall

Chloroplasts

Nucleus

Animal cell

Cell wall

Nucleus

CELL

Cells are the smallest living parts of plants and animals. Single cells can only be seen under a MICROSCOPE. Even a tiny bit of human skin contains millions of them.

Cells are usually round in shape. A few are spiralled and some, like nerve cells, have sprawling tree-like branches.

In 1665, a scientist called Robert Hooke looked at a piece of cork under a microscope and saw that it was made up of many tiny compartments. He named them cells and this term has been used ever since.

Plant cells are different from animal cells. They have an extra-thick cell wall. This gives plants their stiffness as they do not have bones to support them. Animal cells only have a thin cell wall. Plants also have chloroplasts. These give them their green colour and help them use sunlight for growing. At the heart of all cells is a nucleus. The nucleus controls all of the cell's actions. Without it, the cell would die.

The bronze Celtic shield below dates from the 1st century AD. *The design in the centre includes four owl faces.*

CELTS

The Celts were an ancient people of north-western Europe. At one time, over 2000 years ago, they lived all over Britain, France and parts of Spain and Germany. In about 400 BC they even crossed into Italy and attacked Rome.

The Celts were tall, fair and very warlike. They lived in tribes made up of a chief, nobles, free men and slaves. The tribes often fought each other. They were good metal-workers and liked to decorate their weapons and armour with bright designs and curious creatures. And they were gifted musicians and poets. The Celtic religion was known as Druidism, and their priests were called Druids.

When the armies of the ROMAN EMPIRE spread out, many Celts fled to remote regions. In the lands they had once conquered the Celtic way of life was soon lost. It was only in the far-off corners of Europe that their language and way of life survived.

Celtic speech was very common in Ireland, Cornwall, Wales, Scotland and Brittany up until a few hundred years ago. Today, although less common, Celtic speech can still be heard. Irish and Scottish, Gaelic and Welsh are Celtic languages. The Celtic people of Scotland were known to the Romans as the Picts.

The solid gold necklace above was once worn by a Celtic chief. It was found in a field in eastern England.

CEMENT

Cement is a very important building material. It is the ingredient which binds concrete. Cement is made by roasting a mixture composed largely of LIMESTONE and clay, and then crushing it to a fine, grey powder. When water is added it forms a sludge-like mass which quickly sets rock-hard.

Cement is seldom used by itself. Mixed with sand it forms the mortar used to bind one brick to another. Mixed with sand and larger pieces of stone it forms the concrete used to build skyscrapers, bridges and dams.

Cement has been used since ancient times. The Greeks and Romans used a kind of mortar which was stronger than the mortar used in the Middle Ages. The most common type of modern cement is called Portland cement. It was invented in the early 1800s.

The world's most important cereal crops are (from left to right) barley, maize (corn), rice, rye, oats and wheat. Rye and wheat are mostly ground into flour. Oats and maize are often used to feed farm animals. Rice is eaten by more people than any other cereal. Barley is used to make beer.

CEREALS

Cereals are the SEEDS of a group of plants that belong to the GRASS family. Throughout human history they have been the most important of all types of food. In ancient times, cereals were collected from wild plants. Later, when they began to be grown on farms, they became the most important food of early civilizations.

Some cereals such as RICE and maize, are eaten in their natural form. Others, such as WHEAT and rye, are ground into flour before being baked or cooked. Cereals are also used to make alcoholic drinks and to feed farm animals.

CHARLEMAGNE'S EMPIRE

Saxony

LOUIS

Lotharingia

Bavaria

Neustria

CHARLES

Burgundy

LOTHAIR

Aquitaine

Lombardy

CHARLEMAGNE

Charlemagne (AD 742–814) was a great military leader. In the AD 700s he founded an empire that covered most of western Europe.

In the year 768, Charlemagne became the king of the Franks, a people who lived in the country we now call France. Through his skill in war he soon took over northern Spain, Italy and Germany. He fought for the Church in Rome, and in return, the POPE crowned him Holy Roman Emperor on Christmas Day, in the year AD 800.

Charlemagne wanted to build another ROMAN EMPIRE, but after his death his sons fought among themselves and his empire was slowly broken up.

Left: Charlemagne founded the greatest empire in Europe since the Romans. During his reign he brought peace and order to Europe and his court became a centre of art and learning.

CHARLES I

Charles I (1600–1649) is known in history as the only British king to have caused his people to rebel and execute him. He came to the throne in 1625, but he was such a bad king he made enemies almost everywhere and in 1642 the country was split by CIVIL WAR.

Below: King Charles I was beheaded in London in 1649, after being sentenced to death by the English parliament.

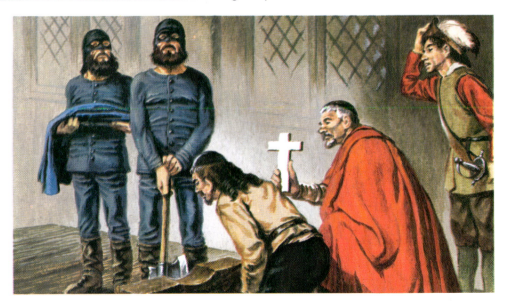

CHARLES II

As King of Britain, Charles II (1630–1685) was liked as much as his father was hated. He spent most of his youth in exile in Europe, while CHARLES I fought to save his crown and his life, and lost both.

In 1660, after being ruled by Oliver CROMWELL for ten years, the English invited Charles II to return and take back the crown. He was a wise ruler and he was very careful in the way in which he treated his people and PARLIAMENT. His court was very lively and gay and his personal charm won him many friends. His subjects called him the 'merry monarch'.

Right: This portrait of King Charles II of England shows him as he was best remembered—a kind, wise ruler who enjoyed the good things in life.

CHAUCER, GEOFFREY

Geoffrey Chaucer (1345–1400) was a great English poet. He was one of the first people to write in the ENGLISH LANGUAGE rather than in Latin. His best known work is the *Canterbury Tales*. It is a collection of stories told by an imaginary group of pilgrims (shown in the picture on the right), as they travelled to Canterbury Cathedral.

CHEESE

Most cheese is made from cows' MILK, but it can be made from the milk of goats, sheep, buffalo and even reindeer. To make cheese, the milk is turned sour so that it will *curdle*.

The solid bits, called the *curds*, are taken away from the liquid, or *whey*, and are pressed into a more solid form and dried. The cheese is then left to ripen.

There are hundreds of different cheeses in the world. Here, rows of Swiss cheeses are left to ripen in cool storage cellars.

CHEMISTRY

Chemistry is the study of materials—solids, liquids and gases. A chemist finds out what things are made of and how they are joined together. If a piece of wood is burned in a fire, this is a *chemical reaction*. The wood turns to ash and, at the same time, heat and light are given off. It took chemists a long time to find out that burning is the joining together of the wood with the gas oxygen from the air. There are lots and lots of chemical reactions.

The true science of chemistry as we know it began only in the 1600s. Chemists at this time began to find out how chemicals really work. Then they discovered the *elements*, simple substances which make up all the millions of different substances on Earth. There are only about a hundred elements, each of them made up of tiny ATOMS. The atoms of elements often join together to make different substances. The salt you put on your food is made up of atoms of the elements sodium and chlorine. An atom of sodium joins with an atom of chlorine to make a molecule of salt, like this:

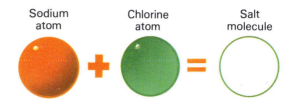

Sodium atom Chlorine atom Salt molecule

Chemistry is today a very important science, and chemists are employed in a vast number of industries.

CHESS

Chess is a game that has been played for hundreds of years. It is played by two people on a board with 64 black and white squares. Each of the two players has 16 pieces which they line up on either side of the board (shown right). Every piece can only be moved around the board in a special way. They are used to attack and retreat, to defend each other, and can be captured and taken out of play. The most important piece for each player is the 'king'. The game is won when one player manages to capture the other player's king.

Black

White

CHESTNUT

There are two quite different TREES that are both called chestnuts. We eat the nuts of the sweet chestnut either boiled or roasted, or preserved in sugar as *marrons glacés*. The 'nuts' of the horse chestnut are not really nuts but large round seeds we call 'conkers'.

Right: Sweet chestnuts are tall trees with spreading branches. Their nuts are delicious to eat.

Sweet chestnut

CHIMPANZEE

Chimpanzees are the most human-looking of all the APES. Fully grown, they are about 1·3 metres (5 ft) tall and are able to walk upright, although they often use their hands to help push themselves along the ground. Chimpanzees come from the jungles of Africa. They live in family groups and are very fond of their young and take good care of them. They are playful and intelligent animals. Tame chimpanzees have been taught to behave like humans in many ways. They can even learn to talk in sign language.

Chimpanzees are just as happy in trees as on the ground. They use their strong arms to swing from branch to branch. They live mainly on fruit and vegetables, but they will also eat insects, grubs and birds' eggs.

CHINA

China is the third biggest nation in the world, and it has a population larger than that of any other country. A fifth of all the people on Earth are Chinese—over 1000 million.

To the north and west, China is cut off from the rest of ASIA by great deserts and by the HIMALAYAS. To the east lies the Pacific Ocean and Japan. The Chinese have ruled within this area almost without a break for the past 3500 years.

The first great Chinese civilization grew up in the great river valleys of the Hwang Ho in the north and the YANGTZE in the south. Today, more Chinese live crowded close to these rivers than in any other part of the country.

By far the greatest number of Chinese are farmers. In modern China, the farmers do not own their farms. Each village or commune owns its own land. Everyone works on it together and the harvest is shared out between them. ▷

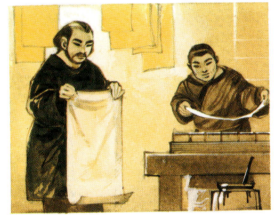

Top: The Chinese discovered how to make paper in about AD 100. They made beautiful paintings on paper scrolls (right) filled with delicately coloured flowers and birds.

Hot summers and cool or cold winters with plenty of rainfall all year round make the heart of China a very good farming region. But much of China cannot be farmed, and growing enough food for the many people who live there is still a great problem. The main crops that are raised are rice in the south and wheat and millet in the north. Silk, tea and cotton are also important and there is a large fishing industry.

The biggest cities of China are the great port of Shanghai—near the mouth of the Yangtze—and Tientsin. The capital is Peking, a fine old city. For centuries the Chinese emperors lived in great splendour in the Forbidden City in the centre of Peking.

In 1949, China was greatly changed when the civil war which had been raging since the 1920s came to an end. The Communist Party led by MAO TSE-TUNG came into power. Mao Tse-Tung persuaded the Chinese people to give up many of their old ways of life. He set out to make China an important industrial centre, and today, China is as powerful as the other large nations.

CHLOROPHYLL

This is a chemical substance that is found in the leaves and stems of almost all PLANTS. It gives them their green colour. Chlorophyll is found inside plant CELLS in tiny bodies called *chloroplasts*.

Plants need chlorophyll to make their food. Sunlight, falling on the leaves, acts with the chlorophyll to turn carbon dioxide from the air, and water, which the plant's roots suck up from the soil, into food made up of SUGARS and STARCHES. At the same time, the plant's leaves give out OXYGEN. This whole process is called *photosynthesis*.

It is a very important part of life on our Earth, as all living things need oxygen in order to breathe.

Plants can only produce chlorophyll when they are grown in the light. Plants kept in darkness often turn white or yellow.

CHOCOLATE

The chocolate we eat is made from the beans of the cacao tree. The beans grow inside pods, which hang from the trunk and the branches of the tree (left).

To make chocolate, the beans are first roasted, then ground up to give an oily liquid called 'chocolate liquor'. Other things may then be added to the liquor. The milk chocolate we buy in shops, for example, has milk and sugar added to it.

CHRISTIANITY

Christianity is one of the world's great religions. More than 1000 million people call themselves Christians. These are people who follow the teachings of JESUS, and who believe that he is the son of God who came to Earth in human form.

Christianity is almost 2000 years old. In fact, we date our calendar from the year in which it was thought that Jesus was born. Christians accept the BIBLE as their holy book and Sunday is their holy day, when they go to church, pray and observe other religious traditions. The most important festivals are Christmas, which marks the birth of Jesus, and Easter, which marks his death and rise to heaven.

In some ways Christianity grew out of the Jewish religion of Judaism. But the teachings of Jesus upset the Jewish and Roman leaders of the time, and in AD 29 he was crucified. After his death, the followers of Jesus, the disciples, spread his teachings far and wide. Today, there are many different forms of Christianity.

CHURCHES

Christian churches are as varied as the countries in which they are found. They come in all shapes and sizes—from tents and tiny wooden huts to towering stone cathedrals. But all churches are used for the same purposes. They serve as places of prayer, as settings for holding religious services and as places that house all kinds of religious objects.

Larger churches, especially traditional Catholic ones, were usually built in the shape of a cross. In most, the altar is built at the east end. It is found at the end furthest away from the main door.

The inside of a cathedral, showing the bell tower, the nave, the altar and the transepts.

Throughout the ages, Churches have been built in many different styles of ARCHITECTURE, depending on the period of history and which country they were built in. Many churches adopted the Romanesque style of architecture known as *Byzantine*. They all had wide, rounded arches and low round domes. In the Middle Ages, in western Europe, a style known as *Gothic* appeared. After the 1000s, cathedrals with pointed spires, narrow soaring arches, richly stained glass windows and lots of stone carvings became very popular. These churches were cool and dark on the inside. The huge space inside them helped to give churchgoers a sense of awe and wonder at being in the presence of God.

Most cathedrals were laid out in the same way on the inside. The worshippers sat in the centre, in a section called the *nave*. They faced toward the altar and the place where the choir sang. On either side were the wings, called *transepts*, which gave the church its cross shape. Sometimes, a number of small chapels were placed inside the transepts.

CHURCHILL, WINSTON

Sir Winston Churchill (1874–1965) was a great British Prime Minister, war leader, and writer. Although he was a senior minister in PARLIAMENT before and during World War I, he was not very powerful. But in 1940, when World War II threatened Britain the country chose him as their Prime Minister. As a leader during war time he showed great courage and determination. His rousing speeches helped the people of Britain to fight on when they stood alone against Germany and her allies.

CINEMA

The art of making moving pictures came from an invention called the *kinetoscope*, built by an American, Thomas EDISON, in 1891. Soon after Edison's machine became known, two brothers, Auguste and Louis Lumière, built a similar machine of their own called a *cinématographe*. This machine projected pictures from a piece of film onto a screen. The pictures were shown one after the other, so quickly that the images on the screen appeared to move. In 1896, in Paris, the Lumière brothers gave the world's first public film show. Soon, people all over Europe and North America were making films.

These early films did not look much like the ones we are used to seeing today. They were only in black and white, the movements were very jerky and they had no sound. At first, films were made to show news and real events, but by 1902 film-makers began to make up their own stories, using actors to play the parts of imaginary people. These films were very popular in France and the United States, and Hollywood in California became the film-making centre of the world. The first 'talkie', or moving picture with sound, was shown in America in 1927. It was called *The Jazz Singer*.

America remained the leader in the film world. Huge amounts of money were spent on films that used hundreds of actors, singers and dancers, lavish costumes and specially designed 'sets' or backgrounds. But Europe too produced many important films, and after World War II, a more realistic type of film became popular, telling stories of everyday life.

Many films made today, like Star Wars, *use a lot of equipment to create special effects.*

CIVIL WAR

Civil war happens when a whole country is divided into two or more groups who fight each other over their different political or religious beliefs. In England, the last civil war lasted from 1642 to 1649 and was fought between the king, CHARLES I, and PARLIAMENT.

Up to this time it had been agreed that although the King ruled the country he could only tax money from the people if Parliament agreed. Charles believed that God had given him the right to do this alone. So in 1629 he got rid of Parliament and ruled without it, taxing the people whenever he needed money.

People became very unwilling to pay their taxes to Charles. In 1640 Charles was forced to recall Parliament because he needed more money. Instead of giving him money, Parliament argued with the King and said he could not rule on his own. Charles angrily dismissed Parliament and later tried to arrest some of its leaders.

In 1642 the King called his friends to arm themselves. They were called Royalists. Parliament had its own army. They were called Roundheads because they had short hair. The Roundheads had a great general called Oliver CROMWELL. He was very strict and trained his army carefully.

After several battles the Royalist forces lost the war and the King was captured. Charles was put on trial and in 1649 he was executed. Parliament began to rule without a king, with Cromwell as its leader.

The Royalists and the Roundheads fought the English Civil War. The Royalists wore rich clothes and had long hair. They were also known as 'Cavaliers' because they were good cavalry soldiers. The Roundheads had short hair and wore plain uniforms.

CIVIL WAR (AMERICAN)

The American Civil War took place in the United States from 1861 to 1865. It was fought between the government (Union), backed by the northern states, and the southern states (Confederacy). In 1861 a number of southern states tried to break away from the USA and form their own country. The main quarrel was over SLAVERY. People in the northern states wanted to free the slaves who still worked on the big farms, or *plantations*, in the south. These quarrels led to civil war.

At first the Confederates, under General Lee, won many battles but they were defeated at the Battle of Gettysburg in 1863. The Union army, under General Grant, began to win the war. In April, 1865, the Confederate army surrendered to General Grant. The slaves were finally freed.

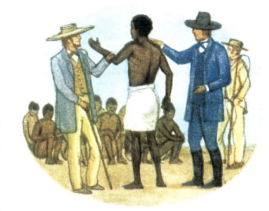

Right: The slaves in America came from Africa. They were caught and sent to America in ships. Many of them died on the way. In America they were sold to farmers and put to work on the cotton plantations. Some slaves also worked on sugar and tobacco farms.

CLIMATE

Climate is the usual WEATHER of a place over a long period of time. The weather can change from day to day but the climate stays the same.

The Sun has the greatest influence on the climate. It heats the land, the seas and the air. Countries near the equator get more of the Sun's rays and usually have a hotter climate than places further north or south. The Sun's rays do not get to the Arctic and the Antarctic easily. They have very cold climates.

When the Sun heats the air it causes winds which can make the climate hotter or colder. The winds may also carry rain or dry air which can make the climate wet or dry.

Together with the winds, the Sun's heat makes ocean currents. The Gulf Stream is a current which travels from Mexico to north-western Europe. In winter the warmth from its water makes the climate of Britain milder.

Mountains also affect the climate. The air up mountains is thinner. It does not soak up the heat of the sun as much as air at the bottom of mountains or in valleys.

The poles get less heat than the equator because the Sun's rays have to travel further through the Earth's atmosphere. The rays also reach the poles at a slant because the Earth is round.

North pole

Sun

Equator

Earth

South pole

CLIPPER SHIPS

A clipper was a fast sailing SHIP of the mid-1800s. Clippers were specially built for speed. They were very long and slim and had many large sails. Because they were slender they could not carry as large a cargo as other ships, so they had to carry valuable cargoes, like tea, grain or wood, instead. Most clippers had three masts on which five or six square sails were rigged. A good captain with a trained crew could set these sails to catch every bit of wind. Some clippers set records for speed. One, called *Lightning*, once sailed 808 km (502 miles) in a day, a record that even steamships could not beat for many years.

Clippers were first built in America in the 1830s, but a few years later they were also being built in England and Scotland. When the tea trade between China and Britain began, the first ship home with this valuable cargo made the most money. Many famous races took place. The most famous clipper ship of all, the *Cutty Sark*, spent many years in the tea and wool trade. Later she was fully restored, and today she can be visited in dry dock at Greenwich in London.

CLOCKS

Long ago people measured time by putting a stick in the ground and watching its shadow move with the Sun. Sundials work in the same way. Sun clocks work only when the Sun is shining, so people began to measure time by watching how long it took a candle to burn or a tank of water to empty.

The first mechanical clocks were made in Europe in the 1200s, although the Chinese probably had clocks as early as the 600s.

European clocks were first used in churches and abbeys to mark the time of services. A clock in Salisbury Cathedral dates from 1386.

Early clocks like these were bad time-keepers and could lose or gain an hour a day. In 1581 the great astronomer Galileo discovered that the PENDULUM could be used to measure time. This helped people to make much more accurate clocks. From then on improvements were made and ordinary clocks are now accurate to within a few minutes a year.

Today's scientists need very accurate clocks. They invented first the electric and then the quartz crystal clock. Now there are atomic clocks that are accurate to less than one thousandth of a second a year.

Right: The Cutty Sark *was built of iron that was covered with timber planks. Between 1885 and 1895 she was the fastest ship in the Australian wool trade. After a 26-year spell as a tramp ship carrying general cargo, she became a training ship, until she was finally restored and brought to Greenwich in London.*

CLOTH

Cloth is material made by WEAVING natural fibres such as wool, flax, silk and linen or man-made fibres such as nylon and rayon. No one knows when cloth was first woven but it was certainly made in prehistoric times. Fabric from as far back as 6000 BC has been found. Once the secret of weaving had been discovered it spread around the world. Only a few people, such as the African bushmen, do not weave cloth.

Cloth was probably first used instead of animal skins to protect people from the weather. From early times cloth has been coloured and decorated. This can be done by dyeing the fibres before they are woven. Or the cloth can be decorated with dyes or paints after it is woven. An even more important discovery was that different ▷

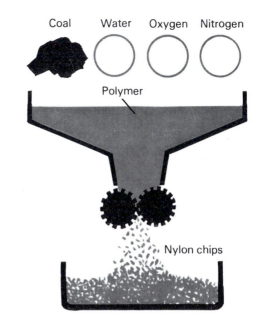

Coal   Water   Oxygen   Nitrogen

Polymer

Nylon chips

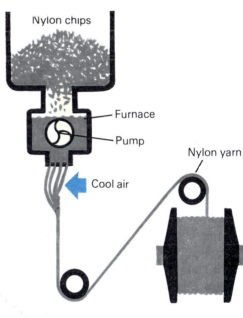

Nylon chips

Furnace

Pump

Cool air

Nylon yarn

Above: Nylon is a synthetic fibre made from coal and other chemicals. These are turned into nylon chips which are melted. The liquid nylon is pushed through tiny holes and comes out as thread which is cooled and gathered on a reel.

coloured threads could be woven together to make patterns or pictures. Tapestries and patterned rugs and carpets are made in this way.

Cloth was first woven by hand. Even today much fine cloth is hand-woven, but in many parts of the world it is woven by machines in factories.

Cloth is used to make many useful and beautiful things, from carpets and curtains to tents and sails. It is also very important for making clothes. Synthetic or man-made fibres are now used in many cloths. They are often more hard-wearing and cheaper than cloth made from natural fibres. Modern cloths are often treated to make them easier to wash and care for.

CLOUDS

Clouds are great clusters of tiny water droplets or ice crystals in the air. A cloud may float more than 10,000 metres (30,000 feet) up, or drift so low that it touches the ground, when it is known as mist or fog.

There is always a certain amount of water *vapour* in the air. It is made up of tiny specks of water. Warm air that contains water vapour often rises and cools. Since cool air cannot hold as much water as warm air, the vapour particles start to form droplets (condense) around bits of dust, pollen and salt that the wind has carried into the sky.

As more water vapour condenses, the droplets grow in size and clouds begin to form. At first they are white and gauzy. As they become heavy with water they become thick and grey. Finally the droplets become so heavy that they clump together and fall to the earth. If the temperature is high enough they come down as rain. Otherwise they land as hail or snow.

Below you can see the main kinds of clouds. Cirrus *are wispy clouds high in the sky. They are made of tiny ice-crystals.* Cirrostratus *clouds are not quite so high, and often mean rain is on the way.* Cirrocumulus *is often called a 'mackerel' sky.* Altostratus *and* Altocumulus *clouds are made up of water droplets. The low clouds are* Stratocumulus, Cumulus, Nimbostratus, Stratus *and* Cumulonimbus. *This last kind of cloud is the huge, dark thundercloud that threatens thunder and lightning.*

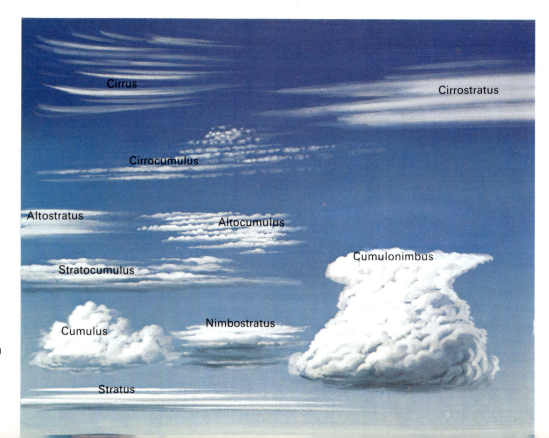

80

COAL

Coal is a fuel which is found in layers, or *seams*, under the ground. It is known as a FOSSIL fuel because it was made millions of years ago from dead plants. Coal is used for heating and in making electricity, gas and chemicals. It is also made into another fuel called coke.

Coal lies in the earth in thick layers called seams. If it is deep underground it can be reached only by digging deep mine shafts. From the main mine shaft are tunnels reaching out in all directions. These tunnels may be several kilometres long. Miners working on a coal seam use powerful cutting tools to dig out the coal. The coal is then loaded on to conveyor belts or wagons and taken away.

COCOA

Cocoa comes from the seeds, or beans, of the cacao tree of South America. The beans are roasted and made into cocoa powder which is used to make chocolate and chocolate drinks.

Cocoa

COCONUT

The coconut is the fruit of the coconut PALM. The inside is white and sweet. It can be eaten fresh or dried into copra. Copra is made into coconut oil and is used in soap, margarine and other things. The hairy husk near the outside is made into coir for weaving mats and rope.

COFFEE

Coffee is a drink made from the beans of the coffee plant. The beans are dried and roasted until they are brown, and then ground.

Coffee

Cocoa beans grow in clusters inside a large pod. Green coffee beans grow inside red berries.

COLOUR

The first man to find out about coloured light was Isaac Newton. He shone sunlight through a piece of glass called a *prism*. (You can see one below). The light that came out of the prism was broken up into all the colours of the rainbow—red, orange, yellow, green, blue and violet. Newton had found out that ordinary white light is made up of many colours added together.

As you can see in the picture below, red, blue and green light can be mixed to make any other colour. Red and green light mixed together give us yellow light. If we add blue to the yellow light, we have white light. All the colours you see in a colour TV set are made up from these three light colours—red, green and blue.

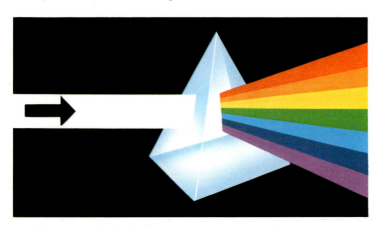

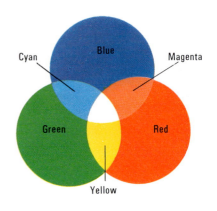

When sunlight falls on rain or spray from a garden hose, we sometimes see a rainbow. Rainbows are caused by the drops of water behaving like tiny prisms. They break up the Sun's light into colours. The colours are always in the same order, from red to violet.

A red flower is red because it takes in all the other colours and throws back only red. A white flower gives back to our eyes all the colours of light. We know that all the colours added together make white. You can see this for yourself by making a circle of card with the colours as shown below. Spin the card quickly and the card looks almost white. When you look at white light you are seeing a mixture of colours.

Mixing paints is quite different from mixing coloured lights. If you mix yellow and blue paint you get green. You can get any colour of paint you like by using yellow, blue and red paints. But you cannot make white paint by mixing different colours.

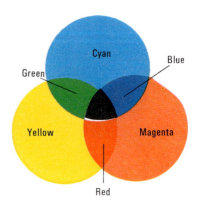

COLUMBUS, CHRISTOPHER

Christopher Columbus (1451–1506) was a sailor and explorer. He discovered America for Spain in 1492. Although Columbus returned to America three more times, he died believing that the land he had reached was Asia.

Like many people of his time, Columbus knew that the Earth was not flat but round. Sailors from Europe used to sail east to the 'Indies' (Asia). They brought back rich cargoes of gold, spices and treasure. Columbus thought that if he sailed west instead he could reach the Indies quicker. The Queen and King of Spain gave him ships and money to make this voyage.

In 1492 Columbus sailed west with three small ships, the *Santa Maria*, the *Pinta* and the *Niña*. The ships sailed for three weeks without seeing any land and the crew became afraid. Then, on 12 October, they reached an island near America. Columbus named it San Salvador. When he returned to Spain Columbus had a hero's welcome.

The Santa Maria *(below) was the flag ship of Columbus's fleet. It was 35 metres (115 feet) long, twice the size of the other two ships in his fleet. When he returned to Spain, the Spanish gave Columbus a coat of arms (below) to honour his discoveries.*

COMETS

Comets travel round the SOLAR SYSTEM in paths, or ORBITS. Sometimes they pass close to the Sun. At other times they move far beyond the path of Pluto, the outermost planet. A complete orbit by a comet is called its period. Encke's Comet has the shortest period of all. It is three and a half years. Others have periods of centuries or even thousands of years.

Comets are clouds of frozen gases, ice, dust and rock. The biggest are only a few kilometres across, but their bright tails may be millions of kilometres long.

Most of the time comets cannot be seen, even through the biggest telescopes. But whenever their orbits bring them back into the middle of the solar system they flare up and look very bright.

As a comet travels towards the Sun, the Sun's rays knock particles out of the comet and push them away to make a long tail. The tail is made of glowing gas and dust. But the tail is so fine that a rocket passing through it would not be harmed.

Only the brightest comets can be seen without a telescope. They are seen as they move past the sun. At this time their tails are at their longest and brightest. The best known of all is Halley's Comet. It appears in the sky every 76 years and is next due in 1986. Ikeya-Seki (below) was first seen in 1965. It is one of the brightest comets found this century, but is not due back for another 880 years.

Above: China became a communist country in 1949.
Left: Lenin was the leader of the Russian communists when they took power in 1917.

COMMONWEALTH

A commonwealth is a group of countries or people who are friendly and help each other. The Commonwealth of Nations is made up from most of the countries that were once ruled by Britain. Most of these countries now have their own governments and laws but many of them still have the queen or king of Britain as their monarch.

The Commonwealth came into being at a meeting held in 1926. Commonwealth countries share some of the same beliefs and trade with each other. The heads of Commonwealth countries that have their own governments meet together often. They talk about their problems and try to help each other. Commonwealth countries also take part in sports meetings called the Commonwealth Games.

COMMUNISM

Communism is a set of ideas about the way a country should be run. The main idea of communism is that people should share wealth and property. This makes people more equal because nobody is very rich or very poor. In most communist countries the people own the factories and farms but it is usually the government which runs them. People who believe in communism are often called Marxists. This is because they follow the ideas of Karl MARX, a thinker, or *philosopher*, of the 1800s.

Many countries have become communist in the 1900s. They include Russia, China and Cuba, and some countries in Eastern Europe and the Far East. LENIN and Mao Tse-Tung were among the great communist leaders of this century.

COMPASS

A compass is an instrument for finding the way. A magnetic compass always points to the Earth's magnetic poles, which are close to the North and South Poles. The magnetic compass has been used for centuries by sailors and explorers to find the right direction.

A magnetic compass works by MAGNETISM. It has a magnetic needle fixed to a pivot so that it is free to swing round. The needle always points north and south when it is at rest. With a compass showing where north and south are, it is easy to travel in a straight line in any direction you wish to go.

The needle always points north and south because the Earth itself is a big magnet. The compass lines up parallel with the Earth's magnetic field.

The needle of a magnetic compass always points north and south (above). Below and right are compasses used by sailors hundreds of years ago. The face of a modern compass is divided into 360 degrees.

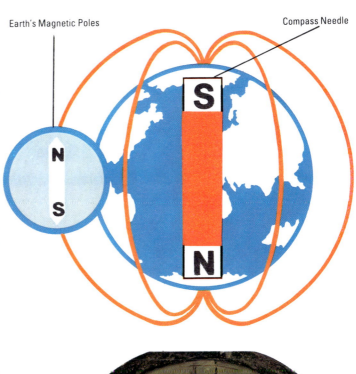

Earth's Magnetic Poles — Compass Needle

COMPUTERS

Computers are playing a bigger and bigger part in all our lives. They can play a game of chess with you, guide a spacecraft, check fingerprints and draw a map of Australia. They can do all these things and many more merely because they can add, subtract and compare one number with another. Computers are special because they can do millions of calculations in a second.

Although the computer works with numbers, the information it uses does not have to start off as numbers. We can feed almost anything into it, but the first thing the computer does is to turn everything into numbers. But the numbers it uses are not quite the same as ours. We use the numbers 0 to 9. All the computer needs is 0 and 1. In fact, it can only count up to 1! This is called the binary system. The computer uses the binary system because it has been designed to work with electrical currents. It can recognize the difference between a big current and a small current flow. If there is a big current, it registers 1; if there is a small current, it registers 0. When we type on the keys of a computer keyboard we are making little electrical currents flow through tiny circuits in microchips. It is these tiny currents that give us the answers we need.

Some conifers are very quick-growing. It is from conifers that we get the timber known as soft-wood. They also give us wood-pulp for paper.

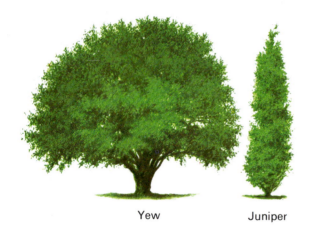

Yew   Juniper

Scots pine

Spruce

CONGO

The Congo is a country in the west of central AFRICA. It used to be enormous, about the size of western Europe. Now it is much smaller, although it is still bigger than Great Britain. It has an area of 342,000 sq km (132,047 sq miles).

The Congo is a hot, wet country. It has great forests and swamps, and a low grassy plain on the coast. The capital is called Brazzaville. The Congo produces a lot of timber, but it also has diamonds, sugar, oil, cocoa and coffee.

When the Congo was a larger country, the river that ran through it was called the Congo river. Now most of the river runs along the Congo's border with ZAIRE. The Congo river is now called the Zaire river. It is 4700 km (2900 miles) long: one of the longest in the world. Many other rivers flow into it. It is used for travel, but only small boats can go any distance on it. Waterfalls block the way for big ships.

CONIFERS

Conifers are TREES and shrubs which have cones instead of flowers for making pollen and seeds. There are about 600 different kinds of conifer. Many of them are found in the cool parts of the world. Some even grow north of the Arctic Circle.

Conifers include pines, firs, spruces, larches and cedars. Most have needle-like leaves which they do not lose in winter.

Cedar of Lebanon

CONTINENTAL SHELF

Continents do not end where their coasts meet the sea. Their true edge lies far out under the sea.

Each continent is ringed by a gently sloping shelf of land under the sea called the continental shelf. This shelf sometimes stretches for hundreds of kilometres from the shore. Beyond the continental shelf is the deep ocean floor.

In the past, the sea level was lower and much of the continental shelf was dry land. Rivers flowed through it to the sea and made valleys or canyons. These canyons are still there, but today they are under the sea.

Most sea life is found on the continental shelf. Sunlight shines through the water, helping plants, fish and other animals to grow.

Most of the continental shelf lies under about 140 metres (460 feet) of water. At its edge, the seabed falls steeply to the deep ocean floor. Here, the water is usually about 4800 metres (15,750 feet) deep. The ocean floor is not flat but has big mountains and valleys.

CONTINENTS

Continents are large areas of land. The Earth has seven continents: Africa, Antarctica, Asia, Australia, Europe, North America and South America.

The continents are not fixed. They are made of lighter rock than the rock on the ocean floor. The great heat in the centre of the Earth has made the surface rocks break into huge pieces called *plates*. When the plates move they move the continents with them. This movement is very slow. A continent moves only a few centimetres in one century.

A few hundred years ago some people saw that the shapes of America, Europe and Africa looked like jigsaw pieces that would fit closely if they were pushed together. This gave them the idea that the continents used to be one big piece of land which broke up. This idea is called continental drift. Today, people who study GEOLOGY believe this idea is true.

Geologists think that the movements of the continents pushed up some pieces of land to make mountains such as the Alps and the Himalayas.

Continent

Continental shelf

Ocean floor

COOK, JAMES

James Cook (1728–1779) was a famous British sea captain and explorer. His expeditions took him round the world and all over the Pacific Ocean. Cook's discoveries led to Australia, New Zealand and many South Pacific islands becoming British colonies.

After serving in the Royal Navy for 13 years, Cook was put in command of an expedition to Tahiti in 1768. After Tahiti, Cook carried on to New Zealand. He

sailed around both North and South islands, and then went on to Australia. Cook landed in Botany Bay in 1770 to claim the continent for Britain.

On his second voyage (1772–1775), Cook set off to look for the 'southern continent', which many people believed lay south of Australia. He crossed the Antarctic Circle and explored the edges of Antarctica. He also charted many unknown Pacific islands.

Cook's third and last voyage began in 1776. He left England with two ships—the *Resolution* and *Discovery*—to try to find a route around North America. Again he sailed to the Pacific. In early 1778 he discovered the Hawaiian Islands. From there Cook sailed north along the west coast of America. He got as far as the Bering Strait off Alaska before being forced back by ice. Returning to Hawaii, he was killed in a scuffle with natives over a stolen boat. Today Cook is remembered as a skilled navigator and a great explorer.

Left: At Botany Bay in Australia, scientists with Cook's expedition gathered and sketched more than 1500 types of plants they had never seen before.

COPERNICUS, NICOLAUS

Nicolaus Copernicus (1473–1543) was a Polish scientist. He is sometimes called the father of modern ASTRONOMY.

Copernicus showed that the Earth is not the centre of the UNIVERSE, as people used to believe. Instead, the Earth and PLANETS revolve round the Sun. Copernicus also showed that the Earth itself moves round, or *rotates*, each day, and stars do not.

COPPER

Copper is a reddish-brown metal. It was probably one of the first metals that people used. About 7000 years ago the ancient Egyptians and people in Iraq began to use copper for their tools and weapons. They also made copper ornaments. At first they used pure copper which they found in the ground. But most copper is found with other metals and minerals in a mixture called ore. People began to heat, or *smelt*, copper ores so that the pure copper melted and flowed out.

Copper is very soft when it is pure. But if it is mixed with other metals it makes alloys such as BRASS and BRONZE, which are harder and better for making tools.

Copper can be beaten into sheets or pulled out into wire. It lets heat and electricity pass through it very easily, so it is often used for making pots and pans and electric wires.

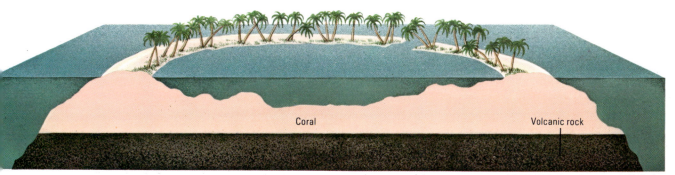

Coral   Volcanic rock

CORAL

Coral is a kind of limestone found mostly in warm, shallow seas. It is made by tiny animals, called coral polyps, that build limestone 'shells' around themselves for protection. Most coral polyps live in groups, or colonies. These may take many shapes, from lacy fans to stubby branches, all in beautiful colours. Other colonies form thick underwater walls known as reefs.

Along some reefs waves may throw up bits of sand and coral which gradually build up on top of the reef until it is above water. The reef then becomes an island. One kind of coral island is the atoll (above), a ringed reef that encloses a central lagoon.

CORK

The cork that is used to make bottle stoppers comes from the smooth bark of the cork oak tree of the Mediterranean. It is a light, spongy material that forms a thick layer about 3 cm (1·5 inches) deep around the trunk of the tree.

Cork is stripped from cork oaks once every nine or ten years until the trees are about 150 years old.

CORTÉS, HERNANDO

Hernando Cortés (1485–1547) was a Spanish soldier and explorer who in 1519 landed on the coast of Mexico. With a force of only 600 men and a handful of horses he conquered the great AZTEC empire. Cortés' horses and guns helped convince the Aztecs he was a god. He marched on their capital, captured the Aztec emperor Montezuma, and by 1521 had taken control of Mexico.

Above: The coral polyp on the left is open, showing its mouth fringed with tentacles. The polyps on the right are closed. In the background the limestone reef built by these animals can be seen.

Hernando Cortés entered the Aztec capital of Tenochtitlán (where Mexico City is today) in 1521 after defeating a large Aztec army. He destroyed a large part of the city and made the Aztec empire a Spanish colony.

COTTON

Cotton grows in warm and tropical places all round the world. It is one of the most important plants grown by people; its fibres and seeds are both used. The fibres are made into CLOTH and the seeds are used for oil and cattle food. The oil is used in soaps, paints and cosmetics.

Cotton has green fruits called bolls. When they are ripe, the bolls split open. Inside them is a mass of white fibres and seeds. The bolls are harvested and the fibres are separated from the seeds. The fibres are spun into yarn and then woven into cloth.

In the past, cotton harvesting was a back-breaking job done by hand. Today, in many parts of the world, machines are used to harvest the cotton.

COW

The cow that gives us milk is a member of the cattle family. Cattle are large grass-eating animals. Grass is difficult to digest, and all cattle have four stomachs to make it easier. During digestion the food is returned to the mouth to be chewed and swallowed again. When a cow does this we say it is 'chewing the cud'. The farm cow comes from an extinct wild cow called an *auroch*, and has been tamed by man for about 6000 years.

Left: There are many types of cow. Some are bred for meat, and others for milk.

CRABS

Most people think that crabs live only in the sea. But there are some kinds that live in fresh water (rivers or lakes) and some tropical kinds that make their home on land.

Crabs belong to a group of animals called CRUSTACEANS. They have hard, thick shells that cover their flat bodies. They also have long, spidery legs for walking underwater, swimming and burrowing. The first pair of legs have pincers which are used for attacking and holding prey. Crabs have their eyes on the end of short stalks. These can be pulled into the shell for safety.

CRETE

Crete is a mountainous island in the Mediterranean. It lies to the south of Greece. Today it is a poor land, the home of half a million people who are mostly Greek and live mainly by farming. About 5000 years ago a great civilization began in Crete. It lasted for more than a thousand years.

This civilization was forgotten about until 1900 when Arthur Evans, a British archaeologist, rediscovered it. He began digging, or *excavating*, the ruins of a palace at Knossos.

Soon Evans found more remains which told him about the old civilization. It had busy towns and traded with ancient Egypt. The people had well-built homes and some of the houses had beautiful wall paintings, or *frescoes*. Evans called this civilization Minoan, after a legendary king of Crete called Minos. The Minoans also had an alphabet and could write. They may have been the first people in Europe to do this.

Suddenly, in about 1400 BC, many of the palaces and cities were destroyed. This may have been caused by an earthquake.

The palace at Knossos probably looked like this (below). It had many buildings, gardens, staircases and courtyards. Minoan craftsmen had great skill. The golden brooch (top) is in the shape of two bees with a piece of honeycomb. The Minoan vase (above) is shaped like a bull's head.

CRICKET

Cricket is a very old game. It was probably first played in the 1300s in England. The early bats were curved, and there were no wickets. But by the early 1800s the game was very much as it is now. The pitch is 22 yards (20 metres) from wicket to wicket; the three stumps are 28 inches (71·1 cm) high and 9 inches (22·9 cm) wide. The ball must weigh between $5\frac{1}{2}$ and $5\frac{3}{4}$ ounces (156 and 163 gm); the bat must not be more than $4\frac{1}{4}$ inches (10·8 cm) wide.

The Marylebone Cricket Club (M.C.C.), whose ground is at Lords in London, was started in 1787. It governed the game for many years.

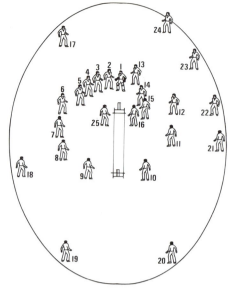

The positions on a cricket field: 1 wicket-keeper; 2 first slip; 3 second slip; 4 third slip; 5 gully; 6 point; 7 cover; 8 extra cover; 9 mid-off; 10 mid-on; 11 mid-wicket; 12 square leg; 13 leg slip; 14 backward short leg; 15 forward short leg; 16 silly mid-on; 17 third man; 18 deep extra cover; 19 long off; 20 long on; 21 deep mid-wicket; 22 deep square leg; 23 long leg; 24 fine leg; 25 silly point.

CRIMEAN WAR

The Crimean War (1854–56) was a struggle between Russia on one side and Turkey, France and Britain on the other. At that time the Turkish Empire was very weak. Russia hoped to make its power greater in the eastern Mediterranean by taking Constantinople.

The British, French and Turks pushed the Russian army back into the Crimean peninsula, where the war was fought. There was much misery and suffering.

For the first time, newspaper reporters and photographers went to the battle-grounds. They reported the terrible conditions of the soldiers to the newspapers.

More than half a million men died in the Crimean War. More were killed by disease and cold than by the fighting.

CROCODILES

Crocodiles and their relatives the ALLIGATORS, caymans and gavials are the largest of living REPTILES. They live in swamps and rivers in warm parts of the world.

Crocodiles have heavy bodies covered with bony scales. Their tails are long and powerful, and they wave them from side to side when swimming. Their jaws have sharp teeth.

On land crocodiles are clumsy and slow, but they can lift their bodies and run short distances if they have to. In the water they move swiftly without a sound.

Crocodiles hunt fish, turtles, birds and water mammals. They usually attack from under the water. Sometimes crocodiles eat land mammals. They float in the water with

The crocodile birds of Africa feed on small ticks and leeches that live on the skin of the crocodiles. The birds also warn the crocodiles when enemies are near by making noises or flying away.

only the tops of their heads showing. When an animal comes to the river bank to drink, the crocodile swims quickly towards it underwater. The crocodile then pulls the animal into the water with its strong jaws and drowns it.

Crocodiles lay white eggs in nests or holes in the ground. As soon as the young hatch out of the eggs they are able to run and catch their own food. Many kinds of crocodile are becoming extinct because people hunt them. Their skin is made into leather for bags and shoes.

CROMWELL, OLIVER

Oliver Cromwell (1599–1658) was the only ruler of Britain never to have been a king or queen. He came to power after the CIVIL WAR of the 1640s. Cromwell was a member of PARLIAMENT. He fought against CHARLES I with the army of Parliament and became its leader.

After Charles I was beheaded, Cromwell became the head of the country but he never made himself king. He was called the 'Lord Protector'. After Cromwell died, CHARLES II became king.

CRUSADES

The Crusades were wars between Christians and Moslems in the MIDDLE AGES. They took place in Palestine, the Holy Land. In 1087, the Turks captured the city of Jerusalem in Palestine. The Turks were Moslems and they stopped Christians from visiting the holy places in Palestine.

The Christian rulers in Europe were very angry about this. A few years later, the Byzantine emperor in Constantinople asked the Pope to help him drive the Turks from the Holy Land. The Pope started the first Crusade. He said he would forgive the sins of all the people who went and fought in the Holy Land.

The armies of the first Crusade were successful. They took Jerusalem from the Turks in 1099. The Crusaders set up Christian kingdoms along the coast of Palestine and Syria and built strong fortresses to defend their new lands.

There were seven more Crusades after the first one. Many of them failed because the Crusaders quarrelled with each other. The Turks took back much of the Holy Land from the Christians. When the Turks took Jerusalem in 1187, the third Crusade set off from Europe. When they got to the Holy Land the Crusaders were defeated by the Turks who had a new general called Saladin.

Later, the Crusaders forgot that they were fighting for their religion. Many of them went to Palestine hoping to take the land and become rich. By 1291, the Turks took the last remaining Christian city at Acre.

During the Crusades European people learnt more about the eastern parts of the world. When they returned to Europe they took back with them many new things including foods, spices, silk clothes and paper. They learnt about medicine, mathematics and astronomy from the Arabs of the east, and trade between east and west began to grow.

The Crusader on the left is wearing a full coat of armour made from mail. The mail was metal chains or rings joined together. This figure comes from a tomb.

Saladin (left) was a famous Turkish general. He fought the armies of the third Crusade and took back many cities from the Christians.

Sometimes the Crusaders had to attack cities or castles with strong walls around them. They would use catapults and battering rams to break down the doors. They built tall towers so they could fire arrows into the enemy and climb over the walls.

CRYSTALS

If you look closely at sugar through a magnifying glass, you will see that it is made up of thousands of tiny glassy pieces with flat sides. They are sugar crystals. Snow is made up of tiny crystals of frozen water. So are the beautiful patterns on a frosty window. Some crystals are so small they can only be seen through a microscope. Others can sometimes be as big as a man.

All crystals have a definite shape. They have smooth, flat sides that meet in sharp edges. The shape of any one type of crystal never changes, but there are many different crystal shapes. The differences between them are caused by the ATOMS in the crystals arranging themselves in different ways.

For example, the salt you eat is made up of two different kinds of atoms—sodium atoms and chlorine atoms. The tiny sodium and chlorine atoms are arranged in cube patterns as in the picture on the right. If you look at salt grains through a magnifying glass, you will see that most of them are little cubes. All salt crystals are built in the same way.

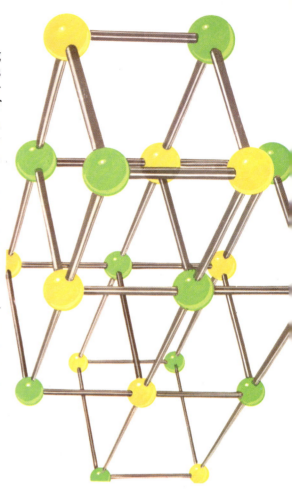

The sharp-pointed crystals on the right are calcite. A clump of crystals like this one can grow to a huge size. The stalactites and stalagmites that grow in caves are made of calcite.

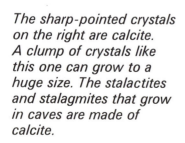

CUBA

Cuba is an island in the Caribbean Sea. It is part of the WEST INDIES. Cuba has 10,346,000 people and covers an area of 114,524 sq km (44,218 sq miles). The capital city is Havana.

Part of the island is hilly, with high mountains in the south-east. In the centre are large cedar and mahogany forests. Cuba has big sugar cane plantations and tobacco farms.

The climate is warm and pleasant, but Cuba lies in the path of hurricanes which come blowing through the West Indies every year. Hurricanes are very strong winds which travel fast and often damage buildings and farms.

Cuba was ruled by Spain after Christopher COLUMBUS went there in 1492. The United States took Cuba from Spain in 1898. In 1902 the island became independent. Cuba became a communist country in 1959 under its leader Fidel Castro.

When Cuba became a communist country in 1959, it turned to Russia for much of its trade and other kinds of help. The leader of Russia then was Nikita Khrushchev (above right), seen here with Fidel Castro.

This piece of sugar is cube-shaped. All its edges are the same length.

CUBE

A cube is an object with six square sides. All the edges are the same length. Sugar and ice are often made in cubes.

The space a cube fills is called its volume. You can find the volume of a cube by multiplying the length of a side by itself and then by itself again. If the length of a side is 3 cm, the volume of the cube is $3 \times 3 \times 3 = 27$ cubic cm.

Many kinds of CRYSTAL have a cube shape. This is because of the way their ATOMS are arranged.

CUBIT

The cubit was a measure of length used by some ancient people—the Egyptians, the Babylonians and the Hebrews. It began as the length of the forearm from the tip of the middle finger to the elbow. The cubit mentioned in the Bible was 43 cm ($17\frac{1}{2}$ inches) long. The ancient Egyptian cubit was about 53 cm (21 inches) in length.

CUCKOO

Cuckoos are a family of birds. There are many kinds of cuckoo. They are found in a lot of countries, but most live in the warm parts of the world. Cuckoos that live in cool countries fly to warm places for the winter.

The European cuckoo is a large bird about 30 cm (12 inches) long. It is blue-grey in colour with stripes underneath. It eats mainly insects. The call of the European cuckoo sounds just like its name. The birds can be heard calling in spring when they ▷

return from Africa.

European cuckoos do not build nests. They lay their eggs in the nests of other birds such as warblers and sparrows. The female cuckoo watches while the other birds build their nests and lay their eggs. When they leave the nest to find food the cuckoo pulls one of the eggs out of the nest with her beak. Then she lays her own egg in its place and flies away. When the other birds return they do not notice the strange egg because it is often the same colour as their own.

After about two weeks the young cuckoo hatches. It pushes the other eggs or baby birds out of the nest. The foster parents feed and take care of the cuckoo until it is ready to fly away. Young cuckoos are greedy and usually grow much bigger than their foster parents.

Two American cuckoos, the black-billed cuckoo and the yellow-billed cuckoo, are very different from the European kind. They are shy birds which live in trees and eat caterpillars. These birds do not have the same call as the European cuckoo and they usually build their own nests and take care of their young.

CURIE, MARIE AND PIERRE

Marie Curie (1867–1934) and Pierre Curie (1859–1906) were scientists who worked together. They studied RADIOACTIVITY and discovered the elements RADIUM and polonium. They married each other in 1895.

Because of their work on radioactivity and their discovery of radium in 1898, they were given the NOBEL PRIZE for physics in 1903. When Pierre was killed three years later, Marie took over his job as professor at the Sorbonne University in Paris. In 1911 she was given a second Nobel Prize, this time for chemistry.

The discoveries of the Curies were very important for medicine and science. In honour of their work, the unit for measuring levels of radioactivity was called the curie.

Reed warbler

Young cuckoo

Young cuckoos grow quite large before they leave their nest. This young cuckoo is already much bigger than its foster parent, a reed warbler.

The town of Darwin, in Australia, was destroyed by a tropical cyclone on Christmas Day, 1974.

CYCLONES

Cyclones are winds which blow inwards in a circle, or spiral. In hot, or *tropical* parts of the world cyclones can be very strong and cause great damage. The wind speed can be as fast as 240 km/hr (150 mph). These strong cyclones are known by different names such as hurricanes, TORNADOES and typhoons.

Cyclones usually come with storms. The winds bring black clouds and heavy rain, and sometimes thunder and lightning.

Cyclones often start at sea. When they move over land they cause terrible damage. They destroy houses, overturn cars and can even pull up trees.

CYPRUS

Cyprus is a large, mountainous island in the eastern Mediterranean. It covers an area of 9251 sq km (3572 sq miles) and has about 656,000 people. The capital city is Nicosia. Cyprus has a warm climate and the farmers grow grapes, lemons, oranges and olives.

Cyprus was ruled by Turkey for 300 years until 1878, when Britain took it over. It became independent in 1960. The people are Greek Cypriots who are Christian, and Turkish Cypriots who are Moslem. These two groups often quarrelled with each other and in the 1960s there was a civil war. Today, Cyprus is split into two parts, one part for the Greek Cypriots and one part for the Turkish Cypriots.

CZECHOSLOVAKIA

Czechoslovakia is a country in eastern EUROPE. It is surrounded by Germany, Poland, Russia, Hungary and Austria. The country has 15,556,000 people and covers an area of 127,869 sq km (49,370 sq miles).

Much of Czechoslovakia is covered in hills and mountains, and there are some big forests. Many of the people are farmers. Czechoslovakia also has coal and iron and an important steel industry.

The capital of Czechoslovakia is Prague. It is a medieval town, filled with churches and old buildings. Most of the people speak either Czech or Slovak, the two main languages of the country. The government has been communist since 1948.

D

DAMS

Dams are walls built across rivers to hold back water. They are used for irrigation, to make electricity, or to provide water for towns. Dams are particularly useful in places where there is not much rain. They store the rainwater in large lakes and release it steadily over the whole year. Some dams are made of enormous quantities of earth and rock. Others are made of concrete and stone. Dam-bursts are when water breaks through the wall of the dam. The severe flooding that may follow can cause great disasters.

There are different kinds of dams. A gravity dam (1) is a huge concrete or stone wall strong enough to hold back a great weight of water. Arch dams (2) are curved and are built across narrow canyons. Buttress dams (3) are strengthened by buttress supports. Embankment dams (4) are made by heaping earth and rock into a triangular shape across a river.

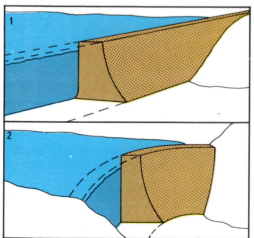

DANCE

All through the ages dance has been important to man. Early prehistoric cave paintings show men dancing. And today Australian aborigines still paint dancing figures on their sacred rocks. Archaeologists think that the earliest dances were about the hunt. Men used to dress up as animals and make rhythmical movements. They believed this would attract the animals they needed for

food and fur. These ancient ritual dances eventually developed into religious ceremonies. People danced to please their gods. They asked them for rain or for a good harvest. Sometimes they asked for success in the hunt or in battle. Dances like these still exist in many parts of the world. But some of them, like the rain dance of the American Indian or the Bolivian temple dance, are now more a tourist attraction than a religious ceremony.

In the Western world the religious meaning of dances disappeared many years ago. Today people dance only for pleasure or entertainment. In the 1920s and 1930s there were hundreds of dance halls. Dances like the foxtrot, quickstep and waltz were popular. Some people still enjoy ballroom dancing and competitions are often shown on television. But young people today prefer a freer form of dance. In modern discothèques where rock and reggae music is played, they make up the dance steps as they go along.

Another kind of dance is the traditional folkdance. Most countries have their own typical dances. In England Morris dancing is popular and in Spain the flamenco is the best known traditional dance.

The other main kind of dance is classical BALLET. This graceful dance obeys certain rules of posture and motion. Ballets are pieces of drama set to music, such as *Swan Lake* and *Sleeping Beauty*. To become a successful ballet dancer needs years of training and constant practice. Top ballet dancers become well known and stars like Margot Fonteyn and Rudolf Nureyev are famous all over the world.

DARWIN, CHARLES

Charles Darwin (1809–1882) was an English biologist. In 1859 he published his great book *The Origin of Species*. Before this almost everyone believed that the world was created by God exactly as the Bible described. Darwin put forward the theory that all living things evolved from earlier forms. They were alive because they had won the struggle to survive.

Within any species of living thing there would be small variations in shape, size or habit. Some of these variations would increase the living thing's chance of survival. For example, a giraffe with a long neck could reach leaves a giraffe with a shorter neck could not. In times of famine, the taller giraffe would survive while the shorter one would die. The taller giraffe that survived would, in time, replace the variety with the shorter neck.

This theory outraged many churchmen. They thought it was against the teachings of the Bible. But its common sense soon made it universally accepted. The Church came to realize that the Bible story was a parable. It saw that the theory of evolution did not threaten religious beliefs.

At the age of 22, Darwin went on a five-year voyage in the Beagle, *to the South Atlantic and the Pacific. During the voyage he studied thousands of plants and animals and developed his theory of the survival of the fittest. The map shows the route followed by the* Beagle, *and Darwin's journeys into South America.*

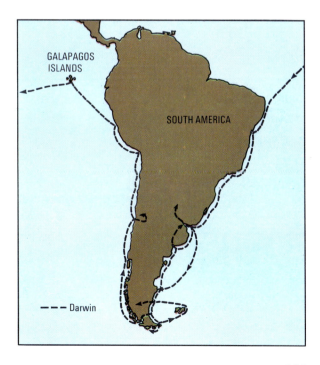

GALAPAGOS ISLANDS

SOUTH AMERICA

- - - Darwin

Sharp ears

Keen sense
of smell

Long neck helps
the deer reach
tasty leaves
and shoots.

The stag has six
points on its
antlers which
shows he is full
grown. He is
called a royal stag.

Mane grows long in
the mating season

The male (right) and female red deer

DEER

Deer belong to the cow and antelope family. They are different from their relatives because they have antlers rather than permanent horns. Male deer grow new antlers every year. Female deer, except for reindeers, do not grow antlers.

Every year in early spring, a lot of blood starts to flow into two bony lumps on the male deer's forehead. The blood carries a bony substance that makes the antlers grow quite rapidly. At first they are covered with a soft, hairy skin known as velvet. In early summer the antlers are fully grown. The blood supply is then cut off and the velvet dies. The male deer rubs off the velvet until his antlers are hard and shiny. Some antlers can be very big indeed. One red deer's antlers have weighed as much as 35 kg (77 lb). A moose's antlers have measured 2 metres (6½ feet).

Deer are mainly found in the Northern Hemisphere. But there are some species in South America and Indonesia.

In autumn male deer become very aggressive. They fight each other over groups of females which they guard very jealously.

Deer vary enormously in size. The biggest is the Alaskan moose which stands up to 2·3 metres (7½ feet) at the shoulder and weighs over 800 kg (1764 lb). The smallest is the Pudu of Chile which can measure as little as 33 cm (13 inches) at the shoulder and weigh as little as 8 kg (17½ lb).

Deer are useful to man because they provide meat and hides. But they also damage the bark of trees. They are naturally wild animals but some of them, such as reindeer, have been successfully domesticated.

The growth of antlers on the male red deer can be very rapid. The biggest antlers ever recorded in Britain were found in Sussex in 1892. They were 85 cm (33 inches) wide.

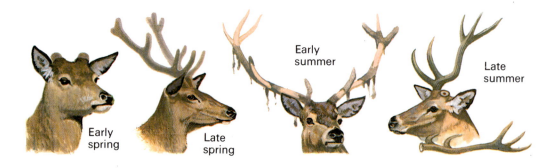

Early spring

Late spring

Early summer

Late summer

DEMOCRACY

Democracy is a type of government, organized by the people, for the people. In a democracy people elect their own government. Representatives of different political parties stand for election and people vote for the one they prefer. The people can also dismiss their government if they want to. In a democracy people can say and read what they like. They cannot be put into prison without a proper trial.

There are many different kinds of democracy. The British form is a monarchy with an elected PARLIAMENT. The American form is a republic with an elected president and an elected Congress. There is no one perfect democracy in the world. But all free nations are trying to work towards a perfect democracy.

Pericles of Athens was a great democratic leader who lived in the 400s BC.

DENMARK

Denmark is a small Scandinavian country in the north of EUROPE. It consists mainly of a peninsula called Jutland surrounded by 600 islands. In the west is the North Sea, to the east is the Baltic Sea, and to the south is West Germany. The capital is Copenhagen. Denmark is a flat country whose soil and climate is ideal for agriculture. Dairy and pig farming are especially important. Denmark is a member of the EUROPEAN ECONOMIC COMMUNITY. It exports a lot of butter and bacon to Britain. The Danes also make and export lager beer. There is little heavy industry. The Danes prefer to concentrate on high quality goods like china, furniture and textiles.

Danish dairy herds are world famous. Danish cream and butter are exported all over Europe. Denmark also produces a lot of cheese (left). The famous statue above is The Little Mermaid, from a fairy tale by Hans Christian Andersen. It stands in Copenhagen harbour.

103

DESERT

Not all deserts are hot and sandy. Some are cold, and some are rocky. But all are very dry. Some scientists say that a desert is any area where less than 8 cm (3 inches) of rain falls in a year. Other scientists may call a place a desert when there is more rain than this but where it evaporates quickly in the sun or sinks rapidly into the ground.

Many big deserts are in the tropics, often deep inside large continents where rain-bearing winds cannot reach them.

There are three main types of desert. The first is rocky, where any soil is blown away by the wind. The second has large areas of gravel. The third is made up of great sand dunes, burning hot by day and bitterly cold at night.

It is difficult for plants and animals to live in such conditions. Some plants, like the CACTUS, store moisture in their fleshy stems. Others have seeds that lie apparently lifeless in the ground for long periods. When a shower of rain falls they burst into life and can flower and produce new seeds within weeks. Many desert animals shelter from the sun by day and come out only at night. Some never drink but get all the moisture they need from their food.

The world's largest desert is the SAHARA in Africa. The driest desert is the Atacama in South America where it may not rain for several years. There are also cold deserts. These include Antarctica and a large part of the Arctic.

DETERGENT

The word *detergent* means any substance that will clean things. SOAP is a detergent. But today the word detergent is usually used to mean synthetic, or man-made, detergents, such as most washing powders. Detergents are similar to soaps. But soaps leave filmy deposits behind, such as the familiar bathtub ring. Detergents can reach soiled areas better than soaps, and do not leave deposits.

DIAMONDS

Diamonds are CRYSTALS. They are harder than anything else in the world. They are formed by great heat and pressure deep beneath the surface of the Earth. Diamonds are made of pure CARBON, the same mineral that is found in ordinary coal. They are usually colourless and have to be cut in a special way to catch the light and 'sparkle'. A diamond cutter is very skilled and uses tools tipped with diamonds, for only another diamond is hard enough to cut a diamond. Diamonds and diamond dust are used in industry for drilling and cutting many other materials.

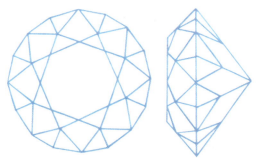

An uncut diamond looks like a dull lump of glass (top). A 'brilliant' cut (above) is shown from the top and from the side. A stone cut this way has 58 flat surfaces, or facets.

DICKENS, CHARLES

Charles Dickens (1812–1870) was a great English writer. His books give us a vivid picture of life in Victorian England in the middle of the 1800s. Many of his stories are about children, especially poor children and orphans. Dickens tried to improve the lives of the poor by making their sufferings more widely known through his books. He also created some of the liveliest and best-known characters in English literature. Some of his most famous books are *Oliver Twist*, *David Copperfield*, *Great Expectations* and *A Christmas Carol*.

DICTIONARY

A dictionary is a book that tells us what words mean. The words are arranged in alphabetical order from A to Z. Often the meanings, or definitions, include the history of the words and how they are used and pronounced. Dictionaries may vary in size from the 12-volume Oxford English Dictionary to dictionaries small enough to slip into your pocket. Dr Samuel JOHNSON was one of the greatest English dictionary-makers.

DIESEL ENGINES

Diesel engines are a type of INTERNAL COMBUSTION ENGINE, where fuel is burned inside the engine. Diesel engines are named after their inventor, Rudolf Diesel, who built his first successful engine in 1897 to replace the steam engine. Diesel engines use a cruder, heavier fuel oil than petrol. They are cheaper to run than petrol engines, but they are heavier and more difficult to start, so they are not widely used in cars. They are more often used to drive heavy machines such as trains, cranes, tractors, ships, buses and lorries.

A diesel engine is very like a petrol engine. But instead of using a spark from a sparking plug to ignite (set fire to) the fuel, the diesel engine uses heat that is made by squeezing air in a cylinder. When air is very tightly compressed, or pushed into a much smaller space than it filled before, it gets very hot. This heat sets fire to the diesel oil, which burns instantly, like a

The diagram below sets out how a diesel engine works. As the piston goes down (1), air is drawn into the cylinder. When the piston goes up, the air is squeezed and becomes very hot (2). When the piston gets to the top, oil is squirted in and bursts into flame. The hot gases expand and push the piston down (3). When the piston goes up again it pushes the spent gases out through the exhaust valve (4).

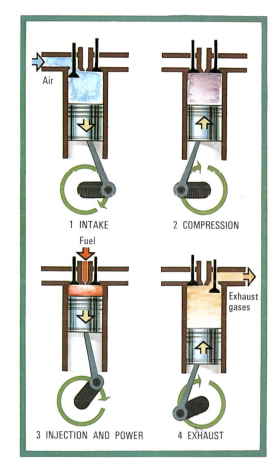

1 INTAKE 2 COMPRESSION
3 INJECTION AND POWER 4 EXHAUST

small explosion, as soon as it is pumped into the cylinder. The burning oil heats the air and forces it to expand again to push the piston and thus drive the engine.

Many RAILWAYS began using diesel engines after World War II. Railways badly damaged in the war took the opportunity to modernize their engines and replaced the old steam LOCOMOTIVES with diesel engines. Diesel engines were first used regularly on the railways of the United States and Denmark in the 1930s. Today, diesel-electric engines are in use all over the world.

DIGESTION

Digestion is the way in which the food we eat is broken down into substances that can be used by the body. It takes place in the digestive tract or *alimentary canal*, a long tube that runs from the mouth to the anus. Digestion starts in the mouth, where the teeth and special chemicals in the saliva help to break down the food. The food then passes down a tube called the *oesophagus*. Muscles in the oesophagus push and squeeze the food down into the STOMACH. There, acids and more chemicals help to turn the food into a creamy liquid. Then a muscle at the lower end of the stomach opens from time to time to release food into the small intestine.

Inside the small intestine, bile from the LIVER and juice from the pancreas help to break down the food still further. Much of it passes through the thin walls of the intestine into the bloodstream. The remainder passes on into the large intestine. There, liquids and salts are absorbed until only solid waste material is left. Bacteria in the large intestine digest any remaining food products. The final waste product is passed out of the body as *faeces*.

Below: A section through the lining of the wall of the small intestine. It is greatly enlarged to show some of the thousands of finger-like villi. *The villi increase the inside surface area of the small intestine so that digested food can more easily pass into the tiny blood vessels in the villi. Each of the villi is only 0·5 to 1·5 mm long.*

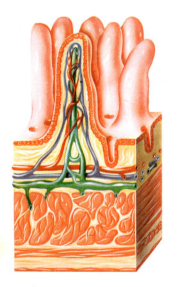

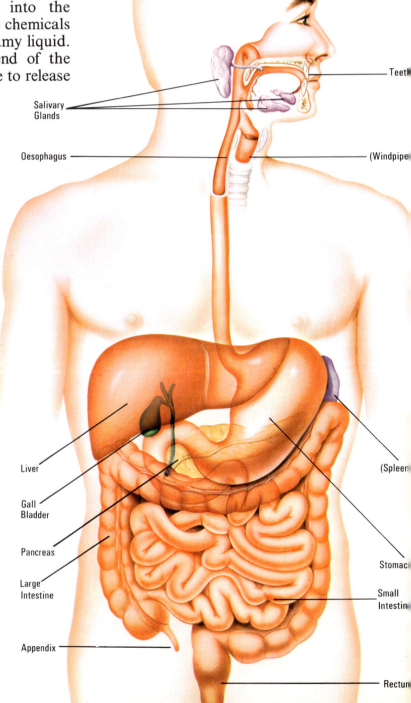

Teeth

Salivary Glands

Oesophagus

(Windpipe

Liver

Gall Bladder

Pancreas

Large Intestine

Appendix

(Spleen

Stomach

Small Intestine

Rectum

DINOSAURS

The word *dinosaur* means 'enormous lizard'. These creatures lived between 65 and 225 million years ago. They developed from primitive REPTILES. Dinosaurs included the largest and most ferocious animals ever to live on Earth.

There were two main groups of dinosaurs, the *Saurischians* and the *Ornithischians*. The Ornithischian dinosaurs were all plant-eaters and most of them went about on all fours. Some of these, like *Stegosaurus* and *Triceratops*, were large and lumbering, but had bony armour and horns to protect them from the teeth and claws of the great meat-eating dinosaurs.

The second of the two main groups, the Saurischians, contained both plant-eaters and meat-eaters. The plant-eaters included the largest-ever dinosaurs, the biggest of which was *Brachiosaurus*. This huge creature was 24 metres (80 feet) long and weighed about 50 tonnes. *Brachiosaurus* had a long neck and a tiny head, a long tapering tail and a thick body. *Brachiosaurus* and other similar dinosaurs such as *Apatosaurus* (BRONTOSAURUS) and *Diplodocus*, ate the leaves at the tops of trees.

Perhaps the most famous of the Saurischian dinosaurs are the great carnivores, or meat-eaters. Tyrannosaurus, which was up to 14 metres (47 feet) from snout to tail, stood on its hind legs. Its forward-pointing toes bore claws as long as carving knives. Sabre-like teeth—some nearly the length of a man's hand—lined the jaws. No flesh-eating beasts that ever lived on land were larger or more menacing than these monsters.

DISCUS

Throwing the discus is an event in the OLYMPIC GAMES. The discus is a wooden plate with a metal rim. Athletes take turns to stand in a circle and throw the discus as far as they can. The longest throw ever is over 71 metres (233 feet).

An ancient statue shows how Greeks threw the discus more than 2400 years ago.

DIVING

People have been diving underwater for thousands of years. The first divers just held their breath. This meant they could make only short, shallow dives.

Modern inventions allow divers to dive deeper and stay down longer. Scuba divers carry their own air supply with them. They wear rubber foot fins and they can swim about freely. Helmeted divers breathe air pumped down through a tube. Heavy weights allow them to work on the sea bed without bobbing up. All divers see through glass face masks and wear special suits to stay warm. Today's divers can study water life, build harbours, and find sunken treasure.

An aqualung diver explores an undersea wreck.

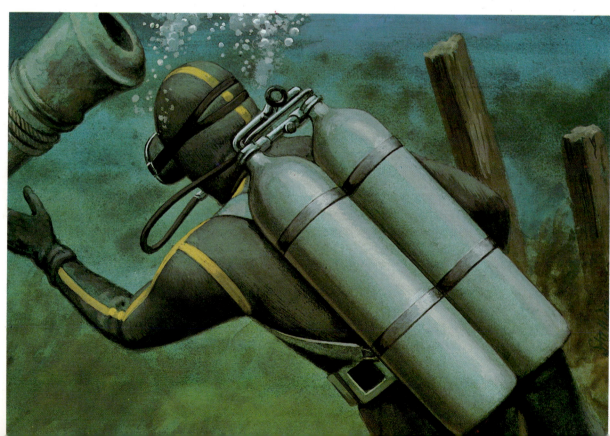

DODO

About 400 years ago a Dutch ship landed explorers on Mauritius, a lonely island in the Indian Ocean. They found doves, fish, and large flocks of birds as big and fat as turkeys. These birds had no proper wings and could not fly. In time people called them dodos, from the Portuguese word *doudo*. This means 'simpleton', or stupid person.

Sailors quickly learnt that dodos were good to eat. Ships that visited Mauritius sailed off with larders full of salted dodo meat. Meanwhile rats and dogs that came from the ships started eating dodo eggs and chicks.

By the 1690s all the dodos were dead. Only drawings, bones, and one stuffed bird remained.

The dodo

DOGS

People have been keeping dogs for perhaps 10,000 years. Most dogs are kept as pets but some do useful work like herding sheep or guarding buildings.

The first dog was probably descended from a WOLF and looked much like a wolf. Today there are more than 100 breeds of dog of many colours, shapes, and sizes. The St Bernard is the largest breed. A St Bernard may weigh nearly twice as much as a man. The Yorkshire terrier is one of the smallest dogs. A full-grown Yorkshire terrier may weigh less than a small pot of jam.

Most of the breeds shown here were developed to be good at special kinds of work. Airedales and terriers make fine rat hunters. Labrador retrievers bring back ducks shot by hunters. Collies round up sheep. Dachshunds were used for hunting badgers. Setters find animals for hunters to shoot. Dobermans are ferocious guard dogs.

All puppies are born blind and helpless, and at first only feed on their mother's milk. But small dogs are fully grown in a year or so. Most kinds of dog live for about 12 years.

Smooth and long haired Dachshunds

English and Irish setters

DOLLS

Children play with dolls all over the world. Dolls may be made of wood, china, plastic, or many other substances. The very first doll may have just been a forked twig that looked a bit like a human being. Home-made dolls can cost nothing. But doll collectors will pay a lot of money for rare old dolls.

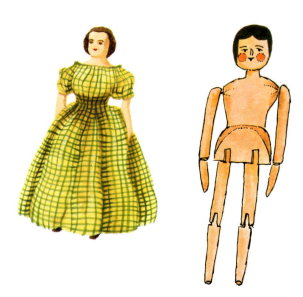

Children played with dolls like these in the 1800s. The dressed doll is made of china. The other doll is made of wood.

DOLPHINS

Dolphins are small, toothed WHALES, with a long snout rather like a beak. The largest dolphins are twice as long as a man and five times as heavy. Most kinds live in the sea but two kinds live in rivers. Dolphins swim in groups called schools. They signal to each other by making whistling sounds.

Dolphins are playful and intelligent. Tame dolphins can learn many tricks. They will jump through hoops and snatch fish from a trainer's mouth. Dolphins can also learn to 'walk' across water on their tails.

Below: The pictures of dolphins. The top picture shows the streamlined shape of a common dolphin. Common dolphins can swim at 40 km (24 miles) an hour. They are among the fastest animals in the sea. The bottom picture shows a dolphin leaping through the air for fun. Wild dolphins often enjoy speeding just ahead of ships for hour after hour.

DON QUIXOTE

Some people think that this long Spanish tale is one of the world's six best books. The story describes the adventures of a crazy old man called Don Quixote. He makes absurd mistakes because he tries to behave like a fairytale knight. Miguel de Cervantes wrote *Don Quixote* in the early 1600s.

DRAGONFLIES

These insects hatch from eggs laid in pools and rivers. The young are called nymphs. Dragonfly nymphs live in water for up to five years. Meanwhile they may shed their skin 11 times. At last they crawl out of the water, grow wings, and fly away.

Above: A full-grown dragonfly is a big flying insect with large eyes. It catches small insects as it flies at up to 90 km (60 miles) an hour.

DRAGONS

Dragons are storybook monsters, but many people once believed that they really lived. Artists showed them as huge snakes or lizards with wings of skin and terrifying claws. They were supposed to breathe fire and swallow people, cows, and horses whole.

Fighting dragons called for great bravery. Legends tell how Hercules, St George and other heroes killed these evil monsters.

Not everyone thought dragons wicked. The Chinese looked upon the creatures as gods.

111

DRAKE, FRANCIS

Sir Francis Drake (about 1540–1596) was a sea captain who helped to make England a great sea power. In the 1570s he led sea raids against Spanish ships and ports in and near the Caribbean Sea. He also became the first Englishman to sail around the world. In 1588 he helped to destroy the Spanish ARMADA and so saved England from invasion.

DRUGS

Drugs are chemicals that affect the way the body works. Doctors give drugs to patients to help them fight disease. Antibiotics attack certain kinds of GERM. These drugs help to cure people suffering from pneumonia and other illnesses. Drugs like aspirin help to deaden pain. The strongest pain-killers are called anaesthetics. Some people need drugs containing VITAMINS, or other substances their bodies must have, but cannot get from food.

Certain drugs come from plants or animals. For instance, the foxglove gives us a drug called digitalis. This makes weak

hearts beat more strongly. Many other drugs are made from MINERALS.

Some people take drugs such as cocaine, cannabis or alcohol just because these give a pleasant feeling. These drugs can make people ill.

Below: Inside a drugs factory these pill-packing machines count thousands of pills into hundreds of containers faster than any person could. Each day people swallow millions of pills to help them cure or prevent dozens of different diseases.

DRUMS

Drums are the most important of those MUSICAL INSTRUMENTS that are played by being struck. The sound is made by hitting a tightly stretched sheet of skin or plastic called a drumhead. A kettledrum has one drumhead stretched over a metal basin. A bass drum or a side drum has two drumheads, one across each end of a large open 'can'

Left: When a drummer hits a taut skin with a drumstick, the skin vibrates (above) and makes a sound. To change the note the drummer slackens or tightens the skin.

Duck · Duck · Duck

Goldeneye · Drake · Drake · Tufted duck · Drake · Teal

DUCKS

These web-footed water birds are related to swans and geese. Ducks look rather like small geese with short necks.

The two main groups of ducks are dabbling ducks and diving ducks. Dabbling ducks feed at the surface of the water. They may put most of their body under the water, but they do not dive. Dabbling ducks include the mallards that swim on pools and rivers in the northern half of the world. (Farmyard ducks were bred from mallards.) Other dabbling ducks include teal and wigeon, and the pretty mandarin and Carolina ducks.

Diving ducks dive completely under water in their hunt for food. Most diving ducks live out at sea. These ducks include the eider duck from which we get eiderdown. Sawbills are also diving ducks. Their long, slim beaks have inside edges like the teeth of a saw. Sawbills are good at grasping fish. The long-tailed duck is a diving duck that can fly at 112 km (70 miles) an hour.

Above: Three pairs of ducks of different kinds. The drakes (males) have brighter feathers than the ducks (females) except when the drakes are moulting. Tufted ducks and goldeneyes are diving ducks. Goldeneyes can dive more than 5 metres (16 feet) deep to catch small water animals. Teal are small dabbling ducks. They fly low and fast and can turn very suddenly.

Below: A pair of mallards on land and in the air. In water they kick their webbed feet backward to swim forward. Ducks stay afloat because they keep their feathers waterproof. They do this by spreading oil over their feathers. The oil comes from a preen gland just above the tail.

Underside of duck

Topside of drake

Strong wing feathers for flying

Preen gland

Webbed feet for paddling

DWARF

Any unusually small kind of adult plant, animal or human being is called a dwarf. Dwarf fruit trees, Shetland ponies, and PYGMIES are all dwarfs.

Some dwarfs happen naturally. Some can be produced by breeding. Others had too little nourishment to make them grow.

There are three kinds of human dwarf. One looks like a tiny normal person. Another has short arms and legs. The third kind has a strangely shaped body.

DYE

Dyes are substances that people use to colour TEXTILES and other materials. Some dyes come from plants. Most dyes are made from chemicals. To dye an object you dip it in water containing dissolved dye. If the dye is *fast* the object will keep its dyed colour however much you wash it afterwards.

DYNAMITE

This powerful explosive was invented in the 1860s by the Swedish chemist Alfred Nobel. Its main ingredient is nitroglycerin. Dynamite is packed in paper tubes. Then someone a safe distance away sends an electric current through a wire to explode the charge. Engineers use dynamite to blast holes in mines, quarries, and building sites.

His invention earned Nobel a fortune. He used much of it to set up the NOBEL PRIZES.

This is how people once made and dyed cloth. The woman is spinning fibres into threads. A frame is used to weave threads into cloth. The man and boy are stirring cloths placed in a vat of dye, which is made from plants. A fire is kept alight beneath the vat to heat the dye.

EAGLES

Eagles are large birds of prey. Most hunt small mammals and birds. Some catch fish or reptiles. The harpy eagle and the monkey-eating eagle catch monkeys. Each of these great birds measures more than 2 metres (7 feet) across its outspread wings. These eagles are the largest in the world.

Many eagles soar high above the ground. Others perch on a tree or rock. When an eagle sees its prey it swoops suddenly and pounces. The eagle seizes its prey with its sharp claws, and tears off chunks of flesh with its strong, hooked beak.

The bald eagle (below left) has a white head but is not really bald. This bird is the national emblem of the United States. It hunts fish in rivers, lakes, and on the coast of North America. The golden eagle (right) lives among mountains in northern lands. It hunts rabbits, hares and grouse.

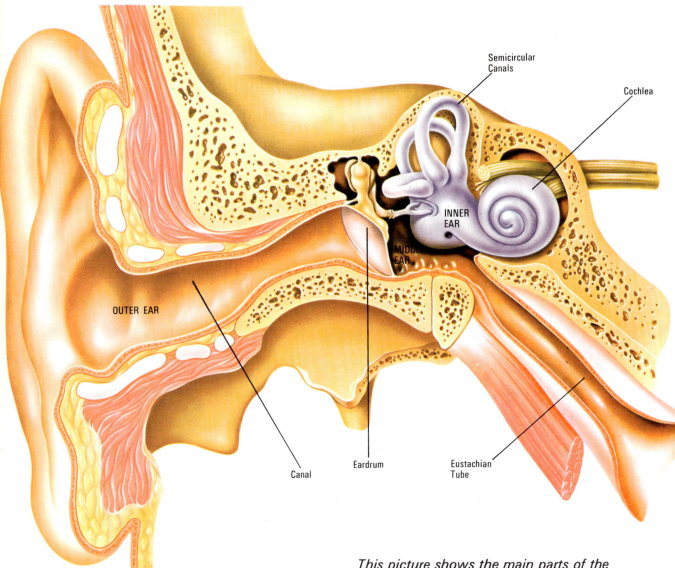

Semicircular
Canals

Cochlea

INNER
EAR

MIDDLE
EAR

OUTER EAR

Canal

Eardrum

Eustachian
Tube

*This picture shows the main parts of the
outer ear, middle ear and inner ear. The
eustachian tube helps to keep air pressure
the same on both sides of the eardrum.*

EAR

Our ears help us to hear and to keep our
balance. Each ear has three main parts.
These are the outer ear, middle ear and
inner ear.

The outer ear is the part we can see, and
the tube leading from it into the head.
Sounds reach the outer ear as vibrations,
or waves, in the air. The cup-like shape of
the ear collects these sound waves and
sends them into the tube.

Next, the sound waves reach the middle
ear. Here, the waves make the eardrum
move to and fro. This is a thin 'skin' across
the entrance of the middle ear. The moving

eardrum sets tiny bones vibrating in the
middle ear.

The vibrations travel on into the inner
ear. Here they set liquid moving in the
cochlea. This looks like a snail's shell. The
nerves inside it turn vibrations into messages
that travel to your brain. The inner ear also
has three hollow loops containing liquid.
These loops send signals to the brain to
help you keep your balance.

Ears are delicate and easily damaged.
Hitting or poking into an ear can sometimes cause an injury that leads to deafness.

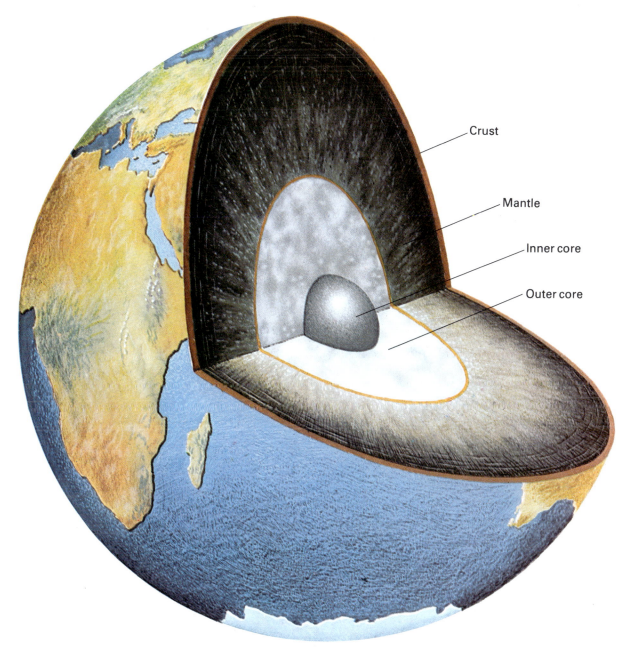

Crust

Mantle

Inner core

Outer core

EARTH, THE

Our Earth is the fifth largest of the PLANETS that move around the SUN. Seen from space the Earth looks like a giant ball. Land and WATER cover the surface, and AIR surrounds the Earth. The Earth has three main layers. The top layer is a thin crust of hard rock. The crust floats on a thicker layer of rock called the mantle. This is so hot that its rocks are at least partly melted. Below the mantle lies the core. Much of this is made of iron so hot that it is liquid.

All living things live on and just above the crust. (GEOLOGY tells us much about

Above: A picture of the Earth cut open to show its crust and inner layers. Most of the outer core is made of iron and nickel so hot that they are liquid. The inner core is even hotter. But the great weight of the rest of the Earth pressing on it makes it solid.

past life on Earth.) Earth is the only planet in the SOLAR SYSTEM to have living things. Other planets are too hot or cold or are surrounded by poisonous gases.

The Earth spins as it speeds through space. It takes a day and night to spin around once and a year to travel around the Sun. The Earth spins in a tilted position. This causes the different seasons of the year.

EARTHQUAKE

People often use the saying 'safe as houses'. But in certain lands houses sometimes topple over because the ground starts trembling. This trembling is called an earthquake. About half a million earthquakes happen every year. Most are so weak that only special instruments called *seismographs* show that they have happened. Only one earthquake in 500 does any damage. But some earthquakes can cause terrible damage and suffering. Three-quarters of a million people are thought to have died when an earthquake hit the Chinese city of Tangshan in 1976.

Small tremors can happen when VOLCANOES erupt, when there is a landslide, or when the roof of an underground cave falls in. The largest earthquakes occur when one huge piece of the Earth's crust slips suddenly against another piece. This slipping may take place deep underground. But the shock travels up through the crust and sets the surface quaking.

A seabed earthquake may set off a huge ocean wave called a TIDAL WAVE. These can rise higher than a house and travel faster than the fastest train.

Above: Some houses have been flattened, and others stand at crazy angles. This was San Francisco after an earthquake struck in 1906. About 500 buildings and 700 people were destroyed by the earthquake and the fires that followed it.

Below: Orange bands show where most of the world's earthquakes happen. They take place where great sections of the Earth's crust are pulled apart or pushed together.

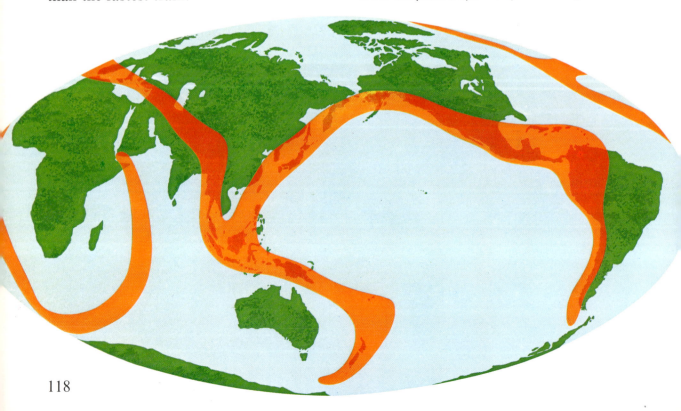

EASTER

Easter is the day when Christians remember the resurrection of JESUS. Most Christians celebrate Easter on the Sunday following the first full moon after the first day of spring in the northern half of the world.

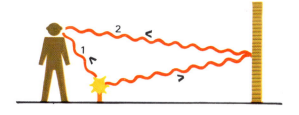

ECHO

An echo is a SOUND bounced back from a wall or some other object. Sound travels at a known, fixed speed, so we can use echoes to find how far off some objects are. A ship's sonar uses echoes to find the depth of the sea. Echoes help BATS to fly in the dark. RADAR depends on echoes from radio signals.

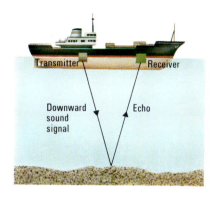

ECLIPSE

An eclipse happens when the shadow of one planet or moon falls on another. If the shadow hides all of the planet or moon there is a total eclipse. If the shadow hides only a part there is a partial eclipse.

The only eclipses you can easily see without a telescope take place when the Sun, Moon, and Earth are in line. When the Earth lies between the Sun and the Moon, the Earth's shadow falls on the Moon. This is an eclipse of the Moon. When the Moon lies between the Earth and the Sun, the Moon's shadow falls on a part of the Earth. An eclipse of the Sun, or solar eclipse, can be seen from that part. Two or three of each kind of eclipse happen every year.

Top: When the firework goes 'bang', some sound waves go straight to the man's ears (1). Others hit the wall and bounce back to the man as an echo (2), heard after the first bang. Above: A ship's echo-sounder sends a sound down to the seabed. The longer the echo takes to return, the deeper the seabed must be. This tells the ship the depth of the water.

Below: This diagram shows a solar eclipse caused as the Moon's shadow falls on the Earth, and a lunar eclipse as the Earth's shadow falls on the Moon. Only the umbra – the dark middle part of each shadow – is shown. A total solar eclipse can only be seen from a small area, in this case in Africa.

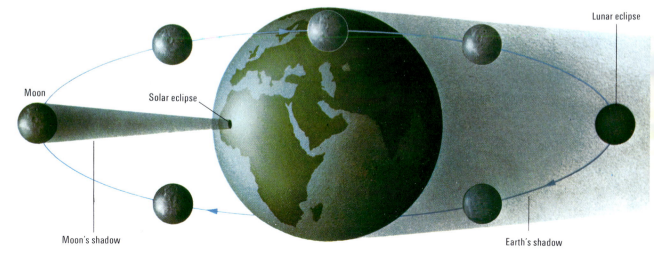

Moon

Solar eclipse

Moon's shadow

Lunar eclipse

Earth's shadow

ECOLOGY

Ecology is the study of living things and their surroundings. Scientists called ecologists try to find out how living things and their surroundings affect each other. Ecology shows us that most plants and animals can only live in a special set of surroundings like a pond, field, forest, or desert. Within each place live plants that are suited to a certain soil, temperature, and so on. All the animals living there eat the plants or one another. So the plants and animals are linked in what ecologists call a food web. If some kinds die out, those that eat them lose their food and may die too.

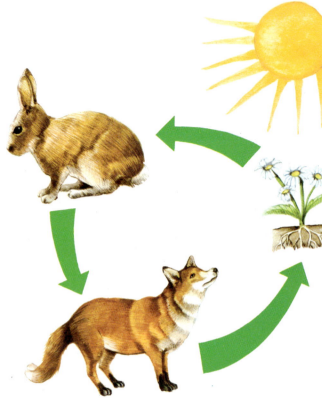

Right: Sunshine gives the plant energy to make food. The rabbit eats the plant. The fox eats the rabbit. Body wastes from the fox nourish the soil and therefore the plants. This balance is an important part of an ecological 'system'.

EDINBURGH

Edinburgh is the capital of SCOTLAND and its second largest city. It is more than 800 years old. Edinburgh stands south of the great sea inlet called the Firth of Forth. Edinburgh Castle is perched on an extinct volcano in the city centre. Each year people from all over the world come to the Edinburgh Festival of plays, films and music.

EDISON, THOMAS

Thomas Alva Edison (1847–1931) was an American inventor. As a boy he spent only three months at school, and his teacher thought him stupid. But he went on to produce over 1000 inventions. The most famous were the electric light and the phonograph for RECORDING and playing back sounds.

Some of Edison's can-shaped 'records' and an early wide-mouthed loudspeaker. Edison cut his first record in tinfoil with one needle and used another needle to play back the sound.

EDWARD (KINGS)

Nine kings of England were called Edward. Edward 'The Confessor' (about 1002–1066) founded WESTMINSTER ABBEY. Edward I (1239–1307) brought Wales under English rule. Edward II (1248–1327) was the first English Prince of Wales. Edward III (1312–1337) began the Hundred Years' War. Edward IV (1442–1483) took the crown from Henry VI in the Wars of the Roses. Edward V (1470–1483) was murdered in the Tower of London. Edward VI (1537–1553) reigned as a boy king for only six years. Edward VII (1841–1910) was Prince of Wales for 60 years. Edward VIII (1894–1972) gave up the throne to marry Mrs Simpson, a divorced American.

Above: Edward VII (left) was 60 when he inherited the throne from Queen Victoria. Edward VIII (right) was king for barely a year, in 1936. He gave up the throne to marry a woman who could not become queen because she was divorced.

Below: This freshwater eel spawns in a part of the Atlantic Ocean called the Sargasso Sea. Some of the young take three years to find their way to Europe.

EELS

Eels are long, slim fish with fins like narrow ribbons. Some eels have tiny scales. Some are covered with slime. European and American freshwater eels swim thousands of kilometres and spawn far out in the Atlantic Ocean. Then they die. The tiny, transparent young that hatch look nothing like their parents. These babies find their way all the way back to their parents' homes in America and Europe. There, they travel up rivers and streams. The young eels grow up in fresh water and stay there until they are ready for their long journey back across the Atlantic.

EGGS

An egg is a female CELL that will grow into a new young plant or animal. Most eggs only grow if they are joined with, or fertilized by, male cells. In most MAMMALS the fertilized eggs grow inside the mother's body. But birds and most reptiles and fish lay eggs that contain enough food to help the developing young grow inside the egg.

Common Crow

Osprey

Guira Cuckoo

Great Bustard

Kiwi

Emu

American Robin

Golden Plover

Coot

Left: Nine kinds of birds' eggs, all smaller than in life.

EGYPT

About 5000 years ago the ancient Egyptians began to build one of the world's first great civilizations. For the next 2500 years, ancient Egypt was one of the strongest, richest nations on Earth.

The people who made Egypt great were short, slim, dark-skinned men and women with black hair. They probably numbered no more than six million. Scarcely any of them lived in the hot sand and rock deserts that cover most of Egypt. Almost all the people settled by the NILE river that runs from south to north across the land.

Each year the river overflowed and left rich mud on nearby fields. Farmers learnt to dig and plough the fields. They could grow two crops a year in the warm, fertile soil. The farmers grew more than enough grain, fruit and vegetable to feed themselves.

The rest of the food helped to feed Egyptian craftsmen, miners, merchants, priests, noble families, and the PHARAOHS who ruled over the entire land.

Most Egyptians were poor and lived in mud-brick huts with palm-leaf roofs. Rich Egyptians lived in large, well-furnished houses and had meat and cakes to eat. They wore fine clothes and jewels.

The most splendid buildings in the land were tombs and temples. Thousands of workers toiled for years to build the mighty PYRAMIDS. In each such tomb, Egyptians would place the MUMMY of a pharaoh. They believed the dead went on living. So they buried food and furniture beside each mummy. Thieves later emptied almost all the tombs. But Tutankhamen's tomb shows us what royal burials were like.

The dry Egyptian air has preserved HIEROGLYPHICS written on fragile paper made from the papyrus plant. Paintings and hieroglyphics tell us a great deal about how

the ancient Egyptians lived. The ancient Egyptians also left many fine statues. They may also have invented glass. They had a calendar and could do sums to work out shapes and sizes.

In time, foreign armies using iron weapons defeated the Egyptians. Their land fell under foreign rule after 525 BC.

Modern Egypt dates from AD 642 when Egypt was conquered by Moslem soldiers from Arabia. Egypt is now a Moslem, mainly Arab, country. It has about 40 million people, more than any other nation in Africa. No other African city is as large as Cairo, Egypt's capital. But Egyptians still depend upon the waters of the river that made old Egypt great.

Right: Ancient Egyptian craftsmen made this fish-shaped glass bottle and the fine wooden box inlaid with ivory.
Below: Attendants take a dead pharaoh to his tomb. Old tomb paintings help to show that scenes like this really took place.

EIFFEL TOWER

The Eiffel Tower rises more than 300 metres (985 feet) above Paris. The tower is really four open, wrought-iron towers that curve inwards and join. Criss-cross bars give the tower its strength. The metal in it weighs about 7000 tonnes. People can reach the top by lifts and stairs. The French engineer Gustave Eiffel designed the tower for a Paris exhibition of 1889. For the next 40 years the Eiffel Tower was the tallest man-made structure in the world.

Right: The Eiffel Tower has platforms from which people can look over Paris. TV and radio signals can be sent out from the top.

EINSTEIN, ALBERT

Albert Einstein (1879–1955) was a great scientist who was born in Germany. His theory of relativity was a new way of looking at time, space, matter and ENERGY. Einstein showed that a small amount of matter could be changed into a vast amount of energy. This made it possible for man to use ATOMIC ENERGY.

As a boy Albert Einstein found school boring. Teachers thought him lazy or stupid.

ELECTIONS

Most countries hold elections from time to time. Elections give people the chance to elect, or choose, a new government. They do this by voting. In Britain each voter goes to a certain building on a day called polling day. He or she is given a paper, or BALLOT, printed with the names of several candidates. The voter marks a cross against the name of the person he wants to represent him in PARLIAMENT. Voting goes on all over the country at the same time. Each area has its own candidates. Those who win the most votes are elected.

In some countries anyone may be a candidate. In others the government chooses candidates. Teams and clubs also hold elections to choose leaders. Members often vote simply by a show of hands when their candidate's name is read out.

ELECTRICITY

Electricity heats and lights our homes. It is the kind of ENERGY that powers electric trains, vacuum cleaners, radios, television sets and many more devices.

The electricity that we use flows through wires as electric current. Current flows when tiny particles called electrons jump between the ATOMS that make up the metal in the wire. Current can flow only if a wire makes a complete loop called a circuit. If a gap is made in the circuit, the current stops flowing. Switches are simply devices that open and close gaps in circuits.

Batteries produce electric current that can be used to start cars, light torch bulbs and work radios. But most of the electricity we use is produced in power stations. In a power station generator, coils of wire are made to rotate between powerful magnets. This makes electric current flow through the coils of wire. This current then flows through other long wires to our homes.

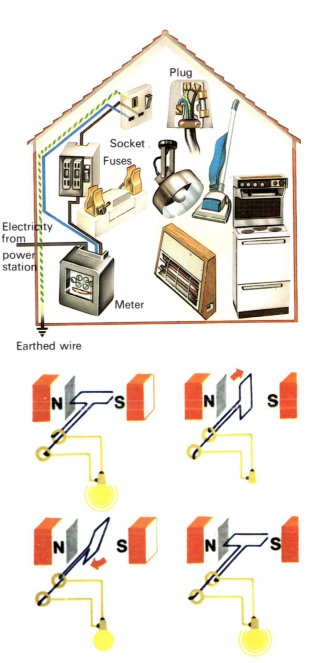

Right, top: Electric current from a power station flows indoors through wires that form a circuit. An electric lamp or cooker works when a plug is pushed into a socket that links it with that circuit. Fuses and earthed wires make electricity safer.
Right: Electricity flows through a wire loop if the loop is made to turn and cut across invisible lines of force between two magnets (N and S). This is how an electric generator works.

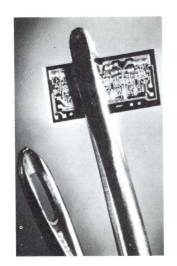

ELECTRONICS

Electronics is an important part of the study of ELECTRICITY. It deals with the way in which tiny particles called electrons flow through certain CRYSTALS, gases, or a VACUUM. Electronic devices like TRANSISTORS and SILICON CHIPS are used in such things as COMPUTERS, radar and radios. Electronics helps us to see the smallest living thing, to guide planes, and to do difficult sums instantly.

This magnified silicon chip is small enough to pass through the eye of a needle. Yet this tiny chip contains an electronic memory circuit made of hundreds of parts. Such chips are used in computers and calculators.

ELEMENTS

Your own body and everything you see around you is composed (made up) of chemical ingredients called elements. In each element all the ATOMS are of the same kind. You can join different elements to make more complicated substances called compounds. But you cannot break an element into a simpler kind of substance.

Chemists have found more than 100 different elements. Ninety-four of these occur naturally. Scientists have produced other elements in laboratories. At ordinary temperatures, some elements are gases, some are liquids, and some are solids.

OXYGEN is the most plentiful element on Earth. Half of the Earth's crust and most of your body is made of oxygen.

Right: An early list of elements made by John Dalton (1766–1844). He found that each element had its own kind of atoms.

ELEPHANTS

Elephants are the largest living land animals. A big bull (male) elephant may stand twice as high as a man and weigh as much as seven family cars. An elephant has larger ears, thicker legs, a longer nose and longer teeth than any other creature. Its skin is nearly as thick as the heel of a man's shoe.

Baby elephants stand no taller than big dogs. Elephants are fully grown after 20 years. They live almost as long as people.

Men teach Indian elephants to move heavy loads. African elephants are harder to tame. Many thousands have been killed just for the IVORY of their tusks. Today most are protected by law.

The African elephant (left) has bigger ears than the Indian elephant. One shot in Angola stood nearly 4 metres (13 feet) high and weighed nearly 12 tonnes.

ELIZABETH I

Elizabeth I (1533–1603) was a famous English queen. She never married, but she reigned for 45 years with the help of wise advisers. She worked for peace between quarrelling religious groups but had her rival MARY QUEEN OF SCOTS put to death. Elizabeth's seamen crushed the Spanish ARMADA and made England powerful at sea. Great English playwrights, poets and scholars lived in her reign. People often call it 'the Elizabethan Age'.

Above left: Queen Elizabeth I. Above right: Elizabeth was fond of fine clothes.

Above: Queen Elizabeth II made her son, Charles, Prince of Wales in 1969. Charles is the heir to the throne.

ELIZABETH II

Elizabeth II (1926–) is Queen of the United Kingdom of Great Britain and Northern Ireland and head of the COMMONWEALTH. Her husband is the Duke of Edinburgh. Her eldest son is Charles, Prince of Wales.

ELM

Elms are broad-leaved trees that shed their leaves in autumn. The leaves have zig-zag edges rather like the teeth of a saw. The seeds have little 'wings' and drift off on the wind. Elms have tough, hard wood used for making furniture. Some kinds of elm have smooth bark, others have rough bark. An elm tree may live more than 200 years.

Many elms have been killed by Dutch elm disease. This is caused by a FUNGUS spread by a beetle that flies from tree to tree.

Right, top: An elm seed and leaf, and an elm tree pictured in early spring.
Right: Beetles made these tunnels in elm bark. The beetles spread fungus that blocks water-carrying tubes in elm trees. All their leaves turn yellow and die.

ENERGY

Having energy means being able to do work. There are various kinds of energy. Muscles and machines have mechanical energy. They can move loads. Coal and food store chemical energy. If you burn coal or eat food they are chemically changed and give up heat energy. We can turn electrical energy into heat, light or sound. When the middle parts of ATOMS split or join they give off RADIOACTIVITY. Radiant energy from the Sun gives us energy in the form of light and heat. Most of the energy on Earth comes in some way from the Sun.

A huge man-made island built to drill for oil under the sea. If you burn oil its chemical energy turns to heat energy. Oil was made from once-living things. The energy that helped them live and grow was the heat and light given out by the Sun.

ENGINEERING

Engineers do a great many different types of jobs. Mining engineers find useful MINERALS and take them from the ground. Metallurgical engineers separate METALS from unwanted substances and make them usable. Chemical engineers use chemicals to make such things as explosives, paint, plastics, and soap. Civil engineers build bridges, tunnels, roads, railways, ports, airports, and so on. Mechanical engineers make and use machines. Such people design JET ENGINES and factory machinery. Electrical engineers work with devices that produce and use electricity. Some specialize in building a particular type of generator. Others work in ELECTRONICS. Most of the main kinds of engineering fall into one or the other of these groups.

Mechanical engineering was the kind of work that went into making the devices below.
Top: The water-frame spinning machine was worked by a water wheel. The machine pulled rough cotton thread over rollers to make it fine. Then the cotton was wound on to spindles to make it strong. Richard Arkwright's water-frame spinning machine made cotton in the late 1700s.
Bottom: This cut-away view shows a Rolls-Royce turbofan engine. Making and looking after a complicated jet engine like this calls for work by very skilled engineers.

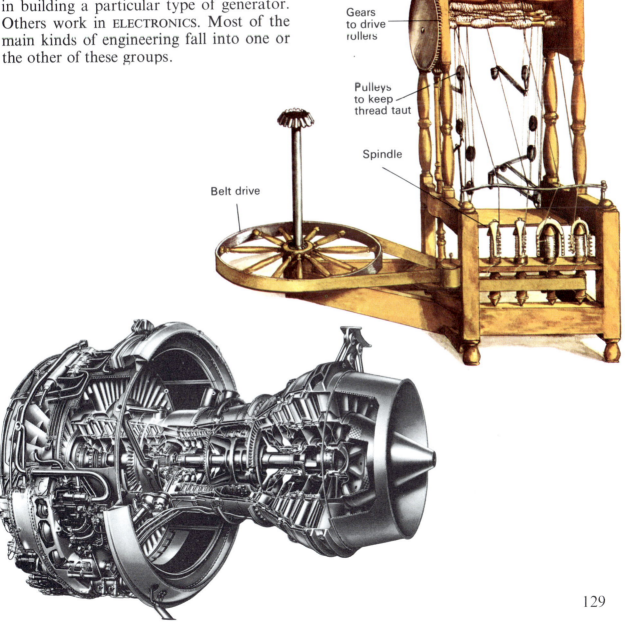

Rollers

Gears to drive rollers

Pulleys to keep thread taut

Spindle

Belt drive

ENGLAND

England is the largest country in the kingdom of GREAT BRITAIN and Northern Ireland. If Great Britain were divided into five equal parts, England would fill three of them. England's neighbours are Scotland and Wales. But most of England is surrounded by sea. Green fields spread over the plains and low hills that cover most of the country. In the north and west there are mountains with moors and forests. Most English people live and work in big cities like London, Birmingham, Liverpool, and Manchester.

England gets its name from the Angles, a group of the ANGLO-SAXONS who sailed to this island and settled down here about 1500 years ago.

ENGLISH LANGUAGE

More people speak English than any other language except Chinese. English is the main language spoken in the United Kingdom, Ireland, Australia, New Zealand, Canada, the United States, and some other countries. Altogether more than 370 million people speak English as their everyday language. Another 100 million or more speak at least some English. Most English words come from old ANGLO-SAXON, French, or Latin words.

EQUATOR

The equator is an imaginary line around the world, half way between the North Pole and the South Pole. A journey around the equator covers 40,076 km (24,902 miles).

The word 'equator' comes from an old Latin word meaning 'equalizer'. The equator divides the world into two equal halves. The half north of the equator is called the Northern Hemisphere. The half south of the equator is the Southern Hemisphere. Distances north and south of the equator are measured in degrees of latitude. The equator itself has a latitude of 0 degrees. (See also LATITUDE AND LONGITUDE.)

On the equator, nights are always as long as days. At midday the Sun always shines from directly or almost directly overhead. So all places on the equator except high mountains are warm all through the year.

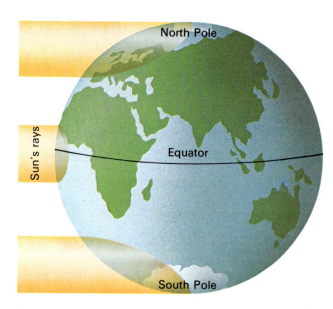

When the Sun's rays reach the poles they are more thinly spread than at the equator. They have also had to travel through more air. This is why it is hotter at the equator than in the polar regions.

ESKIMOS

Eskimos are hardy people who live in the cold, ARCTIC lands of Greenland, North America and north-east Asia. They have slanting eyes, a wide, flat face, and a short, thick body with short arms and legs. This shape helps to keep them warm in the cold, Arctic climate.

Eskimos wear fur clothes. Some live in tents in summer and build snow homes called igloos for the winter. All Eskimos once killed for food. They used bows and arrows and harpoons, and hunted seals, whales, fish, seabirds and deer. Eskimos paddled skin BOATS. Dogs pulled their sledges overland.

Many Eskimos no longer lead this kind of life. They now live and work in towns.

Map Key	Country	Area (sq km)	Capital
32	Albania	28,500	Tirane
25	Andorra	453	Andorra La Vella
19	Austria	84,000	Vienna
13	Belgium	30,500	Brussels
31	Bulgaria	111,000	Sofia
16	Czecho-slovakia	128,000	Prague
8	Denmark	45,000	Copenhagen
4	Finland	337,000	Helsinki
14	France	547,000	Paris
11	Germany, East	108,000	East Berlin
10	Germany, West	249,000	Bonn
23	Gibraltar	6	Gibraltar
34	Greece	132,000	Athens
20	Hungary	93,000	Budapest
1	Iceland	103,000	Reykjavik
6	Ireland, Republic of	70,000	Dublin
27	Italy	301,000	Rome
18	Liechtenstein	160	Vaduz
15	Luxembourg	2,600	Luxembourg
33	Malta	316	Valletta
26	Monaco	1·9	Monaco
9	Netherlands	41,000	Amsterdam
2	Norway	324,000	Oslo
12	Poland	313,000	Warsaw
22	Portugal	92,000	Lisbon
21	Romania	238,000	Bucharest
28	San Marino	61	San Marino
24	Spain	505,000	Madrid
3	Sweden	450,000	Stockholm
17	Switzerland	41,000	Bern
35	Turkey (in Europe)	24,000	—
7	United Kingdom	245,000	London
5	USSR (in Europe)	5,570,000	Moscow
29	Vatican City State	0·44	Vatican City
30	Yugoslavia	256,000	Belgrade

EUROPE

Europe is a peninsula poking out from the western end of Asia. Other small peninsulas jut from the main one and there are many offshore islands. Australia is the only continent smaller than Europe, but Europe holds more people than any continent except Asia.

European people have settled in the Americas, Australia, New Zealand, South Africa, and Siberia. European ideas and inventions helped shape the way of life of many people in lands all around the world.

Mountains cross the countries of southern Europe. From west to east there are the Pyrenees, Alps, Apennines, Balkans, Carpathians, Caucasus, and other ranges. The Caucasus has Mt Elbrus, Europe's highest peak.

In northern Europe low mountains cover much of Iceland, Ireland, Scotland, Wales, Norway, and Sweden. Between the mountains of the north and south lies a great plain. Here flow Europe's longest rivers. The Volga in the USSR is the longest of them all.

All Europe lies north of the hot tropics and most of it lies south of the cold Arctic. So most of Europe is neither always hot nor cold. But Mediterranean lands have hot summers, and countries in the north and east have long, cold winters.

Shrubs and flowering plants grow in the far north. Next come the great northern forests of CONIFERS. Farther south lie most of Europe's farms and cities.

Much of Europe's wealth comes from her factories, farms, and mines. Europe's richest nations include West Germany and Switzerland. The largest European country is the USSR. The smallest European country is the Vatican in Rome.

131

EUROPEAN ECONOMIC COMMUNITY

Above: Flags of the nine Common Market countries. The first six were joined in 1973 by Britain, Ireland and Denmark.

This is a group of Western European nations that work together to help goods, people, and money travel between countries in the community. Its members are Belgium, Denmark, France, Ireland, Italy, Great Britain, Luxembourg, the Netherlands and West Germany. People also call the community the European Common Market.

EVAPORATION

This is the changing of liquids into a vapour. Some liquids evaporate in air. Water evaporates quite quickly in warm, dry, moving air. This is why windy days are good for drying damp clothes. Huge amounts of water evaporate from the sea, land, and plants.

When water boils in a kettle some of it evaporates. As the hot water vapour leaves the spout of the kettle much of it turns back into water droplets and becomes visible as steam.

EVEREST, MOUNT

Mt Everest is the world's highest peak. It rises 8848 metres (29,028 feet) above sea level. The mountain stands in the HIMALAYAS on the borders of Nepal and Tibet. Everest is named after Sir George Everest, a British surveyor. Gales and falling masses of rock and snow sweep the steep, cold slopes. Many climbers tried to reach the top before two finally succeeded, in 1953. They were the New Zealander Edmund Hillary and Tenzing Norgay, a Nepalese Sherpa tribesman.

Tenzing Norgay photographed on Everest by Edmund Hillary on May 29, 1953.

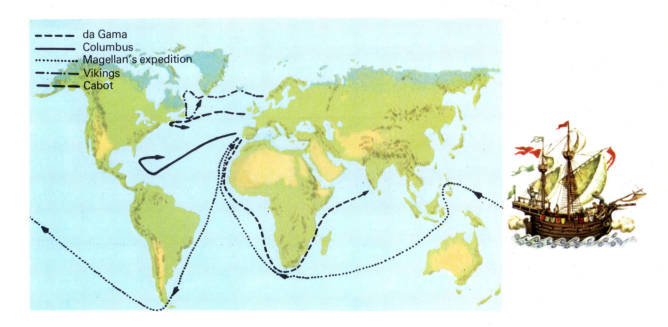

Map legend:
- – – – da Gama
- —— Columbus
- ········ Magellan's expedition
- –·–·– Vikings
- ━━ Cabot

EXPLORERS

Explorers are people who travel to find out about unknown places. There have always been explorers. The Stone Age men and women who wandered across continents were in a way explorers. Phoenician seamen sailed the Mediterranean about 2600 years ago. In the Middle Ages MARCO POLO reached China from Europe. But the great age of exploration began in the 1400s. Sailors like Vasco da GAMA, Christopher COLUMBUS, Ferdinand Magellan, and James COOK discovered the shape, size, and position of continents and oceans. Later, men like David Livingstone and Roald AMUNDSEN explored wild, untamed continents. SPACE EXPLORATION now takes men beyond the Earth.

EXPLOSIONS

Explosions happen when people heat or strike certain solid or liquid substances. These suddenly turn into hot gases. They fill more space than the solids or liquids, so they rush violently outward. High explosives like DYNAMITE explode faster and do more damage than low explosives like GUN-POWDER. Engineers use explosives to break up rocks and old buildings. Armies use explosives to destroy vehicles and cities.

Above: This map shows famous voyages of exploration from Europe to other lands. In 1522 Magellan's ship Victoria became the first to sail around the world.

A carefully planned explosion brings down an old block of flats without harming nearby buildings. The flats fall in seconds. To knock them down brick by brick could take days.

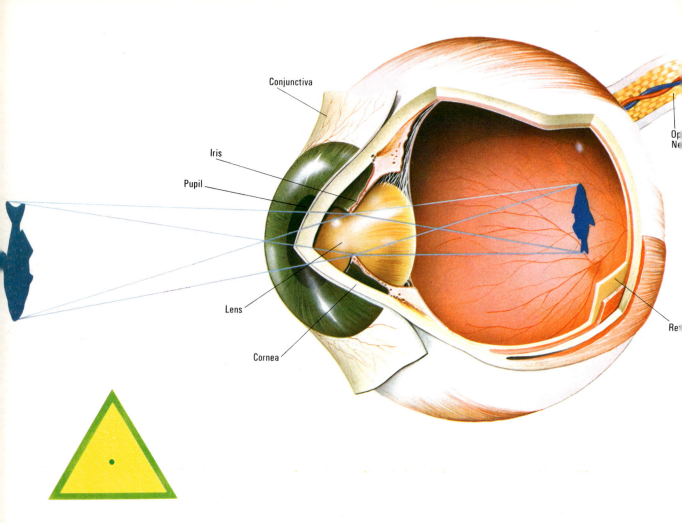

Conjunctiva

Iris

Pupil

Lens

Cornea

Op
Ne

Re

EYE

Our eyes show us the size, shape, and colour of objects in the world around us. Your eyes can see something as small and near as a tiny insect crawling on this page, or as far off and large as the Moon or stars.

A human eye is much larger than the part you can see. The eye is a ball bigger than a marble. It works much like a camera. Both bend LIGHT rays to form a picture of the object that the rays come from.

Light rays enter the eye through a layer of transparent skin called the *conjunctiva*. The rays pass through a hard, transparent layer called the *cornea*. This bends the rays. The LENS brings them into focus on the *retina* at the back of the eye. But you do not 'see' the picture formed here until light-sensitive nerve endings on the retina send the brain a message along the *optic nerve*.

The cutaway diagram shows the main parts of the eye. It also shows how rays of light from an object form a small upside-down image on the retina. Eyes sometimes play tricks. Stare at the spot in the triangle (left) for 30 seconds, then look at white paper. The green has become red and the yellow blue. What you see is called an after-image.

To be able to see properly, all the parts of the eye shown in the picture above have to work correctly. For instance, the *iris* (the coloured part of the eye) can open and close to let more or less light through the *pupil*. This is the dark opening in front of the lens.

Sometimes eyes go wrong. For example, a person with a thin lens cannot see nearby objects clearly. Such conditions can be helped by wearing spectacles. Sometimes people lose their sight entirely. But even blind people can be helped by aids like BRAILLE.

FALCONS

Falcons are a group of birds of prey that are found all over the world. They can be recognized by the dark markings around their eyes and by their pointed wings. Falcons use their large, hooked beaks for tearing flesh. But they kill their prey with their sharp claws. Falcons swoop down on their victims from above, hitting them with their claws. This act is called 'stooping' It is used to kill smaller birds in mid-flight and also to take RODENTS and other small animals on the ground.

The biggest of all falcons is the gyr falcon of the Arctic. It may reach over 60 cm (2 feet) in size. The smallest is the pygmy falcon of southern Asia. It is less than 15 cm (6 inches) long and feeds mainly on insects.

The peregrine falcon is one of the fastest flyers in the world. In a fast dive, it can reach 280 km/hr (175 mph).

FARADAY, MICHAEL

Michael Faraday (1791–1867) was a brilliant English scientist. His studies of chemistry and physics made him world famous. Faraday is best known for his experiments with ELECTRICITY. He showed that it could be made to flow in a wire when the wire was passed between a set of magnets. Today this is how most electricity is produced in big generators.

Hood

Falcon

For several thousand years, falconers have trained birds of prey to hunt for them as a sport. The bird perches on the falconer's wrist. A hood is placed over its head until it is ready to be released. Then the bird flies off to catch its prey and bring it back to the falconer.

FARMING

Farming is man's most important activity. More people work at it than at any other job. And in all, about a third of the land on our planet is farmed.

Farmers grow hundreds of different kinds of crops. But a few, such as WHEAT, RICE and barley, and beans and peas, are by far the most important. They are grown almost everywhere that men plough the soil.

The kinds of crops that are raised in one region depends on several things. The climate, altitude (the height of the land above sea level), and the fertility of the soil are the most important. For example, RICE, ORANGES, and COCONUTS all need a warm, tropical climate in which to grow. COFFEE needs warmth, but does best at a high altitude. Rye, on the other hand, can stand cool climates right up to the Arctic Circle.

Farmers do not only grow our food. They also raise crops such as hay and clover to feed animals. Some plant TOBACCO, COTTON or SUGAR cane. Others raise animals for meat.

FAT

Fat is an important food for both animals and plants. The tissues of these living things contain fat. Fat in a pure state can take the form of a liquid, such as vegetable oil, or a solid such as BUTTER or lard.

Fat is a store of ENERGY. A unit of fat contains twice as much energy as the same amount of PROTEIN or STARCH. Fats play an important part in our diet. We get most vegetable fats from the seeds and fruits of plants, where it is stored. In animals and human beings fat is stored in tiny 'droplets' in a layer under the skin and in the CELLS of the body. Pigs and cattle are our main sources of animal fats. Fats are also important in making SOAPS, perfumes and polishes.

Above: A person who eats more than his body needs will store the extra in fat cells all over his body. The main place where fat is stored is around the waist and hips.

Left: Guy Fawkes and his fellow conspirators plan to blow up Parliament and James I. This became known as the 'Gunpowder Plot'.

FAWKES, GUY

Guy Fawkes (1570–1606) and his group of ROMAN CATHOLIC plotters sought to kill King JAMES I of England by blowing up the House of Lords with gunpowder. They were protesting against some laws which tried to control the rights of Roman Catholics. The plot failed. Fawkes was arrested in the cellars of the House of Lords and, with the other conspirators, was executed.

FEATHERS

The only animals with an outer layer of feathers are BIRDS. Feathers protect birds and keep them warm. They give their bodies a smooth, streamlined shape. Feathers also form the broad surface area of the wing that allows birds to fly.

Feathers are replaced once or twice a year. This process is called moulting. Old feathers that are worn and broken fall out. New ones grow in their place.

Feathers

Shaft   Barb

There are two main kinds of feathers. Strong contour feathers cover the outer part of the bird. Soft down feathers lie between the skin and the contour feathers. Chicks are covered with down before their contour feathers grow.

FERTILIZER

Fertilizers are chemicals. They are dug into the soil to nourish it. In this way fertilizers help plants to grow bigger and healthier by giving them the chemical 'foods' they need to grow. The most important fertilizers are calcium, phosphorus, potassium and sulphur.

Fertilizers are usually added to soils that do not contain enough nutrients. This can happen if the same crops have been planted in the soil year after year, or if the rain has washed all the nutrients out.

FIGS

The fig is a soft, sweet fruit produced by a small-sized tree of the same name, which has large leaves. Figs were first grown in the Mediterranean region, but today are raised in warm climates all over the world.

FINCHES

Finches are a very large family of birds. They are found almost everywhere except Australia. Finches are small; rarely do they grow larger than 20 cm (8 inches) in length. Their short, thick bills are used for cracking and eating seeds. Finches' bills are amazingly strong. A hawfinch such as the one shown below can crack olive and cherry stones with ease. It can exert a pressure of 45 kg (100 lb) to do this.

Below: The woodpecker finch of the Galapagos Islands uses a cactus spine to probe for insects in the bark of trees. On these islands, the naturalist Charles Darwin found 13 different kinds of finches. He realized that because they were so different, they did not compete for the same kinds of food, so all 13 kinds were able to survive. Bottom right: A chaffinch nest.

Hawfinch

The cactus finch, another of the Galapagos finches.

Chaffinch nest

Woodpecker finch

FINGERPRINTS

Fingerprints are marks we leave behind whenever we touch something. You can see them by pressing your fingertips into an ink pad and then on to a sheet of white paper. Everybody has patterns of lines and swirls on their fingers. But each person's fingerprints are different from everybody else's. Because of this, police use fingerprints to help identify criminals. They keep files of millions of different prints. By comparing those on file with those found at the scene of a crime, they can often trace the guilty person.

FINLAND

Finland is a country in northern EUROPE tucked between Scandinavia and Russia. Northern Finland stretches north of the Arctic Circle.

The thousands of lakes and rivers that dot the Finnish landscape form a great inland waterway. About three-quarters of the land is covered by thick forests of spruce, pine and larch trees. The main industries of Finland are logging and the making of wood products such as paper.

Just under 5,000,000 people live in Finland. The capital, Helsinki, has a population of about 800,000.

FIORD

Along the coasts of NORWAY and GREENLAND are a series of steep-sided valleys called fiords. Here the sea has invaded the land. Narrow tongues of water wind inland for miles in narrow mountain gorges.

Fiords were formed when the great glaciers of the ICE AGES gouged out valleys as they flowed to the sea. When the ice melted, the sea flooded the valleys. Fiords are very deep and make perfect shelters for large ocean-going ships.

The spectacular scenery of the Norwegian fiord (right) is typical of the region. Here the slopes of mountains plunge straight into the sea in an unbroken drop.

FIRE

The ability to make and use fire is one of the great advantages people have over the animals. Primitive man found fire frightening, just as animals do. But once he learned to make and control fires, they became a necessary part of life. They kept out the cold, lit up the dark, cooked food, kept him warm, and kept away wild animals. But even today fires that get out of control cause terrible damage and suffering.

FIR TREES

Firs are an important group of CONIFERS. They are mostly found in cool climates. Forests of fir trees grow all over northern Asia, Europe and America.

The leaves of fir trees are short, thin and needle-like. They grow separately along the twigs, unlike PINE needles, which grow in clusters. The fruit of the fir tree is a scaly cone. The tall Douglas 'Fir' is not really a fir—it belongs to a different group of evergreens.

Above: The cone of the balsam fir stands upright on the branch.

FISH

There are more fish than all the other back-boned animals put together. The fish shown on these two pages are just a few of more than 30,000 different kinds. Fish are also the oldest backboned animals. The ancestors of modern fish first appeared on Earth over 500 million years ago.

Fish range in size from tiny gobies less than 12 mm ($\frac{1}{2}$ inch) long to the great whale SHARKS, up to 15 metres (49 feet) long. Their shapes vary from the snake-like EELS to the flatfish that lie on their 'sides' on the seabed.

Right, top: This colourful angel fish lives among coral in the Caribbean. Right, bottom: The colours of the plaice hide it on the sea floor.

Below: The porcupine fish blows itself up into a spiky ball when danger threatens.

The SEAHORSE, another fish, looks nothing like a fish at all. And a few fish-like creatures are not fish. WHALES and DOLPHINS are really mammals—they give birth to live young and feed them on milk.

Fish are cold-blooded. They live in fresh and salt water, and are found everywhere from the tropics to the poles. They breathe through gills, and move by bending their bodies from side to side. Their fins and tails help them to swim well. Over short distances, fish can swim with surprising speed. The record is 70 km/hr (44 mph) for the bluefin TUNA.

Most fish lay eggs in the water. This is called *spawning*. A few, such as some sharks and rays, give birth to live young. Egg-

laying fish release millions of eggs into the water. But only a few of them will survive to become adults. Some fish, such as bass, SALMON and sticklebacks, protect their eggs by building nests. Because more eggs will survive, fewer are laid. Male seahorses and pipefish have a pouch into which the female lays her eggs. The male carries them until they hatch.

FISHING

Fishing is one of the most important activities in the world. In one year, about 60 million tonnes of fish are taken from the seas, rivers and lakes.

Although fish are a good source of food, much of the catch ends up as animal feed, FERTILIZER, or oil used to make SOAPS or for tanning, turning animal skins into leather.

Often, the catch is made far away from home port. The fish must be preserved or they will quickly spoil. In the past fish were often dried, smoked or salted, because there were no refrigerators. Today they are packed on ice or frozen. Some fishing fleets include large factory ships. These take fresh fish straight from the other ships, and can them or package them on the spot.

The best places to fish at sea are where the sloping sea bottom is no more than about 180 metres (600 feet) deep. Here, fish can be found feeding in huge numbers. The Grand Banks off the coast of Newfoundland is one such region. It has been fished for hundreds of years.

Trawl nets are great funnel-shaped 'sacks' that are dragged along the seabed. They are used to catch bottom-feeders like cod and haddock. A purse-seine net is for taking surface-swimming shoals of fish. Gill nets are floating traps which tangle fish that try to swim through. They are used in shallow waters. Long-lines have many baited hooks. They are set along the sea floor to catch large fish such as halibut. Lobster pots are baited wooden traps laid on the ocean floor.

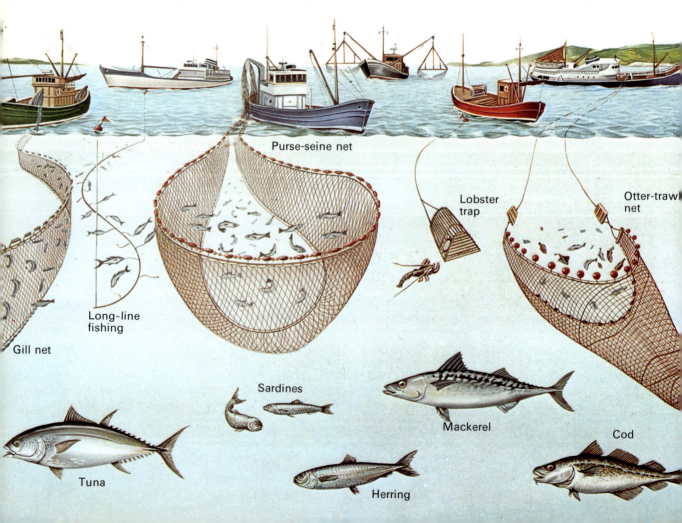

Purse-seine net

Lobster trap

Otter-trawl net

Long-line fishing

Gill net

Sardines

Mackerel

Cod

Tuna

Herring

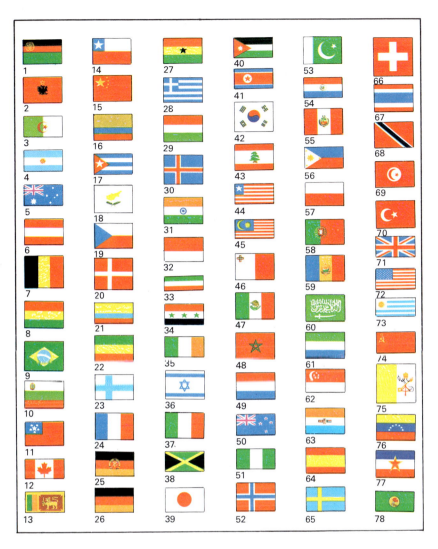

1. Afghanistan 2. Albania
3. Algeria 4. Argentina
5. Australia 6. Austria
7. Belgium 8. Bolivia
9. Brazil 10. Bulgaria
11. Burma 12. Canada
13. Sri Lanka 14. Chile
15. China 16. Colombia
17. Cuba 18. Cyprus
19. Czechoslovakia
20. Denmark 21. Ecuador
22. Ethiopia 23. Finland
24. France 25. E. Germany
26. W. Germany 27. Ghana
28. Greece 29. Hungary
30. Iceland 31. India
32. Indonesia 33. Iran
34. Iraq 35. Ireland
36. Israel 37. Italy
38. Jamaica 39. Japan
40. Jordan 41. N. Korea
42. S. Korea 43. Lebanon
44. Liberia 45. Malaysia
46. Malta 47. Mexico
48. Morocco 49. Netherlands
50. New Zealand 51. Nigeria
52. Norway 53. Pakistan
54. Paraguay 55. Peru
56. Philippines 57. Poland
58. Portugal 59. Romania
60. Saudi Arabia
61. Sierra Leone 62. Singapore
63. South Africa 64. Spain
65. Sweden 66. Switzerland
67. Thailand 68. Trinidad & Tobago
69. Tunisia 70. Turkey
71. United Kingdom 72. USA
73. Uruguay 74. USSR
75. Vatican City 76. Venezuela
77. Yugoslavia 78. Zaire

FLAGS

Flags are pieces of coloured cloth, often decorated with bold markings. They have special fastenings so that they can be flown from masts and poles. Flags are used by countries, armies, and groups such as BOY SCOUTS, marching bands, and sports teams.

Flags have been used as emblems since the time of the ancient Egyptians. Their flags were flown on long poles as battle standards, held by 'standard-bearers'. Flying high in the air, flags helped soldiers to find their companions quickly as they plunged into battle. And they showed which soldiers belonged to which king or general.

Today, national flags are flown as a symbol of a country's history, its power and its importance, or *prestige*. They are also a symbol of people's loyalty to one nation and one government.

Flags are also used for signalling. Since 1857 there has been an international code for flag signals. It is used by ships. A yellow flag, for instance, means that a ship is in quarantine because of illness on board. A blue flag with a white rectangle, known as the 'Blue Peter', means that a ship is about to sail. For thousands of years flags have been important as a way of identifying ships at sea. Ships from countries that were enemies could therefore avoid or challenge each other.

Other well-known signals are a white flag—a sign of truce—and a flag raised to half mast—a sign that people are mourning someone's death.

141

FLEAS

Fleas are tiny wingless insects less than 3 mm ($\frac{1}{8}$ inch) long. They live on the bodies of birds, animals and human beings. Fleas are parasites, and feed on their hosts by biting through the skin and sucking the blood. Fleas can carry GERMS from one host to another. Rat fleas, for example, can give bubonic plague to people.

The flea below is drawn 25 times its size. Fleas can jump as high as 17 cm (7 inches).

Above: Sir Alexander Fleming. Below: The penicillium mould from which the anti-biotic penicillin is made.

Below: This spearhead was skilfully chipped from a lump of flint. It was made by Stone Age people living in France more than 15,000 years ago.

FLEMING, ALEXANDER

Sir Alexander Fleming (1881-1955) was a British doctor who discovered the anti-biotic drug penicillin. It is one of the most important drugs known. Penicillin fights infections caused by many kinds of GERMS and bacteria. Although the drug fights the infection it does not usually harm the body. Penicillin has saved thousands of lives.

Fleming discovered the drug by accident in 1928. He found an unknown kind of mould growing in his laboratory. From this he was able to make penicillin. For his work, Fleming was awarded the NOBEL PRIZE in 1945.

FLINT

Flint is a glassy MINERAL that is a form of QUARTZ. It is found in beds of chalk and limestone. A lump of flint is dull white on the outside and shiny grey to black on the inside.

Flint is very hard, but it can be easily chipped into sharp-edged flakes. In ancient times men made tools and weapons out of flint. Because it will give off a spark when struck against iron, it can be used for starting a FIRE. A spark from a flint also ignited the powder in a flintlock GUN.

FLOWERS

There are about 250,000 different kinds of flowering plants in the world. Their flowers come in a dazzling array of colours, sizes and shapes. Some grow singly. Some grow in tight clusters. Many have showy colours, a strong scent and produce a sweet nectar. Others are quite drab and plain-smelling.

Whatever they look like, flowers all have the same part to play in the life of the plant. Flowers help plants to reproduce themselves. Inside a flower are male parts, called *stamens*, and female parts known as *pistils*. The stamens contain hundreds of powdery grains of POLLEN. These fertilize the pistil. Then a FRUIT begins to form and grow. Inside the fruit are the SEEDS for a new generation of plants. The seeds are scattered in different ways. They may be blown by the wind, or carried off by birds and animals. From them new plants will grow.

Right: People use flowers for many purposes. They keep them in their homes because they are lovely to look at and smell sweet. Flowers are also used to make decorations, and their scents have been used for centuries in the making of perfumes.

FLY

Flies are a large group of winged insects. They have two pairs of wings, one pair for flying and another set of small wings behind the main pair to help them to balance in flight.

Many flies are dangerous. They spread deadly diseases such as cholera and dysentery. They pick up GERMS from manure and rotting food and carry them into homes where they leave them on our fresh food.

Some flies bite and feed on the blood of animals. Hornflies and gadflies attack cattle and horses in great swarms. Tsetse flies, which live in the tropics, spread sleeping sickness among humans. Blowflies lay their eggs in open wounds on the skin of animals. The maggots that hatch eat into the flesh and cause great harm.

Flies have three pairs of legs and one pair of antennae (1). They have two huge 'compound' eyes (2) that are made up of hundreds of tiny 'eyes'.

Above: International soccer – Stanley Matthews (left) made 698 League appearances. Centre, Pelé of Brazil playing in the 1970 World Cup. Right, Ajax Amsterdam after winning the 1973 European Cup final.

FOOTBALL

There are several kinds of football. They differ in the shape of the ball, the size of the teams and the rules.

Soccer is played all over the world. The ball is round, the field anywhere from 90 to 118 metres (100 to 130 yards) long, and each team has 11 players. Teams score by kicking the ball into the goal at the opposite end of the field. The ball may not be carried.

American football uses an oval ball. The game consists mostly of tackling, passing and running, with very little kicking. The players—11 on each side—are protected by helmets and pads. This type of football is sometimes very violent.

Rugby football is played in Britain, the COMMONWEALTH and parts of Europe. The ball is oval, and each team has 15 players. The ball may be kicked or carried. Australian football has slightly different rules, and there are 18 men to a side.

FORD, HENRY

Henry Ford (1863–1947) was a pioneer MOTOR CAR maker in America. He was the first to use assembly lines. By building his cars out of standard parts he was able to turn out hundreds a day. His cars were designed so that many people could afford to buy them. Ford's biggest success was the Model T. His Detroit factories turned out 15 million Model Ts during the 19 years it was in production. The 1916 coupé and 1923 sedan (below) are two other models built by Ford.

FOREST

Forests are large areas of tree-covered land. Tropical rain forests are found near the EQUATOR. In their hot and steamy climate many kinds of tree and plant grow very quickly. In some places the trees grow so closely together that the sunlight cannot reach the dark, bare forest floor.

Coniferous forests are nearly always found in cold northern lands. These forests are mostly made up of one kind of tree, such as spruce, FIR or PINE. Few other plants grow there. In temperate lands like Europe and the cooler parts of Australia and Africa, there are deciduous forests with trees like OAK and beech.

FOSSILS

Fossils are the hardened remains or impressions of animals and plants that lived a very long time ago. A fossil may be a shell, a bone, a tooth, a leaf, a skeleton or even sometimes an entire animal.

Most fossils have been found in areas that were once in or near the sea. When the plant or creature died its body sank to the seabed. The soft parts usually rotted away but the hard skeleton became buried in the mud.

Over millions of years more and more mud settled on top of the skeleton. Eventually these layers of mud hardened into rock, and the skeleton became part of that rock. Water seeping through the rock slowly dissolved away the original skeleton. It was replaced by stony MINERALS which formed exactly the same shape.

These fossils lay buried until movements in the Earth's crust pushed up the seabed and it became dry land. In time water, ice and wind wear away the rock and the fossil comes to the surface. The oldest known fossil is over 3000 million years old.

Because teeth are so very hard many have become fossils. Fossilized teeth are often the only parts left of an ancient mammal.

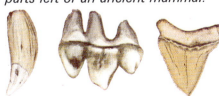

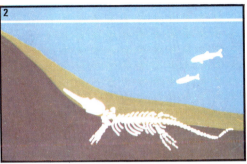

This diagram shows how a creature like this fish-like reptile, could become a fossil. When it dies its body sinks to the seabed. Its bones are covered with silt which gradually turns to rock. Later the seabed becomes dry land and the rocks above the fossil slowly wear away, exposing the fossil. Fossils of small snail-like sea creatures are quite common and can be found in layers in rocks by the seaside.

FOX

Foxes belong to the same animal family as dogs. The most common kind is the red fox, which is found in Europe, North Africa, North America and parts of Asia. It eats small birds, animals and insects, and occasionally poultry or lambs.

Foxes are seldom seen because they are shy and only come out at night. They live in holes called 'earths' which they either dig themselves or take over from rabbits or badgers. Recently, some foxes have been found in cities. They live under the floors of buildings or in any hidden place they can find. They eat scraps from the dustbins.

Foxes are very cunning animals. Sometimes they catch rabbits and other prey by chasing their own tails very fast. This fascinates the rabbit who watches without realizing that the fox is gradually getting nearer and nearer. When the fox gets close enough it suddenly straightens out and grabs its dinner.

FRANCE

France is the largest country in Western EUROPE. It has a population of 54,414,000 (1978). In ancient times France was inhabited by CELTS, but Julius CAESAR conquered it and for 500 years it was part of the Roman Empire. The Franks, from whom the country got its name, invaded in the AD 400s. Since then France has remained one country with one official language.

France is a very varied and beautiful country with large plains to the north and west, a big central plateau and mountains to the east and south. It has a temperate climate and is very fertile. Farmland covers about half the country and many of the people are employed in farming, fishing or forestry work. France produces a lot of grain, fruit and vegetables, and it is famous for its WINES.

The history of France is long and turbulent. For centuries the French and English were enemies and fought many wars. The French people had their own troubles too. For many years they suffered under the rule of greedy kings and nobles. Then in 1789 the people started the FRENCH REVOLUTION. They overthrew their king and made France a republic.

But the country was soon taken over by NAPOLEON who made himself Emperor. He went to war and conquered most of the countries of Europe before he was finally defeated at Waterloo in 1815. Since then France has fought three wars against Germany, two with Britain as her ally. ▷

Below: A fully grown male fox will weigh about 7 kg (15½ lb) and stand about 35 cm (14 inches) at the shoulder.

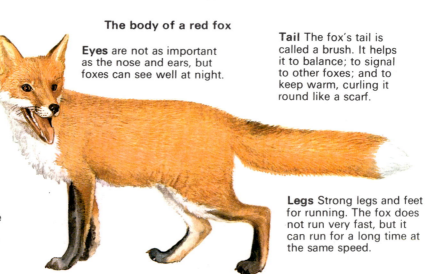

The body of a red fox

Ears are large to pick up as much sound as possible. A fox can hear even better than a dog.

Nose The fox's sense of smell is very keen. With its wet nose it can tell which way the wind is blowing, so it knows exactly where any smell is coming from.

Teeth Long ones at the front for tearing meat and sharp side ones for slicing it.

Eyes are not as important as the nose and ears, but foxes can see well at night.

Tail The fox's tail is called a brush. It helps it to balance; to signal to other foxes; and to keep warm, curling it round like a scarf.

Legs Strong legs and feet for running. The fox does not run very fast, but it can run for a long time at the same speed.

Today, France is one of the wealthiest nations in Europe. It was one of the first members of the EUROPEAN ECONOMIC COMMUNITY. It has many beautiful historical buildings and palaces, and it is famous for the number of important writers, artists and musicians who have been born there. The capital city of PARIS is visited by thousands of people every year.

FRANCIS OF ASSISI

St. Francis (1182–1226) was born in Assisi in central Italy. When he was 22 he suffered a severe illness. Afterwards he decided to devote his life to the service of God. He lived in poverty and gathered round him a band of monks who became known as the Franciscans. St. Francis was very fond of birds and animals whom he called his brothers and sisters.

FRANKLIN, BENJAMIN

Benjamin Franklin (1706–1790) was an American politician and scientist. He was born in Boston, the youngest of 17 children. Franklin became a printer and then went on to publish a yearly almanac which made his fortune.

He became involved in the War of Independence, which brought America freedom from British rule. He helped draw up the peace treaty at the end of the war and was one of the men who signed America's Declaration of Independence.

His scientific inventions include bifocal glasses, and a rod that protects buildings from being struck by lightning.

FRENCH REVOLUTION

For many centuries the poor people of FRANCE suffered under the rule of their kings and nobles. Rich people built themselves lavish palaces and mansions while many other people starved in misery. French kings forced the peasants and shopkeepers to pay taxes to pay for their extravagant way of life, and for the wars they were always fighting.

There was no PARLIAMENT to stop the king from treating his subjects badly and eventually, in 1789, the French people exploded into revolution. King LOUIS XVI was imprisoned but tried to escape. Violent leaders like Danton and Marat took over the Revolution and the king and queen and many nobles were beheaded.

Then followed the 'Reign of Terror', when the Revolutionary leaders began to quarrel amongst themselves and many of them were beheaded too. The people tired of bloodshed and in 1795 they set up a government called 'The Directory'. But it ruled the country badly, and in 1799 it was overthrown by NAPOLEON.

FRICTION

When two things rub together it causes friction. Friction makes it harder to move something across a surface. Smooth objects cause much less friction than rough objects, so when things need to go fast we try to reduce friction. This is why the rails and wheels of railways are smooth. When we want things to slow down we add friction, like putting on the brakes in our cars. If two things rub together at great speed the friction produces HEAT. If you rub your hand very fast against your leg you can feel the heat made by the friction.

FROGS

Frogs are amphibians. This means that they can live both on land and in water. Frogs are found all over the world except in very ▷

cold lands that are always frozen. There are hundreds of different kinds. The biggest is the Goliath frog of Central Africa. This frog can be over 80 cm (31 inches) long and weigh over 3 kg (6½ lb). The smallest is a tree frog from the United States which is less than 2 cm (¾ inch) long.

Frogs breathe through their skins as well as their LUNGS. It is important that frogs keep their skins wet because if the skin became too dry it could not breathe and the frog would die. This is why you will never find a frog very far away from water, and why they like to stay in the shade.

Common frogs feed on insects, grubs and slugs. They catch their food with the long sticky tongue which is attached to the front of their mouths. A frog can flick its tongue in and out in a fraction of a second. Really big frogs eat snakes, small animals and other frogs, as well as insects. Tadpoles eat small water creatures although they themselves often make a tasty meal for adult frogs.

FRUIT

To most of us 'fruit' means juicy foods which grow on certain plants and trees. Apples, oranges and pears are three examples. These fruits taste good and are important in our diet. They give us mineral salts, sugar and VITAMINS. The water, skins and seeds of fruit help our DIGESTION.

To scientists who study plants, fruits are the ripe SEED cases of any flowering plant.

The fruits protect the seeds as they develop and help spread them when they are ripe. Some fruits scatter seeds. Others are eaten by birds and animals that spread the seeds.

FUNGUS

A fungus is a simple PLANT with no true roots, stems or leaves. Fungi do not have

Eggs (spawn) laid in spring

Tadpole hatches two weeks later

From tadpole to frog

Tadpole with gills outside

Tadpole with gills inside

Back legs grow after about six weeks

Front legs grow about three weeks later

Froglet is ready to leave water about eleven weeks after the eggs were laid

Frog is fully grown after about three years

Moist skin for breathing

Strong back legs for jumping and swimming

Webbed feet for swimming

Long sticky tongue attached to front of mouth

Eyes which are covered by a special see-through eyelid for when the frog is under the water

148   **The body of a common frog**

the CHLOROPHYLL that helps green plants to make food. So fungi have to find a ready-made supply of food. Some feed as parasites on living plants or animals. Others feed on animal and plant remains.

There are more than 50,000 kinds of fungi. Some have only one CELL. Other fungi are chains of cells. These produce tiny thread-like growths that spread through the substance they feed on. Many fungi grow a large fruiting body which sheds spores that produce new fungus plants. The mushrooms we eat are the fruiting bodies of a fungus.

Right, top: Fly agaric fungi growing among the leaves on the forest floor. They feed on tree roots and rotting leaves.

FUR

Fur is the thick hairy coat that some mammals grow. There are two kinds of fur fibre. Short soft fur grows close to the skin. Longer, stiffer hairs cover this underfur and prevent the fur from becoming matted.

Fur keeps in body heat. Mammals with thick fur stay warm even in the coldest weather. Animals with very thick fur live in the coldest parts of the world.

Since STONE AGE times people have worn furs to keep them warm. Wearing furs today is a sign of luxury. Some of the best furs come from the chinchilla, fur seals, mink, muskrat, silver fox and ermine (the white winter coat of the stoat).

FURNITURE

Furniture is used for resting things on and for storing things in. Beds, chairs and tables all support some kind of load. Chests and cupboards hold such things as blankets, sheets and china.

The first pieces of furniture were simple slabs of stone and chunks of wood. In time, people tried to make furniture that was beautiful as well as useful.

Wealthy Egyptians carved and painted beds, chairs and tables 4000 years ago. The Romans used bronze and marble, and made tables with legs carved in animal shapes. From the end of the Middle Ages onwards many different styles of furniture have been made.

More recently, people have tried using new materials and machines to make furniture with clean, simple shapes. Today you can buy metal or plastic furniture.

FUSE

This word has two meanings. One kind of fuse is a safety device in an electric circuit. Fuse wire is made so that it will melt at a low temperature. If too much ELECTRICITY flows through the circuit the wire 'fuses', or melts. This breaks the circuit and stops the flow of electric current.

In this way, an electric fuse stops the wire in the circuit from becoming too hot and possibly setting fire to nearby objects. Electric current must pass through fuse wire to get from the main power line to the electric wiring in a house. Inside the house, each electric plug also has a fuse.

The other kind of fuse is a device that sets off EXPLOSIONS. A safety fuse burns slowly until the flame reaches the explosive. A detonating fuse explodes itself and this explosion sets off a much larger amount of DYNAMITE.

GALAXY

Someone once called galaxies 'star islands in space'. A galaxy is made up of a huge group of STARS. Our Sun is just one star of about 100,000 million stars that belong to the MILKY WAY galaxy. A beam of light would take about 100,000 years to shine from one side of the Milky Way to the other. Yet the Milky Way is only a middle-sized galaxy.

Beyond our galaxy there may be as many as 10,000 million more. The nearest large one is the Andromeda galaxy. The light we see it by took more than two million years to reach us.

Some galaxies have no special shape. Others have spiral arms made up of many millions of stars. The Milky Way and Andromeda galaxies both look like this. There are also galaxies that look like saucers or like balls. Astronomers used to think that these changed into galaxies with spiral arms. Now some astronomers believe that the spiral galaxies shrink into the other kind instead.

RADIO ASTRONOMY has shown that radio waves are sent out from many galaxies. Astronomers call these radio galaxies. Strong radio waves also come from strange star-like objects known as *quasars*. A quasar is smaller than a galaxy yet it may give out 100 times more energy. Some people think that a quasar may be the beginning of a new galaxy. Scientists think that galaxies may form where GRAVITY pulls huge clouds of gas together.

This is a picture of the Andromeda Galaxy. Our Milky Way Galaxy would look like this if seen from space.

GALILEO

Galileo Galilei (1564–1642) was an Italian mathematics teacher who might be called the first true scientist. Instead of believing old ideas about the way the world worked, Galileo made careful experiments to find out for himself. He learnt that a PENDULUM took the same time to make a long swing as it did to make a short one. He showed that light objects fell as fast as heavy ones when pulled toward the Earth by what we know as GRAVITY. He built a TELESCOPE and became the first man to use this tool for studying the Moon and planets. What he saw made Galileo believe COPERNICUS' idea that the Earth was not the centre of the UNIVERSE. The Church punished him for his belief in this idea. But later scientists like Isaac NEWTON built new knowledge on Galileo's discoveries.

GALLEON

This kind of heavy, wooden sailing ship was used for carrying fighting men and cargoes over oceans in the 1500s. A galleon was four times as long as it was wide. It had a special deck to carry cannons. There were square sails on its two front masts and three-cornered *lateen* sails on its one or two rear masts. Lateen sails helped galleons to sail against the wind. Galleons were faster and easier to manage than some other ships. But some Spanish galleons were clumsy and topheavy.

GAMA, VASCO DA

Vasco da Gama (about 1469–1524) discovered how to sail by sea from Europe to India by way of southern Africa. This Portuguese navigator left Lisbon with four ships in July 1497. In East Africa he found a guide who showed him how to sail across the Indian Ocean. Da Gama reached Calicut in southern India in May 1498. But Arab traders who were jealous of the Portuguese tried to stop him trading with the Indians. On the journey home, 30 of his 90 crewmen died of scurvy, and only two of the four ships got back to Lisbon.

GANDHI

Mohandas Karamchand Gandhi (1869–1948) is sometimes called the 'father of modern India'. This frail-looking Hindu lawyer helped to free INDIA from British rule by showing Indians peaceful ways of disobeying British laws. From 1893 to 1915 he lived in South Africa, where he tried to win equal rights for Indians under British rule.

In 1915 Gandhi moved back to India. He became the leader of those people who wanted Indian not British rule in India. When the British passed a law against this work he called the people out on strike. In 1920 he told the Indians to spin cloth for their own clothes instead of buying it from Britain. In 1930 he broke a British law by making salt from seawater instead of buying salt from the government.

People admired Gandhi's beliefs, his kindness to all men, and his simple way of life. But he spent seven years in prisons for disobeying British laws. In 1947 Britain gave India independence. Soon after, one of his fellow HINDUS shot Gandhi for preaching peace to Moslems, people who follow the religion of ISLAM.

Right: A cross-section of a galleon with three gun decks. Hammocks were hung from the ceilings of the gun decks.

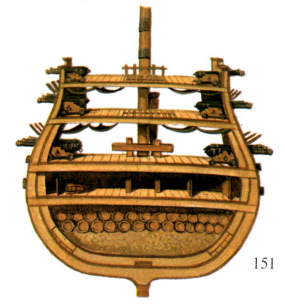

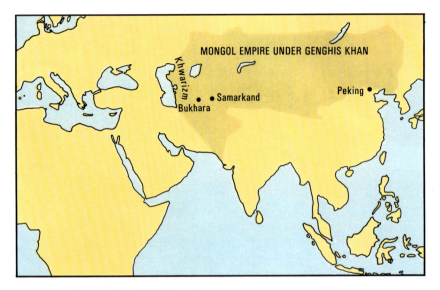

GENGHIS KHAN

Genghis Khan (1167–1227) was a Mongol chief who cruelly attacked many Asian peoples and won a mighty empire. His real name was Temujin ('ironsmith'). Legend has it that he was born holding a clot of blood, a hint of the many people he would kill.

At 13 he took his dead father's place as chief of a small Mongol tribe of NOMADS. He soon won power over nearby tribes as well. In 1206 he became known as Genghis Khan, 'Very Mighty King'. Genghis Khan formed a huge army of tough, hard-riding nomads on the great grasslands of central Asia. Then he set off to conquer the lands around him. His troops pushed south-east to Peking in China, and south into Tibet and what are now Pakistan and Afghanistan. In the south-west they invaded Iran and southern Russia.

No city could drive off the fierce Mongol archers. Genghis Khan forced prisoners of war to lead his army. He punished cities that resisted him by killing most of the people. At Nishapur in Iran, his troops built pyramids of severed heads.

Genghis Khan was once supposed to have said that nothing made him happier than smashing enemies and taking their possessions. After he died other Mongol rulers won more land and made the empire even larger.

This map shows the empire won by the cruel Mongol leader Genghis Khan (above). After his ambassador was killed in Khwarizm, he spent three years smashing all of that kingdom's biggest cities. Samarkand and Bukhara as well as Peking in China suffered horribly from Mongol armies.

Below: This old Asian painting shows people paying their respects to Temujin when he took the title Genghis Khan. Soon after, he set out to seize the world.

GEOGRAPHY

Geography is the subject we study when we want to learn about the surface of the Earth. Geographers study everything on the Earth—the land, sea, air, plants, animals and even man. They explain where different things are found, how they got there, and how they affect one another.

There are many different areas, or branches, of geography. For instance, physical geography describes things like mountains, valleys, lakes, and rivers. Meteorology describes weather. Economic geography deals with farming, mining, manufacturing, and trade.

Maps and charts are the geographer's most useful tools.

Below: Geographers study deserts, rivers, and other things on the Earth's surface. Geologists study rocks on and under it.

GEOLOGY

Geology is the study of the Earth itself. Geologists discover what things the Earth is made of, where they are found, and how they got there. Geologists study the chemicals in ROCKS and MINERALS. They also try to find out how rocks are formed, and how they are changed by movements beneath the surface of the Earth. VOLCANOES and EARTHQUAKES give us useful clues about movements deep down underground.

Geologists also study the history of the Earth. They have found rocks 3800 million years old, and FOSSILS showing that EVOLUTION began over 3400 million years ago.

Geologists help engineers to choose where to build a road or tunnel. They help miners to find coal, oil, or gas beneath the ground. By studying rocks brought back by astronauts they may even be able to tell us what the Moon is made of.

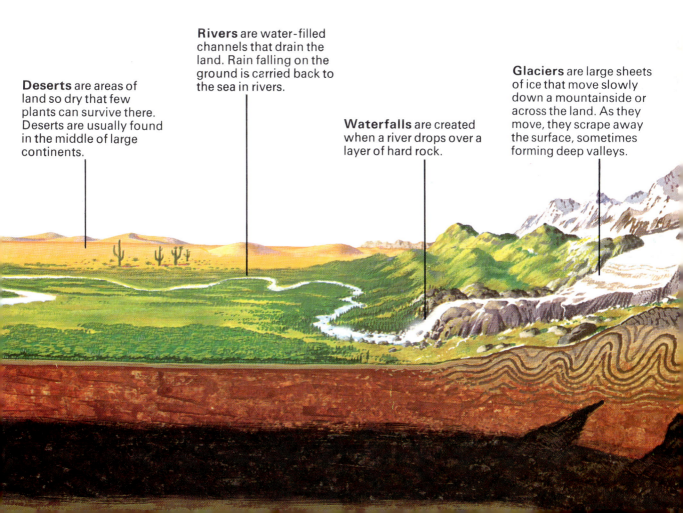

Rivers are water-filled channels that drain the land. Rain falling on the ground is carried back to the sea in rivers.

Deserts are areas of land so dry that few plants can survive there. Deserts are usually found in the middle of large continents.

Waterfalls are created when a river drops over a layer of hard rock.

Glaciers are large sheets of ice that move slowly down a mountainside or across the land. As they move, they scrape away the surface, sometimes forming deep valleys.

GEOMETRY

Geometry is a branch of MATHEMATICS. It can help you to find out the shape, size and position of an object, or how much a container holds. People draw lines and measure ANGLES to help them solve geometric problems.

GEORGE (KINGS)

Six British kings were called George.

George I (1660–1727) was a German ruler who inherited the British throne. JAMES I was his great grandfather.

George II (1683–1760) was the last British king to lead troops into battle. He reigned when Britain was winning Canada and India.

George III (1738–1820) ruled as the INDUSTRIAL REVOLUTION began. He lost what became the UNITED STATES. In old age he went mad.

George IV (1762–1830) was a spendthrift who loved to be in fashion. As Prince Regent he took his mad father's place from 1811.

George V (1865–1936) was a naval officer before he was king. He reigned during WORLD WAR I.

George VI (1895–1952) reigned during WORLD WAR II. He was the father of ELIZABETH II.

Top left: George I, A German. Top right: George III, called 'Farmer George'.

Above: George V broadcasts a Christmas message to his people.

GERMANY

Germany used to be one great nation. After WORLD WAR II the land was divided into two nations: West Germany and East Germany. Both lie in the middle of EUROPE, and their peoples speak the same language, German.

West Germany is a little larger than the United Kingdom, and has more people than any other nation in Western Europe. Farms and cities stand on the low plain in the north and in the valley of the River Rhine. The south has low, wooded mountains and sharp tall peaks belonging to the Alps.

Above left: A map of East and West Germany. Left: Fine grapes grow on the steep slopes above the River Moselle.

West Germany's farms produce more pigs and barley than any other western European nation. No other western European country produces so much coal or steel, or so many cars and television sets. West Germany's mines and factories make her the richest nation in Europe. Her capital is Bonn.

East Germany is less than half the size of West Germany. There is only one East German for roughly every three West Germans. Like West Germany, East Germany has low, flat land in the north and forested mountains in the south. The rivers Elbe and Oder flow north toward the Baltic Sea. East Germans mine more soft brown coal than any other nation. East Germany is a communist country. The capital is East BERLIN.

Factories cover much of the Ruhr, the part of West Germany where the River Ruhr flows into the Rhine. These factories use coal from the many nearby mines.

GERMS

Many diseases are caused by living things so tiny that you can only see them through a MICROSCOPE. These living things are germs. Germs include certain bacteria, viruses, and some kinds of FUNGUS. Some germs get into the body with breathed-in air. Others can get in through a cut that is not clean.

GEYSERS

Geysers are hot springs that now and then squirt out steam and scalding water. They work like this. Water fills a deep crack in the ground, often near VOLCANOES. Hot rock heats the water deep underground, but the weight of the water above it stops the hot water from boiling until it is much hotter still. Then it turns to steam that forces the water upward, emptying the crack. The next eruption happens when the crack is full again.

There are many geysers in some parts of Iceland, the United States, and New Zealand. The tallest geyser ever known was the Waimangu geyser in New Zealand. In 1904 this squirted steam and water nearly 460 metres (about 1500 feet) into the sky.

GHANA

Ghana is a nation in West AFRICA. It is a bit smaller than the United Kingdom. The country is hot, with plenty of rain in the south where Ghana meets the Atlantic Ocean. The land here is low, with tropical forests and farms. The north is drier and grassy.

Most of Ghana's 12 million people are Negroes. They grow cocoa and mine diamonds and gold. Electricity comes from Lake Volta. This man-made lake covers more land than any other man-made lake in the world.

Below: Geysers spouting and gushing in the great geyser area around the Waikato river in the North Island of New Zealand.

GIBRALTAR

This small British colony is a rocky peninsula that juts out from southern Spain. Most of Gibraltar is a mountain called the Rock. Britain won Gibraltar from Spain in 1704. Gibraltar's ships and guns guard the western end of the MEDITERRANEAN SEA.

GILLS

FISH, CRABS and many other water animals breathe by forcing water past gills. Gills are flat or feathery pieces of thin 'skin'. They take oxygen from water and give out carbon dioxide waste. Many fish have hard gill covers to protect their soft gills.

Gills

Fish have gills on each side of their heads. This is a bitterling, a freshwater fish.

A giraffe has two short, bony horns between its ears. Its nostrils can be shut to keep out dust. Inside its mouth is a long, worm-like tongue that tears leaves from twigs.

GIPSIES

Gipsies are a special group of people found in Europe and North America. They have dark hair, skin, and eyes. Many speak a language called Romany. Some live in houses, others travel all the time and live in caravans. Gipsies trade in cars and horses and make metalwork or tell people's fortunes. They are famous for their songs and dances.

The name 'gipsy' comes from the word Egyptian. Europeans once thought gipsies came from Egypt, but they probably came from India 600 years ago.

GIRAFFE

Giraffes are the tallest animals. An adult male may stand three times taller than a tall man. They have long legs and a long neck. Yet this neck has only seven bones, the same as any other MAMMAL. Giraffes live in the hot grasslands of Africa. They feed on shrubs and trees and spread their forelegs wide when they bend their necks to drink.

GLASS

People use glass in windows, eye-glasses, mirrors, tumblers, bottles, electric light bulbs, and many other objects.

Glass is made of sand mixed with some lime, soda, and other chemical ingredients. Then the mixture is melted in a furnace. When it flows, it is called molten glass. Workers can shape the molten glass in several ways. They may pour it in a mould, or shape it by blowing through a tube into a blob of molten glass stuck to the far end. If they pour molten glass on a bath of molten tin, the glass forms a smooth sheet that is used for windows.

Most glass is brittle and breaks easily. But some kinds are so tough that you could use them to hammer nails into wood.

GOLD

This is a lovely yellow metal that never goes rusty. It is so soft that you can beat it into thin sheets, or pull it out into a wire.

People find thin veins of gold in cracks in certain rocks. It was left there by hot gases and liquids rising from deep underground. If water washes out the gold, lumps called nuggets may collect in the beds of streams and rivers. Half of the world's gold is mined in just one part of South Africa.

Because gold is beautiful and scarce, it is also very valuable. Most of the world's gold is kept in brick-shaped bars in banks. People make jewellery from gold mixed with other substances to make it harder. But gold is useful, too. Dentists sometimes put gold fillings in people's teeth.

GOOSE

Geese are water birds related to DUCKS and SWANS and between the two in size. Geese have webbed feet and swim well. They have longer legs than ducks and swans and can walk more easily. Geese come on land to eat leaves and grains. Most of the 15 kinds of geese nest in the Arctic, but in winter they fly farther south in flocks. Tame geese give us eggs, meat, and down feathers for stuffing pillows.

Snow goose

Left: A lovely wine glass made 500 years ago in Venice, a city famous for its glass.
Below: Making glass. Cullet is broken glass added to speed up melting in the furnace.

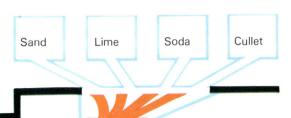

Sand   Lime   Soda   Cullet

GORILLA

Gorillas are the largest of the APES. A big male may be as tall as a man. Gorillas live in family groups in the warm forests of central Africa. They eat fruit, roots, tree bark and leaves. Every night they make beds of twigs in the low branches of trees.

GRASS

Grasses are flowering plants with long, thin, leaves growing from hollow stems. BAMBOO is as tall as a tree but most grasses are short. Sheep and cattle eat grass. We eat the seeds of cultivated CEREAL grasses like WHEAT and RICE.

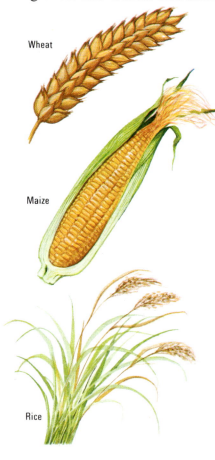

Wheat

Maize

Rice

GRASSHOPPER

These insects have feelers, wings, and long back legs. A grasshopper can jump 20 times its own length. Grasshoppers eat leaves, and those called LOCUSTS damage crops. Many males 'sing' by rubbing their back legs on their wings.

Above: Wheat, maize, and rice are the world's three most important crops of cultivated grasses.

Right: A Lesser Marsh grasshopper which lives by rivers and in wet meadows.

GRAVITY

Gravity is the pull that tries to tug everything toward the middle of the EARTH. It is gravity that makes objects tend to fall, stops us flying off into space, and keeps the MOON circling the Earth. When we weigh something, we are measuring the force with which gravity pulls that object down. The more closely packed the substances in an object are, the heavier it seems.

Not just the Earth, but all PLANETS and STARS exert a pulling force. Scientists call this gravitation. The larger and denser a star or a planet is and the nearer it is to other objects, the more strongly it pulls them toward it. The SUN is far from the planets, but it is so huge that its gravitation keeps the planets circling around it. The Moon is small and its gravitation is weak. An astronaut on the Moon seems to weigh far less than he weighs here on Earth.

Left: Galileo found that light and heavy objects tend to fall at the same rate.

GREAT BRITAIN

The United Kingdom of Great Britain and Northern IRELAND is the eleventh largest nation in Europe. ENGLAND, WALES and SCOTLAND make up the island of Great Britain, which takes up most of the BRITISH ISLES. Northern Ireland, Scotland, and Wales are mountainous. The highest mountain is Ben Nevis in Scotland. Plains and valleys cover much of England. The longest river is the Thames, which flows through southern England. The British climate is mild.

About 56 million people live in the United Kingdom. Few other countries are so crowded. Four out of five people live in cities such as Belfast, Glasgow, and LONDON. London is the capital. Great Britain grows half of the food she needs. Her mines and factories help to pay for the food that is bought from abroad.

Left: Queen Elizabeth II opening Parliament. Members of Parliament are chosen by the people and form the government that makes Great Britain's laws.

GREAT LAKES

This is the world's largest group of fresh-water lakes. They are a bit larger than the whole of Great Britain. Lake Michigan lies in the UNITED STATES. Lakes Superior, Erie, Huron and Ontario are shared by the United States and CANADA. The largest lake of all is Superior. The lakes were formed when a huge sheet of ice melted 18,000 years ago.

Rivers and canals connect the lakes to each other and to the Atlantic Ocean. Ships can reach the sea from lake ports that lie 1600 km (1000 miles) inland. Lots of factories are built around the lakes to take advantage of the water supply. Most of the goods that the factories produce are taken to other parts of the country by boat.

Below: Part of the Great Wall of China. In places it stands wider and taller than a house. Soldiers once rode on horses along its top, which is flat and covered with bricks.

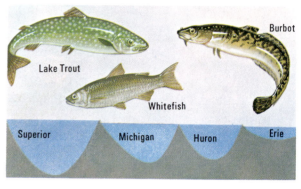

Some of the kinds of fish that live in the four inner Great Lakes. The fishing industry there is very important. In 1932 it was almost ruined when the Welland Ship Canal was built. This connected Lake Erie to Lake Ontario. Sea fish were able to get into the lakes through the canal and they ate the freshwater fish. The problem was solved by putting in new fish that were enemies of the sea fish but left the others alone.

GREAT WALL OF CHINA

More than 2000 years ago the first emperor of CHINA, Ch'in Shi Huang Ti, built this wall to keep out China's enemies from the north. The Great Wall is the longest wall in the world. It stretches for 3460 km (2130 miles) from the Yellow Sea in the east to Asia in the west.

The wall is made from earth and stone. Watchtowers were built every 180 metres (200 yds) along it. Chinese sentries sent warning signals from the towers if anyone attacked the wall. The signal was smoke by day and a fire at night.

GREECE

Greece is a country that lies in southeast EUROPE. Mountains cover most of the land, and peninsulas poke out into the sea like giant fingers. Greece includes the island of CRETE and many smaller islands in the Aegean and Ionian seas. Greek summers are hot and dry. Winters are mild and wet.

More than nine million people live in Greece. Many work in the capital city Athens. Greek farmers produce crops like lemons, grapes, wheat and olives. Millions of tourists visit Greece every year.

Ancient Greece

The first great people in Greece were the Minoans and the Mycenaeans. The Minoans lived in Crete. They had rich cities and farms and led a peaceful life. The Mycenaeans lived on the mainland of Greece. They were warriors and sailors. The heroes of HOMER'S poems were probably Mycenaean. Both these civilizations ended in about 1200 BC.

Around this time, new groups of people began to move into Greece. They came from the north and spoke Greek. Instead of making Greece one kingdom, they built separate cities. They often fought wars with each other. Sometimes they joined together to fight other enemies, such as the Persians. Two of the strongest cities were Athens and Sparta. In the 400s BC Athens was ruled by a DEMOCRACY. It became very powerful.

The Greeks loved the theatre, art and poetry. They had many great thinkers, or *philosophers*, including ARISTOTLE, Plato and Socrates. Greek cities had many graceful buildings. They were decorated with beautiful SCULPTURE. The Greeks also started the first OLYMPIC GAMES. In 339 BC Greece was conquered by Philip, the father of ALEXANDER THE GREAT.

Above: Gathering grapes on the big Greek island of Crete. Like mainland Greece, Crete produces much wine and olive oil.

Right: Many ancient Greek cities had their own money. The top coin comes from Athens. It is made of silver. The coin below is made of a mixture of gold and silver.

161

GUNPOWDER

Gunpowder is a dark powder used for making weak EXPLOSIONS. People make gunpowder by mixing special amounts of charcoal, sulphur, and saltpetre. When someone sets fire to the mixture, it burns quickly and gives off lots of gas and smoke. If the gunpowder has been packed into fireworks or a gun barrel, there will be an explosion.

The Chinese may have invented gunpowder nearly 1000 years ago. In 1242 the monk Roger Bacon wrote a recipe for making gunpowder.

Cannon, 1460

Vigilant rocket

GUNS

Guns are weapons that fire bullets or other missiles from a long tube open at one end.

Guns were probably invented in the 1200s. By the 1300s guns were firing missiles that could pierce armour and break down castle walls.

Early guns were large weapons, far too heavy for one man to carry. The first gun was a big bucket with a small hole in the bottom. Soldiers put GUNPOWDER in the bucket. Then they piled stones on top. They lit the gunpowder through the hole. When the gunpowder exploded the stones flew out. The large, long, guns called cannons were first used about 1350. Cannons fired big metal cannonballs. In the 1800s came guns which fired pointed shells that exploded when they hit their target. A spiral groove cut in the gun barrel made the shells spin as they flew through the air. Soldiers could fire such shells farther and hit their targets more often than with cannonballs.

Troops first used small arms in the 1300s. Small arms are guns that one man can carry. Inventors developed short-barrelled pistols and revolvers for firing at nearby targets. They developed muskets, rifles, and machine guns for long-distance shooting. In modern guns a hammer sets off an explosion that drives a shell or bullet from the barrel.

Tank gu 1917

Above: Four artillery officers stand around a small cannon. This type of gun was used in the American Civil War in the 1860s.

GUTENBERG, JOHANNES

Johannes Gutenberg (about 1398 to about 1468) was a German goldsmith sometimes called the father of PRINTING. In his day, people slowly copied books by hand or printed them from wooden blocks where each letter of every page had to be carved separately. About 1440, Gutenberg learnt to make metal letters called type. He could pick them up and place them in rows to build pages of type. Each page was held together by a frame. Gutenberg fixed the frame to a press, and quickly pressed the inked surface of his type onto sheets of paper. Gutenberg's movable type helped him to make copies of a book faster and more cheaply than ever before.

GYMNASTICS

Gymnastics are exercises that help to make and keep the body fit. The word gymnastics comes from a Greek word for 'naked', because the ancient Greeks did their gymnastic exercises with no clothes on.

The OLYMPIC GAMES have separate gymnastic exercises for men and women. Women perform graceful steps, runs, jumps, turns and somersaults on a narrow wooden beam. They hang from a high bar and swing to and fro between it and a lower one. They leap over a vaulting horse.

Women also perform floor exercises on a big mat, to music. They do handsprings, somersaults, cartwheels, jumps and other movements in a graceful flowing way, without stepping off the mat.

The men's Olympic exercises are different. They hang from a high bar and swing up and down, to and fro, and over and over in giant circles. Using two raised, level bars they swing, vault and do handstands. They grip hoops that jut up from a leather-covered pommel 'horse', and swing their legs and body this way and that without touching the horse. They leap over a vaulting horse. They hang and swing from two rings slung from ropes. They also perform floor exercises.

This toy gyroscope is tilted, yet balances on the tip of a pencil. It seems to defy gravity. As its wheel slows down it will wobble and fall, like a slowing top.

GYROSCOPE

A gyroscope is a wheel that spins in a special frame. No matter how the frame tilts, the wheel's axle points in the same direction. Even the pull of GRAVITY and the Earth's MAGNETISM do not affect the axle.

On a ship or aircraft, a COMPASS made from a gyroscope always points to the north. Gyroscopes can also keep an aircraft on course without the pilot steering.

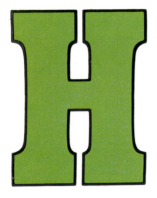

HADES

In Greek myth, Hades was the god of the underworld. (The Romans called him Pluto.) In his underground kingdom, Hades ruled sternly over the dead. In time people gave his name to the underworld itself. Christians came to use Hades as another name for Hell, the home of the devil, where wicked people who died were supposed to be punished for ever.

HAIR

Hair grows like living threads from the skins of MAMMALS. It has the same ingredients that make nails, claws, hoofs, FEATHERS and reptiles' scales. Hair helps to keep the body warm, and protects the skin. There are several kinds of hair. Cats have plenty of soft, thick FUR. Porcupines are protected by sharp, stiff hairs called quills.

HALLOWEEN

Halloween is a festival held on October 31, the day before All Saints' Day. (Halloween roughly means 'holy evening'.) Men used to believe that ghosts, demons, and witches roamed the land on Halloween night. Today, people celebrate Halloween by giving parties.

HAND

Our hands can grip all kinds of objects. We can even hold a fine needle by pressing it between a thumb and finger. Most MAMMALS have hand bones rather like ours. But their 'hands' are shaped as wings, paws, flippers and so on. Such hands can fly, dig, or swim but they cannot make and use tools.

HANDEL, GEORGE FREDERIC

George Frederic Handel (1685–1759) was a German-born British composer, famous for the oratorio *Messiah* and the orchestral *Fireworks Music* and *Water Music*. He wrote about 40 operas and 21 oratorios.

HANNIBAL

Hannibal (247–183 BC) was a Carthaginian general who invaded Italy. In 218 BC he left Spain, and marched an army over the Alps into Italy. He fought the Romans for 15 years but never quite crushed them.

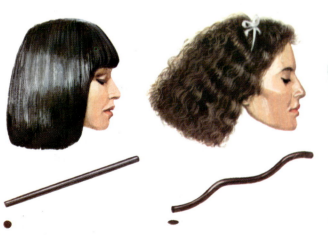

Left: Mongoloid people have straight hair. Caucasoid (white) people usually have wavy hair. Negroid people have hair that is coiled like a spring. Each type of hair seen end-on also looks different.

HAROLD, KING

Harold II (about 1022–1066) was the last of the ANGLO-SAXONS to rule England. In 1053 he became Earl of Wessex. In 1064 he was shipwrecked off France and caught by his cousin William of Normandy (WILLIAM THE CONQUEROR). Harold was freed when he promised to help William become king of England. But the English nobles chose Harold as king. He died at the Battle of HASTINGS, where William's Norman invaders defeated the English.

HARP

This musical instrument has long and short strings stretched over a tall frame that stands on the floor. One side of the frame is hollow. This helps to give the harp its special sound. A harpist plays by plucking the strings with fingers and thumbs. Harps are the oldest stringed instruments. People made harps in Iraq more than 4000 years ago.

Above: This old painting of musicians shows what harps looked like in Egypt more than 3000 years ago. The harpist twisted pegs on the frame to tighten or loosen the strings.

HARPSICHORD

A harpsichord looks rather like a HARP laid on its side and put in a box on legs. The first successful ones date from the 1500s. A harpsichord player plays a keyboard like a PIANO's. Each key lifts a piece of wood called a jack. A quill or a bit of leather fixed to the jack plucks a string.

This harpsichord was made in the 1700s. It had one keyboard, but some others had two or three keyboards. Harpsichords give a rich sound, but it cannot be made loud or soft as easily as the sound from a piano. So when pianos were invented, harpsichords were forgotten for more than a century.

The Norman knights at first failed to pierce the Anglo-Saxons' wall of shields.

HARVEY, WILLIAM

William Harvey (1578–1657) was an English doctor who showed that BLOOD flows around the body in an endless stream. Harvey proved that a beating heart squeezes blood through arteries and flaps in the heart, and that VEINS stop the blood flowing back. He worked out that the amount of blood pumped by a heart in an hour weighs three times more than a man.

HASTINGS, BATTLE OF

In 1066 this battle made Norman invaders the masters of England.

WILLIAM THE CONQUEROR sailed 7000 Norman troops and some war horses from France to England in about 450 open boats. Meanwhile, ANGLO-SAXONS under King HAROLD were defeating Norse invaders in northern England.

Harold quickly marched south. He met William at Senlac near Hastings. The Anglo-Saxons defended a hilltop with axes, spears, swords, and shields. The Normans attacked with arrows, lances, spiked clubs and swords. The battle lasted all day. Then the Normans pretended to run away. When some Anglo-Saxons followed, Norman cavalry cut them down. Then the Normans showered arrows on the rest and attacked once more. By evening, Harold was dead and his army was beaten.

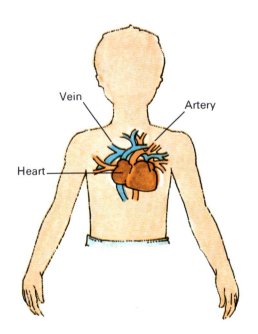

Your heart is inside your chest. Arteries pump blood from the heart to the body. Veins carry blood back to the heart.

HEART

The heart is a muscle in the body. It pumps BLOOD round the body through VEINS and arteries. In an adult person, the heart goes on working at between 70 and 80 beats a minute until death.

The ancient Greeks believed the heart was the centre of life. They knew that when someone died the heart stopped beating. But they did not understand how the heart worked. In the 1600s an English doctor called William HARVEY (1578–1657) discovered that the heart pumps blood around the body.

The blood carries oxygen from the LUNGS and energy from the food we eat. Arteries carry this rich red blood to feed the body. Veins carry away waste products and return the dark 'tired' blood to the heart.

When the heart stops beating, the body is starved of oxygen and quickly dies. But doctors can sometimes massage a stopped heart back to life. People with diseased hearts can be given 'spare parts' to repair them and even a new heart, transplanted from someone who has just died.

HEAT

Heat is a form of ENERGY. We can feel it but we cannot see it. We feel heat from the SUN, or when we sit in front of a fire. When something burns, heat is produced. The Sun gives out enormous amounts of heat, which is produced by atoms joining together or 'fusing' inside the Sun. This same kind of energy can be released by a hydrogen bomb

Water will take up heat until it boils. More heat is needed to keep it boiling and then to change it into steam.

on Earth. It is because we get just the right amount of heat from the Sun that our Earth and ourselves are what they are. A few degrees less heat from the Sun and our world would be a lifeless frozen waste. A few degrees more heat and life as we know it could not exist.

Most of the heat we use comes from burning fuels. But heat can also be made by FRICTION, or rubbing. Heat is also produced when electricity travels through a coil of wire. This is what makes the bar of an electric fire glow red.

We can measure how hot a thing is by finding its temperature. This is done with a THERMOMETER. When a substance gets hot, the molecules, or tiny particles, of which it is made move around more quickly. Often the substance expands (gets bigger) as this happens. Metals expand the most.

HELEN OF TROY

Helen of Troy was said by the ancient Greeks to be the most beautiful woman in the world. She was the wife of Menelaus, King of Sparta, but ran away with Paris, Prince of Troy. Menelaus followed with a great army, and so began the TROJAN WAR. The story is told by the poet HOMER.

HELICOPTER

The helicopter is an unusual and useful AIRCRAFT. It was invented in the 1930s and today is used for all kinds of jobs, especially rescue work. This is because helicopters can land in areas too small for ordinary aircraft. Helicopters can fly in any direction and hover in mid-air. Instead of fixed wings they have a moving wing called a rotor which acts as a wing and a propeller. A smaller rotor on the tail stops the helicopter from spinning round and is also used for turning.

Russian Mi-10

American Boeing-Vertol 107–11

German FW-61

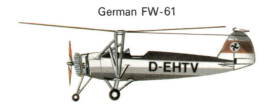

The German FW-61 had two rotors fixed side by side. It was the first successful helicopter. Some modern helicopters, like the Boeing-Vertol, have a rotor at each end of the fuselage. But the huge Russian Mi-10 relies on one big rotor.

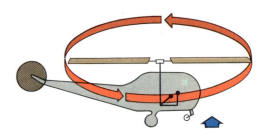

To fly upwards, the rotor blades are kept at the same angle or 'pitch'.

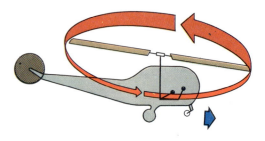

To fly forwards, the blades are tilted forwards to 'bite' into the air.

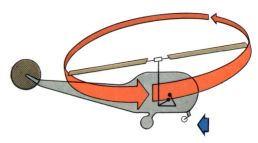

To fly backwards, the blades are tilted in the opposite direction.

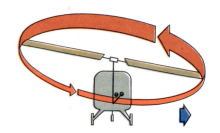

To fly sideways, the blades are tilted either to left or right.

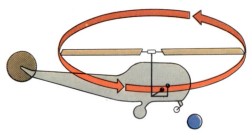

To hover, the blades are angled so as to balance up and down forces.

HENRY (KINGS)

Eight English kings have been named Henry. Henry I (1068–1135) was the youngest son of WILLIAM THE CONQUEROR. Henry II (1133–1189) was the first of the Plantagenet line of kings. He quarrelled with Thomas à Becket, Archbishop of Canterbury, and his knights murdered him. He also quarrelled with his sons Richard and John. His grandson, Henry III (1207–1272) was a weak king, ruled by the barons.

During the WARS OF THE ROSES, the families of York and Lancaster fought for the English throne. Three Lancastrian kings were called Henry: Henry IV, or Henry Bolingbroke (1367–1413), Henry V (1387–1422), and Henry VI (1421–1471). Henry V was a brilliant soldier, famous for beating the French army at Agincourt. But poor Henry VI went mad and was probably murdered.

The first of the TUDOR kings was Henry VII (1457–1509), who restored peace. His son, Henry VIII (1491–1547) was a clever, popular but ruthless king. He had six wives, and three of his children reigned after him: EDWARD VI, Mary I and ELIZABETH I.

HERALDRY

In the MIDDLE AGES, a knight in full ARMOUR was hard to recognize, for his face was hidden by his helmet. So knights began to use special designs worn on their surcoats and shields. These designs became special family emblems which no one else could wear. They were called coats-of-arms.

Heralds were officials who kept records of coats-of-arms and awarded new ones. The College of Heralds in London still does this. There are special names for the colours and patterns used in heraldry.

HERBS

Herbs are plants with soft, rather than woody, stems. But the name herbs is also given to certain plants which are added to food during cooking. They are valued for their scent and flavour. A common herb is mint, which is made into mint sauce and served with roast lamb.

Common herbs used in cooking include sage, thyme, parsley, garlic, chervil, rosemary, basil, fennel and chives. Most can be grown quite easily, although they came originally from the warm, sunny lands of the Mediterranean region.

Herbs can be used fresh from the garden, or they can be cut and dried for storage. People have grown and used herbs for hundreds of years. In the days before modern medicine, herbs were used to treat many illnesses. Even today some herbs are still used in this way.

HIBERNATION

When an animal hibernates, it goes to sleep for the winter. It does this because in winter food is scarce. Going to sleep during the cold weather saves animals from having to look for food and possibly starving to death. Animals which hibernate are mostly plant- or insect-eaters.

Some of the common herbs used in cooking. Mint, sage and thyme have an attractive smell. Parsley is chopped and added to soups, stews and sauces. Garlic is a member of the onion family. Eating garlic may make your breath smell for hours!

Before hibernating, animals eat as much food as they can find. The dormouse, for instance, stuffs itself until it is fat and round. As autumn approaches, it makes a snug nest, curls into a ball and falls into a sound sleep. In fact, its heart beats so slowly that the dormouse looks quite dead. Its body uses hardly any energy while in hibernation, in order to make its store of fat last as long as possible. In spring, a thin and hungry dormouse wakes up and comes out of its nest to look for food.

In cold countries many animals hibernate. Not all sleep right through the winter. Squirrels wake up on mild days and eat food they had hidden away in the summer. But all hibernating animals find a warm, dry place to sleep, where they are safe from hungry enemies.

HIEROGLYPHICS

Hieroglyphics were an ancient form of writing. Our ALPHABET has 26 letters. But 5000 years ago the ancient Egyptians used picture-signs instead of letters. Later, these signs became hieroglyphics, marks which stood for things, people and ideas.

Hieroglyphic writing was very difficult and only a few people could do it. When the Egyptian empire died out, the secret of reading it was lost. No one could understand the hieroglyphs carved on stones and written on papyrus scrolls. Then, in 1799, a Frenchman found the 'Rosetta Stone', which is now in the British Museum in London. On it was writing in two known languages, and also in hieroglyphics. By comparing the known languages with the hieroglyphics, experts were at last able to understand what the signs meant.

HIMALAYAS

The highest range of mountains in the world is the mighty Himalaya. The name means 'land of snow'. The Himalayas form a great barrier range across Asia, dividing India in the south from Tibet (part of China) in the north. Many of Asia's greatest rivers rise among the Himalayas, fed by the melting snows.

Egyptian hieroglyphs written on papyrus. Papyrus was a kind of paper made from a type of reed. The reeds were cut, beaten into thin strips, and pressed together into sheets.

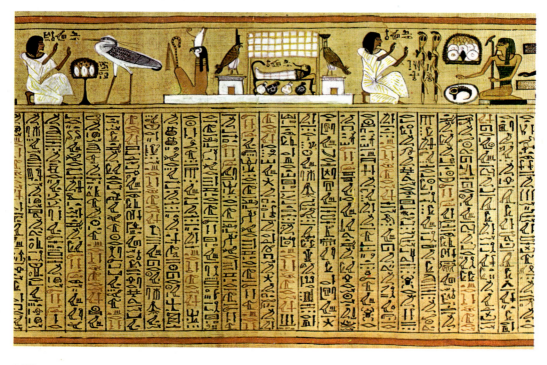

The hippo's eyes and nostrils are on top of its head. In this way it can see and breathe with ease while almost hidden in the water. The bulky hippo moves quite gracefully in water, even running along the river bed!

HIPPOPOTAMUS

The name hippopotamus means 'river horse', but in fact the hippo is related to the pig, not the horse. It is a huge, heavy animal and lives in Africa. Of all the land animals, only the elephant is bigger. An adult hippo can weigh over 4 tonnes.

Hippos live near rivers and lakes. They spend most of their time in the water and are good swimmers. In spite of its fearsome-looking jaws, the hippo eats only plant food. It browses on water weeds and grasses, and at night often comes ashore to feed. A herd of hungry hippos can ruin a farmer's crops in a single night.

Hippos are not usually dangerous if left alone. But they can inflict serious wounds with slashes from the tusks in their lower jaws.

HISTORY

History is the story of the past. The people who write down history are called historians. They usually write about important events such as wars, revolutions and governments, because these affect nations. However, historians are also interested in the lives of ordinary people and in what they did and thought about.

Nowadays, we think of history as being written down in history books. But in earlier times, before books and printing, history was passed on by word of mouth. People told stories about their kings, their wars, their adventures, and also about their own families. It was in this way that the stories of ancient Greece were collected by the poet HOMER to form the *Iliad* and the *Odyssey*. Some early stories such as these were made up in verse, and sung to music. This made it easier for people to remember the stories correctly.

In ancient Egypt, scholars recorded the reigns of the PHARAOHS, and listed the victories they won in battle. Often these accounts were written in HIEROGLYPHICS on ▷

Until aircraft were invented few outsiders had ever been into the Himalayas. There are no roads or railways. The only way to travel is on foot, over steep mountain tracks. Horses, YAKS, goats and even sheep are used to carry loads.

The highest mountain in the world lies in the Himalayas. This is Mount EVEREST, which is 8848 metres (29,028 feet) high.

HINDUS

Hinduism is one of the world's great religions. Most Hindus live in Asia, and particularly in INDIA. Their religion is a mixture of old ideas and beliefs.

Hindus believe that God is present in all things. Only priests or Brahmins can worship the supreme God. Ordinary people worship lesser gods, such as Vishnu, God of Life. The most important holy books of the Hindus are the *Vedas*. Hindus believe that certain animals, such as the cobra and the cow, are sacred and must never be killed or eaten.

stone tablets. The Chinese, Greeks and Romans were also very interested in history. It was they who first took the writing of history seriously, and they wrote of how their civilizations rose to power. During the Middle Ages in Europe, it was the priests and monks who preserved ancient books and kept the official records and documents. These records include the *Domesday Book*, which tells us much of what we know about Norman England. History became an important branch of study in the 1700s and 1800s. Famous historians were Edward Gibbon (1737–1794) and Lord Macaulay (1800–1859).

Historians get their information from hidden remains such as things found buried in old graves, as well as from old books. The study of hidden remains is called ARCHAEOLOGY. But history is not just concerned with the long distant past. After all, history is *our* story. What is news today will be history tomorrow.

HITLER, ADOLF

Adolf Hitler (1889–1945) was the 'Fuhrer', or leader, of GERMANY during WORLD WAR II. An ex-soldier, born in Vienna, Austria, he became leader of the Nazi Party which came to power in Germany in 1933.

Germany was still weak after its defeat in WORLD WAR I. The Nazis promised to avenge this defeat and create a new German empire. In 1939 Hitler led Germany into World War II. German armies conquered most of Europe. Millions of people were killed in special death camps set up by the Nazis. But by 1945 Britain, the USA, Russia and the other Allies had defeated Germany. Hitler killed himself in the ruins of Berlin to avoid capture.

HOLLAND

Holland, or the Netherlands as it is also known, is a low-lying country in Western EUROPE. The sea often floods the flat land near the coast, so sea walls have been built

for protection against storms. Living so near the sea, the people of Holland (who call themselves the Dutch) have a long and successful history of seafaring, trade and exploring.

Holland is a land of canals, windmills, neat farms and bulb fields which burst into colour in spring. It was once part of a group of countries called the Low Countries, but it became self-governing in 1759. Important cities are AMSTERDAM, the capital, and Rotterdam, which is the busiest port in Europe. Holland is a prosperous country and one of the first members of the EURO-PEAN ECONOMIC COMMUNITY. It has a queen, but is governed by a democratic parliament. The population of Holland is about 14,000,000.

HOMER

Homer was a Greek poet and story-teller. He probably lived around 800 BC, but we know nothing else about him. All we have are two great poems said to be by Homer: the *Iliad* and the *Odyssey*. These poems tell us much of what we know about ancient Greek history and legend. The *Iliad* tells the story of the TROJAN WAR. The *Odyssey* tells of the adventures of Odysseus as he returned to Greece after the war.

HONG KONG

Hong Kong is a tiny British colony off the coast of China. Part of it is a small island, and the rest is a narrow strip of land called the New Territories which is actually part of mainland China. Hong Kong has been governed by Britain since 1842.

Hong Kong has a fine harbour surrounded by mountains. The capital is Victoria, and another busy city is Kowloon. Hong Kong is a fascinating mixture of East and West. The people live by trade, fishing and farming. Tall blocks of flats have been built to house them, but there is still not enough room for all of the 5,000,000 people who crowd this small island, which is only about 18 km (11 miles) long and 8 km (5 miles) wide.

HORN, CAPE

Cape Horn is the tip of land at the southern end of SOUTH AMERICA. To cross from the Atlantic Ocean into the Pacific Ocean, a ship had to go through the stormy seas off Cape Horn. In the days of sail, this was a perilous adventure and many ships were wrecked on the rocky coast. Today, ships can take a short cut through the PANAMA CANAL.

HORSE

The horse was one of the first wild animals to be tamed by man. Today there are very few wild horses left. Many so-called 'wild' horses are actually descended from domestic horses which have run wild.

The horse is valued for its speed and strength. But the first horse was a small rather dog-like creature, with a way of life quite unlike that of modern horses. Called *Eohippus*, or 'dawn horse', it lived millions of years ago. It had four toes on its front feet and three toes on its back feet, and it probably hid from its enemies in the undergrowth.

Later, horses came out to live on the wide grassy plains. There was no undergrowth to hide in, so they escaped from enemies by running away. Gradually, their legs grew longer, and they lost all their toes except one. Finally, after millions of years of evolution, there appeared the modern horse which has only one toe. In fact, it runs on tiptoe! Its toe has become a tough nail or HOOF.

In the wild, horses live in herds. The leader of the herd is the strongest male, or stallion. He defends the females, or mares, and their young foals. Horses can usually outrun their enemies (such as wolves), but they can also kick and bite.

This picture shows the names given to different parts of the horse's body. Almost all the horses kept today are ridden for pleasure and sport. There are very few working horses used today.

173

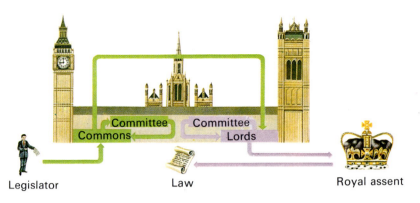

Legislator   Law   Royal assent

HOUSES

Modern houses are airy, light and comfortable. They are built to keep out the cold and wet and to stay warm. Large windows, electricity, hot and cold running water and good heating systems make them very cosy to live in.

Houses date back to prehistoric times. Some of the first are found in the Middle East. They were simple little boxes with flat roofs. Often doors and windows were simply open spaces to let in air. Built of sun-dried bricks, their main purpose was to keep off rain and to stay cool in the hot summer sun.

Houses in Greek and Roman times could be quite large. In towns they might be apartment 'blocks', perhaps five storeys high. Wealthy Romans built themselves splendid villas that were even fitted with running water and heating systems.

In the MIDDLE AGES houses were mostly crude wooden affairs. They had just one or two rooms on a single level and everyone, including the animals, crowded into them to live, sleep and eat. Nobles' homes were more elaborate. They were often made of stone, and had several floors and many rooms, each for a different purpose.

As towns and cities grew in size, thousands of cheap apartments or small cheap houses were built to house workers. Today, houses are built from a wide variety of different materials, and in many shapes and sizes. Tall blocks of flats are mostly built of steel and concrete, while small suburban houses are usually made of bricks or stone.

All new laws must pass through both the Houses of Parliament and be approved by the king or queen before they become law.

HOUSES OF PARLIAMENT

The Houses of Parliament form the main bodies of the British PARLIAMENT, the House of Commons and the House of Lords.

The House of Commons was set up during the reign of HENRY III, and it is the more important. The members of the Commons are known as MPs. They are chosen by the people of the country during public ELECTIONS. The political party which has the most members elected to sit in the Commons has the right to form the government and to choose the PRIME MINISTER. There are 635 members of the Commons, and only commoners (people who do not have certain titles) can become MPs.

The House of Commons is responsible for passing all the laws that are made. Before new laws are passed they are called 'bills'. A bill is discussed by the MPs and sent to special committees for more study. Then, if a majority of MPs support a bill it will be sent to the House of Lords.

Members of the House of Lords are not elected by the public. People become members because they have either inherited a title, or have been given one. The House of Lords is not as powerful as the Commons. The members cannot turn down a bill but they can make some changes to it.

After a bill has been approved by both Houses, it goes to the monarch for royal approval.

HOVERCRAFT

Depending on how you look at one, a hovercraft is either a plane with no wings or a ship that rides out of the water.

Hovercraft ride on a cushion of air no more than a few metres thick. They work best over flat surfaces like water but can also cross beaches and flat land. The only danger is that big boulders or bushes may snag their bottoms if they venture over rough ground.

Hovercraft are much faster than ships. Since they do not have to push against any water but simply skim smoothly through the air, they can easily manage speeds of 120 km/hr (75 mph). Their advantage over planes is the size of the load they can carry. A large craft can load dozens of cars and up to 400 passengers at a time. And of course they do not need to land at harbours or runways. At the end of a trip they simply climb up the beach to settle on a simple concrete landing pad.

The hovercraft was invented in 1955 by the British engineer Christopher Cockerell. The first working model sailed four years later and had soon crossed the Channel from England to France. Today, fleets of hovercraft shuttle back and forth every day carrying hundreds of cars and passengers.

HUMIDITY

All air has some water in it, although we cannot see it. Humidity is the amount of water in the air. If the air contains only a little water vapour, the humidity is low. When air holds a lot of moisture, we say the humidity is high. The warmer the air, the more moisture it can hold. Humidity affects the way we feel. When the humidity is high we feel 'sweaty' and uncomfortable. This is because the sweat does not evaporate easily from our skin. But too low a humidity is not very good for us. Some people use *humidifiers* in their homes to put more moisture into the air.

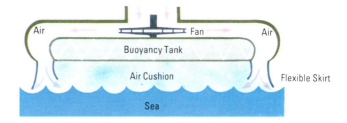

Above: Hovercraft ride on a cushion of air. Huge fans suck in air at the top. They then force the air downward and under the bottom so forcefully that it can lift the entire weight of the craft. Skirts at the sides hold in the air cushion and help the craft ride higher. The buoyancy tank makes sure the hovercraft will float should the air cushion stop working.

HUMMINGBIRD

These birds are among the smallest in the world. They are found only in the New World, from Canada to the tip of South America. The tiniest of the 320 known kinds lives in Cuba. It is less than 5 cm (2 inches) when fully grown; hardly bigger than a large bumblebee. ▷

A hovering hummingbird reaches deep into an hibiscus flower with its slender beak to suck up the flower's sweet nectar.

The feathers of hummingbirds are coloured in brilliant metallic hues of blue, green, red and yellow. The colours flash in the sun so that they look like glittering jewels on the wing.

Hummingbirds can beat their wings up to 70 times a second. This is what causes their distinctive humming sound. It also lets them hover in mid-air and fly backwards and sideways like a helicopter. In this way, they dart from flower to flower and feed while flying. They take nectar and tiny insects from deep within the cups of flowers.

HUNGARY

This is a small, central European country with a population of less than 11 million. It covers an area of some 93,000 sq km (35,900 sq miles), not much bigger than Scotland.

Hungary has no coastline. The mighty Danube river flows across the country on its way to the Black Sea, dividing it almost in two. Ships can sail up-river as far as Budapest, the capital and biggest city.

Hungary is low-lying and fairly flat. To the east it becomes a vast grassy plain. Here herds of sheep, cattle and horses are grazed. The climate is hot and dry in summer, and bitterly cold in winter. Agriculture is very important, and there are also rich sources of coal, oil and bauxite for making aluminium.

After WORLD WAR I and the collapse of the Austro-Hungarian Empire, Hungary became an independent republic. Since WORLD WAR II it has had a communist government and has been closely linked with the Soviet Union.

HYDROFOIL

Much of a ship's engine power goes into overcoming the drag of the water around the ship's hull. A hydrofoil solves this problem by lifting the ship right out of the water. It does this with a set of under-water struts attached to the hull of the

craft at the bow and stern. These water wings lift the hull as the ship gathers speed. As the water's drag grows less, the craft shoots ahead, travelling far faster than it normally could go.

HYDROGEN

Hydrogen is a gas. It is thought to be the most abundant ELEMENT in the whole universe. It is the single most important material from which stars, including our SUN, are made.

Hydrogen is the lightest of all elements. It is more than 14 times as light as air. It is colourless, has no smell and no taste. Hydrogen burns very easily. Great masses of hydrogen are always being burned in the Sun. It is this fierce burning that gives us light and heat from the Sun.

Coal, oil and natural gas all contain hydrogen. It is also a very important part of all plant and animal bodies.

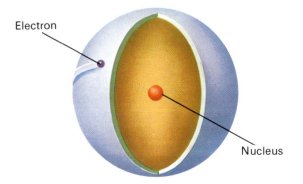

Above: A hydrogen atom is the simplest of all. It contains only one electron that circles a nucleus with one proton in it.

Hydrofoils operate best in calm, sheltered waters. They make excellent ferries on short routes.

ICE AGES

The Ice Ages were times when vast sheets of ice covered parts of the Earth. Each period lasted for thousands of years. In between were warmer periods. The last Ice Age ended about 20,000 years ago but the ice might return again.

During the Ice Ages the weather was very cold. Endless snow fell and glaciers grew and spread. At times the glaciers covered much of North America and Asia, and Europe as far south as London. In some places the ice piled up more than a thousand metres high. This made the sea level lower than it is today. A land bridge was formed between Asia and North America. The first people in America came across this land bridge from Asia.

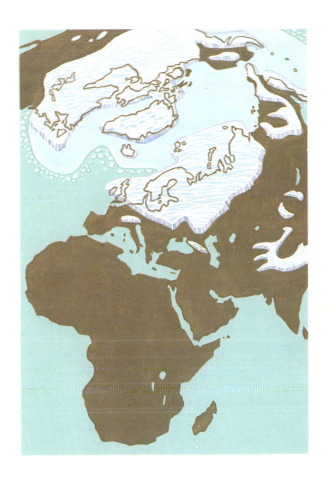

Above: The ice sheets of the last Ice Age spread over an area of 45 million sq km (17 million sq miles).

Below: This great iceberg is shaped like a huge table. It has broken free from an ice shelf in Antarctica.

Left: The seas around Iceland are full of fish such as cod, herring and haddock. Here, a trawler's net comes up from the sea. It is bulging with fish. Fishing and canning and freezing food are the most important jobs in Iceland.

ICEBERGS

Icebergs are parts of glaciers and ice shelves that have broken away and float in the sea. They are found in the waters of the ARCTIC and the ANTARCTIC.

Icebergs can be very big. Some weigh millions of tonnes. Most of an iceberg is hidden under the surface of the sea. Some icebergs may be 145 km (90 miles) long. They can be 120 metres (400 feet) high above water. An iceberg this high would be about another 960 metres (3200 feet) deep under water.

Icebergs are dangerous to ships. Some icebergs float south from the Arctic into the Atlantic Ocean. In 1912, a ship called the *Titanic* hit an iceberg in the Atlantic. It sank and 1500 people on it were drowned.

ICELAND

Iceland is a small, mountainous island, about 100,000 sq km (40,000 sq miles) in size. It was first discovered by VIKINGS in AD 874. The island lies just south of the Arctic in the north Atlantic, between Greenland and Norway. Warm waters from the Gulf Stream keep most of the harbours free of ice all the year round.

Iceland has many VOLCANOES. About 25 of its volcanoes have erupted. There are many hot water springs too. Some are used to heat homes. The north of Iceland is covered by glaciers and a desert of stone and lava.

There are about 234,000 people in Iceland. Most live in the south and east where the land is lower. They live by farming and fishing. The capital city is Reykjavik.

IGUANA

Iguanas are a group of large LIZARDS. They live in hot parts of America, on some Pacific islands and in Madagascar. They may reach almost 2 metres (6 feet) in length. About two-thirds of this is tail.

Iguanas spend most of their time in trees, often near rivers and lakes. They feed on fruit, leaves and flowers. Iguanas are good swimmers. They can dive into the water to escape from danger.

Above: The large marine iguana lives in big herds in the Galapagos Islands. It stays close to the seashore and feeds on seaweed.

INCAS

The Incas were people who lived in SOUTH AMERICA. They ruled a great empire from the 1200s until the 1500s. The centre of their empire was in PERU. In the 1400s the empire grew. It stretched thousands of kilometres, from Chile in the south to Ecuador in the north.

The Inca king and his nobles ruled over the people in the empire. They were very strict and told the farmers and craftsmen what to grow and make. The Incas built many roads through the empire so they could reach the distant parts.

In the 1500s, Spanish soldiers led by Pizarro reached America. They captured the Inca king and said they would free him in return for gold. Incas brought their treasure to free the king, but the Spanish still killed him.

The Incas built great cities high in the Andes mountains. One of these was Machu Picchu (left). The Incas fled to Machu Picchu after the Spanish arrived and killed their king in the 1500s.

INDIA

India has a population of 698 million. It has more people than any other country except China. India is part of ASIA. It is a large country with an area of 3,287,590 sq km (1,269,345 sq miles).

To the north of India are the HIMALAYAS. Many people live in the fertile northern plains. The plains are crossed by the great Ganges and Brahmaputra rivers. The south of India is high, flat land, with mountains called the Ghats along the coast.

India is very hot and dry in summer. Parts of the country are almost DESERT. But winds called *monsoons* bring a lot of rain to the north-east every year.

Most Indians are farmers. They live in small villages and grow rice, wheat, tea, cotton and jute. India is also a fast-growing industrial country. Cities, such as Calcutta and Bombay, are among the biggest in the world. The capital is New Delhi.

Hindi and English are the two main languages, but there are hundreds of others. Most Indians are HINDUS, but many follow the religion of ISLAM. There are also many other religions in India, including Buddhism and Christianity.

Below: Indians have many festivals at which they make music and dance. Below right: These women are picking tea. They put the leaves in baskets slung from their heads.

Below: In the 1800s India was taken over by the British. Here, some British people are visiting a rich Indian family in their palace. India now has its own government.

INDONESIA

Indonesia is a country in south-east ASIA. It is a chain of about 3000 islands around the EQUATOR. The islands stretch over a distance of 4800 km (3000 miles).

Indonesia has 150 million people. More than half of them live in Java. Java is the biggest island. The capital city, Djakarta, is in Java. Most Indonesians are farmers. They grow many things, including rice, tea, rubber and tobacco.

Left: These Indonesian women live in Java. They are dyeing cloth in bright patterns.

INDUSTRIAL REVOLUTION

The industrial revolution was a great change which took place in Europe in the 1700s and 1800s. People began to make things on MACHINES in factories. The new machines were run by STEAM ENGINES. They made things much faster than people could by hand. Mining and metals became more important and the RAILWAYS began. Many people moved from the countryside and began to work in factories in the towns.

Left: Women worked in coalmines during the industrial revolution. Others spent long hours in factories like this one (below).

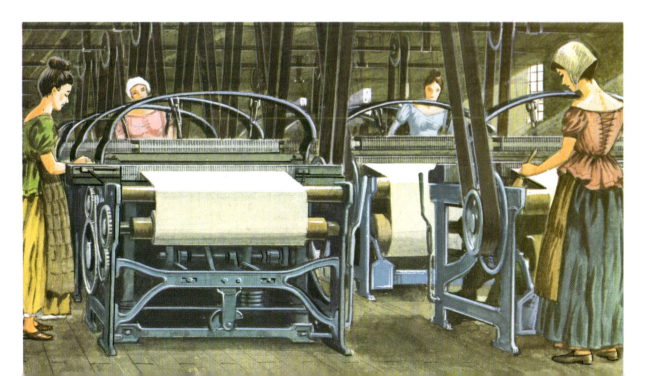

INFLATION

Inflation is a word used to mean rapidly rising prices. Every time prices go up, MONEY is worth less because people need more money to buy the same things. In turn, people ask for higher WAGES. If wages are higher, then the cost of making things in factories goes up. This often makes prices rise again. Because prices and wages affect each other like this, inflation is hard to stop. There are many reasons why inflation starts. If inflation becomes very bad, money can become worthless.

INK

People write and draw with ink. A lot of ink is also used in PRINTING.

Ink has been used since ancient times. The Egyptians were making it 5000 years ago. They made it from CARBON and gum. To make coloured inks they used DYES.

The Chinese also used ink from early times. They wrote with a brush dipped in the ink. People in Europe first used pens made from long feathers, or *quills*. Many people now use ballpoint pens which have the ink already inside them.

The Chinese were using ink by 2500 BC. They made it by mixing soot, oil, resin and gum. It was used with brushes, not pens, and so was made into solid blocks.

Below left: In 1885, Louis Pasteur made a vaccine against rabies. He inoculated a child who had been bitten by a rabid dog. The boy lived.

INOCULATION

Inoculation is a way of protecting people from diseases. It is also called *vaccination*.

Inoculation works by giving people a very weak dose of a disease. The body learns to fight the GERMS which cause the disease. In this way, the body becomes protected, or *immune*, from the disease.

Immunity from a disease may last from a few months to many years, depending on the kind of disease and vaccine. There are many kinds of inoculation. They are used against diseases such as typhoid, cholera, measles and polio. Many people used to fall ill and die with these diseases. Now more people are saved every year through inoculation.

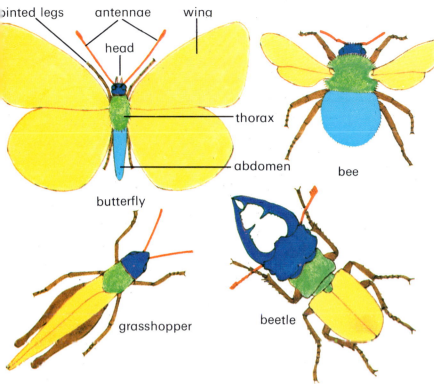

jointed legs antennae wing

head

thorax

abdomen

butterfly

bee

grasshopper

beetle

INSECTS

There are about 35 million different kinds of insect in the world. Every year, hundreds of new kinds are found. Some of the main kinds are BEETLES, BUTTERFLIES, MOTHS, BEES, ANTS, grasshoppers, and the FLY.

Insects do not have backbones. Animals without backbones are called *invertebrates*. Insects live everywhere except in the sea. Some insects live in hot, volcanic pools. Others live in the cold Antarctic. They can feed on almost anything: plants, animals, plastic and even chemicals. Some insects are very small. Tiny WASPS called fairy flies are only about 0·25 mm (one-hundredth of an inch) long. Some insects grow very big. Giant stick insects may be 30 cm (12 inches) long.

The bodies of insects have three parts: the head, the *thorax* and the *abdomen*. The head has eyes and a pair of feelers, or *antennae*. It also has a mouth for biting or sucking. The thorax has three parts, each with a pair of legs. The thorax often has two pairs of wings as well. Inside the abdomen lies the gut.

Insects breathe through tiny holes in the sides of their bodies. These are called *spiracles*. Tubes from the spiracles take air to all the CELLS of the body.

Many insects are pests. They damage crops and spread diseases. Some MOSQUITOS carry MALARIA. The tsetse fly spreads sleeping sickness. Flies and FLEAS also pass on diseases. Swarms of locusts can destroy tonnes of crops in a few hours. Some insects are useful. They eat harmful insects or lay their eggs inside them. Many insects help plants. They take POLLEN from one flower to another, like the honeybee.

Many insects go through four stages in their lives. At each stage they are different. The insect is born as an egg. The egg hatches into a grub, or *larva*. After a while the larva stops eating and turns into a chrysalis, or *pupa*. The adult insect grows inside the pupa and breaks out of it when it is fully formed.

Adult insects do not live long. Most live for a few weeks. Adult mayflies live only a few hours. Some insects live longer. A queen bee may live for seven years. Termite queens live even longer.

INSTINCT

People have to learn to read and write, but bees do not learn how to sting. They are born to sting when there is danger. This kind of behaviour is called instinct. Parents pass on instincts to their young through HEREDITY.

Animals do many things by instinct. Birds build their nests this way. Simple animals, such as insects, do almost everything by instinct. They have a set way of finding food, attacking enemies or escaping. Animals that act entirely by instinct do not have enough INTELLIGENCE to learn new ways of doing things.

INSURANCE

Insurance is a way of getting money to replace something which is lost or damaged. Many people pay a little money to an insurance company every year. If someone loses or damages something they have insured, the company gives them money to replace it.

INTELLIGENCE

When someone uses experience and knowledge to solve a new kind of problem, he shows intelligence. Intelligence depends on being able to learn. Creatures that act only by INSTINCT lack intelligence. People, apes and whales are the most intelligent creatures.

Above: Insects act mostly by instinct. Weaver ants make nests by joining leaves together. Hundreds of ants may work together on the same nest.

Left: The potter wasp lays its eggs inside 'pots' of soil. Each egg has its own pot. The wasp puts a caterpillar in each pot. When the young wasps hatch they eat the caterpillars.

Left: Birds also act by instinct. The ovenbird builds a nest of mud, grass and leaves. The nest looks like an old kind of oven.

Left: This dormouse is sleeping, or hibernating, in its winter nest. It does not have to remember to do this every autumn. The dormouse acts by instinct.

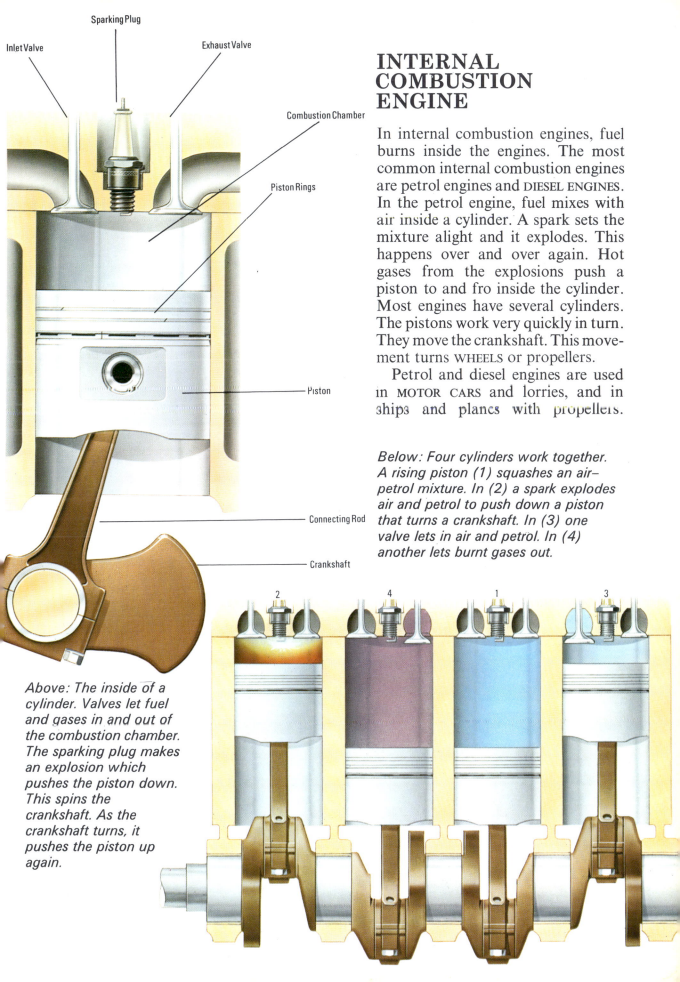

Inlet Valve

Sparking Plug

Exhaust Valve

Combustion Chamber

Piston Rings

Piston

Connecting Rod

Crankshaft

INTERNAL COMBUSTION ENGINE

In internal combustion engines, fuel burns inside the engines. The most common internal combustion engines are petrol engines and DIESEL ENGINES. In the petrol engine, fuel mixes with air inside a cylinder. A spark sets the mixture alight and it explodes. This happens over and over again. Hot gases from the explosions push a piston to and fro inside the cylinder. Most engines have several cylinders. The pistons work very quickly in turn. They move the crankshaft. This movement turns WHEELS or propellers.

Petrol and diesel engines are used in MOTOR CARS and lorries, and in ships and planes with propellers.

Below: Four cylinders work together. A rising piston (1) squashes an air–petrol mixture. In (2) a spark explodes air and petrol to push down a piston that turns a crankshaft. In (3) one valve lets in air and petrol. In (4) another lets burnt gases out.

Above: The inside of a cylinder. Valves let fuel and gases in and out of the combustion chamber. The sparking plug makes an explosion which pushes the piston down. This spins the crankshaft. As the crankshaft turns, it pushes the piston up again.

2   4   1   3

IRAN

Iran is a country in ASIA. It lies between the Caspian Sea in the north and the Persian Gulf in the south. The country is nearly seven times larger than Great Britain but it has fewer people. Deserts, snowy mountains and green valleys cover most of the land. Much of Iran has hot summers and cold winters.

Iranians speak Persian. (Persia is the old name for Iran.) Their religion is ISLAM. Tehran is the capital city.

Many Iranians are NOMADS who travel around with flocks of sheep or goats. Each time they camp, the women set up simple looms and weave beautiful rugs by hand. Some Persian rugs and carpets take years to make. They are bought by people in many countries. Iran's most important product is oil. The country is one of the world's biggest oil producers.

Iran has a long history. In about 550 BC the Persians had a leader called Cyrus. Cyrus and his army made an empire that stretched from Greece and Egypt to India. The Persian empire was then the largest in the world.

ALEXANDER THE GREAT conquered Persia about 330 BC. Later, the country was ruled by ARABS and MONGOLS. During this century Iran was ruled by emperors, or *shahs*. In 1978 the government of Iran changed and the shah left the country. Religious leaders now rule Iran.

IRAQ

Iraq is an ARAB country in south-west ASIA. Much of Iraq is a dry, sandy and stony plain. It is cool in winter and very hot in summer. The Tigris and Euphrates rivers flow through the plain to the Persian Gulf. Their water helps the farmers to grow rice, cotton, wheat and dates. Iraq is also one of the biggest oil producers in the world. Pipelines carry the oil from the north of the country across the desert to ports in Syria and the Lebanon.

Many Iraqis are NOMADS. They live in the deserts with their sheep and goats. But 3 million of the 13 million people work in the capital city of Baghdad.

Some of the first cities in the world were built near Iraq's big rivers. Ur was one of the earliest cities. It was built by a Bronze Age people called the Sumerians. The Bible says that Ur was also the home of Abraham. Later, the Babylonians built their famous city, Babylon, in Iraq. The ruins of Babylon can still be seen.

Below left: This royal palace was built at Persepolis in Persia (Iran) 2500 years ago. It was owned by Darius, who ruled the Persian empire. The palace stood on a platform reached by steps.

Below right: This beautiful mosque is in Isfahan, a city in Iran. A mosque is a Moslem place of worship.

IRELAND

Ireland is the second largest island of the BRITISH ISLES. It is like a saucer. Mountains form the rim. The middle is a low plain. Through this flows the Shannon, the longest river in the British Isles. Irish weather is often mild and rainy. Meadows and moors cover much of the land. Northern Ireland is part of the United Kingdom of GREAT BRITAIN and Northern Ireland. Its capital city is Belfast. Southern Ireland is the Republic of Ireland, or Eire. The capital city of Eire is Dublin.

Above: A map of Ireland showing the two parts.

Above: The ancient Chinese were the first people to use iron.

IRON AND STEEL

Iron is the cheapest and most useful of all metals. Much of our food, clothes, homes, cars, tools and machines are made with machines and tools that are made from iron.

Iron is mined or quarried as iron ores, or MINERALS. The ore is melted down, or *smelted*, in a blast furnace. The iron is then made into cast iron, wrought iron or different kinds of steel.

Cast iron is hard but not as strong as steel. Molten cast iron is poured into moulds to make such things as engine blocks. Wrought iron is soft but tough. It is used for chains and gates. Steel is hard and strong. Steel alloys are used to make many different things, from bridges to nails.

Right: Molten iron is poured into a furnace at an iron and steel foundry in Canada.

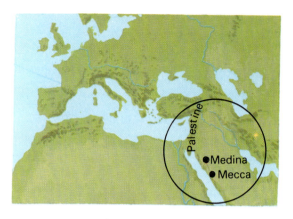

Above: Mohammed preached Islam in Mecca and Medina. Palestine is the home of Judaism and Christianity. Mohammed took ideas from these religions. All three teach belief in one God.
Left: This beautiful mosque is at Samarra in Iraq. The building behind is a minaret. Holy men stand on minarets to call Moslems to prayer.

Below: A 600-year-old painting of the angel Gabriel. Moslems believe he was the messenger of Allah (God).

ISLAM

Islam is a religion started in AD 622 by MOHAMMED. It has more followers than any other religion except Christianity. Islam means 'submission'. Its followers are called Moslems. Moslem means 'submissive one'. Moslems believe they must submit, or give in, to God's will. They believe in one God and in Mohammed as his prophet. Moslems pray five times a day and give gifts to the poor. They go without food until dark for one month a year and try to visit Mecca before they die. They also try to obey the rules for good living, set out in the KORAN, the holy book of Islam.

Islam began in Arabia. Today it is the main religion in North Africa and most of south-west Asia.

ISLAND

An island is a piece of land surrounded by water. Some islands are chunks of land that became separated from CONTINENTS. Other islands are VOLCANOES that have poked up above the sea. Yet others stand inland, in lakes and rivers. GREENLAND is the largest island in the world.

ISRAEL

Israel is a country in south-west ASIA. It lies between the Mediterranean Sea, Red Sea and Dead Sea.

Farmers grow oranges, cotton and grain on fertile plains. More than half the land is mountain or desert where few plants grow. Summers are hot and winters are mild.

There are four million Israelis. Half of them live in or near three cities. One of these is JERUSALEM, the capital. Most Israelis are JEWS. Israel is also the home of many ARABS. The main language is Hebrew.

ITALY

Italy is a country in southern EUROPE. It is shaped like a leg stuck out in the Mediterranean Sea to kick Sicily. Sicily and Sardinia are big Italian islands.

Much of Italy is mountainous. The sharp, snowy peaks of the Alps cross northern Italy. The Apennines run like a backbone down the middle. Between the Alps and Apennines lies the plain of Lombardy. Italy is famous for its lovely mountain lakes and hot, sunny summers. Rain falls mostly in winter.

Crops grow on almost half the land. Italy produces more pears and olives than any other country. The farmers also grow a lot of grapes and lemons. Other foods grown in Italy are wheat, rice, oranges, apples and tomatoes.

Big factories in northern Italy make cars, chemicals, machines and much else.

The capital is ROME. Many tourists visit Rome to see the VATICAN CITY and the ruins of the ROMAN EMPIRE. Many of Italy's 56 million people are descended from the Romans.

IVAN THE TERRIBLE

Ivan IV, the Terrible (1530–1584), was the first emperor, or *tsar*, of RUSSIA. He was a cruel man who killed his own son. But he helped to make Russia great. In his reign MOSCOW became the Russian capital, and Russians began to spread east to SIBERIA.

IVORY

Ivory comes from the long teeth, or *tusks* of some animals. Walrus and narwhal tusks and hippopotamus teeth are made of ivory. Larger pieces of ivory come from ELEPHANT and mammoth tusks. Mammoths died out thousands of years ago, yet Russians still find their tusks in Siberia.

Elephant ivory bends and can be cut and polished. People use it to make ornaments, piano keys and jewellery.

This ivory carving of a woman's head was made in about 715 BC, in Iraq.

JACKAL

Jackals are a kind of wild DOG. Some are brown or greyish and live in eastern Europe, Asia and North Africa. Africa has other kinds too. Jackals hide in bushes by day. At night they hunt small animals and find food in rubbish heaps.

JADE

Jade is a kind of MINERAL. It is a hard stone that is usually green, blackish green or white. Jade can be carved and polished to make delicate ornaments and jewellery. The Chinese have been making jade carvings for more than 3000 years.

People in many lands learnt to carve jade in STONE AGE times. They could not chip it

This open ring was carved from jade in China about 2000 years ago. Old pieces of Chinese jade are very valuable.

into shape. Instead, they had to grind or saw it. To cut it they laid wet sand on the jade. They rubbed the sand grains to and fro with a slate or flat piece of sandstone. Then they shaped the jade with pieces of sandstone. To make holes in the jade they used sharp sticks or bones pressed on wet sand and twisted to and fro. Craftsmen still shape jade by hand. But now they use metal tools, and carborundum instead of sand.

JAGUAR

No other American wild CAT is as heavy or perhaps as dangerous as the jaguar. From nose to tail a jaguar is longer than a man, and may be nearly twice his weight. The jaguar is yellow with black spots like a LEOPARD. But many of the jaguar's spots are in rings. Jaguars live in the hot, wet forests of Central and South America. They leap from trees onto wild pigs and deer. They also catch turtles, fish and alligators.

Left: A jaguar crouches on a tree in wait for its prey. The jaguar is heavy and strong. It can swim and catch fish.

JAMAICA

Jamaica is a tropical island in the Caribbean Sea. The name Jamaica means 'island of springs'. It is a beautiful island, with hundreds of streams flowing from springs on the sides of its green mountains.

There are two million people in Jamaica. Most of them are Negroes. They are descended from African slaves. Many work on farms that grow bananas, coconuts, coffee, oranges and sugar cane. Jamaica also mines bauxite. Kingston is Jamaica's capital city.

Right: This Jamaican boy cuts sugar cane with a big knife. A factory will make sugar from the sweet juice in the stalks.

This portrait of James I shows him wearing a ruff. This was a large, stiff collar shaped like a wheel.

JAMES I

James I (1566–1625) was the first of the STUARTS to rule England. He became King James VI of Scotland in 1567 when his mother, MARY, QUEEN OF SCOTS, gave up the throne. He also became King James I of England when his cousin, ELIZABETH I, died in 1603. Since then, Scotland and England have always shared the same king or queen.

James believed that God gave him the right to rule as he pleased. This led to quarrels with PARLIAMENT.

JAPAN

Japan is a long, narrow string of islands off the mainland coast of ASIA. Altogether they make a country larger than Great Britain but smaller than Spain.

Mountains cover most of Japan. The highest is a beautiful volcano. It is called Fujiyama, or Mount Fuji. Parts of Japan have forests, waterfalls and lakes. Northern Japan has cool summers and cold, snowy winters. The south is hot in summer and mild in winter.

Japan is a crowded country. It has more than 120 million people. To help feed them, farmers grow huge amounts of rice and fruits. The Japanese also eat a lot of fish and seaweed. They catch more fish than any other country. Japan does not have many MINERALS. The Japanese buy most of their minerals from other countries. But no other country makes as many ships and television sets as Japan does. The Japanese also make a lot of cars.

Most people in Japan live in towns or cities. The capital city is Tokyo.

JASON

Jason is the hero of an ancient Greek story. He tried to get back a kingdom stolen from his father by Pelias, Jason's uncle. Pelias let Jason have the kingdom in return for the Golden Fleece. Jason married a princess called Medea who helped him to steel the fleece.

JAVELIN THROW

A javelin is a kind of light spear. In ancient times soldiers threw javelins at enemies. In 708 BC, throwing the javelin became part of the early OLYMPIC GAMES. Today, athletes still compete in throwing the javelin.

JAZZ

Jazz is a kind of music. The players use unexpected rhythms. They also play any notes they like, but they must fit the music made by the rest of the band. In this way, jazz musicians often *improvise*, or make up music as they go along. Jazz began in the United States in the 1800s. It grew from songs sung by Negro slaves brought from Africa.

Right: Jellyfish live at different depths of the sea. The big Portuguese man o' war floats on the surface.

JELLYFISH

A jellyfish is a sea animal. It is related to the SEA ANEMONE. The jellyfish looks like a bell made of jelly. To float upwards, it pushes water down by squeezing the bell shut. Tentacles hang from the bell. These catch small animals. The jellyfish stings the animals. It then pushes the food into its mouth under the bell.

JENNER, EDWARD

Edward Jenner (1749–1823) was a British doctor. He inoculated a boy with cowpox germs. Cowpox disease is like SMALLPOX but it is less dangerous. The boy did not catch smallpox. Jenner's INOCULATION made the boy's body strong against smallpox.

Left: A statue of Edward Jenner inoculating a child against smallpox.

JERUSALEM

Jerusalem is the capital of ISRAEL. It is a holy city of the Jews, Christians and Moslems. David, Jesus and other famous people in the Bible lived or died here.

Jerusalem stands high up in hilly country. It has many old religious buildings. Huge walls surround the city's oldest part. In 1948 Jerusalem was divided between Israel and Jordan. But Israel took the whole city during a war in 1967.

JESUS

Jesus was a JEW. He started CHRISTIANITY. The New Testament of the BIBLE says that Jesus was God's son.

Jesus was born in BETHLEHEM. His mother was called Mary. When he grew up he travelled about, teaching and healing sick people. Some Jewish priests were jealous of Jesus. They told their Roman rulers that he was making trouble. The Romans killed Jesus on a cross, but he came to life again and rose to heaven. Followers of Jesus spread his teachings through the world.

Above: Part of Jerusalem. In the middle is the Dome of the Rock, a Moslem mosque. It is thought to be where the Jewish Temple once stood.

This old picture shows one of Jesus's miracles. He is making a blind beggar see again.

193

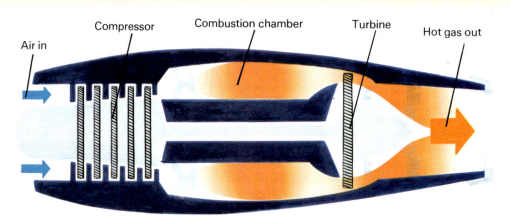

Air in   Compressor   Combustion chamber   Turbine   Hot gas out

JET ENGINES

A swimmer swims forward by pushing water backward. A jet engine works in a similar way. It drives an AIRCRAFT forward by pushing gases backward. Engines that work like this are called *reaction* engines. ROCKETS are also reaction engines. The main difference between jets and rockets is that jets take in oxygen from the air to burn their fuel, but rockets have their own supply of oxygen.

There are four main kinds of jet engine. These are turbojets, turboprops, turbofans and ramjets. The pictures on this page show how each kind of engine works.

Jet engines have replaced propeller-driven piston engines in many kinds of

In a turbojet, sucked-in air is squashed by spinning compressor blades. Oxygen and fuel burn in a combustion chamber. Hot gas rushes out, spinning a 'windmill' called a turbine. This works the compressor.

plane. There are many reasons for this. Jet engines weigh less than piston engines. They also go wrong less often. Their moving parts spin instead of moving to and fro. This stops the plane from shaking about. Jet engines burn cheap paraffin (kerosene) instead of costly petrol (gasoline). Jet engines can also carry planes faster and higher than piston engines can. Some jet fighters can travel at 3400 km/hr (2100 mph). Others can climb to about 30,500 metres (100,000 feet).

JEWS

A Jew is someone who believes in Judaism or has Jewish parents. The first Jews were HEBREWS descended from Abraham's grandson, Israel. They lived in PALESTINE.

In AD 70, the Romans destroyed the Jewish temple in JERUSALEM. Many Jews scattered to other countries, where millions had already gone. In some European countries people did not like the Jews because they were not Christian. In World War II the followers of HITLER killed millions of Jews. In 1947 the UNITED NATIONS gave the Jews ISRAEL as a country of their own. Many Jews went to live there.

Left: Today, the Jews of Israel have a strong army. They have fought several wars against neighbouring countries.

JOAN OF ARC

Joan of Arc (1412–1431) was a French girl who believed that God told her to free France from its English invaders. At 17 she left the farm where she worked, and persuaded France's King Charles VII to let her lead his army. She won five battles. Then she was captured and burnt as a witch. But she had saved France. In 1920 the Pope made her a SAINT.

Joan of Arc led the French army into battle. She saved France from the English.

JUPITER (PLANET)

Jupiter is the largest of the PLANETS in our SOLAR SYSTEM. It is twice the size of all the other planets put together. You could cram 1300 planets like the Earth into the space filled by Jupiter. Jupiter's force of GRAVITY is great. Anyone on Jupiter would weigh twice as much as on the Earth.

Astronomers believe that most of Jupiter is hot, liquid HYDROGEN. It is so hot that it would be a glowing star if it were ten times larger.

Jupiter spins so fast that a day and night last less than ten hours. But a YEAR on Jupiter is 12 times longer than one of ours. This is because Jupiter is farther from the SUN than we are.

Jupiter can be seen through a big telescope. Clouds hide the surface. Jupiter spins so fast that it pulls the clouds into dark and bright stripes. The strange red spot near the bottom of the picture is probably a storm. The storm has been ranging for hundreds of years. The small, dark spot is a shadow. It is made by one of Jupiter's moons. Jupiter has 16 moons. The four largest are as big as Africa. One is covered with ice. Another has eight fiery volcanoes.

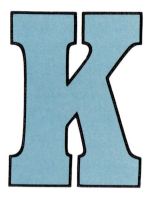

KANGAROO

Kangaroos are MARSUPIALS that live in New Guinea and Australia. Most of them live on grassy plains and all of them feed on plants. They move about in troops, springing along on their big, powerful hind legs and large feet. Their long tails help them to balance.

There are more than 50 kinds of kangaroo. Red and grey kangaroos are the largest. A red kangaroo may be taller and heavier than a man. Grey kangaroos can bounce along at 40 km/hr (25 mph) if chased. Wallabies are smaller kinds of kangaroo. The smallest of all are rat kangaroos. They are about the size of a rabbit.

KENYA

Kenya is a country in east AFRICA. It is just a bit larger than France. The south-west border touches Lake Victoria. The Indian Ocean is on the south east. The EQUATOR goes across the middle of the country. Much of the land is covered by mountains and flat-topped hills. The rest looks like a huge open park. It is a hot, dry country.

Kenya belongs to the COMMONWEALTH. Most of the 16 million Kenyans are African. They belong to a number of different tribes. Many grow maize, tea and coffee. Kenya sells a lot of tea and coffee abroad. Some tribes like the Masai keep cattle. Many tourists visit Kenya to see the wild animals roaming the huge nature reserves. The capital is Nairobi.

KIDNEYS

All VERTEBRATES (animals with a backbone) have two kidneys. Kidneys look like reddish-

Mother kangaroos carry their babies in pouches from the time they are born until they are nearly six months old. Baby kangaroos are called 'joeys'.

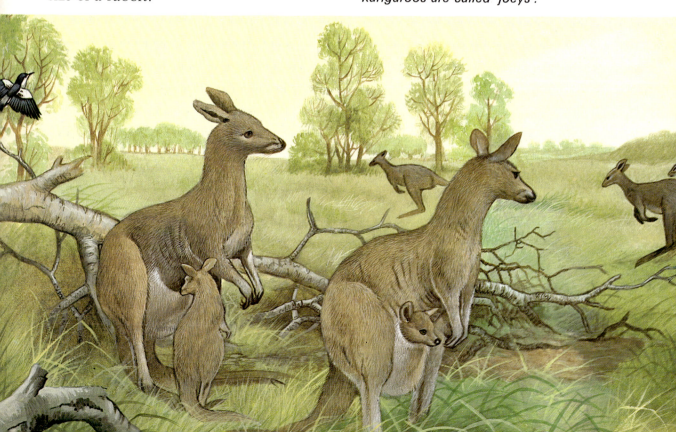

brown beans. Human kidneys are about the size of a man's fist. They lie on each side of the backbone, at just about waist level.

Kidneys clean the BLOOD. They filter out waste matter and poisons and strain off any water the body does not need. Blood pumped from the HEART flows into each kidney through an artery. The blood flows on through tubes which get smaller and smaller. These tubes act as filters. Blood cells, tiny food particles and other useful things stay in the blood to be used by the body. Filtered blood flows out of the kidney through a VEIN. All the waste matter and extra water mix together to make urine. This drips slowly into the bladder.

KINGFISHER

Most kingfishers are small, brightly-coloured birds with large heads and beaks like daggers. Birds of the king-fisher family live in many lands, but most live in the tropics.

Kingfishers nest in burrows in river banks or in holes in trees. The nest is made of fish bones, so it is very smelly. Not all kingfishers fish for their food. One New Guinea kingfisher eats worms. Australia's kookaburra eats lizards, snakes, insects and even other birds.

A kingfisher rises from the water clutching its dinner. Kingfishers perch very still on a branch or hover over the water watching for fish. Then they quickly plunge and grab.

KITE

This is a light frame covered with paper or thin cloth. A long string is attached to the kite at one end. Someone holds the other end of the string and the wind lifts the kite into the air. It hangs in the sky like the graceful bird from which it gets its name. Wide open fields with no trees or overhead wires are the best places for flying kites.

Most people fly kites for fun. They can be useful too. A kite lifted the aerial that received the first RADIO signal sent across the Atlantic Ocean. Kites have guided rescuers to shipwrecked men in lifeboats.

KIWI

This strange bird from New Zealand gets its name from the shrill cries made by the male. The kiwi is a stocky brown bird as big as a chicken. It has tiny wings but cannot fly. Instead it runs on short, thick, strong legs. Kiwi feathers look very much like hair.

Kiwis are shy birds that live in forests. By day they sleep in burrows. At night, they hunt for worms and grubs. Kiwis can hardly see. They smell out their food with the help of nostrils at the tip of their long, thin beaks. The females lay very large eggs but it is the male who sits on them and waits for them to hatch.

197

KOALA

Koalas are MARSUPIALS that look like small, chubby bears. Koalas live in east and south-east Australia. They live much like a SLOTH. Koalas climb about slowly among the branches of trees and hardly ever touch the ground. Their only food is eucalyptus leaves. Forest fires and hunting nearly wiped them out but many koalas now live safely in reserves.

Right: Koalas live in the trees where they are safe. A mother koala carries her baby either in her pouch or clinging to her back.

KORAN

The *Koran* is the sacred book of ISLAM. Its name means 'a recitation'. It has 114 chapters of Arabic verse, and teaches that there is one God whose prophets (messengers) included Abraham, JESUS, and MOHAMMED. The book teaches Moslems to be humble, generous, and just.

KOREA

Korea is a peninsula which juts out from CHINA into the Sea of Japan. The land has many mountains and small valleys. Forests cover most of the country. Korean farms produce much rice and silk. Korean factories make steel and many more products.

Korea was divided into two separate nations in 1945. The two countries are now known as North Korea and South Korea.

Left: Pusan is South Korea's second largest city. It is also a busy port.

KREMLIN

This is the oldest part of MOSCOW. It was once the fortress home of RUSSIA's *tsars*. Inside the high wall that surrounds it stand old palaces and cathedrals crowned by golden domes shaped like giant onions.

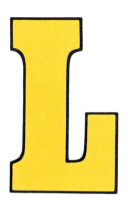

LABORATORY

A laboratory is a place where scientists work. Laboratory workers make experiments and test things to find out more about them. Some people now learn foreign languages in special rooms called language laboratories.

LACE

Lace is a delicate fabric. It is patterned with tiny holes. People make collars, shawls, scarves and tablecloths from lace. Lace is made from threads of cotton, linen, nylon or silk, and sometimes gold or silver. Lace-makers twist, knot or loop the threads in special ways. Lace made by hand is expensive. Much lace is now made on machines.

Above: A ladybird flies away. Its wings are usually hidden under the wing cases.

Left: In a language laboratory each pupil learns from a tape-recorded lesson.

LADYBIRD

Ladybirds are small BEETLES. They were named after the Virgin Mary. From above, ladybirds look nearly round. They have shiny wing covers. The wing covers are usually red or yellow with black spots. Young ladybird grubs, or *larvae*, are quite different. They have long, soft bodies. Ladybirds eat greenflies and other pests. They hibernate in the winter.

LAKES

Lakes are large areas of water surrounded by land. The world's largest lake is the salty Caspian Sea. It lies in the Soviet Union and Iran. The largest freshwater lake is Lake Superior, one of the GREAT LAKES.

Many lakes were formed in the ICE AGES. They began in valleys made by glaciers. When the glaciers melted they left behind mud and stones that formed DAMS. The melted water from the glaciers piled up behind the dams.

LAPPS

Lapps are a people who live in Lapland. Lapland is a place in the ARCTIC. It lies in the far north of Sweden, Norway, Finland and Russia. Lapps are short people. Many have straight, black hair and yellowish skin. They keep warm by wearing clothes made from wool and reindeer skins. Their clothes have bright colours.

Some Lapps are NOMADS. They travel the land with herds of REINDEER. They sleep in tents and eat reindeer meat. Other Lapps are fishermen or farmers. They live in small huts in villages.

The Lapps live with herds of reindeer. Lapps eat reindeer meat. They make their clothes and tents from reindeer skin.

LASERS

A laser is something that strengthens light and makes it shine in a very narrow beam. Many lasers have a ruby CRYSTAL or gas inside them. Bright light, radio waves or electricity are fed into the laser. This makes the ATOMS of the crystal or gas jump around in a very excited way. The atoms give off strong light.

The light of lasers can be used for many things. Doctors use small laser beams to burn away tiny areas of disease in the body. They also repair damaged eyes with laser beams. Dentists can use lasers to drill holes in teeth. Some lasers are so strong they can cut through DIAMONDS. Lasers are used in factories to cut metal and join tiny metal parts together.

Lasers can also be used to measure distance. The laser beam is aimed at objects far away. The distance is measured by counting the time it takes for the light to get there and back. Laser beams can also carry radio and television signals. One laser beam can send many television programmes and telephone calls at once without mixing them up.

A flash tube sets a ruby crystal glowing with a beam of light. The light bounces between mirrors and grows stronger. When it is very strong it shines through a mirror at one end as a laser beam.

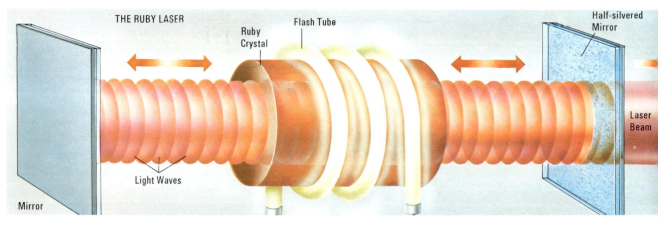

THE RUBY LASER
Ruby Crystal
Flash Tube
Half-silvered Mirror
Laser Beam
Light Waves
Mirror

LATITUDE AND LONGITUDE

Every place on Earth has a latitude and a longitude. Lines of latitude and longitude are drawn on maps. Lines, or *parallels*, of latitude show how far north or south of the EQUATOR a place is. They are measured in degrees (written as °). The equator is at 0° latitude. The North Pole has a latitude of 90° north, and the South Pole is 90° south.

Lines, or *meridians*, of longitude show how far east or west a place is. They are also measured in degrees. Greenwich, in London, is at 0° longitude. A place halfway around the world from Greenwich is at 180° longitude.

LEAD

Lead is a soft, heavy blue-grey metal. It does not RUST. Lead is used for many things including water pipes and roofs. Lead shields protect ATOMIC ENERGY workers from dangerous radiation. Lead is mixed with TIN to make pewter mugs and other things. Alloys of tin and lead are also used in solder. Solder is used for joining pieces of metal. Many things are now made without lead because lead can become poisonous when it is mixed with certain other things.

Above: Lines of latitude and longitude are measured in degrees. Each measurement lies at a certain angle to the centre of the Earth.

The sticky bud of a horse chestnut tree bursts open to let the leaves out.

LEAF

Leaves are the food factories of green PLANTS. To make food, leaves need light, carbon dioxide and water. Light comes from the Sun. Carbon dioxide comes from the air. Air enters a leaf through little holes called *stomata*. Water is drawn up from the ground by the plant's roots. It flows up the stem and into the leaf through tiny tubes called veins. Inside the leaf is a green colouring called CHLORO-PHYLL. The chlorophyll uses light, water and carbon dioxide to make SUGAR. The way it does this is known as *photosynthesis*. Sugar then passes through tubes to the other parts of the plant.

In autumn many trees lose their leaves. First they shut off the water supply to the leaves. This destroys the green colour and gives the leaves yellow, red and orange tints.

LEMONS

Lemons are oval yellow FRUITS. They have a sour taste. Their juice is used in drinks, to flavour food, and in perfumes. Lemon trees need a warm climate. Most lemons come from the United States and Italy.

LENIN, VLADIMIR

Vladimir Ilyich Lenin (1870–1924) helped to make RUSSIA the first communist country in the world. Before his time, Russia was ruled by emperors, or *tsars*. Like Karl MARX, Lenin believed in COMMUNISM. He wanted every country run by the workers, and no longer split into rich and poor groups. For many years Lenin lived outside Russia. He wrote books, and for communist newspapers. In 1917 he went back to Russia. He became the leader of a group of communists called Bolsheviks. The Bolsheviks overthrew the government. Lenin then ruled Russia until he died.

LENS

Lenses are used to make things look bigger or smaller. They are usually made of glass or plastic. The lens inside your EYE is made of PROTEIN. Sometimes eye lenses do not work properly. Then people cannot see clearly. The lenses in spectacles make their eyesight better. Lenses are used for many other things. The lenses in MICROSCOPES, binoculars and TELESCOPES make far away things or small things seem much larger.

Each lens has two smooth sides. Both sides may be curved, or one may be curved and the other flat. There are two main kinds of lens. Lenses where the edges are thicker than the middle are called *concave* lenses. Concave means 'hollowed out'. When LIGHT rays pass through a concave lens, they spread out. If you look at something through a concave lens, it looks smaller than it really is.

Lenses where the middle is thicker than the edges are called *convex* lenses. Convex means rounded, like the outside of a circle.

Above: Pieces of glass are made into curved shapes for different kinds of lenses. Some are thick and some are thin.

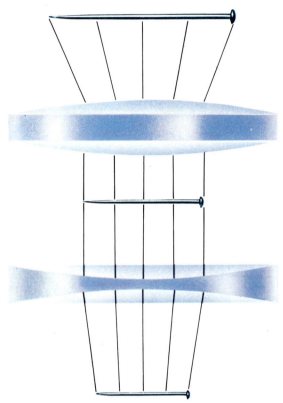

Above: The top lens is convex (thickest in the middle). The bottom lens is concave (thickest at the edges). The pin in between them looks larger through the convex lens, and smaller through the concave lens.

When light rays pass through a convex lens, they come together. If you look at things through a convex lens, they seem larger.

Craftsmen who make lenses know exactly how to shape them for the things they are made for. They may fit different lenses together, or shape each side of a lens differently. Short-sighted people use spectacle lenses with a concave and a convex side. But the concave side is curved more than the convex side.

LEONARDO DA VINCI

Leonardo da Vinci (1452–1519) was an Italian artist and inventor. He lived during the Renaissance. One of his most famous paintings is the *Mona Lisa*. It is a picture of a woman who is smiling mysteriously. Many people have wondered what she was smiling at. Leonardo made thousands of drawings of human bodies, water, plants and animals. He wrote many notes on the things he drew.

Leonardo worked as an engineer for Italian nobles and for the French king. He designed forts and canals. The canals had locks so that boats could travel up and down hills. Leonardo also drew ideas for things long before they were invented. His drawings include a helicopter, a flying machine and a machine gun.

Leonardo was interested in many other things, including music and architecture. He was a good musician and singer.

Right: Leonardo da Vinci made this beautiful painting of the Virgin Mary and baby Jesus.

LEOPARD

Leopards are large, wild cats just a bit smaller than LIONS. They live in Africa and south Asia. Most leopards are spotted like JAGUARS, but some are nearly black. These are called panthers.

Leopards are very fierce, strong and agile hunters. They catch and eat antelopes, goats, dogs and sometimes people. They often hunt from trees, lying in wait on a branch. If they cannot eat all their catch at once, they may haul the carcase high up into a tree. This is to stop lazier hunters like lions or hyenas from stealing it.

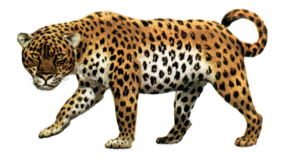

Most leopards have blotchy spots called rosettes. Unlike jaguars, leopards have no spot in the middle of the rosettes.

LIBYA

Libya is a large country in North AFRICA. It is more than three times the size of France, but very few people live there. This is because most of Libya lies in the SAHARA.

Most Libyans are ARABS who farm the land. Libya is also rich in oil.

LICHENS

A lichen is a simple PLANT. It has no roots, leaves or flowers. Some lichens grow as crusty patches on rocks, trees or walls. They grow very slowly. A patch no larger than your hand may be hundreds of years old. Other lichens grow as shrubby tufts. Lichens can live in places that are too bare, dry, cold or hot for any other plant.

LIGHT

Light is a kind of ENERGY that we can see. Some objects—stars, lamps, certain chemicals—produce light. Most things do not produce light. We can only see them because they reflect light. For instance, we can only see the Moon because it reflects light from the Sun.

Sunlight is the brightest light we normally see. Summer sunlight can be as bright as 10,000 candles burning close enough to touch. Bright sunlight seems white but it is really made up of the colours of the RAINBOW. Isaac NEWTON showed this. He made a sunbeam shine through a specially shaped chunk of glass called a prism. Red, orange, yellow, green, blue, indigo and violet rays of light came out of the prism. The prism had split the sunbeam into separate beams, each with its own *wavelength*. This is easy to understand if you think of light travelling in waves. The distance between the tops of the waves is the wavelength. We see each wavelength as a different colour. Long waves are red, short waves are violet and wavelengths in between show up as the other colours.

Light travels very fast, more than 300,000 km (186,000 miles) each second. Even so, it takes eight minutes for the light from the Sun to reach Earth. A light year is the distance a beam of light travels in one year. Scientists use light years to measure how far away PLANETS and STARS are from the Earth. Some are millions of light years away.

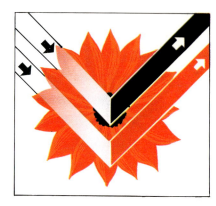

Above: A red flower is red because it reflects only the red colour in light and absorbs the others. Its black centre absorbs all colours.

Above: Straight objects seem bent in water because light rays bend when they pass from air to water.

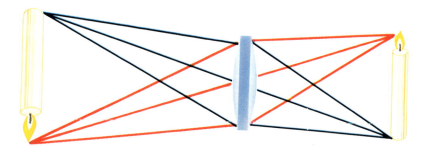

Below: The angler fish lives at the bottom of the sea where light cannot reach. To attract other fish, which it eats, the angler fish has a 'fishing rod' growing above its mouth. The rod produces a chemical which glows.

Above: Light travels in straight lines. When a ray of light hits glass or water, it will bend. Lenses are specially shaped pieces of glass, which bend light in several ways. A camera lens bends light rays from a candle to make an upside down image on the film inside the camera.

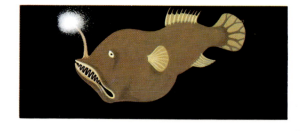

LIGHTNING

Lightning is ELECTRICITY that you can see. It is a sudden flow of electric CURRENT between two clouds, between a cloud and the ground, or between two parts of the cloud. There are three types of lightning. Streak lightning flashes in a single line from cloud to earth. Forked lightning happens when the lightning divides to find the quickest way to earth. Sheet lightning happens inside a cloud and lights up the sky, like the flash bulb on a camera.

LIMESTONE

Limestone is a rock containing the chemical substance *calcium carbonate*. Most limestone was made from the limy plants and the skeletons of millions of tiny animals that lived in prehistoric seas. Dead plants and animals piled up on the seabed and were pressed together until they hardened into rock. You can see their FOSSILS in some types of limestone.

Water wears away limestone. It trickles through small cracks in the rock and widens them. This is how rivers eat out underground caves in limestone rock.

People QUARRY limestone because it is very useful. Builders use it in blocks. Burnt limestone becomes lime. This is used to make CEMENT and FERTILIZER. It is also used in steel and glass making.

Above: Lightning flashes over a harbour at night. Lightning can happen when an electric charge develops in a cloud and an opposite charge builds up in the ground below it.

Below: Fossil animals in this limestone mountain show that its rocks formed under the sea 250 million years ago. Movements of the Earth later forced them upward.

LINCOLN, ABRAHAM

Abraham Lincoln (1809–1865) was President of the United States from 1861 to 1865. He grew up in a log cabin. He had very little schooling, but studied by himself and became a lawyer. As President, he fought the American CIVIL WAR to make his divided country into one nation again. He was murdered by an actor, John Wilkes Booth, just as the war was over.

Right: Abraham Lincoln, 16th US president.

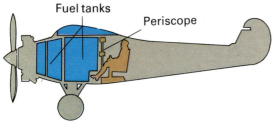

LINEN

Linen is cloth made from the stringy stems of FLAX plants. The stems are soaked in water and beaten to separate the strands. These are combed smooth and then spun into yarn. The yarn is woven into cloth. Linen is very strong and soaks up water easily. It is used to make sheets, tablecloths, handkerchiefs and towels. It is very hard wearing.

Ancient Egyptians grew flax and made linen more than 4000 years ago. Today, Russia grows more flax than all the other nations together.

Models from an ancient Egyptian tomb show how Egyptians made and wove linen.

LINDBERGH, CHARLES

Charles Augustus Lindbergh (1902–1974) was an American pilot who became the first man to fly the Atlantic Ocean alone. His single-engine aircraft, *Spirit of St. Louis*, left New York on May 20, 1927. He landed at Paris in France on May 21, $33\frac{1}{2}$ hours later, after flying about 5800 km (3600 miles) non-stop. Lindbergh's flight showed people that air travel was possible. Later he helped to plan air routes to South America and over the Atlantic Ocean.

Left: Lindbergh and his monoplane. Fuel tanks took up so much space that he had to use a periscope to see ahead. The plane carried no radio, parachute, or sextant to help him check his position. It flew at only 200 km/hr (124 mph).

LION

Lions are large, tawny coloured wild cats. An adult male weighs about 180 kg (400 lb) and measures about 2·7 metres (9 feet) from nose to tail. Females (lionesses) are slightly smaller and have no mane.

Lions usually live in family groups called prides. A pride has one male, one or two females and all their cubs. Lions often hunt together. No other big cats seem to do this. They hunt mainly antelope and zebra, creeping up on their victims through the long grass. One lion may leap out to scare the prey into another lion's path. Lionesses do most of the hunting as they have to feed their cubs as well as themselves.

Lions used to roam wild over southern Europe, India and Africa. Now they live in south and east Africa and a tiny part of India. Most lions today lead protected lives in nature reserves. Hundreds of captive lions live in zoos all over the world.

Lions resting after a meal. A large meal may satisfy a lion for several days.

LISTER, JOSEPH

Joseph Lister (1827–1912) was an English surgeon who found a way to stop his patients dying of infection after operations. He used antiseptics to kill GERMS on surgeons' hands and instruments.

LIVER

Your liver is a flat, triangular organ tucked under your right ribs. It is larger than your stomach. The liver is a kind of chemical factory and store cupboard. It produces the digestive juice that burns up the fat you eat. It makes the PROTEINS used in blood. It gets rid of any poisonous substances in the blood or changes them so that they are harmless. Minerals and VITAMINS are stored in the liver until the body needs them.

Frilled lizard

LIZARDS

Lizards are REPTILES with dry, scaly skins and long tails. Most have four legs but some have none. These look like snakes. Some lizards are born live like MAMMALS, but most of them hatch from eggs.

There are about 3000 kinds of lizard. Most live in hot countries. Lizards that live in cooler places spend the winter in HIBERNATION. Lizards eat insects mainly, but the IGUANA likes fruit. Very large lizards sometimes eat small animals.

Most lizards are only a few centimetres long. But the Komodo dragon is longer and heavier than a man.

The tiny frilled lizard (top) spreads a frill to scare enemies. The bearded lizard (centre) runs on two legs over hot sand. Europe's green lizard is an insect eater.

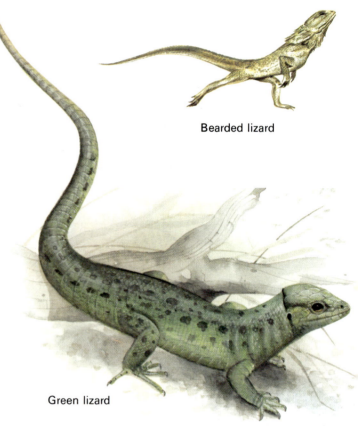
Bearded lizard

Green lizard

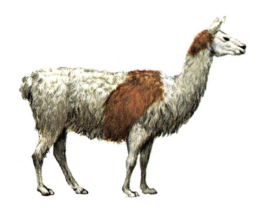
The sure-footed llama can travel 30 km (20 miles) a day on mountain paths.

LLAMAS

The llama belongs to the camel family, but has no hump. It stands about 1·5 metres (5 feet) high at the shoulder and may weigh twice as much as a man. Long, thick hair keeps it warm on the cold slopes of the Andes Mountains in South America, where it lives.

All llamas come from wild ancestors who were tamed at least 4500 years ago by the INCAS. Today, South American Indians still use llamas to carry heavy loads. They make clothes and ropes from the llama's wool and candles from its fat.

LOBSTERS

Lobsters are crustaceans. They are related to shrimps and CRABS. One kind of lobster can weigh up to 20 kg (44 lb). The lobster's body has a hard SHELL. It has four pairs of legs for walking and a pair of huge claws for grabbing food. When a lobster is afraid it tucks its tail under its body. This drives water forwards and pushes the lobster backwards to escape.

Lobsters hide among rocks on the sea bed. They feed on live and dead animals. A female lobster can lay thousands of eggs.

The Norway lobster is small. It lives near the shores of Europe.

LOCKS AND KEYS

There are two main kinds of locks. In the simplest kind, when the key is turned a piece of metal, called a bolt, moves out and fits into a slot. The key has a few notches that have to fit with similar notches in the lock. The Yale lock was invented in 1860. In it the key can turn a cylinder when all the little pins in the lock are pushed to the right height by the notches on the key.

LOCOMOTIVES

Locomotives are railway engines. They pull trains along RAILWAYS. Locomotives run on coal, oil, gas or electricity.

The first locomotives were STEAM ENGINES, which burned coal. In 1804 a British engineer, Richard Trevithick, built a steam locomotive. It carried ten tonnes of iron ore and 70 men. But it moved only at walking pace. In the 1820s, George Stephenson built engines that travelled as fast as a horse.

Since then, engineers have built powerful locomotives that go much faster. One American locomotive was so strong it pulled 250 trucks. One modern French locomotive can travel at 300 km (186 miles) an hour.

Most modern locomotives have DIESEL ENGINES or motors worked by electricity. The electricity can come from wires above the track. Locomotives on UNDERGROUND RAILWAYS take their electricity from the rails.

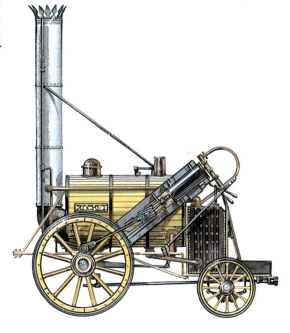

In 1829, George Stephenson built a locomotive called the Rocket. It pulled trains on the Liverpool and Manchester Railway. The Rocket was very fast for those days. It reached a speed of 58 km (36 miles) an hour.

LOCUSTS

Locusts are grasshoppers that sometimes breed in huge numbers. They fly far across land and sea to find new feeding places. A big swarm may have thousands of locusts. When they land, the locusts eat everything green. Swarms of locusts have destroyed many farms in warm lands.

Locusts swarm and fly away only when there are too many of them. Farmers try to kill the young locusts before they are able to fly.

LONDON

London is the capital of GREAT BRITAIN. It has about seven million people. The River THAMES runs through London.

People from all over the world visit London to see Buckingham Palace, the HOUSES OF PARLIAMENT, Westminster Abbey and the Tower of London. There are many museums, theatres and parks in London, also offices and factories.

London began as a Roman settlement called *Londinium*. The Black Death came to London in the 1600s, followed by the Great Fire of 1666. The city was badly bombed in WORLD WAR II.

A swarm of locusts flies through a field. The swarm looks like a big cloud. When locusts fly, they grow extra-long wings and look darker.

LUNGS

Lungs are for BREATHING. People have lungs, and so do many animals. Lungs bring OXYGEN to the body from the air. They also remove waste carbon dioxide from the BLOOD.

Your lungs are two large, sponge-like masses in your chest. They fill with air and empty as you breathe in and out.

You breathe in air through the nose. The air flows down the windpipe, or *trachea*. Where the lungs begin, the trachea divides into two hollow branches called bronchial tubes, or *bronchi*. Each divides into smaller tubes called *bronchioles*. These end in cups called air sacs, or *alveoli*. This is where the lungs give oxygen to the blood and take away carbon dioxide.

Lungs need clean air. Smokers and people who live in smoky towns, or work in some kinds of dusty air, may get lung diseases.

MACHINERY

Machines make our jobs easier. They carry us from place to place, and make the goods we need. Until the INDUSTRIAL REVOLUTION, there were very few machines. In the Middle Ages the most powerful machines were mills and wheels driven by wind and water. Today, machines are a part of life.

STEAM ENGINES were known to the ancient Greeks, but were used only as toys. The machine age did not begin until the 1700s. Later, in the 1800s, came other forms of power, such as the petrol engine and the electric motor. The INTERNAL COMBUSTION ENGINE, which uses oil as fuel, has been used since the early 1900s for the MOTOR CAR. JET ENGINES drive the aircraft of today.

MAGNETISM

A magnet attracts metals, particularly iron and steel. The Earth is a huge natural

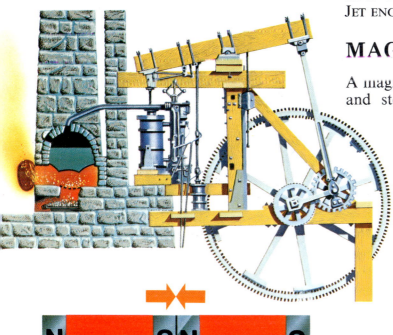

Left: James Watt built this improved steam engine in 1788.

If the North pole of one magnet comes near the South pole of another, the two are pulled together. But two South poles repel each other. So do two North poles.

magnet. Invisible lines of magnetic force spread out round the planet, joining the North and South magnetic poles. We call this the Earth's *magnetic field*.

The needle in a COMPASS is a magnet. It always turns to face magnetic North. In ancient times people noticed that a kind of iron ore called a lodestone suspended from a string would always swing in the same direction. A lodestone is a natural magnet. Another name for it is magnetite.

An electromagnet is made by coiling wire round a metal core and passing electricity through the coil.

MALARIA

Malaria is a tropical disease. It is carried by the *Anopheles* MOSQUITO, which can infect the humans it bites. Drugs are used to treat malaria. Scientists try to destroy the mosquitoes and the swamps in which the insects breed.

MALAYSIA

Malaysia is a country in South-east ASIA. It is in two parts, West Malaysia on the Malay Peninsula, and East Malaysia, which is part of the island of Borneo. The capital, Kuala Lumpur, is in West Malaysia.

Malaysia has about 14,700,000 people, mostly Malays and Chinese. Its main exports are rubber, timber and tin.

A Malaysian rubber tree is tapped for latex, the liquid from which rubber is made.

MALTA

Malta is an island in the MEDITERRANEAN SEA. It lies south of Sicily. Since ancient times it has been a vital naval base, for it guards the Mediterranean trade routes to the East. For centuries Malta was ruled by the Knights of St. John, but in 1813 it became British. During World War II, Malta survived heavy bombing raids and the whole island was awarded the George Cross medal.

Since 1962 Malta has been self-governing. Today, it is a republic. The capital is Valletta, with its splendid Grand Harbour.

The orang-utan is one of the primates, the highest order of mammals.

MAMMALS

Mammals are not the largest group of animals on Earth. But they are the most intelligent and show a greater variety of forms than any other group of animals.

All mammals have warm blood and a bony skeleton. Many have hair or fur on their bodies to keep them warm. Female mammals give birth to live young, which they feed on milk from special glands in their bodies. Some mammals (such as mice) are born naked, blind and helpless. Others (such as deer) can run within hours of being born.

Mammals were the last great animal group to appear on Earth. They came long after fish, amphibians, reptiles and insects. When DINOSAURS ruled the Earth, millions of years ago, the only mammals were tiny creatures which looked like shrews. But after the dinosaurs died out, the mammals took over. During EVOLUTION, the mammals multiplied into many different forms, which spread all over the world.

Scientists divide the mammals into three families. The most primitive mammals still lay eggs, like the reptiles and birds. There are only two left, the echidna and the platypus. Then come the MARSUPIALS.

These mammals give birth to tiny, half-developed young which have to be carried in their mother's pouch until they are big enough to look after themselves. The best known marsupial is the KANGAROO. Almost all the marsupials live in Australia.

The 'placental' mammals, the highest group of all, give birth to fully developed young. There are many different kinds, including flying mammals (BATS); gnawing animals or RODENTS; sea mammals (WHALES and DOLPHINS); and burrowing animals (for example, moles). There are insect-eaters, plant-eaters and flesh-eaters. The flesh-eaters, or CARNIVORES, include the powerful CATS, WOLVES and BEARS. The most intelligent of all the mammals are the primates. This family includes MONKEYS, APES and man.

Above: A female elephant and her calf. Young mammals are cared for by their mother and feed on her milk.

MARCONI, GUGLIELMO

Guglielmo Marconi (1874–1937) was the man who, most people say, invented RADIO. His parents were rich Italians. When he was only 20 he managed to make an electric bell ring in one corner of a room with radio waves sent out from the other corner. Soon he was sending radio signals over longer and longer distances. In 1901 he sent the first message across the Atlantic. In 1924 he sent signals across the world to Australia.

Left: Guglielmo Marconi with equipment similar to that which he used to send the first wireless signal across the Atlantic.

MARCO POLO

Marco Polo (1254–1324) was an Italian traveller. He is famous for the long journey he made to far-away China at a time when the people of Europe knew little about the East. His father and his uncle were merchants from Venice and they decided to take the young Marco with them when they set out for the East in 1271. They crossed Persia and the vast Gobi desert. In 1275 they reached Peking and were welcomed by Kublai Khan, a great MONGOL conqueror. The Polos stayed for many years during which Marco travelled all over China in the service of the Khan. They left China in 1292 and arrived home in Venice in 1295. Later, Marco's stories of his travels were written down. The *Travels of Marco Polo* is one of the most exciting books ever written.

MARS (GOD)

Mars was one of the oldest and most important of the Roman gods. He was the son of Jupiter and Juno and became the god of war. His son, Romulus, was supposed to have been the founder of ROME. The temples and festivals of Mars were important to the Romans. The month of March was named for him. It was the first month in the Roman year.

MARS (PLANET)

The planet Mars is only about half the size of the Earth. It takes about two years to travel around the Sun. The surface of Mars has huge volcanoes and great gorges, far bigger than those on Earth. Most of Mars is covered with loose rocks, scattered over a dusty red surface. This is why Mars is called the 'Red Planet'. It has a North Pole and a South Pole, just like our Earth—both covered with snow or frost.

Seen through a telescope, the red surface of Mars is criss-crossed by thin grey lines. Some early astronomers thought that these lines were canals which had been dug by man-like creatures. They said these canals

Above: The landscape of Mars is red and rock-strewn. This picture was taken by the Viking 1 spacecraft.

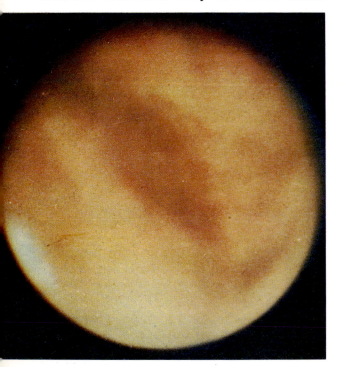

Left: This is what Mars looks like viewed through a telescope from the Earth. Until the recent space probes, these photos were all we had to tell us about the Red Planet.

had been dug to irrigate the soil, since Mars has very little water. But space probes to Mars in 1965, 1969 and 1976 found no trace of the canals. The American Viking spacecraft landed on Mars and took samples of the planet's soil. But it was unable to find any kind of life on Mars.

The planet has two tiny moons—Phobos and Deimos. Phobos, the larger of the two, is only about 24 km (15 miles) across.

Because Mars has a smaller mass than the Earth, things on its surface weigh only about 40 percent of what they would weigh on Earth. A day on Mars is about the same length as an Earth day.

MARSUPIALS

Marsupials are MAMMALS with pouches—animals like KANGAROOS, WALLABIES, KOALAS and OPOSSUMS. They all live in Australia, except the American opossum. A newly-born marsupial is very tiny. It crawls into its mother's pouch and stays there, feeding on her milk, until it can look after itself.

MARX, KARL

Many people think that Karl Marx (1818–1883) was the greatest political thinker and writer there has ever been. Marx was born in Germany and his ideas were the starting point of COMMUNISM. He believed that people who own property, the capitalist class, keep those who work for them down so the owners can become richer. He also thought that the workers would one day rise against the capitalists and take control. Marx's ideas later led to the Russian Revolution.

MARY QUEEN OF SCOTS

Mary, Queen of Scots (1542–1587) was the last Roman Catholic ruler of SCOTLAND. The daughter of James V of Scotland, she was educated in France, and did not return

Above: The little wallaby is like a small kangaroo. Like all marsupials, it rears its young in a pouch.

to Scotland until she was 19. By that time she thought of herself as more French and Catholic than Scottish and Protestant.

Mary was the heir to the English throne after the Protestant ELIZABETH 1. In 1567 Mary was forced to give up the Scottish throne. Later she was imprisoned for 20 years in England. People said she was plotting against Queen Elizabeth. She was executed on the Queen's orders in 1587.

Left: Mary, Queen of Scots had to escape in secret from Scotland to England in 1567.

MASKS

The use of masks is very ancient. People wore masks on their faces as a kind of magic and in religious ceremonies. Masks were worn by actors in ancient China and Greece to show that they were a certain kind of character. They were also worn in religious plays in the Middle Ages and by medieval jesters. Nowadays masks are still worn by circus clowns, in modern dance, at parties, and during Mardi Gras carnivals in Latin America.

MATHEMATICS

We all use mathematics every day. We add up the coins in our pockets to find out how much money we have. We look at a clock and work out how much time we have left before going somewhere. In every business people are constantly using some kind of mathematics; often, nowadays, with the help of calculators and computers. The branch of mathematics that deals with numbers is called ARITHMETIC. *Algebra* uses symbols such as *x* and *y* instead of numbers. GEOMETRY deals with lines, angles, and shapes such as triangles and squares.

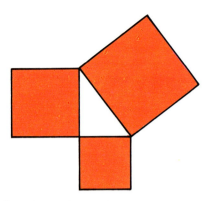

The Greek mathematician Pythagoras proved that the square on the longest side of a right-angled triangle equals the sum of the squares on the other two sides. This is one of the principles of modern geometry.

The Maya site of Tikal in Guatemala was a ceremonial centre built deep in the jungle. As many as 45,000 people lived there.

MAYA

The Maya Indians first lived in Central America in the 400s AD. They grew maize and sweet potatoes and kept pet dogs. Later they built cities of stone, with richly decorated palaces, temples, pyramids and observatories. Even today, many of these wonderful buildings are still standing, hidden in the jungle. The Maya were also skilled in astronomy and mathematics, and they had an advanced kind of writing.

The Maya people did not have any metals until very late in their history. They built with only stone tools. And they had no knowledge of the wheel. Their lives were controlled by religion. They worshipped a sun god, rain gods, soil gods, and a moon goddess who looked after women.

MEDITERRANEAN SEA

The Mediterranean is a large sea surrounded by three continents—Africa, Europe and Asia. It flows out into the Atlantic Ocean through the narrow Strait of GIBRALTAR. It is also joined to the Black Sea by a narrow passage.

In ancient times the Mediterranean was more important than it is now. In fact, it was the centre of the Western world for a long time. The Phoenicians were a seafaring people who travelled around the Mediterranean from about 2500 BC. Then the Greeks and Romans sailed the

Below: This Turkish trawler is harvesting sponges in the Mediterranean. The diver collects them.

sea. The Romans were in control of the whole Mediterranean for nearly 500 years. They even called it *Mare Nostrum*, which means 'our sea'.

The SUEZ CANAL was opened in 1869. It cuts across Egypt, joining the Mediterranean to the Red Sea. The canal was very useful because it shortened the distance by sea between Europe and the East. It is still very useful to cargo ships.

Nowadays people know the Mediterranean best for its sunshine and its beaches. Countries such as Spain, France and Italy welcome tourists who want to lie in the Mediterranean sun.

MENDEL, GREGOR

Gregor Mendel (1822–1884) was an Austrian priest who became famous for his work on heredity. Heredity is the passing on of things such as eye colour, skin colour, and mental ability from parents to their children.

Mendel grew up on a farm, where he became interested in plants. When he entered a monastery he began growing peas. He noticed that when he planted the seeds of tall pea plants, only tall pea plants grew up. Then he tried crossing tall peas with short peas by taking pollen from one and putting it in the other. He found that again he had only tall plants. But when he crossed these new mixed tall plants with each other, three-quarters of the new plants were tall and one quarter were short. Mendel had found out that things like the tallness or shortness are controlled by tiny *genes*, passed on from each parent. He also found out that some genes are stronger than other genes.

MERCURY (GOD)

Mercury was a Roman god who was the same as the Greek god Hermes. He was the messenger of the gods and is usually shown as a young man with winged sandals and carrying a winged stick.

MERCURY (METAL)

Mercury, or quicksilver, is the only metal that is a liquid at ordinary temperatures. When mercury is poured on to a table it forms little bead-like drops. Most metals dissolve in mercury to make *amalgams*, such as fillings for teeth. Mercury is used in THERMOMETERS and BAROMETERS.

Gregor Mendel's experiments with cross-breeding peas helped him to draw up the Laws of Heredity.

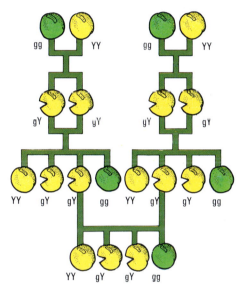

Mendel discovered that the gene for yellow in peas was stronger than that for green. A cross between green and yellow peas produced all yellow, but green turned up in later generations.

An electric current passed through mercury vapour will make the vapour glow. Mercury vapour lamps are used in street lighting and sunlamps.

217

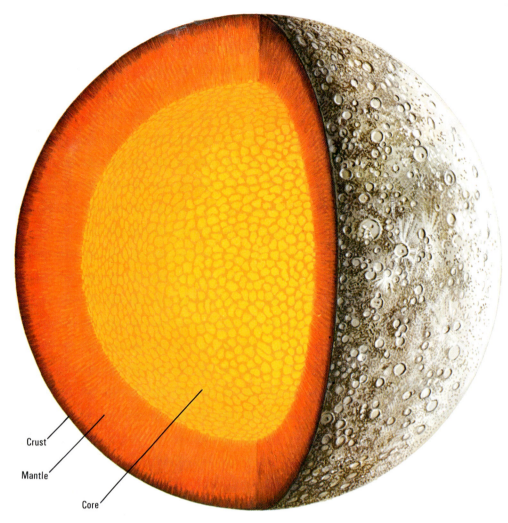

Crust

Mantle

Core

MERCURY (PLANET)

The planet Mercury is the smallest planet in the SOLAR SYSTEM. It is also the closest to the Sun. A day on Mercury lasts for 59 of our days. During the long daylight hours it is so hot that lead would melt. During the long night it grows unbelievably cold. Little was known about Mercury's surface until the space probe Mariner 10 passed within 800 km (500 miles) of the planet. It showed Mercury to have a thin atmosphere and big craters like those on the Moon.

Mercury travels very fast through space —at between 37 and 56 km (23 and 35 miles) per second. This great speed and its nearness to the Sun give it the shortest year of all the planets (the time it takes Mercury to go once round the Sun). Mercury's year lasts only 88 of our Earth days.

Above: Mercury is one of the heaviest planets for its size. Astronomers believe it has a very large iron core. The surface crust is scarred with craters where meteors have bombarded it.

Below: Mercury compared in size with the Earth. It is not much bigger than the Moon.

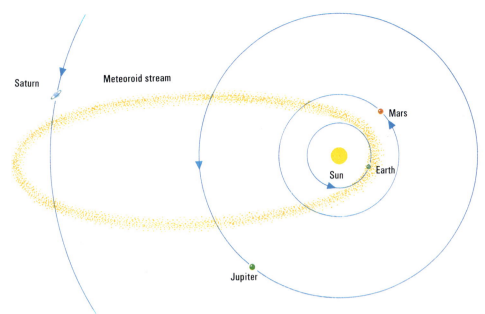

Saturn

Meteoroid stream

Mars

Sun

Earth

Jupiter

METEORS

A meteor is a tiny piece of metal or stone. It travels through space at great speed. Millions of meteors fall on the Earth every day. Most of them burn up before they reach the ground. On clear nights you can sometimes see shooting stars. They are meteors. Sometimes a large meteor reaches the ground. Then it is called a meteorite. Meteorites often make large holes.

Mexicans are descended from Mexican Indians and Spanish people. Most Mexicans are a mixture of both.

Meteors sometimes travel in swarms. They circle the Sun in long orbits. Meteors are probably small pieces from comets.

METRIC SYSTEM

The metric system is used for measuring weight, length and volume. It is based on units of ten, or decimals. It was first used in France in the late 1700s. Now it is used all over the world.

MEXICO

Mexico is a country in NORTH AMERICA. It lies between the United States in the north and Central America in the south. To the east is the Gulf of Mexico, a big bay. On the west lies the Pacific Ocean.

Mexico has an area of 1,972,547 sq km (761,605 sq miles). Much of the country is hilly with fertile uplands. The highest mountains reach over 5700 metres (18,000 feet). In the south-east, the low Yucatan peninsula sticks out far into the Gulf of Mexico.

Mexico is a tropical country. But most of the land is high. This makes the climate cool and dry. The north has desert in places.

The capital of Mexico is Mexico City. The population of Mexico is over 71 million. The first people in Mexico were Indians, such as the AZTECS.

MICHELANGELO

Michelangelo Buonarotti (1475–1564) was a painter and sculptor. He lived in Italy at the time of the RENAISSANCE. Michelangelo is famous for the wonderful statues and paintings he made of people. He spent many years painting pictures in the Sistine Chapel in the VATICAN CITY. Many of his statues are large and very life-like. His statue of David is 4 metres (over 13 feet) high.

Michelangelo began carving this statue when he was only 23. It shows the Virgin Mary holding Jesus. Jesus has just died on the cross.

MICROSCOPE

A microscope is an instrument used for looking at tiny objects. It *magnifies* things, or makes them look bigger. Things which are invisible to the naked eye are called *microscopic*. Many microscopic plants and animals, including bacteria, can be seen if you look at them through a microscope.

Microscopes work by using lenses. The simplest microscope is a magnifying glass. It has only one LENS. The lenses in many microscopes work by bending light rays. Small microscopes can magnify 100 times. Big microscopes used by scientists may magnify up to 1600 times. The electron microscope is much more powerful. It can magnify up to 2,000,000 times. Instead of bending light rays, it bends beams of electrons. Electrons are parts of ATOMS.

Anton van Leeuwenhoek was a Dutchman who lived in the 1600s. He made one of the first microscopes. Using his microscope, he showed that fleas hatch from tiny eggs. Before this, people thought fleas came from sand or mud. They could not see the eggs.

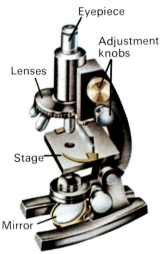

Above: This is a standard microscope. The lenses are inside a tube. You look through the eyepiece. The things you are looking at are put on pieces of glass called slides. Slides are placed on the stage. The mirror helps to light the slides.

MIGRATION

Many animals make long journeys to breed or find food. Most make the journey every year. Some make the journey only twice in their life. These journeys are called migrations. Animals migrate by INSTINCT. They do not have to plan their journey.

Birds are the greatest migrators. Swallows leave Europe and North America every autumn. They fly south to spend winter in Africa or South America. These places are warm and the swallows find plenty of food there. The trip may be 10,000 km (7000 miles) long. In spring, the swallows fly north again to breed.

But birds are not the only animals that make long trips. Butterflies, fish and mammals migrate too. Whales and fish make long journeys through the sea to find food

The monarch butterfly migrates in huge numbers every winter. It flies from Canada and the northern USA south to Mexico, and to the Atlantic and Pacific oceans.

and breed. The EELS of Europe's lakes and rivers swim thousands of kilometres across the Atlantic Ocean to breed. After breeding they die. The young eels take years to swim back to Europe. Monarch butterflies of North America fly south for the winter.

MILK

Milk is a food that all baby MAMMALS live on. It comes from the breasts, or mammaries, of the baby's mother. The baby sucks the milk from its mother's teat or nipple.

At first, the milk is pale and watery. It protects the baby from diseases and infections. Later, the milk is much richer and creamier. It contains all the food the baby needs. Milk is full of FAT, SUGAR, STARCHES, PROTEIN, VITAMINS and MINERALS. After a while the baby grows teeth and starts to eat other kinds of food.

People use milk from many animals. These include cows, sheep, goats, camels, and even reindeer. The animals are kept in herds. Sometimes they live on farms. Reindeer do not live on farms but wander about in the wild.

Milk is used to make many other foods. Cream, butter, yoghurt, cheese and some ice cream are all made from milk.

MILKY WAY

When you look at the sky on a clear, moonless night you can see a pale cloud of light. It stretches across the heavens. If you look at it through binoculars or a telescope, you can see that the cloud is really millions of stars. All these stars, and most of the other stars we see, are part of our GALAXY. It is called the Milky Way.

Astronomers think that the Milky Way has about 100,000 million stars like our Sun. The Milky Way stretches over a distance of about 100,000 LIGHT-years. Our own SOLAR SYSTEM is 30,000 light-years from the centre of the Milky Way.

The Milky Way has a spiral shape. Its trailing arms turn slowly around the centre. They take 200 million years to make a full circle. From Earth, we see the Milky Way through the arms of the spiral. Our Sun and its planets, including Earth, are a tiny speck way out on one of the Milky Way's long arms.

The Milky Way is not a special galaxy. There are thousands of other galaxies with the same shape. There may be millions and millions of other galaxies in the UNIVERSE.

MINERALS

The rocks of the Earth are made up of materials called minerals. There are many different kinds of mineral. Some, such as GOLD or platinum, are made up of only one ELEMENT. Others, such as QUARTZ and SALT, consist of two or more elements. Some minerals are metallic, such as COPPER or SILVER. Other minerals are non-metallic, like sulphur.

Pure minerals are made up of ATOMS arranged in regular patterns, known as CRYSTALS. Minerals form crystals when they cool from hot GASES and liquids deep inside the Earth. Crystals can grow very large if they cool slowly. But large or small, crystals of the same mineral always have the same shape. The exception is CARBON. It takes one crystal shape when it is DIAMOND and another when it is graphite.

Altogether there are over 2000 minerals. Yet most of the Earth's rocks are made up of only 30 minerals. The most common mineral of all is quartz. Most grains of sand are quartz. Pure quartz is made up of large, well-shaped crystals and has a milky colour.

Halite

Cassiterite

Pyrite

Minerals come in many shapes and colours. Halite (top) is rock salt. Cassiterite (centre left) is an important ore of tin. Pyrite, or Fool's Gold (centre right), contains iron and sulphur. Malachite and azurite (left), two ores of copper, are often found in the same piece of rock.

MINING

Mining means digging MINERALS out of the Earth. It is one of the world's most important industries. When minerals lie in one place in large quantities they are known as ores. People mine minerals like GOLD, SILVER and TIN. They also mine COAL.

Mines can be open pits or underground tunnels. When the ore is close to the surface the soil that lies on top of it is simply lifted away. Giant diggers then scoop up the rock that contains the minerals. Underground mines can be as deep as 3·2 km (2 miles) below the surface. Another form of mining is DREDGING. Here minerals are scooped up from the beds of rivers and lakes.

MOHAMMED

Mohammed (AD 570–632) was the founder and leader of the RELIGION known as ISLAM. He was born in Mecca in Saudi Arabia. At the age of 40 he believed that God asked

Malachite and Azurite

him to preach to the ARABS. He taught that there was only one God, called Allah.

In 622 he was forced out of Mecca, and this is the year from which the Moslem calendar dates. After his death his teachings spread rapidly across the world.

MOLLUSCS

Molluscs are a large group of animals. There are about 70,000 different kinds. After insects they are the most numerous of all animals. They are found everywhere from deserts and mountains to the depths of the sea.

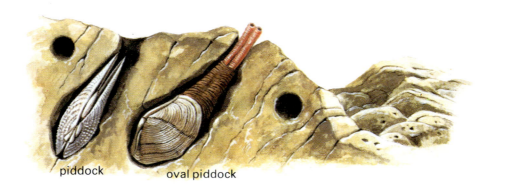

piddock   oval piddock

Piddocks (above) can make holes in soft rocks. Squids (below) swim in the sea and feed on prawns and shrimps. Both are molluscs, as are snails, whelks, slugs, oysters, octopuses, clams and mussels.

Molluscs have soft bodies and no backbones. Instead, a hard outer SHELL protects their body. Some molluscs, such as SQUID and cuttlefish, have their shell inside their body. Certain kinds of slug have no shell at all.

Some shells are only a few millimetres wide. Others, like the giant clam, are over a metre wide. As a mollusc grows, its shell grows with it. The shell is made of a hard limy material formed from the food the mollusc eats. Shells have many strange shapes and patterns and some of them are very beautiful.

The largest mollusc is the giant squid. This can grow to as much as 12 metres (40 feet).

MONEY

We use money every day to pay for things we buy. We pay with either coins or paper notes. This sort of money is known as cash. There is also another kind of money. It includes cheques, credit cards and travellers' cheques.

Almost anything can be used as money. In the past people have used shells, beads, cocoa beans, salt, grain and even cattle. But coins are much easier to use than say, cattle. For one thing, they do not die suddenly. They are also easy to store and to carry around.

Coins were first used in China. They were also used by the ancient Greeks as early as 600 BC. They were valuable because they

were made of either gold or silver. They were stamped with the mark of the government or the ruler of the country for which they were made. The stamp also showed how much each coin was worth.

Later, people began to use coins made of cheaper metals. The metal itself had no value, but the coins were still worth the amount stamped on them. They also started to use paper money. It no longer mattered that the money itself had no real value. It was backed by the government and banks, which people could trust. This is the kind of money we use today.

MONGOLIA AND THE MONGOLS

Mongolia is in the heart of ASIA. It lies between the Soviet Union and China. The country has a population of only 1,650,000. Its capital is Ulan Bator.

Mongolia is a high, flat country. It is mostly desert or rolling grassland with mountain ranges in the west. The Gobi Desert covers a large part of the land.

The people of Mongolia are descended from the Mongols. In the MIDDLE AGES these people controlled an empire that stretched from China to Europe.

Mongols were NOMADS who lived on the great plains of central Asia. They herded huge flocks of sheep, goats, cattle and horses, which they grazed on the vast grasslands of the region. They lived in tent villages that they could quickly pack up and take with them when they moved on to find new pastures.

The Mongols were superb horsemen and highly trained warriors. In the 1200s they formed a mighty army under the great GENGHIS KHAN. Very soon, swift-riding hordes of Mongols swept through China, India, Persia and as far west as Hungary.

Under Genghis Khan, and later his grandson, Kublai Khan, the Mongols conquered half the known world. But they were unable to hold their empire together. In less than 100 years the Mongol empire had been taken over by the Chinese.

Today more than half the Mongolian people live and work as farmers. They keep over 20 million animals in herds.

Golden spider monkey

Long-nosed proboscis monkey

Black howler monkey

MONKEYS

Monkeys are MAMMALS that belong to the same group of animals as APES and man. Most monkeys have long tails and thick fur all over their body. A few have fur only on the rump. Monkeys are usually smaller than apes. Their hands and feet are used for grasping and are very similar to those of humans.

There are about 400 different kinds of monkey.

Golden spider monkeys and black howler monkeys live in South America. Long-nosed proboscis monkeys and mandrills come from Africa. The mandrill spends most of its time on the ground.

Mandrill

Most live in the tropics, especially in forests, in Africa, Asia and South America. South American monkeys have long tails that they use like an extra arm or leg when swinging through the branches of trees.

On the ground monkeys usually move about on all four limbs. But when they are using their hands to hold something they can stand or sit up on two legs.

Monkeys live in family groups known as troops. They spend a lot of time chattering, playing, fighting and grooming each other. Each troop of monkeys has its own special place where it lives and feeds. It will fight fiercely to defend this area against other invading groups.

MOON

The Moon is our nearest neighbour in space. It loops around the EARTH, never coming closer than 355,000 km (221,900 miles). It travels at about 3660 km/hr (2287 mph) and takes $27\frac{1}{3}$ days to complete the circuit.

The Moon is the only other part of the universe that human beings have visited. The first man-made object to reach it was a Russian spacecraft which landed on September 13, 1959. Ten years later, the first men stepped on to the Moon's surface. They were the American astronauts, Neil Armstrong and Edwin Aldrin.

What they found was a waterless, airless, dusty world. It was covered with thousands of craters, some as small as a footprint, others stretching across 320 km (200 miles). The craters were holes made by meteorites crashing into the Moon. The astronauts brought back samples of Moon rock for scientists to examine. The rock shows that the Moon must be at least 4600 million years old.

Above: The Moon is only one quarter the size of Earth. It is just a bit larger than the width of Australia.

Below: Because the Moon takes the same time to spin once on its axis as it does to go round the Earth, we only ever see one side of it.

WAXING

WANING

New Moon

Crescent phase

Gibbous phase

Full Moon

Last quarter

Crescent phase

MORMONS

People who belong to a religious group founded by Joseph Smith in 1830. The name comes from the *Book of Mormon*, which Mormons believe is a sacred history of ancient American peoples. The Mormons began in New York, but were persecuted for their belief and driven out. They finally settled in Salt Lake Valley, Utah.

A market place in Morocco where farmers bring their produce to sell.

MOROCCO

Morocco is a country right at the top of north west AFRICA. It is nearly twice the size of Great Britain and has two coastlines. On the west is the Atlantic Ocean and to the north is the Mediterranean Sea.

Most of Morocco's 21 million people are farmers. They grow wheat, maize, fruit, olives and nuts. Some keep sheep, goats and cattle. Most of the people are Moslems. The capital of Morocco is Rabat. The country is ruled by a king.

MORSE CODE

Morse code is a simple way of sending messages. It is an alphabet of dots and dashes. Each letter has its own dot and dash pattern. The code was invented by Samuel Morse, an American artist, to send messages along a telegraph wire. The telegraph operator presses a key at one end to send a signal along the wire to a sounder at the other end. A short signal is a dot and a long signal is a dash. The first message was sent in 1844.

Morse code can also be signalled by lights, or simply tapped out with your fingers.

A	·—	S	···
B	—···	T	—
C	—·—·	U	··—
D	—··	V	···—
E	·	W	·——
F	··—·	X	—··—
G	——·	Y	—·——
H	····	Z	——··
I	··	1	·————
J	·———	2	··———
K	—·—	3	···——
L	·—··	4	····—
M	——	5	·····
N	—·	6	—····
O	———	7	——···
P	·——·	8	———··
Q	——·—	9	————·
R	·—·	0	—————

Above: Moscow has some beautiful churches. This is the Church of St Basil.
Above right: Every year on May Day, a big parade is held in the vast Red Square in front of the Kremlin.

MOSCOW

Moscow is the capital of RUSSIA. It is also the biggest city in the country. Over eight million people live there.

Moscow lies on a plain across the River Moskva. It is the largest industrial and business centre in the country. Everything is made in Moscow, from cars to clothes. It is also the political and cultural centre of the Soviet Union.

Moscow was first made the capital of Muscovy in 1547, during the reign of IVAN the Terrible, the first *Tsar* (emperor) of Russia. It grew up around the KREMLIN, an ancient fort from which the Muscovy princes used to defend their country. Moscow remained the capital of the Tsars until 1712 when Peter the Great moved it to St. Petersburg. The city remained very important, even after it was nearly all burnt down during NAPOLEON's occupation of 1812.

After the Revolution of 1917, Moscow once more became the seat of government.

MOSQUITOS

Mosquitos are a small kind of FLY. They have slender, tube-shaped bodies, three pairs of long legs and two narrow wings. There are about 1400 different kinds. They live all over the world from the tropics to the Arctic, but must be able to get to water to lay their eggs.

Only female mosquitos bite and suck blood. They have special piercing mouths. Males live on the juices of plants. When the female bites, she injects a substance into her victim to make the blood flow more easily. It is this that makes mosquito bites painful.

Some kinds of mosquito spread serious diseases. Malaria, yellow fever and sleeping sickness are passed on by mosquitos.

A mosquito. Only the female sucks blood.

MOSSES

This is a very common kind of PLANT that grows in low, closely packed clusters. There are more than 12,000 different kinds. They are very hardy plants and flourish everywhere, except in deserts, even as far north as the Arctic. Most mosses grow in damp places. They spread in carpets on the ground in shady forests, or over rocks and the trunks of trees.

Mosses are very simple kinds of plants, like LICHENS. They were among the first to make their home on land. They have slender creeping stems that are covered with tiny leaves. Instead of proper roots that reach down into the soil, mosses simply have a mass of tiny hairs that soak up moisture and food. Mosses do not have flowers. They reproduce by spores, just like ferns. One kind, called sphagnum moss, grows in bogs and is the plant that makes peat.

MOTHS

It can be hard to tell moths and BUTTERFLIES apart. These are the signs to look out for. Moths usually fly in the evening and at night, while butterflies can be seen in the daytime. Moths have plumper bodies than butterflies. Moth antennae are like tiny combs, or have feathery hairs on them. Butterfly antennae end in tiny knobs. When butterflies rest on a plant, they hold their wings upright. Moths spread their wings out flat.

Moths belong to one of the biggest insect groups. There are over 100,000 kinds of moth and they are found all over the world. The smallest scarcely measure 3 mm ($\frac{1}{8}$ inch) across. The largest may be bigger than a man's hand. Some moths have very striking colours that warn their enemies that they are poisonous or bad tasting. Moths have a very good sense of smell. They find their food by 'sniffing' their way from plant to plant. A male moth can follow the scent of a female 3 km (2 miles) away.

Moths are born as eggs, usually in the

Above: Common clubmoss, one of the oldest kinds of plant on Earth. It has not changed for 400 million years.

spring. They hatch into CATERPILLARS. The caterpillar feeds on leaves until it is full grown. Then it spins itself a silk cocoon. This protects the caterpillar while its body changes into a moth. A few kinds of moth do not spin cocoons, but bury themselves in the ground or in piles of leaves until they grow into moths.

The magpie moth and the burnet moth caterpillars are both striped black and yellow or orange. Among animals, this usually means 'beware – I am poisonous to eat'.

magpie moth

burnet moth

MOTOR CAR

In about a hundred years the motor car has changed the world. It has also itself been changed. The clumsy 'horseless carriage' has become the fast, comfortable and reliable car of today.

Most cars have petrol engines. If petrol is mixed with air and a spark takes place in the mixture, it explodes. This explosion, repeated again and again very quickly, is made to turn the wheels of the car. (You can read more about this in the article on the INTERNAL COMBUSTION ENGINE.) The driver can make the car go faster by pressing the *accelerator* peddle. This makes more petrol go into the engine.

Cars are pushed along by either their front or back wheels. The engine is usually at the front. As the engine's *pistons* go up and down, they turn the *crankshaft*. The crankshaft is joined to the *clutch* and the *gearbox*, as you can see in the picture. The clutch is only a way of cutting off the engine from the gearbox. When the driver presses the clutch peddle he separates the crankshaft from the gears. Then he can safely change into any gear he wants. If the driver wants as much power as he can get he uses a low gear—first gear. He wants plenty of power for starting or going up a steep hill. When he drives along a clear road he will use top gear.

Behind the gearbox is a long rod that runs right to the back of the car—the propeller shaft. This rod turns at the speed the driver wants. (He uses his gears and the accelerator to do this.) The rod turns other gears on the axle between the back wheels. So the back wheels are made to drive the car at the speed the driver wants.

Top: In 1886 Gottlieb Daimler built this car in Germany. He bought a coach which should have been pulled by a horse, removed the shafts and fitted an engine to it. Above: This Model T Ford of 1909 was one of many million sold between 1908 and 1927. The Model T was the first car that was both cheap and reliable.

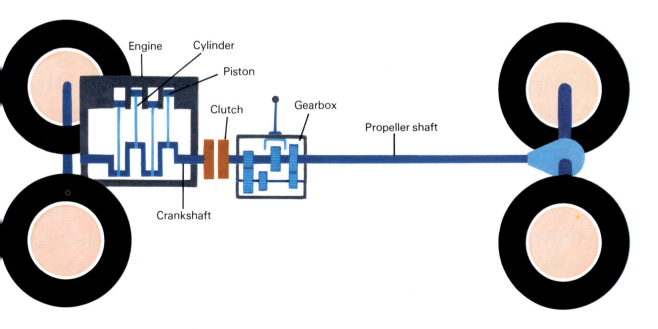

If we go up a high mountain in the hot tropics it is almost like travelling at sea level from the equator to the polar regions. As we go up, tropical forests become deciduous forests. Then we reach cone-bearing trees, followed by low shrubby plants. Above these are lichens and mosses, then nothing but snow and ice.

Snow-line

Tree-line

MOUNTAINS

A large part of the Earth's surface is covered by mountains. The greatest mountain ranges are the Alps of Europe, the Rockies and the Andes of America and the Himalayas of Asia. The Himalayas are the greatest of them all. They have many of the world's highest peaks, including the biggest, Mount EVEREST.

There are mountains under the sea, too. And sometimes the peaks of under-sea mountains stick above the sea's surface as islands. One mountain called Mauna Loa which rises from the floor of the Pacific Ocean is very much higher than Everest.

Mountains are formed by movements in the Earth's crust. Some mountains are formed when two great land masses move towards each other and squeeze up the land in between. The Alps were made in this way. Other mountains are VOLCANOES, great heaps of ash and lava that poured out when the volcano erupted.

But even the greatest mountains do not last for ever. The hardest rock gets worn away in time by rain, wind, sun and frost. Rivers cut valleys, glaciers grind their way down, wearing away the mountains after untold centuries into gentle hills.

When the height of a mountain is given, it means the height above sea level. This can be a lot more than the height from the base.

In the far distance in this picture are the mighty Himalayas, the world's highest mountains. These great peaks were pushed up millions and millions of years ago when the whole of India moved slowly north and collided with the rest of Asia.

MOUSE

A mouse is a RODENT, like its relative the rat. And, like the rat, the house-mouse is a pest to human beings. It can do a great deal of damage to stores of food, usually at night. One mouse can have 40 babies a year, and when the young are 12 weeks old they can themselves breed. People have used cats to catch mice for thousands of years. The wood mouse, field mouse, harvest mouse, and dormouse are mice which live in the countryside. White mice can be kept as pets.

Right: Mice need their sharp ears and sensitive whiskers to protect them against enemies.
Below: Mozart playing a harpsichord.

MOZART, WOLFGANG AMADEUS

Wolfgang Amadeus Mozart (1756–1791) was an Austrian and one of the greatest composers of music that the world has known. He began writing music at the age of five. Two years later he was playing at concerts all over Europe. Mozart wrote over 600 pieces of music, including many beautiful operas and symphonies. But he earned little money from his hard work. He died in poverty at the age of 35.

MUMMY

A mummy is a dead body that has been preserved. Belief in a life after death has led many peoples to try to preserve the bodies of their dead. The body would then be ready to come back to life in the next world.

The ancient Egyptians made mummies of their dead for more than 300 years. The bodies of PHARAOHS and rich people were treated with stuff to preserve them, covered with a kind of tar and then wrapped in linen cloths. The mummy was placed in a casket on which a face was painted. This casket was placed inside another coffin, and the coffin was sometimes put inside another, larger box.

The bodies of the poor were dried in salt and wrapped in coarse cloths.

The mummy and coffin of an unknown Egyptian priestess. Notice the carefully bound wrappings.

231

MUSCLES

Muscles are the things that make the parts of our bodies move. When you pick up this book or kick a ball you are using muscles. There are two different kinds of muscles. Some work when your brain tells them to. When you pick up a chair, your brain sends signals to muscles in your arms, in your body and in your legs. All these muscles work together at the right time, and you pick up the chair. Other kinds of muscles work even when you are asleep. Your stomach muscles go on churning the food you have eaten. Your heart muscles go on pumping blood. The human body has more than 500 muscles.

Right: Some mushrooms of the woods include deathcap (top left), stinkhorn (top right), chanterelle (bottom left) and fly agaric (bottom right).

MUSHROOMS AND TOADSTOOLS

Mushrooms grow in woods, fields and on people's lawns—almost anywhere, in fact, where it is warm enough and damp enough. Some mushrooms are very good to eat. Others are so poisonous that people die from eating them. Many people call the poisonous ones toadstools. Mushrooms are in the FUNGUS group of plants. They have no green colouring matter (CHLOROPHYLL), so they feed on decayed matter in the soil or on other plants.

MUSIC

People have been making some kind of music all through history. The very earliest men probably made singing noises and beat time with pieces of wood. We know that the ancient Egyptians enjoyed their music. Paintings in the tombs of the pharaohs show musicians playing pipes, harps, and other stringed instruments. The ancient Greeks also liked stringed instruments such as the lyre. But we have no idea what this early music sounded like, because there was no way of writing it down.

As instruments improved, new ones were added to the orchestra. BACH and HANDEL, who were both born in 1685, used orchestras with mostly stringed instruments like the violin. But they also had flutes, oboes, trumpets and horns. Joseph Haydn was the first man to use the orchestra as a whole. He invented the *symphony*. In this, all the instruments blended together so that none was more important than the others.

A new kind of music began with the great German composer BEETHOVEN. He began writing music in which some of the notes clashed. This sounded rather shocking to people who listened to his music in his day. Later musicians tried all kinds of mixtures of instruments. In the 1900s new kinds of music were made by composers such as Igor Stravinsky and Arnold Schönberg. Others since then have used tape recorders and electronic systems to produce new sounds which are often rather strange to our ears.

But music still has three things: *melody*, *harmony*, and *rhythm*. The melody is the tune. Harmony is the total sound when several notes are played together. A group of notes is called a *chord*. Rhythm is the regular 'beat' of the music. The simplest kind of music is just beating out a rhythm on a drum.

232

Bassoon

Piccolo

Flute

Oboe

Clarinet

Trumpet

Cor Anglais

Trombone

Double bass

Cello

Tuba

Horn

Cymbals

Triangle

Many sounds have no particular musical note. When a chair falls on the floor we hear a crash. This is an unpleasant sound. Pleasant sounds have a note – a definite pitch. That kind of sound is usually made by musical instruments.

MUSICAL INSTRUMENTS

There are four kinds of musical instruments. In wind instruments, air is made to vibrate inside a tube. This vibrating air makes a musical note.

All *woodwind* instruments such as clarinets, bassoons, flutes, piccolos and recorders have holes that are covered by the fingers or by pads worked by the fingers. These holes change the length of the vibrating column of air inside the instrument. The shorter the column the higher the note. In *brass* wind instruments, the vibration of the player's lips makes the air in the instrument vibrate. By changing the pressure of the lips, the player can make different notes. Most brass instruments also have valves and pistons to change the length of the vibrating column of air, and so make different notes.

Stringed instruments work in one of two ways. The strings of the instrument are either made to vibrate by a bow, as in the violin, viola, cello and double bass; or the strings are plucked, as in the guitar, harp or banjo.

In *percussion* instruments, a tight piece of skin or a piece of wood or metal is struck to make a note. There are lots of percussion instruments— drums, cymbals, gongs, tambourines, triangles and chimes.

Electronic instruments such as the electric organ and the synthesizer make music from electronic circuits.

MUSSOLINI, BENITO

Mussolini (1883–1945) was a dictator who started the Italian Fascist Party. In 1922 he bluffed the king of Italy into making him Prime Minister. Soon he made himself dictator. He wanted to make Italy great; he built many new buildings and created new jobs. But he also wanted military glory and led Italy into World War II on the side of Hitler. His armies were defeated by the Allies and Mussolini was finally captured and shot by his own people.

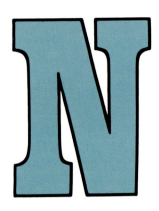

Above: Cats have claws that they can draw back or 'retract' when they are not needed. This picture shows the bones and muscles in the cat's foot that make this possible.

NAILS AND CLAWS

Nails and claws are made of hard skin, like animals' horns. They grow at the end of toes and fingers. When they are broad and flat they are called nails, but if they are sharp and pointed they are claws. Human nails are of little use. But BIRDS, MAMMALS and REPTILES use their claws to attack and to defend themselves.

A close look at an animal's claws will tell you about its way of life. CATS and birds of prey have very sharp claws. They are hooked for holding on to and tearing prey. ANT-EATERS have long, strong, curved claws for tearing termites' nests apart.

Right: Woodpecker claws are useful for tree climbing, and osprey claws help to grip prey. Swifts have claws for clinging. Coot and duck claws are for swimming, and the ostrich's for running. A finch's claws help it to perch securely.

NAMES

Names help us to identify people. Most people have more than one name. A first name is a personal name chosen by our parents. Our last name, or *surname*, is a family name. It can often tell us something about our ancestors. The names 'Smith' and 'Shepherd', for example, are the names of jobs. Some people have names of places as surnames, such as 'Bedford'. Other surnames just add 'son' to the father's name, such as 'Jackson' or Johnson'.

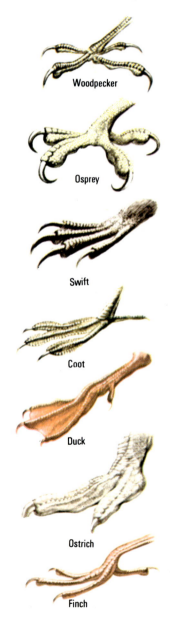

Woodpecker

Osprey

Swift

Coot

Duck

Ostrich

Finch

NAPOLEON BONAPARTE

In 1789 the people of FRANCE rebelled against the unjust rule of their king and his nobles. This revolution was supported by a young man who had been born in the island of Corsica 20 years before. His name was Napoleon Bonaparte (1769–1821).

Napoleon went to the leading military school in Paris, and by 1792 he was a captain of artillery. Three years later he saved France by crushing a royalist rebellion in Paris. Soon Napoleon was head of the French army and won great victories in Italy, Belgium and Austria. In 1804 he crowned himself emperor of France in the presence of the Pope. Then he crowned his wife, Josephine.

But Napoleon could not defeat Britain at sea. He tried to stop all countries from trading with England, but Russia would not cooperate. So Napoleon took a great army into Russia in the winter of 1812. This campaign ended in disaster. His troops were defeated by the bitter weather. Then he met his final defeat at the battle of Waterloo in 1815. There he was beaten by the British under WELLINGTON and the Prussians under Blücher. He was made prisoner by the British on the lonely Atlantic island of St Helena, where he died in 1821.

Napoleon was a small man. His soldiers adored him and called him 'the little corporal'. His speedy rise to power was helped by his first wife, the beautiful Josephine. Napoleon drew up a new French code of law. Many of his laws are still in force today.

Napoleon Bonaparte was 36 when this portrait was painted.

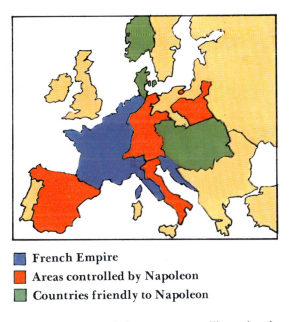

■ French Empire
■ Areas controlled by Napoleon
■ Countries friendly to Napoleon

Napoleon was one of the greatest military leaders of all time. The map above shows the vast area conquered by 'the little corporal'.

NAVIGATION

Navigation means finding the way, usually in a ship or an aircraft. For hundreds of years, navigators at sea used the changing positions of the Sun and stars to work out their LATITUDE. The difference between the time on the ship and the time set at 0° longitude at Greenwich, helped them to work out their position.

Today, many navigational instruments are electronic and are very accurate. Radio stations and satellites send out signals from which a ship can find its position. Then the navigator uses a COMPASS to keep his ship on the right course.

NELSON, HORATIO

Horatio Nelson (1758–1805) was a famous British admiral at the time when Britain was at war with the French, led by NAPOLEON BONAPARTE.

Nelson was born in Norfolk, the son of a country clergyman. He joined the navy when he was 12 and was captain of a frigate by the time he was 20. He was made a rear-admiral in 1797. By then he had already lost an eye in battle. Soon he lost an arm too.

In 1798 he led his ships to victory against the French at Alexandria in Egypt. While he was in the Mediterranean he met and fell in love with Lady Hamilton, the wife of the British ambassador to Naples. Nelson loved Lady Hamilton all his life. Many people thought this was shocking as they were both married to other people.

Nelson's most famous battle was his last. It was fought against a French fleet led by Admiral Villeneuve. For nearly 10 months in 1805, Nelson's ships chased Villeneuve's across the Atlantic and back. Then, on October 21, they met off the Cape of Trafalgar in southern Spain. Nelson defeated the French but was killed on board his ship, the *Victory*.

Before the battle Nelson sent a message to all the ships in his fleet: 'England expects every man to do his duty.'

NEPTUNE (GOD)

Neptune was the Roman name for the Greek god Poseidon, the god of the sea. People believed that when he was angry he sent storms and floods. He carried a three-pronged spear called a trident. The Romans believed that Neptune caused earthquakes by striking the ground with his trident, and that once when he struck the ground the first horse appeared.

NEPTUNE (PLANET)

The PLANET Neptune is named after the Roman god of water and the sea. It is a large planet (much bigger than Earth) far out in the SOLAR SYSTEM. It is about 4493 million km (2793 million miles) from the SUN. Only PLUTO is further away. It takes Neptune 165 years to circle the Sun. (The Earth takes 365 days.)

Being so far from the Sun, Neptune is a very cold place. Scientists think its atmosphere is rather like JUPITER's, which is mostly made up of the gas HYDROGEN. Neptune has two moons, Triton and Nereid. Triton is about the size of the planet MERCURY.

Early astronomers were unable to see Neptune, but they knew it had to be there. They could tell there was something affecting

If a piece were cut out of Neptune it would probably look like this. Scientists think it is made up of hydrogen surrounding a core of rock and ice. This core is probably about the same size as the Earth.

Below: As Neptune is so far away, no one knows its exact size. But we think it is about four times as wide as the Earth.

Rocky core

Ice

Hydrogen

Tailor bird

Fairy tern

Oven bird

Weaver bird

The tailor bird sews itself a nest from leaves. The weaver bird makes a 'basket', while the oven bird makes a nest of mud. The fairy tern makes no nest at all.

the ORBIT of the nearby planet URANUS.

In 1845 two astronomers, Adams in England and Leverrier in France, used mathematics to work out where Neptune should be. Astronomers used this information the next year, and spotted Neptune.

NERVES

Nerves are tiny fibres made up of CELLS. They reach all through the body. When a part of the body feels something, the nerves send a message through the SPINAL COLUMN to the BRAIN. If we feel pain, a message is sent back to make us move away from whatever is hurting. Nerves also carry the senses of sight, hearing and taste.

NESTS

A nest is a home built by a creature, where it has its young and looks after them. BIRDS build nests when they are ready to lay EGGS. Sometimes the female builds the nest, sometimes the male will give her some help. Some nests are very complicated, and may be lined with wool, hair or feathers. Others are simple or rather untidy.

A few MAMMALS such as MICE and SQUIRRELS make nests for their young, but these are not as complicated as birds' nests.

Some INSECTS make the most complicated nests of all. These are not at all like birds' nests. They are often built for a whole group, or colony, of insects. There will be one queen, who lays eggs, and hundreds or even thousands of workers to look after them. Most BEES and WASPS make this sort of nest. Some wasps build their nests out of paper. Termites make huge mud nests.

NEW GUINEA

New Guinea is one of the world's largest islands. It lies to the north of Australia. Its people are dark skinned with curly hair.

The island is divided into two parts. The west is called Irian Jaya, and belongs to INDONESIA. The east is called Papua New Guinea. About three million people live there. It used to belong to Australia but became independent in 1975. The capital is Port Moresby. Most of the people live in the central highlands.

New Guinea's main exports are tea, cocoa, copra (coconut), copper and gold. The official language is English but some 700 different languages are spoken.

NEWSPAPERS

Newspapers are just what their name says they are—papers that print news. They first appeared in the 1400s, just after PRINTING began. Printers produced pamphlets telling people what was happening in the country and what they thought about it.

Modern newspapers first appeared in the 1700s. Today, there are newspapers in almost every country in the world, in many different languages. Some are printed every day, some every week.

One of the oldest newspapers is *The Times* which is printed in London. It began in 1785 when it was called the *Universal Daily Register*. It changed its name to *The Times* in 1788. Other famous newspapers are the *New York Times* and the *Washington Post* in the United States, *Pravda* in Russia, and *Le Monde* in France.

NEWTON, ISAAC

Sir Isaac Newton (1642–1727) was an English mathematician and scientist who made some of the world's greatest scientific discoveries. He left Cambridge University in 1665 when plague shut the University. In the 18 months before the University re-opened, Newton did much of his most important work.

He invented a new kind of mathematics called *calculus*. Today, calculus helps designers to shape things like aircraft wings.

Newton's experiments showed that white LIGHT is a mixture of all the colours of the rainbow (the spectrum). By studying the spectrum of light from a star or other glowing object, scientists can now find out what that object is made of. Newton's studies of light also led him to build the first of all reflecting TELESCOPES.

Newton also discovered GRAVITY. He realized that the same kind of force that makes apples fall from trees also gives objects weight and keeps PLANETS going round the SUN.

Modern JET ENGINES work in a way that was first described by Newton in 1687.

NEW YORK

New York City is the largest city in the UNITED STATES. More than 11 million people live in New York and its suburbs.

The city stands mainly on three islands that lie at the mouth of the Hudson River. The island of Manhattan holds the heart of New York, and many of its most famous sights. Some of the world's greatest skyscrapers tower above its streets. Fifth Avenue is a famous shopping street, and Broadway is known for its theatres. Perhaps New York's best-known sight is the Statue of Liberty, one of the largest statues on Earth. It stands on an island in New York Harbor.

Ships from every continent dock at New York's port, which is the largest anywhere. New York is one of the world's great business centres. Its factories produce more goods than those of any other city in the United States.

Europeans first settled there in 1624. The

Dutch bought Manhattan from the Indians for a handful of cloth, beads and trinkets. The Dutch named their settlement New Amsterdam. Later, the English seized it and renamed the colony New York in honour of the Duke of York (later James II).

NEW ZEALAND

New Zealand is a remote island nation in the Pacific Ocean, south-east of Australia.

New Zealand is actually two main islands. North Island is famous for its hot springs and volcanoes. South Island has a range of mountains, called the Southern Alps, and many lovely lakes and waterfalls.

New Zealand also has plains and valleys. Here, the mild climate helps farmers to grow grains, vegetables and apples. They also raise millions of sheep and cattle. New Zealand is the world's third largest producer of sheep and wool.

There are over three million New Zealanders. Two in three people live in a city or town. Auckland is the largest city,

Right: The snow-crowned peaks of the Southern Alps rise beyond Lake Wakatipu on the South Island of New Zealand.

Skyscrapers on Manhattan in New York, one of the world's largest cities. Manhattan is an Indian word, meaning 'Heavenly Land'.

but the capital is Wellington. Both are in North Island.

New Zealand is a member of the COMMON-WEALTH. Many of its people are descended from British settlers. Others are Maoris, descended from Pacific islanders, who lived in New Zealand before the British came.

NIAGARA FALLS

The Niagara Falls are waterfalls on the Niagara River in North America. Water from most of the GREAT LAKES flows through this river. Each minute about 450,000 tonnes of water plunges about 50 metres (165 feet) from a cliff into a gorge.

The Falls stand on the border between Canada and the United States. The water pours down on each side of an island.

239

NIGERIA

This nation in West AFRICA is named after the Niger River that flows through it to the Atlantic Ocean. Nigeria has over 88 million people, more than any other nation in Africa. The capital is Lagos.

All Nigeria is hot. Dry grass and scrubby trees are scattered across the country. But swamps and forests line the coasts.

Nigerians are mainly Negroes. There are a great number of different tribes and many of them speak different languages.

Half the people believe in the religion of ISLAM. Most of the people grow maize, yams or other food crops. Nigeria is one of the world's main cocoa growers, and one of Africa's top two oil producers.

NIGHTINGALE, FLORENCE

Florence Nightingale (1820–1910) founded modern NURSING. She was wealthy and could have had an easy life, but instead she chose to work hard for the sick. In those days countless patients died in dirty hospitals run by untrained or drunken nurses. Florence Nightingale trained as a nurse, and ran a women's hospital in London.

In 1854 she took 38 nurses to Turkey to tend British soldiers wounded in the CRIMEAN WAR. Her hospital was a dirty barracks that lacked food, medicines and bedding. She cleaned it up, found supplies, and gave the wounded every care she could. Her work saved many hundreds of lives.

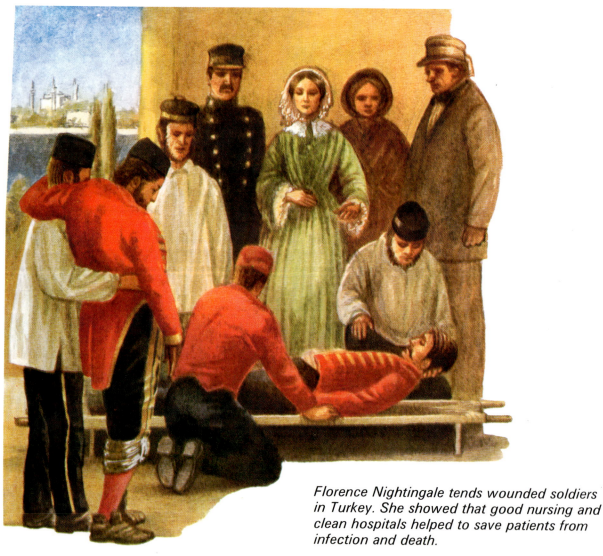

Florence Nightingale tends wounded soldiers in Turkey. She showed that good nursing and clean hospitals helped to save patients from infection and death.

The Nile rises near the equator. It flows through several great lakes on its way to the sea.

NILE

The Nile river in Africa may be the longest river on Earth. (Some people think that the AMAZON is longer.) The Nile was once shown to measure 6670 km (4145 miles). It rises in Burundi in central Africa and flows north through Egypt into the Mediterranean Sea. It is very important to the farmers who live around it.

NOBEL PRIZES

These money prizes are given each year to people who have helped mankind in different ways. Three prizes are for inventions or discoveries in physics, chemistry, physiology and medicine. The fourth is for literature. The fifth prize is for work to make or keep peace between peoples. Money for the prizes was left by the Swedish chemist Alfred Nobel, who invented the explosive DYNAMITE.

NOMADS

People without a settled home are nomads. Many nomads live in lands too dry to farm. Such people keep herds of animals and sleep in tents. They travel to find fresh pasture for their animals. Many nomads still live in or near the great deserts of Africa and Asia.

Below: Saharan nomads use tents that are light enough to carry.

NORTH AMERICA

North America stretches north from tropical Panama to the cold Arctic Ocean, and east from the Pacific Ocean to the Atlantic Ocean. Only Asia is larger than this continent.

North America has the world's largest island (Greenland), and the largest freshwater lake (Lake Superior). It contains the second largest country (CANADA), the second longest mountain range (the Rocky Mountains), and the third longest river (the Mississippi River). North America's natural wonders include the NIAGARA FALLS and the Grand Canyon (the largest gorge on land).

The cold north has long, dark, frozen winters. No trees grow here. Farther south stand huge evergreen forests. Grasslands covered most of the plains in the middle of the continent until men ploughed them up. Cactuses thrive in the deserts of the southwest. Tropical trees grow quickly in the hot, wet forests of the south.

Peoples from all over the world have made their homes in North America. First came the ancestors of the AMERICAN INDIANS and ESKIMOS. Later came Europeans, who brought Negro slaves from Africa. Most North Americans speak English, French or Spanish, and are Protestant or Roman Catholic Christians. They live in more than 30 nations. The UNITED STATES and Canada are large, powerful and rich. But many of the nations of Central America and the WEST INDIES are small and poor.

Only one person in every ten people in the world lives in North America. Yet North Americans make half the manufactured goods on Earth. This is because North America's farms and mines produce huge amounts of food and minerals to feed the workers and supply materials for their factory machines.

NORTH SEA

This part of the Atlantic Ocean separates Great Britain from Scandinavia and other

A huge concrete oil rig being towed into the North Sea. Lowered into position, it drills for oil deep in the seabed.

northern parts of mainland Europe. The North Sea is quite shallow as seas go. If you lowered St Paul's Cathedral in London into the middle of the North Sea, the top would show above the waves. Winter storms often make this sea very dangerous for ships.

The North Sea is an important waterway. Some of the world's largest, busiest ports stand on its shores. Its waters are rich in fish, and the seabed holds oil and gas.

NORWAY

Norway is Europe's sixth largest country. This long, northern kingdom is wide in the south but narrow in the centre and the north. Mountains with forests, bare rocks and snow cover much of Norway. Steep inlets called FIORDS pierce its rocky coast.

North America's three largest nations are Canada, the United States and Mexico. Greenland belongs to Denmark, a nation in Europe. Small nations take up most of Central America (the mainland south of Mexico) and the West Indies islands.

Summers in Norway are cool and the winters long. It is very cold in the ARCTIC north, but the rainy west coast is kept fairly mild by the Gulf Stream.

Four million people live in Norway. Their capital is Oslo. Norwegians catch more fish than any other Europeans, and their North Sea oil wells are among Europe's richest.

NUCLEAR ENERGY

The nucleus, or 'heart', of an ATOM is made of tiny particles. Splitting nuclei (nuclear fission) and joining nuclei (nuclear fusion) gives huge amounts of energy. Nuclear fission produces the ATOMIC ENERGY used in nuclear power stations and atom bombs. Nuclear fusion is used in hydrogen bombs. One day it may be used in power stations.

Below: Four kinds of nut. Hazelnuts grow on hazel shrubs. Acorns grow on oak trees. Peanuts grow in soil on plants related to peas. Coconuts grow on palm trees. Coconuts and peanuts grow in the tropics.

Hazelnut

Peanut

Acorn

Coconut

NUMBERS

In STONE AGE times people showed a number like 20 or 30 by making 20 or 30 separate marks. In certain caves you can still see the marks that they made.

In time people invented special signs or groups of signs to show different numbers. Such signs are called *numerals*. For centuries many people used Roman numerals. But these are rather clumsy. For instance, the Roman numerals for 38 are XXXVIII. Our much simpler system uses Arabic numerals that were first used in India.

NURSING

People who are very ill, old or handicapped need nursing in their homes or in a hospital. Nursing can mean feeding, washing and giving treatment ordered by a doctor. It is hard work and needs special skills. Men and women train for years before becoming nurses. Modern nursing owes much to the example set by Florence NIGHTINGALE.

NUTS

Nuts are FRUITS with a hard, wooden shell. The seeds are called kernels. The kernels of many nuts are good to eat and rich in PROTEINS and FAT. Peanuts are crushed and made into peanut butter. Some people bake bread from chestnuts ground into flour.

NYLON

This is a strong, tough, elastic material made in factories. Its ingredients come from such things as coal, petroleum, air and water. Machines can make nylon stockings, carpets, dresses, tubes and brush bristles. Nylon articles are not damaged by mildew, cleaning fluids or most kinds of oil.

O

OAK TREES

Oaks are trees with NUTS called acorns. Some oaks measure over 11 metres (38 feet) around the trunk. They grow slowly and may live for 900 years. There are about 275 kinds of oak. Most have leaves with deeply notched (wavy) edges. But evergreen oaks have tough, shiny, smooth-edged leaves.

Oak wood is hard and slow to rot. People used to build sailing ships from it. Tannin from oak bark is used in making leather. CORK comes from cork oak bark. Some people eat the acorns of certain oaks.

OASIS

An oasis is a place where plants grow in a DESERT. It may be a small clump of palm trees, or much larger. Egypt's NILE Valley is a huge oasis. Oases are found where there is water. This can come from rivers, wells or springs. These may be fed by rain that falls on nearby mountains and seeps through rocks beneath the surface of the desert. People can make oases by drilling wells and digging IRRIGATION ditches.

Above: The common oak grows in Europe, North Africa and parts of Asia. Its acorns grow in scaly cups on stalks.

Below: Water drawn up from wells helps to irrigate this oasis. Walls protect it from the shifting desert sands that lie outside.

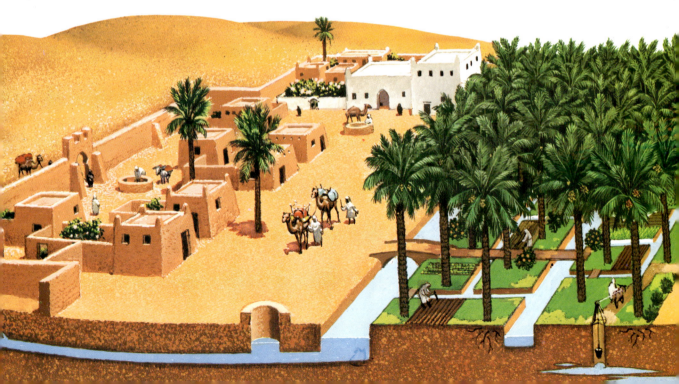

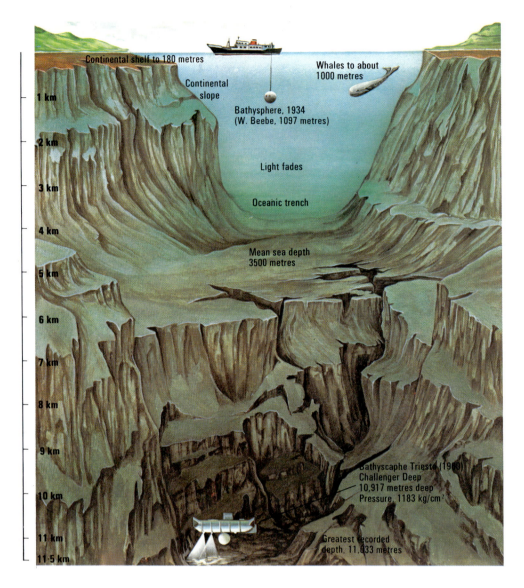

Continental shelf to 180 metres

Continental slope

Whales to about 1000 metres

1 km

Bathysphere, 1934 (W. Beebe, 1097 metres)

2 km

Light fades

3 km

Oceanic trench

4 km

Mean sea depth 3500 metres

5 km

6 km

7 km

8 km

9 km

Bathyscaphe Trieste (1960) Challenger Deep 10,917 metres deep Pressure, 1183 kg/cm²

10 km

11 km

Greatest recorded depth, 11,033 metres

11·5 km

OCEANS

Oceans cover nearly three-quarters of the surface of the Earth. If you put all the world's water in 100 giant tanks, 97 of them would be full of water from the oceans. The oceans are always losing water as water vapour, drawn up into the air by the Sun's heat. But most returns as RAIN. Rain water running off the land takes salts and other MINERALS to the oceans. For instance, enough sea water to fill a square tank one kilometre long would hold four million tonnes of magnesium. Oceans supply most of the magnesium we use.

There are four oceans. The largest and deepest is the PACIFIC OCEAN. The second ▷

Above: Underwater explorers have found that the ocean floor has valleys, cliffs and volcanic peaks. In the deepest parts the floor is being pulled down inside the Earth.

Below: Two views of the world as seen from space. They show us that the oceans cover nearly three-quarters of the Earth.

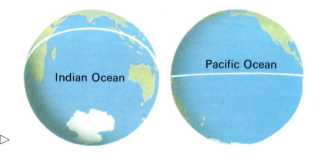

Indian Ocean

Pacific Ocean

largest is the ATLANTIC OCEAN. This is only half as large as the Pacific Ocean. The Indian Ocean is smaller but deeper than the Atlantic Ocean. The Arctic Ocean is the smallest and shallowest ocean of all.

The oceans are never still. Winds crinkle their surface into WAVES. Winds also drive the Gulf Stream and other currents that flow like rivers through the oceans. Every day the ocean surface falls and rises with the TIDES. In winter, polar sea-water freezes over. ICEBERGS from polar seas may drift hundreds of kilometres through the oceans.

Oceans are home to countless living things. The minerals in sea water help to nourish tiny plants drifting at the surface. The plants are food for tiny animals. These animals and plants are called plankton. Fish and some whales eat the plankton. In turn, small fish are eaten by larger hunters.

OCTOPUS

There are about 50 kinds of octopus. They are soft-bodied MOLLUSCS that live in the sea. Octopus means 'eight feet', but the eight tentacles of an octopus are usually called arms. The largest octopus has arms about 9 metres (30 feet) across, but most octopuses are no larger than a man's fist. Suckers on the tentacles grip crabs, shellfish or other prey. An octopus's tentacles pull its victim towards its mouth. This is hard and pointed, like the beak of a bird.

Each octopus hides in an underwater cave or crevice. It creeps about the seabed searching for food. Its two large eyes keep a watch for enemies. If danger threatens, the octopus may confuse its enemy by squirting an inky liquid. The ink hangs in the water like a cloud.

OIL

Oils are FATS and other greasy substances that do not dissolve in water. But when we say 'oil' we usually mean mineral oil. Mineral oil was formed millions of years ago from dead plants and animals. The oil was trapped under rocks. Engineers drill holes down through the surface rocks to reach the mineral oil beneath. It gushes up or can be pumped up to the surface.

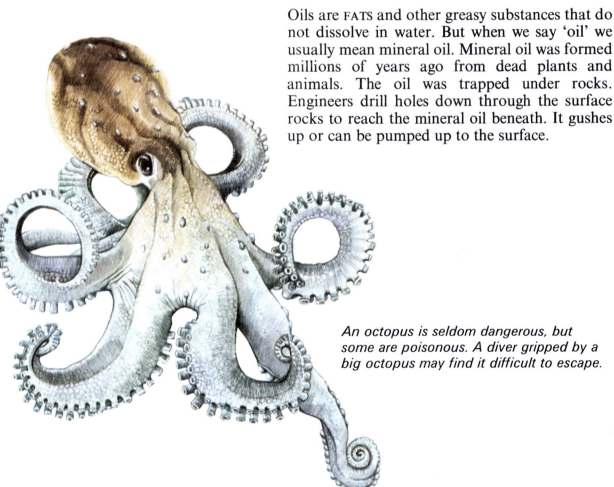

An octopus is seldom dangerous, but some are poisonous. A diver gripped by a big octopus may find it difficult to escape.

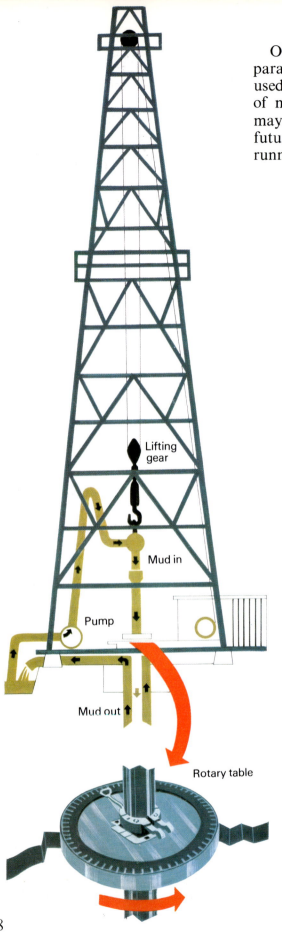

Oil refineries separate the oil to make petrol, paraffin and lubricating oil. Mineral oil is also used in making artificial fertilizer, many kinds of medicine, paint, plastics and detergent. We may run short of many of these things in the future, because the world's supplies of oil are running out.

OLIVES

These fruits grow on trees with slim, grey-green leaves and twisted trunks. Each FRUIT is shaped like a small plum. Farmers pick olives when they are green and unripe, or when ripe, they hit the trees with sticks to knock the olives on to sheets spread on the ground. Olives taste bitter and have a hard stone in the middle. People eat olives and cook food in olive oil made from crushed olives.

Most olives come from Italy, Spain and other countries by the Mediterranean Sea.

Lifting gear

Mud in

Pump

Mud out

Rotary table

OLYMPIC GAMES

This athletics competition is the world's oldest. The first known Olympic Games took place at Olympia in Greece in 776 BC. The Greek Games ended in AD 394. The modern Olympic Games began in 1894. They are held once every four years, each time in a different country. Athletes from different nations compete in races, jumping, gymnastics, football, yachting, and many more contests. The winners gain medals.

Left: A drilling rig drills for oil with a steel 'bit' at the end of lengths of pipe. The pipe is lowered by lifting gear and turned by a rotary table. Soft mud pumped down the pipe comes back up outside it, bringing bits of rock.

OPERA

An opera is a play with music. The 'actors' are singers who sing all or many of their words. An ORCHESTRA accompanies them.

The first opera was performed in Italy, nearly 400 years ago. Famous composers of serious opera include MOZART, Verdi, Puccini and Wagner.

Light, short operas are called operettas. Operettas of the 1800s gave rise to the tuneful musical comedies of the 1900s.

Right: The Australian Joan Sutherland is a famous opera singer.

ORANGES

Oranges are citrus FRUITS, like lemons and grapefruits. Orange seeds lie in juicy segments surrounded by a soft rind with a shiny orange or yellow skin. Orange juice is rich in sugar and VITAMINS.

People eat more oranges than any other citrus fruit. Sweet oranges are eaten raw. Bitter oranges are used in marmalade. Half of the world's oranges come from the United States and Brazil. But orange trees grow in many of the world's warm countries.

Sorting and packing freshly picked oranges in a Greek orange grove. Some of the fruit may be sent to other countries.

OPOSSUM

Opossums are MARSUPIALS found in North and South America. Some look like rats, others look like mice. The Virginia opossum is as big as a cat. This is North America's only marsupial. It climbs trees and can cling on with its tail. A female has up to 18 babies, each no larger than a honeybee. If danger threatens, the Virginia opossum pretends to be dead. If a person pretends to be hurt, we say he is 'playing possum'.

Left: A mother opossum and her babies. Newborn babies live in their mother's pouch. Later, she carries them on her back.

ORANG-UTAN

This big, red-haired APE comes from the islands of Borneo and Sumatra. Its name comes from Malay words meaning 'man of the woods'. A male is as heavy as a man, but not so tall. Orang-utans use their long arms to swing through the branches of trees as they hunt for fruit and leaves to eat. Each night they make a nest high up in the trees. A leafy roof helps to keep out rain.

Man is the orang-utan's main enemy. Hunters kill mothers to catch their babies and sell them to zoos. Orang-utans are already scarce. They could become extinct.

Right: A male orang-utan from Borneo. His cheeks have huge flaps of skin. Some males are almost too heavy to climb and spend a lot of time on the ground.

ORBIT

An orbit is the curved path of something that spins around another object in space. Man-made satellites and the MOON travel around the Earth in orbits. Each planet, including the Earth, has its own orbit around the SUN. Every orbit is a loop rather than a circle. An orbiting object tries to move in a straight line but is pulled by GRAVITY towards the object that it orbits.

Below: This diagram shows how different groups of instruments are often arranged in a symphony orchestra. Violins, violas, cellos and double basses are kept apart, but they are all stringed instruments.

ORCHESTRA

An orchestra is a large group of musicians who play together. The word *orchestra* once meant 'dancing place'. In ancient Greek theatres, dancers and musicians performed on a space between the audience and the stage. When Italy invented OPERA, Italian theatres arranged their musicians in the same way. Soon, people used the word orchestra to describe the group of musicians, and not the place where they performed.

The modern orchestra owes much to Haydn. He arranged its MUSICAL INSTRUMENTS into four main groups: strings, woodwind, brass, and percussion. Most orchestras have a conductor.

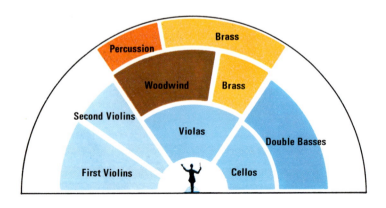

ORCHIDS

There are more than 15,000 kinds of these lovely flowering plants. Most live in warm, rainy forests. Many grow on trees. Their roots draw nourishment from the damp air. Usually each kind of orchid is fertilized by one kind of insect. But some can be pollinated by snails or hummingbirds. A rare orchid costs as much as a new car.

Right: Tropical orchids living on trees. Their spongy roots grow in moist air.

OSTRICH

This is the largest living BIRD. An ostrich may weigh twice as much as a man and stand more than 2 metres (7 feet) high. Ostriches cannot fly. If an enemy attacks, an ostrich runs away or kicks hard enough to rip a lion open. Scared ostriches never hide their heads in sand, as people used to think.

Ostriches live in Africa. They roam in herds, led by a male. The females lay large, white eggs in a nest dug in the sand. Ostriches can live for 50 years or more.

OTTERS

Otters are large relatives of the weasel. They have long, low bodies and short legs. An otter is a bit heavier than a dachshund dog. It hunts in water for fish and frogs. Thick fur keeps its body dry. It can swim nimbly by waggling its tail and body like an eel, and using its webbed hind feet.

Otters are wanderers. By night they hunt up and down a river, or roam overland to find new fishing grounds. They love to play by sliding down a bank of snow or mud.

OWLS

These birds of prey hunt mainly by night. They have soft feathers that make no sound as they fly. Their large, staring eyes help them to see in the dimmest light. Owls also have keen ears. Some owls can catch mice in pitch darkness by listening to the sounds they make. An owl can turn its head right round to look backwards.

When an owl eats a mouse or bird, it swallows it complete with bones and fur or feathers. Later, the owl spits out the remains in a pellet. You can sometimes find owl pellets on the ground.

There are over 500 kinds of owl. Some of the largest and smallest owls live in North America. The great grey owl of the north is as long as a man's arm. The elf owl of the south is shorter than a sparrow.

Above: Unlike other birds, an owl has eyes at the front of its head (instead of on either side). This helps it to find prey and to judge distances exactly. When an owl pounces, it seldom misses.

Above: The farmers of ancient Egypt used oxen for ploughing the land. Farmers in many countries still use oxen today.

OXEN

Oxen are a group of big, heavy animals that include domestic (farm) cattle, bison, wild and tame buffalo, and the YAK. Oxen have split hooves and a pair of curved horns. They eat grass. The heaviest domestic cattle can weigh two tonnes.

Many of us use the word 'ox' only for domestic cattle, especially the kinds that are kept for meat or for pulling carts or ploughs. People probably began domesticating cattle 9000 years ago in Greece.

OXYGEN

Oxygen is a gas. It is one of the most abundant ELEMENTS on Earth. It makes up one part in every five parts of AIR. Oxygen is found in water and many different rocks. Most of the weight of water, and half that of rocks, comes from the oxygen.

FIRE needs oxygen to burn. Almost all living things need oxygen for BREATHING and to give them the energy just to stay alive. Animals need extra oxygen to move about. PLANTS give out oxygen into the air.

OYSTERS

Oysters are MOLLUSCS with a soft body protected by a broad, hinged shell. This is rough on the outside. The inside of a pearl oyster's shell is smooth, shiny mother-of-pearl. Pearl oysters make PEARLS.

Several kinds of oyster are eaten as a food. People farm oysters in shallow coastal water. Oysters cling to empty shells, rocks or wooden posts on the seabed. When they have grown large enough they are harvested.

Below: A jar covers a candle burning in water. Burning uses up the oxygen in the air in the jar. Water rises in the jar by an amount equal to that of the oxygen used.

P

PACIFIC OCEAN

This is the largest and deepest of all the OCEANS. Its waters cover more than one-third of the world. All the CONTINENTS would fit inside the Pacific Ocean with room to spare. Its deepest part is deep enough to drown the world's highest mountain.

The Pacific Ocean lies west of the Americas, and east of Australia and Asia. It stretches from the frozen far north to the frozen far south. There are thousands of tiny islands in the Pacific. Most were formed when VOLCANOES grew up from the seabed. Sometimes earthquakes shake the seabed and send out huge TIDAL WAVES.

PAINTING

Painting is a form of ART in which people use coloured paint to make pictures on canvas, plaster, wood, or paper. Today most people paint for their own pleasure. But this was not always so.

In the Middle Ages most artists worked for the Church. Their paintings showed scenes from Bible stories. Such paintings helped people who could not read to understand the Bible.

By the 1400s Europe's rich princes and merchants were paying artists to paint pictures to decorate their homes. The pictures might be family portraits, still-life scenes of flowers and fruit, or landscapes showing their cities and country estates.

In the 1800s many artists began trying out new ideas. For example, some tried to give a feeling of the light and shade in a landscape. Others used bright, flat colours to bring out the patterns in still-lifes and landscapes. In the 1900s Pablo PICASSO and other artists began to experiment with abstract paintings. These concentrate on the basic shapes, colours and patterns of the things painted.

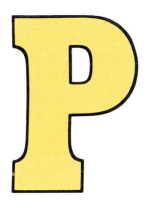

Left: Vittore Carpaccio painted these Italian women and their pets nearly 500 years ago. Old paintings can show us how people used to dress and behave.

PAKISTAN

Pakistan lies between India and Iran. There are more than 75 million Pakistanis. Most of them follow the religion of ISLAM.

Much of Pakistan is hot and dry, but crops such as wheat and cotton grow with the help of water from the Indus river. The Indus flows from the HIMALAYAS to the Arabian Sea. The capital is called Islamabad.

PALESTINE

Palestine is a land on the eastern shore of the Mediterranean Sea. Most of the stories in the BIBLE took place there. Palestine gets its name from the Philistines who once lived in part of it.

By 1800 BC the Hebrews had made Palestine their home. Later they ruled it as two nations, called Israel and Judah. Both of these nations were then taken over by foreign rulers.

Today, most of Palestine lies in the Jewish nation of ISRAEL. The rest is part of Jordan, Lebanon and Syria.

PALM TREES

A palm tree has leaves that sprout straight out of the top of its trunk, rather like the fingers of an outspread hand. There are more than 1000 kinds of palm. Not all are trees. Some are shrubs and others are vines. Most palms grow in warm climates.

Palms are useful plants. People make mats and baskets from their leaves. We eat the fruits of some palms, such as COCONUTS.

PANAMA CANAL

The Panama Canal crosses Panama in Central America. Ships use it as a short cut between the Atlantic and Pacific Oceans. Before it was finished in 1914, ships from the United States' east coast had to sail right round South America to reach the west coast. Sets of locks on the CANAL (right) raise and lower ships as they cross the hilly countryside of Panama.

PANDAS

There are two kinds of panda. Both live in the forests of east Asia. The giant panda looks like a black and white bear. It lives in BAMBOO forests in China. The red panda is not much larger than a cat. It has a bushy tail and reddish fur. Both kinds eat plants. Their nearest relatives are the raccoons of North and South America.

Above: A giant panda is often one of the favourite animals in a zoo. But nowadays few zoos have pandas as they are becoming very scarce in China, where they come from.

PAPER

Paper gets its name from papyrus, a plant that grows in swamps in Egypt. The ancient Egyptians made a kind of paper from papyrus. But the Chinese invented paper as we know it. About 1900 years ago they learnt to separate the fibres from mulberry bark. They soaked these, then dried them, making a flat, dry sheet that they could write on. Paper is still made of plant fibres. Some of the best paper is made of COTTON. Newspaper is made from wood.

PARIS

Paris is the capital of FRANCE, and France's largest city. More than eight million people live there. The River Seine divides the city into the left bank and the right bank.

If you gaze down on Paris from the Eiffel Tower you will see many parks and gardens, fine squares and tree-lined avenues. Other famous landmarks are the cathedral of Nôtre Dame, the basilica of the Sacré Coeur, the Arc de Triomphe and the Louvre Palace, now a famous museum.

Paris is famous for its women's fashions, jewellery and perfume. Another important industry is car manufacturing.

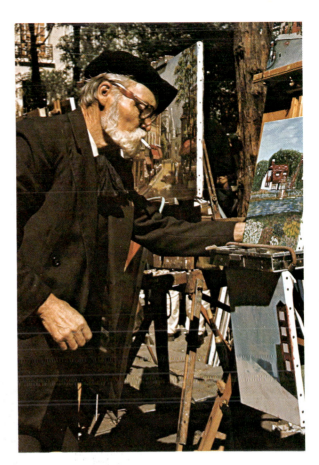

Above: Many artists live and work in a part of Paris called Montmartre.

Inside the Chamber of the House of Commons. The British Parliament was a model for parliaments in many other lands.

PARLIAMENT

A parliament is a meeting of people held to make a nation's LAWS. One of the first parliaments was Iceland's *Althing*, which was founded more than 1000 years ago.

In Great Britain, the HOUSES OF PARLIAMENT stand by the River Thames in London. Members of Parliament chosen by the people sit in the House of Commons. Certain noblemen and churchmen sit in the House of Lords. The British Parliament was started in 1265. It grew gradually out of a meeting of nobles who advised the king. In the 1300s it was divided into the two Houses, and by the 1700s Parliament had become more powerful than the king.

255

PASSPORT

A passport is a travel document issued by the government of a nation. The passport gives a citizen of that nation permission to travel abroad. Many countries refuse to let foreigners in without a passport.

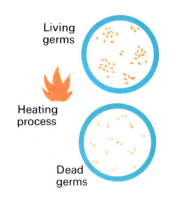

Right: Pasteur killed most germs in milk by heating and then cooling it quickly. Most milk is now pasteurized *in this way.*

PASTEUR, LOUIS

Louis Pasteur (1822–1895) was a great French scientist. He proved that bacteria and other germs cause diseases. Pasteur injected weakened germs into animals and people to stop them catching the diseases those germs usually caused. He invented *pasteurization*: a way of heating milk and cooling it quickly to make it safe to drink. Pasteur also found out how tiny yeast cells turn sugar into alcohol.

PEACOCK

Peacocks are male peafowl. Peafowl are big birds that live in Asia. Peacocks attract their mates by spreading out the long, blue-green feathers that grow just above the tail (below). Big spots on the feathers look like rows of eyes.

PEARLS

Pearls are gems formed in living OYSTERS. Many look like tiny silvery balls. They are made of *nacre*. This is the same substance that forms mother-of-pearl, the shiny lining inside an oyster shell.

If a grain of sand gets inside the shell the oyster covers the grain with layers of nacre. In time these layers form a pearl. People often put beads in oysters to persuade them to make pearls. Such *cultured* pearls come mainly from Japan. Most natural pearls are found in the Persian Gulf.

An oyster split open to reveal the pearls that it has formed. People open an oyster by cutting through the tough muscle that holds both shell halves together.

PELICANS

Pelicans are large water birds. They have a pouch under the beak which they use to scoop up fish. Pelicans are the biggest birds with webbed feet. The outstretched wings of a large pelican can measure almost 3 metres (10 feet). There are six kinds of pelican. Most of them live in warm parts of the world.

PENDULUM

This is a hanging weight that is free to swing to and fro. When the weight is pulled to one side and then released, GRAVITY sets it swinging to and fro in a curved path called an *arc*. Each swing takes the same amount of time, no matter whether the swing is big or small. This makes pendulums useful for keeping time in CLOCKS. After a while a pendulum stops. But a pendulum clock keeps its pendulum swinging with a device called an escapement. This makes the 'tick-tock' sound.

Right: In this clock a pendulum (1) is swung by an escapement (2) that controls a toothed wheel turned by a slowly falling weight (3).

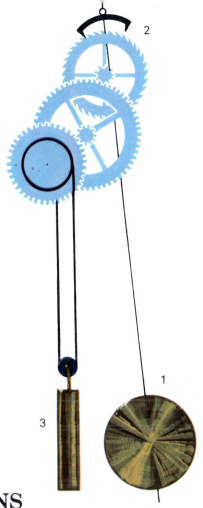

PENGUINS

Penguins are swimming birds. They cannot fly, because their wings are shaped as flippers. Penguins use their wings to 'row' themselves through the sea. They swim and dive well. A penguin in the water can leap up nearly 2 metres (6 feet) to land on a rock or ice.

All penguins come from the southern part of the world. Emperor penguins live in the ANTARCTIC. In winter each female lays one egg on the ice. Her mate rolls the egg onto his feet and warms it for months until it hatches.

Below: A male Adélie penguin brings his mate a stone to help to build their hard, cold nest.

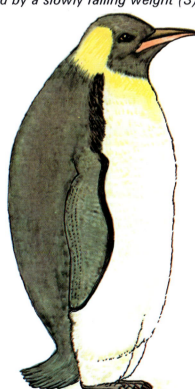

The emperor penguin is the biggest of all the penguins

PERU

Peru is the third largest nation in SOUTH AMERICA. You could fit France, Great Britain, Spain, West Germany and Yugoslavia inside Peru with room to spare.

Peru touches five other countries. Western Peru is washed by the Pacific Ocean. The sharp snowy peaks of the high Andès Mountains cross Peru from north to south like a giant backbone. Between the mountains and the ocean lies a thin strip of desert. East of the mountains hot, steamy forests stretch around the AMAZON.

About 18 million people live in Peru. Many are Indians, or descended from Spanish settlers, or a mixture of the two. The capital is Lima, near the sea. Peruvians grow sugar cane and coffee. The sheep and LLAMAS in the mountains produce wool. Peru mines copper, iron and silver. Its ocean fishing grounds usually hold more fish than those of any other nation in the world.

People have been building towns in Peru for several thousand years. The most famous people were the INCAS who ran a mountain empire. In the 1530s the Spaniards seized Peru and ruled it for Spain. Since the 1820s Peru has been an independent nation.

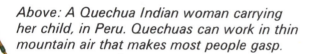

Above: A Quechua Indian woman carrying her child, in Peru. Quechuas can work in thin mountain air that makes most people gasp.

A pharaoh, richly dressed in kilt and cloak. His double crown shows he ruled the north and south. His crook and flail show the care and power that he exercised.

PHARAOHS

We use the word *pharaoh* to mean 'king' when we talk of the kings of ancient EGYPT. (The ancient Egyptians gave their kings other titles as well.) 'Pharaoh' comes from *peraa*, which means 'great house'. This was the royal palace where the pharaoh lived.

Egyptians believed that each pharaoh was the same god in the shape of a different man. He lived in certain ways said to have been fixed by the gods. The pharaoh was said to look after all the needs of his people. He was supposed to rule everything.

PHOTOGRAPHY

The word *photography* comes from Greek words that mean 'drawing with light'. When you take a photograph, rays of LIGHT produce a picture on the film in your CAMERA.

What happens is this. First you look through a viewfinder at the subject you want to photograph. Then you press a knob that lets light from the subject enter the camera. The light passes a LENS that produces an image of your subject on a film in the camera. But the image shows up only when the film is developed (treated with chemicals). A developed film is called a *negative*. This shows black things white, and white things black. From negatives you can print *positives*, the final photos.

Above: One of the first kinds of camera. It used metal plates for making prints. These were called daguerreotypes, *after their French inventor, Louis Daguerre.*

PIANO

A piano is a keyboard instrument with up to 88 keys. When you press a key a padded hammer hits two or three wires. These vibrate and produce a sound. Short wires produce high notes; long wires, low notes. The sounds can be long, short, loud or soft.

PICASSO, PABLO

Pablo Picasso (1881–1973) was the most famous artist of this century. He was born in Spain but lived mostly in France.

People said Picasso could draw before he learnt to talk. Early on he painted poor people and circus performers. He disliked paintings that looked like photographs, and admired the curving shapes of African

Picasso painted this nightmarish picture in 1937 to show the misery and horror of war. It is called Guernica, after a town bombed in the Spanish Civil War.

sculpture. Picasso began painting people as simple shapes like cubes, and as if they could be seen from several sides at once. Picasso did hundreds of paintings in many styles. He also did sculpture and pottery.

PIGEONS AND DOVES

Pigeons and doves are birds that eat seeds or fruit. Many make soft cooing sounds. Pigeons are larger than doves. The crowned pigeon is bigger than a chicken, but the diamond dove is almost as small as a lark.

Tame pigeons all come from rock doves, which nest on cliffs. Homing pigeons will fly great distances to return home. A bird once flew 1300 km (800 miles) in one day.

PIGS

These farmyard animals have a long, heavy body; short legs ending in hoofed toes; a long snout; and a short, curly tail. Males are called boars. Females are called sows. The heaviest boars weigh over a tonne.

Pigs provide us with bacon, ham, pork and lard. Different parts of a pig's body are used to make brushes, glue, leather and soap.

Domestic pigs are descended from the wild boar of Asian and European forests.

PINEAPPLES

Pineapples earned their name because they look like large pine cones. Pineapples are big, juicy fruits from the tropics. They grow on top of short stems belonging to plants with long, spiky leaves. Three-quarters of all pineapples come from Hawaii.

PINE TREES

These CONIFERS are more plentiful than any other kind. Pine trees have larger cones and larger needle-shaped leaves than other conifers. The tallest pine is North America's sugar pine. It can grow to 64 metres (210 feet). Pines can live in places too cold or dry for most other trees.

260

The nine planets of the Solar System. Mercury is the smallest, and Jupiter the largest. The planet nearest the Sun is Mercury. The planet farthest from the Sun is Pluto. Planets do not give out light. They only reflect the light from the Sun.

Below: The upper picture shows the knobbly cones of a lodgepole pine. The lower picture shows an open pine cone releasing seeds.

PLANETS

The word planet comes from a Greek word meaning wanderer. Long ago, skywatchers gave this name to 'stars' that seemed to move instead of keeping still like the rest. We now know that planets are not STARS but objects that travel around stars.

The EARTH and other planets of our SOLAR SYSTEM travel around the star we call the SUN. Each planet travels in its own ORBIT. But they all move in the same direction, and, except for Mercury and Pluto, they lie at about the same level.

Astronomers think the planets came from a band of gas and dust that once whirled around the Sun. They think that GRAVITY pulled parts of this band together as blobs that became planets.

The nine planets in the solar system are MERCURY, VENUS, EARTH, MARS, JUPITER, SATURN, URANUS, NEPTUNE, and PLUTO.

PLANTS

Most living things are either animals or plants. Plants differ from animals in several ways. For instance, green plants can make food with the help of CHLOROPHYLL. Each plant CELL is surrounded by a wall of cellulose. Most plants cannot move about.

Below: Plant orange seeds in a flower pot and keep it somewhere warm and light. The seeds may grow into young orange trees.

Below: Androsace is found on windy mountains. It grows in low clumps that cannot be uprooted by the wind. Its leaves and flowers are thick and help trap warm air.

There are more than 300,000 kinds of living plant. The smallest are one-celled plants so tiny that you need a microscope to see them. The largest plants are TREES that can weigh as much as 2000 tonnes.

Plants are divided into different groups, designed for life in different places. A SEAWEED is an alga, a floppy type of plant found in water. LICHENS grow on bare rock, but MOSSES need wet soil. These are both low-growing plants. Most true land plants have stems that are strong enough to hold their LEAVES above the ground. These plants include many ferns and plants that grow from SEEDS. Among these are the CONIFERS and plants producing FLOWERS.

Plants are the most important of all living things. They make the food all animals depend on. Plants also provide such useful substances as wood and cotton.

PLASTICS

Plastics are man-made substances and can be moulded into many different shapes. They are used to make anything from furniture and car seats to shoes and bags or cups and plates.

Most plastics are largely made from

chemicals obtained from mineral oil. Coal, limestone, salt, and water are also used. Plastics can be hard, soft, or runny. They can be made to look like glass, metal, wood or other substances.

Hard plastics are used in radio and camera cases. But fine threads of the hard plastic NYLON make soft stockings.

Plastic bags and squeezy bottles are made of soft plastics like *polyethylene*. (Poly means 'many'.) Each particle of poly-ethylene is made up of many of the particles that form the gas called ethylene.

POETRY

Poetry is one of the oldest forms of writing. Poets choose words carefully, for their sound as well as their meaning. Poems are usually written in verses. The lines have a rhythm built up by strong and weak sounds. Sometimes rhyme is used for extra rhythm.

POISON

Poisons are chemical substances that kill or damage living things. Some poisons get

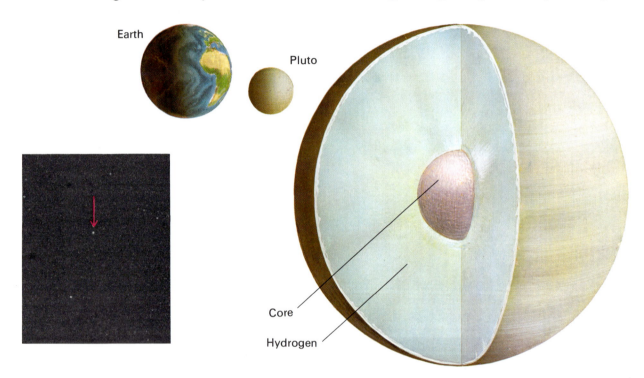

Earth

Pluto

Core

Hydrogen

PLUTO (PLANET)

The planet Pluto is named after the Greek god who ruled the dreary world of the dead. Pluto must be bitterly cold as it is farther away from the Sun than any of the other PLANETS. It is almost 40 times farther from the Sun than the EARTH.

Pluto spins and moves around the Sun much more slowly than the Earth. A day on Pluto may equal nearly a week on Earth. One year on Pluto lasts almost 248 of our years.

Pluto is only half as wide as the Earth, and weighs one-sixth as much.

Pluto is probably made up in much the same way as the Earth, with an iron core and a rocky surface. The red arrow (left) points to Pluto as seen from Earth. It is so small and far away it was not discovered until 1930.

into the body through the skin. Some are swallowed. Poisonous gases are harmful if someone breathes them in with air.

Different poisons work in different ways. Strong ACIDS or alkalis 'burn'. NERVE poisons can stop the heart. Some other poisons can make the body bleed inside.

DRUGS called antidotes can cure people who are suffering from certain poisons.

Below: A policeman stops traffic to let people cross a busy street. Police of different countries wear different uniforms but their tasks are very much the same. They keep order and fight crime.

POLAND

This is the seventh largest country in EUROPE. Poland lies in eastern Europe, south of the Baltic Sea. Most of Poland is low farmland although forests sprawl across the Carpathian Mountains in the south. Poland's largest river is the Vistula. This rises in the mountains and flows into the Baltic Sea. Rivers often freeze in Poland's cold, snowy winters.

There are about 36 million Poles. Most of them speak Polish, and many are Roman Catholics. Their capital is Warsaw.

Poland grows more flax and potatoes than almost any other land. Only three other countries mine more coal than Poland. Its factories make machinery and ships.

POLICE

Police work for a government to keep law and order in their country. Their main task is to see that everyone obeys their country's LAWS. Part of this job is protecting people's lives and property. Police also help to control crowds and traffic. They help people hurt by accidents, and they take charge of lost children.

Policemen try to prevent crime, and track down and capture criminals. This can be dangerous and sometimes they are killed.

POLLEN

Pollen is a fine yellow powder found on many FLOWERS. Each kind of flowering plant has pollen grains of a special shape and size. Some are so small that 6000 would make a row no longer than a man's thumb.

Pollen grains contain male CELLS. When these meet *ovules* (female cells) on the same flower or another flower they produce SEEDS. But to do this the pollen grains must first reach the *stigma*. When pollen reaches the stigma, it grows down inside a stalk to reach the ovule. This process is called *pollination*.

Some flowers are pollinated by the wind. Others are pollinated by insects.

Pollen basket

POMPEII

Two thousand years ago, Pompeii was a small Roman city in southern Italy. A sudden disaster killed many of its citizens and drove out the rest. But the same disaster preserved the streets and buildings. Today, visitors to Pompeii can learn a great deal about what life was like inside a Roman city.

In AD 79 the nearby volcano VESUVIUS erupted and showered Pompeii with volcanic ash and cinders. Poisonous gases swirled through the streets. About one citizen in every ten was poisoned by fumes or burnt to death by hot ash. The rest escaped. Ash and cinders soon covered up the buildings. In time the people living in the surrounding countryside forgot that Pompeii had ever been there.

For centuries Pompeii's thick coat of ash protected it from the weather. At last, in the 1700s, people began to dig it out. The digging has gone on until today. Archaeologists discovered buildings, streets, tools, and statues. They even found hollows left in the ash by the decayed bodies of people and dogs killed by the eruption. The archaeologists poured plaster in these hollows. They let the plaster harden, then they cleared away the ash. They found that the

Above: This garden at Pompeii has been made to look the same as it did 2000 years ago. There are statues, a fountain, and a covered walk with a tiled roof.

plaster had formed life-size models of the dead bodies.

More than half Pompeii is now uncovered. You can step inside its Roman homes and temples, and tread stone streets with wheel ruts worn by carts of long ago.

POPES

'Pope' is a title of the head of the ROMAN CATHOLIC CHURCH. (The word 'pope' comes from *papa*, which means 'father'.) The Pope is also the Bishop of Rome. He rules the VATICAN CITY inside the city of Rome.

Roman Catholics believe that Jesus made St Peter the first Pope. Since then there have been hundreds of Popes. Each time one dies, churchmen choose another. The Pope makes church laws, chooses bishops, and can declare people SAINTS.

PORTUGAL

This is a narrow, oblong country in southwest EUROPE. It is sandwiched between the

Atlantic Ocean and Spain, a country four times the size of Portugal.

Much of Portugal is mountainous. Rivers flow from the mountains through valleys and across plains to the sea. Portugal's mild winters and warm summers help its people to grow olives, oranges and rice. Its grapes produce port, a wine named after the Portuguese city of Oporto. Portugal's woods yield more CORK than those of any other nation. Its fishermen catch sardines and other sea fish. Portugal has mines and factories.

There are about 10 million Portuguese. They speak Portuguese, a language much like Spanish. Their capital is Lisbon.

Left: A fisherman mends nets at Nazaré in western Portugal. Fishing provides work for 30,000 people in Portugal. The country cans sardines for sale abroad.

POST OFFICE

The post office is a government organization that brings the letters we receive and takes the letters that we send. Many towns and villages have a building called a post office, where postal work is done.

To send a letter you must first address its envelope, then add a stamp bought from a post office. The stamp is to pay for what happens after you have put the letter in a mailbox for collection.

Letters collected by local postmen are cancelled (marked so the stamps cannot be used again). Then they are sorted according to the towns they are to go to. The sorted letters travel quickly overland by train. Letters going overseas usually go by plane.

When letters reach the end of their journey, they are sorted according to streets and house numbers. A postman then delivers them.

France

Denmark

Victorian Britain

United States

Left: Mailboxes from different lands, and a modern postal sorting office where a machine separates letters and parcels. Sorting is speeded up if the items are marked with district postal codes.

POTATOES

Potatoes are valuable foods. They are rich in STARCHES and contain PROTEINS and different VITAMINS. Potatoes must be cooked to give nourishment that we can use.

Potato plants are related to tomatoes. Each plant is low and bushy with a soft stem. Each potato grows on a root as a kind of swelling called a tuber. When its tubers have grown, the plant dies. But new plants spring up from the tubers.

Potatoes were first grown by South American Indians. Spanish explorers brought potatoes back to Europe. Today most are grown in Europe and Asia.

Right: This potato plant has been removed from the soil to show its roots and tubers. The old, dark tuber fed the growing stem and roots. Then the leaves and roots made food to produce young tubers.

Young tuber

Old tuber

POTTER, BEATRIX

Beatrix Potter (1866–1943) was a British writer who wrote the words and painted the pictures in a series of books for young children. The most famous one is probably *The Tale of Peter Rabbit*, but she wrote many others about different animals too.

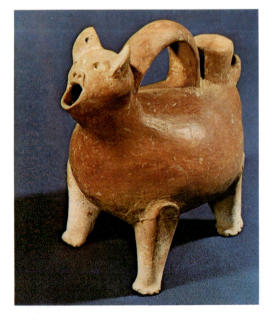

POTTERY

All kinds of objects made of baked CLAY are called pottery. Many cups, saucers, plates, bowls, pots, vases and other tools and ornaments are made of this very useful substance.

People have been making pottery for thousands of years. Early pots were thick, drab and gritty. They leaked, and they cracked if heated. In time people learnt to make pottery that was more useful and more beautiful. Today, there are two main kinds of pottery. These are porcelain and

Left: A Chinese potter made this animal-shaped vessel about 4000 years ago. Early on, potters discovered how to make shaped pots and how to paint decorations on them.

266

stoneware. Porcelain is fine pottery made with white China clay. Thin porcelain lets the light show through. Stoneware (also called earthenware) is often made of blue, brown, grey, red or yellow clay. Stoneware is usually thicker than porcelain and it does not let the light show through.

To make a pot, a potter puts a lump of moist clay on a spinning disc rather like a record turntable. He uses thumbs and fingers to shape the clay into a pot. He leaves this pot to dry. Next he may coat it with a wet mixture called a glaze. Then he fires (heats) the pot with others in an oven called a kiln. Firing makes the pots rock hard and turns their glaze into a smooth, hard, shiny coat. This makes pots leakproof. It also decorates them. Different glazes produce different colours.

Left: Two ancient pots from the Middle East. The one with simple patterns and a human shape (top) was made in what is now Turkey. The finely shaped pot below it came from Crete.

Above: Day-old chicks soon grow into adults.

POULTRY

All birds kept for meat or eggs are known as poultry. To most people, poultry means chickens, DUCKS, geese and TURKEYS. But guinea fowl, OSTRICHES, partridges, PEACOCKS, pheasants, and PIGEONS can be kept as poultry too.

Chickens outnumber other kinds of poultry. There are probably more chickens than people, and they lay enough eggs to give everyone on Earth several hundred eggs each year. Chickens also produce meat more cheaply than sheep or cattle. This is because it costs less in food to produce a kilogram of chicken meat than it costs to make a kilogram of beef or lamb or mutton.

PREHISTORIC ANIMALS

Prehistoric animals are those that lived before history began, about 5000 years ago. We know about them from their FOSSILS found in rocks. Different kinds of creature lived at different times. Each kind came from another by the process of evolution.

The first prehistoric animals probably looked like little blobs of jelly. They lived in seas perhaps 1000 million years ago. ▷

Larger animals without backbones came later. By 600 million years ago there were jellyfish and sponges much like those alive today. There were also strange beasts with jointed bodies. From these, much later, came crabs, insects, millipedes and spiders.

The first backboned animals were strange, armoured fishes that lived about 500 million years ago. In time there were some fishes that could breathe dry air and crawl about on land on stumpy fins. These fishes gave rise to prehistoric AMPHIBIANS. Some looked like SALAMANDERS the size of crocodiles. From amphibians came early REPTILES, and all the other backboned animals.

About 200 million years ago began the Age of DINOSAURS. Some dinosaurs may have weighed 250 tonnes and were as long as several buses. These were the largest land animals ever. Above them flew the first BIRDS. There were also pterodactyls, strange furry beasts with wings like bats. One kind was the largest animal that ever flew. Meanwhile big reptiles with limbs shaped as paddles hunted fishes in the seas.

About 65 million years ago the dinosaurs, pterodactyls, and strange sea reptiles died out. The new masters of the land were pre-historic birds and MAMMALS. Some gave rise to the birds and mammals of today.

PREHISTORIC MAN

Prehistoric man lived long ago before there were any written records of history. We know about these early times from the tools, weapons and bodies of ancient people, which are dug out of the ground. Prehistory is divided into the STONE AGE, the Bronze Age and the Iron Age. The ages are named after the materials that people used to make their tools and weapons.

The Stone Age lasted for a long time. It began around 2½ to 3 million years ago when man-like creatures began to appear on the Earth. They were different from the ape-like animals which lived at the same time. They had larger brains, used stone tools and could walk upright. They lived by hunting animals and collecting plants.

Around 800,000 years ago, a more man-like creature appeared. Scientists call this kind of early man *Homo erectus*. This means 'upright man'. *Homo erectus* is probably the ancestor of more advanced types of man, called *Homo sapiens*. This means 'intelligent man'. One kind of *Homo sapiens* was Neanderthal Man, who appeared about 100,000 years ago. Neanderthal Man finally died out and was replaced by modern man, who is called *Homo sapiens sapiens*. Modern man first appeared in Europe and Asia around 35,000 years ago.

Towards the end of the long Stone Age, prehistoric people first began to use metals. The first metal they used was copper. They made copper tools about 10,000 years ago. About 5000 years ago, people invented bronze. Bronze is a hard ALLOY of copper and tin. This was the start of the Bronze

Right: These were two kinds of big, mammal-like reptile that roamed South Africa more than 200 million years ago. Those with blunt teeth ate plants. But these beasts were killed and eaten by others that had sharper teeth and an appetite for meat.

268

Age, when the earliest civilizations began. The Bronze Age ended about 3300 years ago, when people learned how to make iron tools. Iron is much harder than bronze. With iron tools, people could develop farming and cities more quickly than ever before. The start of the Iron Age marks the beginning of modern times.

PRESBYTERIANS

Presbyterians are PROTESTANTS whose churches are governed by ministers and elders, called *presbyters*.

A French religious thinker called John Calvin (1509–1564) first thought of this idea. There are now about 50 million Presbyterians. Many of them live in France, Hungary, the Netherlands, Northern Ireland, Scotland, Switzerland and the United States.

PRESIDENTS OF THE UNITED STATES

The president of the UNITED STATES is the world's most powerful elected person. He is head of state, like the queen or king of Britain. He is also head of the government, like a PRIME MINISTER. The president is also the commander-in-chief of the army, navy and air force. The American people elect a president for a four-year term. A president may serve two terms. From 1789 to 1980, the USA had 39 presidents. The first was George WASHINGTON. Other famous presidents of the past include Thomas Jefferson, Abraham Lincoln, and John Kennedy.

Winston Churchill (sitting on the left of the picture) was prime minister of Britain during World War II. He is seen here with Franklin Roosevelt (on the right), who was president of the United States in the 1930s and 1940s.

Above: Abraham Lincoln was the 16th president of the United States. He served from 1861 to 1865.

PRIME MINISTER

A prime minister is a head of government. Britain and many other countries have a prime minister. The prime minister is usually the leader of the political party (or group of parties) with the greatest number of seats in PARLIAMENT. He chooses a group of people to help him run the government. These people are called *ministers*. The group is called a *cabinet*.

PRINTING

Printing is a way of copying words and pictures by mechanical means.

In *relief* printing, ink is put on to raised images, such as letters. The letters are then pressed against paper. The most common method is called *letterpress* printing. In *intaglio* or *gravure* printing, the image is not raised but cut away, or etched.

In other kinds of printing, the ink is put on to a flat surface. *Offset lithography* uses printing plates that are made photographically. The plates are treated with chemicals so that the greasy ink sticks only to the images to be printed.

The earliest printing, using wooden blocks, was done in China, probably as early as the AD 500s. Johannes GUTENBERG of Germany founded modern printing in the 1400s.

In this printing works in the 1500s, the man on the left picks out metal letters and arranges them on a stick, forming a line. The lines are put in the tray on the right, and inked. A sheet of paper is placed over the tray and pressed down by a clamp.

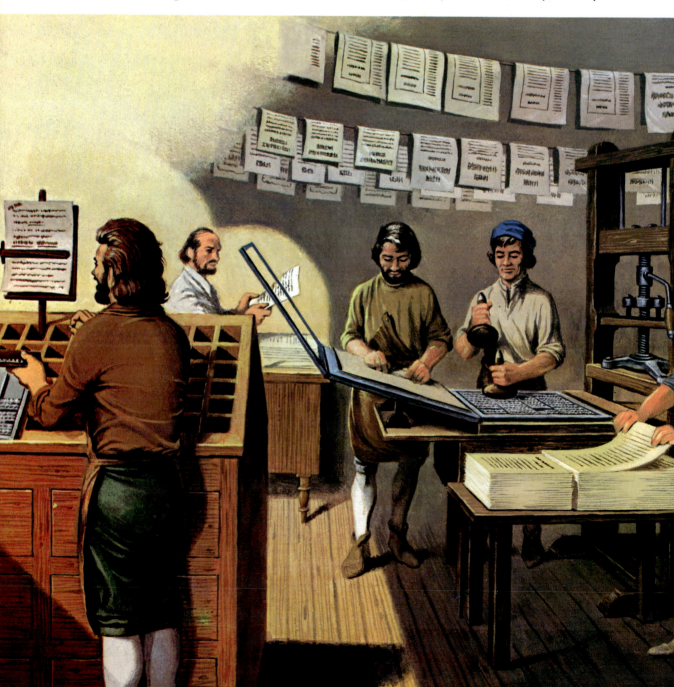

PROTEINS

Proteins are substances in food which are vital to life. They contain CARBON, HYDROGEN, OXYGEN and nitrogen. They build up body tissue, especially muscle, and repair broken-down CELLS. They also give heat and energy, help us to grow, and help to protect us from disease. Our bodies do not store extra protein, so we must eat a regular supply.

Foods which come from animals provide most of our proteins. But some plant foods, such as groundnuts, peas and beans, are also rich in protein.

Right: Meat and fish are rich in protein. So are cheese, eggs and nuts. Most vegetables lack protein, but they contain important minerals and vitamins.

PROTESTANTS

Protestants are Christians who do not belong to the Roman Catholic or the Eastern Orthodox churches. Protestants believe that the things written in the BIBLE are more important than any rules made by church leaders. There are some passages in the Bible which can be explained in different ways. Protestants believe that people should make up their own minds about what these mean.

Protestantism began with the Reformation, when Martin Luther led a movement to change the ROMAN CATHOLIC CHURCH. In 1529, the Roman Catholic Church in Germany tried to stop people from following Luther's ideas. Luther's followers protested against this and were then called Protestants. Early Protestant groups included the Lutherans, Calvinists (PRESBYTERIANS) and Anglicans. Later groups included the Baptists, Congregationalists, Methodists and QUAKERS.

Roman Catholics met at the Council of Trent in Italy between 1545 and 1563. They made changes to strengthen the Church against Protestantism.

PUFFINS

Puffins are birds of the auk family. The Atlantic puffin lives in the North Atlantic Ocean. It is a black and white bird, with orange feet and an odd, flattened, orange bill. It breeds in summer. In winter it goes far out to sea, feeding on fish. Puffins swim well underwater.

PULLEYS

A pulley is a simple MACHINE. It consists of a wheel on a fixed axle. A rope or belt passed over the wheel is tied to a load. When the rope is pulled, the load is raised. Such pulleys raise loads that are too heavy or difficult to lift otherwise.

A *movable pulley* runs along a rope. One end of the rope is fixed to a support. The load hangs from the pulley itself. When the other end of the rope is pulled, the pulley moves the load along the rope. Pulleys are used in machines such as cranes.

Above: Puffins usually nest in colonies on rocky coasts and islands. Their nests are holes or burrows in the ground.

Below: The invention of the wheel led to a useful lifting device, the pulley. The pulley was invented in about 800 BC.

PUPPETS

Puppets are dolls or figures that are made to move. Some, such as marionettes, are moved with strings. Others, like glove puppets, are moved with the hand. Puppets have been popular for over 2000 years. They are often used to 'act' out a story or a short play.

PYGMIES

Pygmies are small people. They are found in parts of central Africa, Asia and some Pacific islands. They are mostly NOMADS and live in bands. They hunt and gather plant foods. Today, they are dying out.

PYRAMIDS

Pyramids are huge, four-sided buildings. They have a square base. The sides are triangles that meet in a point at the top.

The Egyptians built pyramids as royal tombs. The first was built in about 2650 BC at Sakkara. It is 62 metres (204 feet) high. The three most famous pyramids are near Giza. The Great Pyramid, built in the 2600s BC by the PHARAOH Khufu, is 137 metres (449·5 feet) high. Khafre, who ruled soon after Khufu, built the second pyramid. It is 136·4 metres (447·5 feet) high. The third, built by Khafre's successor Menkaure, is 73·1 metres (240 feet) high. About 80 pyramids still stand in Egypt.

Central and South American Indians also built pyramids as temples from the 100s to the 500s AD. One huge pyramid is at Cholula, south east of Mexico City. It is about 54 metres (177 feet) high.

PYTHONS

Pythons are large SNAKES. They live in Africa, south-eastern Asia and a few kinds are found in Australia. Some grow as long as 9 metres (30 feet). They are *constrictors*. This means they squeeze their prey to death, before swallowing it whole.

Above: An explorer and his wife stand with two African pygmies, who are sometimes called Negrillos. *Pygmies are usually between 1·3 and 1·4 metres (4 feet 5 inches to 4 feet 8 inches) in height.*

Hundreds of men were needed to do the back-breaking job of building Egypt's pyramids (above). The workers were peasants, who could not farm their land during the yearly floods.

QUAKERS

The Quakers are also known as the Society of Friends. They are a PROTESTANT group that began in England during the 1650s.

They were called Quakers because some of them shook with emotion at their meetings. Early Quakers were often badly treated because of their belief that religion and government should not be mixed. Quakers have simple religious meetings and do not have priests.

QUARRYING

Unlike mines, quarries are always open to the sky. They are huge pits where rocks are cut or blasted out of the ground.

As long ago as prehistoric times, people had quarries where they dug up FLINT to make into tools and weapons. They used bones as picks and shovels.

Nowadays, rock is quarried in enormous amounts. Explosives blast loose thousands of tonnes. This is scooped up by bulldozers and diggers, and taken to crushers. The rock is ground into stones for use in roads, railways, concrete and cement. Not all rock is removed in this way. Stone that is used in building and paving is cut out of the ground rather than blasted. Electric cutters, wire saws and drills are used to cut the rock.

Marble, used by sculptors and for building work, is quarried by hand. Then it is polished to bring out its beautiful colours.

QUARTZ

Quartz is one of the most common MINERALS in the world. It is found everywhere. SAND is mostly made of quartz, and many rocks have quartz in them.

Quartz forms six-sided CRYSTALS. It is very hard, harder even than steel. In its pure form it has no colour and is as clear as glass. But most is smoky white or tinted with various colours. Many semi-precious GEMS, such as agate, amethyst, opal and onyx, are quartz.

Quartz is an important mineral. It is used in many things, including abrasives (such as sandpaper), lenses and electronics.

Quartz is so hard it can cut glass. It often remains in the ground when other softer minerals have worn away.

QUEBEC

Quebec is the largest province in CANADA. Over five million people live there. It stretches from the United States in the south, up into the Arctic. The St Lawrence River lies in south Quebec. This great river runs from the GREAT LAKES to the Atlantic Ocean.

The far east is hilly. The mountains here are the northernmost finger of the Appalachian range. The north of Quebec is a vast wilderness of lakes and forests. It is part of a plateau of ancient rock called the Canadian Shield.

Most people live in towns and cities along the St Lawrence valley. Much of Quebec's farmland is found here. The largest city, Montreal, is also the second biggest French-speaking city in the world. Quebec was first settled as a colony of France from the early 1600s to 1763. Afterwards it was taken over by the English.

Quebec City is the capital of the province. This view of it, from across the St Lawrence River, was painted in 1754. At that time Quebec was still a colony of France.

Raccoons eat a lot of water animals. They often play with their food in the water before they eat it. People have thought they were washing their food.

RABBITS

Rabbits originally came from Europe. Today they are found all over the world. They are small MAMMALS with short tails and long, pointed ears. Rabbits live in burrows in the ground. Each one is the home of a single family. A group of burrows is known as a warren. Rabbits leave their burrows at dusk to feed on grass and other plants.

Inside this rabbit burrow are a mother and her young (1), the main sleeping chamber (2) and a tunnel-digger at work (3).

RACCOONS

In North America, raccoons are common creatures of the wild. They have long grey fur, a short pointed nose and a bushy tail ringed with black. They may grow to as much as 90 cm (3 feet) long.

Raccoons live in forests. They make their homes in tree holes and are good climbers. At night, they leave their hollows to hunt for food. They will eat almost anything: fruit and plants, eggs, insects, fish, birds and small mammals. But their main food comes from rivers, and so their tree holes are usually found close by.

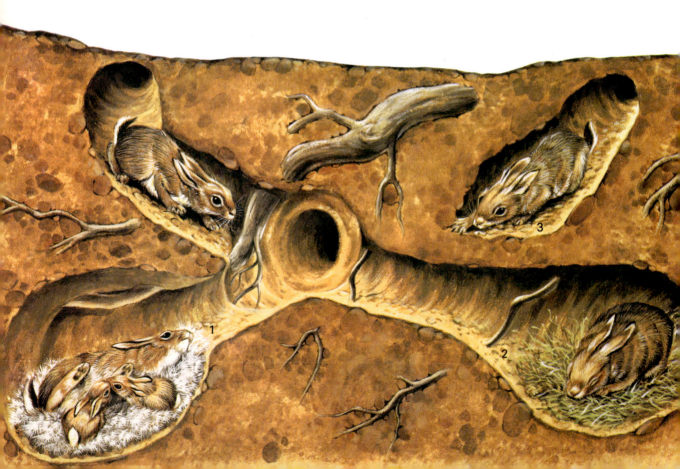

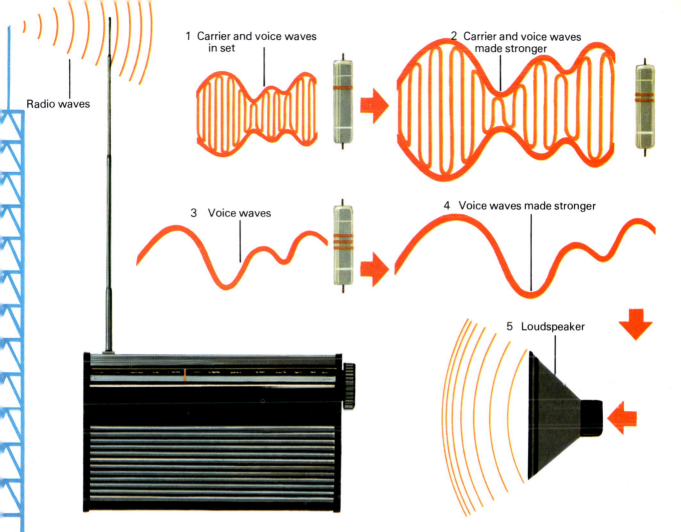

Radio waves

1 Carrier and voice waves in set

2 Carrier and voice waves made stronger

3 Voice waves

4 Voice waves made stronger

5 Loudspeaker

RADIO

The common household object we call a radio is only the receiving end of a great system of radio communications. Most of the system is never even seen.

A radio programme begins in a studio. There, voices and music are turned into electronic signals. These are made stronger (amplified), and then sent out from tall masts as radio waves. These are picked up by the radio set in your home and changed back into sounds we can hear. Radio waves travel at the speed of light. This is so fast that a signal can circle the world $7\frac{1}{2}$ times in one second.

The first person to make radio waves was Heinrich Hertz in 1887. But it was Guglielmo MARCONI who sent the first messages in 1894. His first signals went a few metres. Seven years later he sent signals across the Atlantic.

Radio waves set up a weak electric current when they reach a radio set (1). This current is amplified (2). The voice wave is separated (3). The voice wave is amplified again (4) and comes out through the loudspeaker (5).

RADIOACTIVITY

The atoms of some substances are always shooting off tiny particles and rays that we cannot see or feel. This is called radio-activity. These strange rays were discovered in 1896. And it was found that nothing could be done to stop the rays shooting out. It was also found that in time these radio-active substances changed into other sub-stances, and that they did this at a steady rate. If a piece of radioactive uranium was left for millions of years it would turn into a piece of lead. Scientists use radioactive carbon in animal and plant remains to find out how many thousands of years ago they lived.

RADIO ASTRONOMY

A heavenly body, such as a STAR, does not only give off LIGHT waves. It sends out many kinds of radio waves too. Radio astronomers explore the UNIVERSE by 'listening' to the radio signals that reach Earth from outer space. These signals are not made by other forms of life. They come from natural events, such as exploding stars or heated clouds of gases. By studying these signals, radio astronomers can find out many things about different parts of the universe.

Radio telescopes have giant aerials—often dish-shaped. They pick up faint signals that have come from places much deeper in space than anything ever seen by ordinary TELESCOPES. The first large radio telescopes were built after World War II. Today, the biggest in the world is at Arecibo in Puerto Rico. Its huge receiving dish has been built across an entire mountain valley. It is 305 metres (1000 feet) wide.

RADIUM

Radium is an ELEMENT. It is found only in URANIUM ore and was first discovered by Marie CURIE. She was examining some uranium and realized that it had much more RADIOACTIVITY than it should have had. Radium is very radioactive, and is dangerous to handle.

In its pure form, radium is a whitish metal. About five tonnes of uranium ore have to be mined to make just one gram of radium. Each year, less than 75 grams (2·64 oz) are produced in the entire world. Most comes from Canada and Zaire.

Radium is used in medicine to treat cancer. COMPOUNDS of it are also used to make luminous dials that glow in the dark.

This telescope at Jodrell Bank in Britain uses its receiving bowl to focus weak radio signals onto the receiver stalk at its centre. It can detect stars that may not be seen by ordinary telescopes.

RAILWAYS

Railways have been in use since the 1500s. At first, rails were made of wood and wagons were pulled by horses. These railways were used to haul carts in metal mines. Railways are useful because heavy loads can be pulled along them very easily.

Steam LOCOMOTIVES came into use in the early 1800s. In 1825, the first-ever steam engine to be used on a public railway began to run between Stockton and Darlington in England. The engine, called the *Rocket*, was built by George Stephenson. A few years later, the *Rocket* was hauling 20-tonne loads over a 56-km (35-mile) run in under two hours.

In the railway building boom that followed, tens of thousands of kilometres of track were laid down by the 1850s. Today, there are about 1,250,000 km (785,000 miles) of railway lines in the world. The longest railroad in the world is the Trans-Siberian line in Russia. It runs from Moscow to Nakhodka, a distance of 9334 km (5799 miles). The trains make 97 stops.

Above: Early wagons had flat wheels and rode on L-shaped rails (1). Modern wheels have flanges (projecting edges) (2), which hold the wheel on the rails. To climb steep slopes, wheels have special cogs (3).

Below: A section of modern railway line shows how the steel track is fixed onto sleepers with spikes. The whole thing rests on a bed of crushed stones.

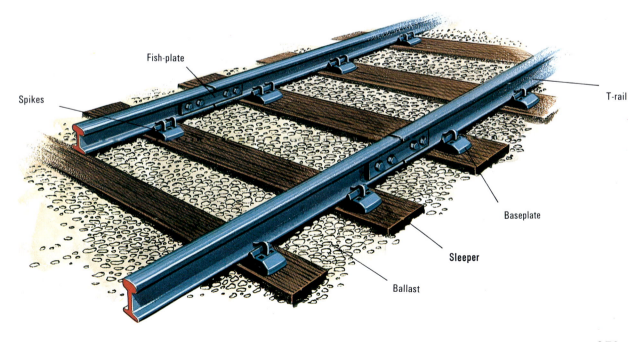

Fish-plate

Spikes

T-rail

Baseplate

Sleeper

Ballast

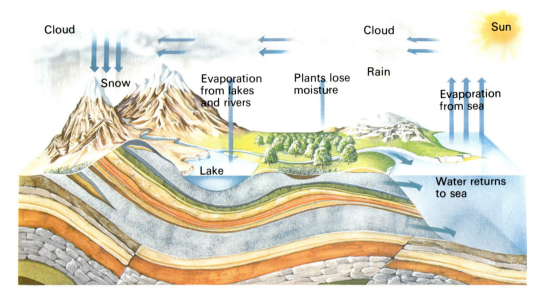

RAIN

When rain pours down, it is only the sky returning the same water to Earth that originally evaporated from the land and sea.

Rain forms when water vapour in the air starts to cool. As the vapour cools it turns first of all into tiny droplets, which form wispy CLOUDS. The droplets grow and the clouds thicken and turn a dull grey. At last the drops become so heavy that they start to fall. Depending on how cold it is, the drops hit the ground as either rain or SNOW.

The amount of rain that falls is widely different from place to place. In the Atacama Desert in Chile, less than 25 mm (1 inch) of rain falls in 20 years. But in eastern India, monsoon rains drop 1080 cm (2743 inches) every year.

RAINBOWS

The gorgeous colours of a rainbow are formed by sunlight shining on drops of rain. The best time for rainbows is right after a shower, when the clouds break up and sunlight streams through.

Rainbows can only be seen when the Sun is behind you and low over the horizon. When the Sun's rays strike the raindrops, each drop acts as a prism and splits the LIGHT into a spectrum of colours ranging from red to violet. The lower the Sun, the higher the rainbow and the fuller its curved arch.

This diagram of the water cycle shows how evaporated water forms clouds and returns to Earth as snow or rain.

According to legend, a pot of gold is buried at the end of every rainbow. The reason the Earth is not crowded with rich people is because rainbows never touch the ground.

RALEIGH, WALTER

Sir Walter Raleigh (1552–1618) was an English knight at the court of ELIZABETH I. He was a soldier, explorer, historian and poet. He tried unsuccessfully to set up a colony in Virginia, in the newly discovered land of North America. He introduced potatoes and tobacco smoking to the English. But his boldness and dashing way of life made him many enemies, and he was executed for treason during the reign of JAMES I.

RATS

Rats are RODENTS. They are found all over the world in enormous numbers, and can live happily in towns and cities. They will eat almost anything. They are harmful to man because they spoil huge amounts of food and they spread diseases. Some rats carry a type of FLEA, which can cause bubonic plague in human beings.

The most common rats are the brown and the black kinds. They grow to between 18–25 cm (7–10 inches) long, though the brown rat is the larger.

RATTLESNAKES

Rattlesnakes are a group of poisonous American SNAKES. There are 30 different kinds, and they are found from Canada to Argentina. Their name comes from the rattle at the tip of their tail. It is made of loose, horny bits of skin that make a whirring noise when the snake shakes its tail. This sound can be heard up to 30 metres (100 feet) away.

A bite from any rattlesnake will cause a painful wound and sometimes even death. The largest type is the eastern diamondback, which lives in the southern coastal region of the United States. It may reach as much as 2·4 metres (8 feet) in length.

Below: When it strikes, the rattlesnake's mouth opens wide, and its fangs, which usually lie flat against the roof of its mouth, swing down ready to strike.

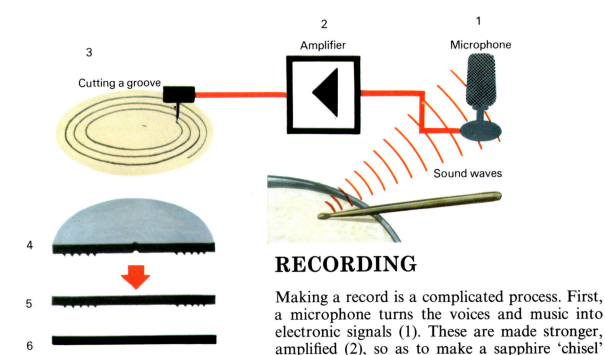

3 — Cutting a groove

2 — Amplifier

1 — Microphone

Sound waves

4

5

6

5

RECORDING

Making a record is a complicated process. First, a microphone turns the voices and music into electronic signals (1). These are made stronger, amplified (2), so as to make a sapphire 'chisel' vibrate as it cuts a very fine groove into a smooth disc (3). This is the master disc.

A metal copy in reverse is made from the master disc so that the grooves stand out as ridges (4) on the copy. Next, metal stampers are made (5). They are used to press thousands of records (6).

Below: Recording tape is a long ribbon coated with magnetic particles. Electric signals from the microphone recording the sounds cause a magnetic field to form at the tape head. This magnetic field arranges the particles on the tape in a way that is a code for the original sound. When the tape is played back, this code is 'read' by the tape machine.

Magnetic particles in tape before recording

Magnetic particles after recording

Below: A modern recording studio is crammed with equipment that can alter and improve sounds, such as music, which are recorded there.

Above: This fridge is a 1927 model but the first ones came into use in the 1860s.
Below: A refrigerator cooling system.

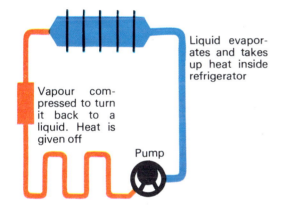

Liquid evaporates and takes up heat inside refrigerator

Vapour compressed to turn it back to a liquid. Heat is given off

Pump

REFRIGERATOR

Refrigerators are used to keep food cold. The simplest ones are really just boxes, with an electric motor running a cooling system. They are made of a material that keeps the inside of the fridge cold for some time, even when the motor is not running. The average TEMPERATURE inside a fridge is 2 to 7°C (35 to 45°F).

The cooling system has a special gas in it. This gas is first compressed (squeezed) to turn it into a liquid. The liquid then flows through hollow tubes inside the fridge into an evaporator, which turns it back into gas. This gas is pumped on around the system. As it goes round the inside of the fridge it draws out any heat from the inside.

When it is pumped outside the fridge the gas is compressed again. This turns it back into a liquid and it gives out the heat it picked up on the inside. The liquid is pumped round and round, turning from liquid to gas and back again. As this goes on, the air inside the fridge becomes colder and the heat is taken to the outside. The process works like a sort of heat sponge.

The Lapps of Scandinavia keep tame reindeer. They herd them all the year round. Meat and milk are used for food, and the hides are turned into leather.

REINDEER

Reindeer are a type of DEER that live in the far north of America, Asia and Europe. In America they are also known as caribou. Reindeer are tall MAMMALS with brown coats and white belly markings. Both males and females have great branches of antlers.

Reindeer live in large herds. In their summer breeding grounds on the open tundra (treeless plains), they feed on grasses and other vegetation. At the end of the summer there is a huge MIGRATION further south where they spend the winter. Reindeer are hunted by ESKIMOS for their skin, meat and antlers. The Lapps keep reindeer herds.

REPTILES

Reptiles are the most advanced of all cold-blooded animals. They live on land and in the sea. In all, there are about 6000 different types of reptile.

Except for the North and South Poles, reptiles live in all parts of the world. Most, however, live in warm regions. This is because they are cold-blooded and must get their warmth from their surroundings.

When it is cold they become very sleepy and cannot move fast enough to catch food or escape enemies. Most reptiles that live in cold places spend the winter in HIBERNATION.

Reptiles played a very important part in the EVOLUTION of the Earth. About 200 million years ago, the first reptiles left the water and began to roam over the land. They soon became the strongest form of life on Earth. They ruled the planet for close to 100 million years. One group of reptiles, the DINOSAURS, were the most spectacular creatures ever to walk the land. The biggest weighed over 50 tonnes.

Strong Survivors

Reptiles are still well suited for life on land. They have thick, leathery skins that stop their bodies drying up in hot weather. Those that eat meat have powerful jaws and sharp teeth, and some have poison fangs for killing their prey. Most reptiles lay eggs. The eggs have hard shells or tough leathery skins to protect them. A few reptiles, such as some sea snakes and lizards, give birth to live young.

Today, there are four main groups of reptiles: ALLIGATORS and CROCODILES, LIZARDS and SNAKES, TORTOISES and TURTLES, and the rare tuatara. The biggest reptiles are the alligators and crocodiles. The estuarine crocodile of south-east Asia grows to 6 metres (20 feet) in length, and is the biggest of them all.

There are over 5000 kinds of lizards and snakes. They live everywhere, from deserts to jungles and faraway ocean islands. Some have poisonous bites with which they kill their prey.

Tortoises and turtles are well protected by their hard shells. Tortoises live mostly on land. The biggest are the lumbering giants of the Pacific and Indian Ocean

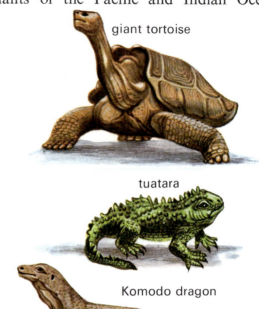

giant tortoise

tuatara

Komodo dragon

The giant tortoise of the Galapagos Islands is the largest of its kind. The Komodo dragon of Indonesia is the largest lizard. The tuatara has survived 150 million years. It now lives only on a few islands off New Zealand. The crow-sized Archaeopteryx was half-reptile, half-bird. Though it had a feathered tail and wings, it was not a good flyer. It also had a toothed beak and wings with claws on them.

islands. They may live as long as 150 years and reach 225 kg (500 lb) in weight. Bigger still are the marine leatherback turtles. Some of them can weigh up to 700 kg (1540 lb).

One of the strangest reptiles of all is the tuatara, which looks rather like an IGUANA. It is a living FOSSIL and so is put in a group all by itself. It was common about 150 million years ago. Today, only a few live on the islands off the coast of New Zealand. It is one of the very few reptiles that can live happily in a cool climate.

A cornered grass snake plays dead. But its stillness and wide-open jaws are only to fool its enemies.

RHINOCEROS

Sometimes described as a 'tank on legs' the rhinoceros is one of the largest and strongest of all land animals. A full grown male can weigh as much as 3·5 tonnes.

This massive beast has a tough leathery skin and sprouts one or two horns on its snout. These may grow as long as 127 cm (50 inches).

The rhinoceros lives in Africa and in south-eastern Asia. There it feeds on leafy twigs, shrubs and grasses.

Although an adult rhino has no natural enemies, it is so widely hunted for its horns that it has become a dying species. When ground into a powder, its horns are believed to be a powerful medicine. Some people claim it can be used to detect poisoned wine. However, the rhino's ability to charge swiftly over short distances makes it a dangerous animal to hunt. Many hunters have been hurt or killed by wildly charging rhinos.

The white rhino is the largest of all. Here a mother and young graze side by side.

285

RICE

Rice is a member of the GRASS family. Its grains are one of the most important CEREAL crops in the world. It is the main food of most Asian people.

Young shoots of rice are planted in flooded fields called paddies. Here they grow in 5-10 cm (2-4 inches) of water, until they are ready to be harvested. Young rice has long narrow leaves and fine clusters of flowers (left) that turn into the grains that we eat.

RIVERS

Rivers are one of the most. important geographical features in the world. They range in size from little more than swollen streams to mighty waterways that flow thousands of kilometres.

The greatest rivers in the world are the AMAZON, the Mississippi and the NILE.

Rivers shape the land more than any other force. They erode mountains, carve out valleys, form flat plains and build great deltas where they drop their silt at the edge of the sea.

River valley

Flood plain

Delta

They all drain huge areas of land. The basin of the Amazon for example, stretches over an area larger than all of western Europe.

Some rivers serve as roads that allow ocean-going ships to sail far inland.

ROADS

Early roads were built soon after the invention of the WHEEL, but the Romans were the first great road builders. Some of their long, straight roads still survive. The Romans made roads of gravel and stones. The surface paving stones were arched in the middle so that rain ran off into ditches.

Modern road building began during the INDUSTRIAL REVOLUTION. In the early 1800s, a Scottish engineer, John McAdam, became the pioneer of modern road making. But the stony surfaces of his roads were not good for vehicles with rubber tyres. Later, *macadamized* roads were built. They are covered with tar or asphalt to make them smooth. Many roads, especially motorways, are now made of CONCRETE.

Right: The Romans built straight roads made from stones and gravel. John McAdam (1756–1836) built roads from layers of stones, with the largest stones at the bottom and the smallest on top. When pressed down by traffic, they had a hard surface.

Below: These robot welders are putting together cars in a Japanese factory. Machines controlled by computers now do many such tasks.

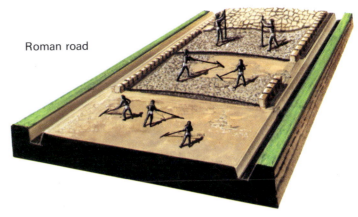
Roman road

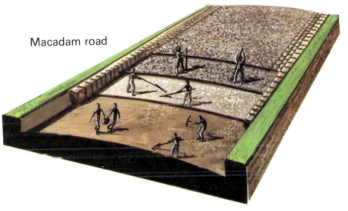
Macadam road

ROBIN HOOD

Robin Hood was an English hero who lived as an outlaw in Sherwood Forest, in Nottinghamshire. He and his band of men robbed the rich and helped the poor. He was supposed to have lived in the 1100s, but most historians think that he never really existed.

ROBOTS

Robots are machines that do jobs by themselves. Some robots look like people. In SCIENCE FICTION, we read of robots that can walk, talk and think. The word robot comes from a Czech word, *robota*. This means 'slave'. The term was first used in a Czech play about mechanical men.

Robot devices also include such things as 'electric eyes' which open doors and work automatic washing machines and traffic signals. Robots have many uses in industry. For example, they are used to weld or spray cars on assembly lines.

287

ROCKETS

A firework rocket and the rocket that took men to the Moon work in much the same way. Both burn fuel to produce hot gases. The gases shoot out backwards. This makes a pressure inside the rocket that thrusts it forward. The gases do not move rockets by pushing against the air. This means that rockets can move in empty space.

Rockets used to launch satellites and spacecraft were developed after World War II. They are *multi-stage* rockets, that is, several rockets that are joined together. Each stage fires in turn. The Chinese used rockets as weapons as early as the 1200s.

The Saturn V *rocket was used for the American Apollo flights. It is a three-stage rocket. Each stage drops away after use. Small rocket engines power the spacecraft after it is launched. Below: A* Saturn V *rocket takes off in the USA.*

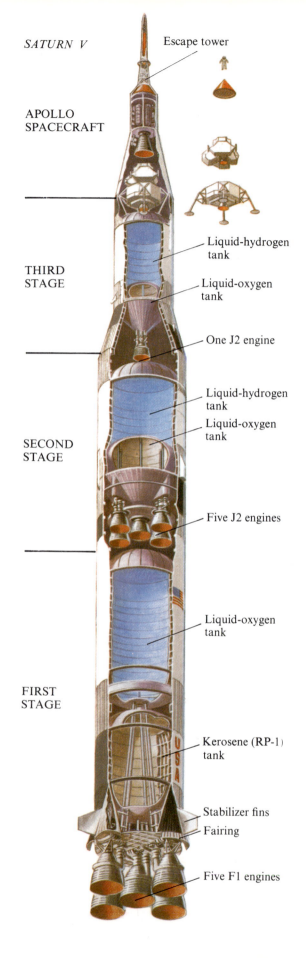

SATURN V

Escape tower

APOLLO SPACECRAFT

THIRD STAGE

Liquid-hydrogen tank

Liquid-oxygen tank

One J2 engine

Liquid-hydrogen tank

Liquid-oxygen tank

SECOND STAGE

Five J2 engines

Liquid-oxygen tank

FIRST STAGE

Kerosene (RP-1) tank

Stabilizer fins

Fairing

Five F1 engines

RODENT

Rodents are a group of gnawing animals. They have large, sharp front teeth that grow all the time. The animals wear down these teeth by gnawing their food. They also use their teeth to dig burrows in the ground for their homes and nests. BEAVERS even cut down trees with their teeth.

The 2000 or so rodents also include the MOUSE, RATS, porcupines and SQUIRRELS. The South American capybara is the largest rodent. It looks like a giant guinea pig. It grows to a length of 1·25 metres (4 feet) and weighs over 45 kg (100 lb). The smallest rodent is the European harvest mouse. It grows only about 135 mm (5·3 inches) long.

RODEO

Rodeos are exciting shows where American cowboys show off their skills. In barcback riding, a cowboy rides a bronco (a half wild or bad-tempered horse). In saddle-bronco riding, the cowboy rides one-handed, using one rein, a saddle and a halter. Bull riding and calf roping are other events. In steer wrestling, the cowboy chases a young bull, or steer, on horseback, grabs its head and pulls the steer down. A comic contest is catching a greased pig. The first recorded rodeo was held in 1869.

Above: Rodeos are popular shows in North America. People take part in different contests. Each event is based on the kind of work cowboys did in the 1800s.

The Pope is seen here in St Peter's, the great church in the Vatican City. This is the centre of the Roman Catholic Church.

ROMAN CATHOLIC CHURCH

The Roman Catholic Church is the oldest and largest of all Christian churches. It has about 585 million members. The POPE is the head of the Church. He lives in the VATICAN CITY.

Roman Catholics follow the teachings of JESUS Christ. The Church also helps its followers by giving them rules for good living. The main church service is called the Mass. Roman Catholics also go to church to confess (tell) their sins.

Roman Catholics give great honour to the SAINTS. The most important saint is Mary, the mother of Jesus.

ROMAN EMPIRE

The ancient Romans built up a vast empire around the Mediterranean Sea. ROME, in Italy, was the centre of the empire. Legend says that Rome was founded in 753 BC. In the 500s BC, it was ruled by the Etruscans. It was not until 509 BC that Rome began to rule itself. Then it was run by officials, called consuls, and magistrates. They were *patricians* (rich people). The consuls shared power with the Senate, a council of men from rich families. Many years passed before the *plebeians* (poor people) won the right to become officials.

In the 200s BC the power of Rome began to reach out to all Italy. It took over the island of Sicily from the powerful city of Carthage, and in 146 BC Rome completely destroyed Carthage. Roman power spread in all directions. But the Romans quarrelled with each other and fought CIVIL WARS between 133 and 27 BC. In 49 BC, Julius CAESAR became dictator. He ruled Rome until he was murdered in 44 BC. Another civil war followed, then Caesar's adopted son, Octavian, became the first Roman emperor. He was renamed Augustus, and made peace throughout the empire.

In the early days of Roman rule, many Christians were killed. But in AD 313, Emperor Constantine gave Christians freedom of worship. He also set up the city of Byzantium, or Constantinople, in the east of the Empire. In 395, the Empire was split into two. The western half had its capital at Rome, and Byzantium was the capital of the eastern half. In the 400s, the western empire was attacked by tribes from the north. It collapsed and was split into small kingdoms. The eastern empire lasted until the Turks took it in 1453. But Roman architecture, art, engineering, law and literature greatly influenced European ideas.

The map below shows the size of the Roman Empire at the time of the first emperor, Augustus. Roman rule stretched from Britain to the shores of the Caspian Sea.

Above: Augustus (63 BC–AD 14) was the first emperor of Rome. He brought peace to the empire after years of civil war. Many new buildings and roads were built during his rule.

Below: A carving of a husband and wife from a tombstone. Male citizens of Rome wore a toga,

ROMANIA

Romania is a small country in south eastern EUROPE. It has beautiful mountains and many forests. Most people are farmers, but there are also mines, and oil is produced too.

ROME

Rome is the capital of ITALY. With a population of 3,700,000, it is also Italy's largest city. Rome stands on the River Tiber, about 27 km (17 miles) from the Mediterranean Sea. Many tourists visit Rome to see the great ruins of ancient Rome, and the beautiful churches, fountains, palaces and art galleries.

This open-air market is in Rome, one of the world's most beautiful cities.

ROSES

Roses are among the most popular of all FLOWERS. There are thousands of different roses. Many have been bred from the wild sweet-briar and the dog rose. Some roses flower only in early summer, but most garden roses now flower for many months.

Right: Roses are lovely flowers. There are thousands of kinds. Their colours include red, pink, yellow and white.

RUBBER

Rubber is an important material with many uses in industry and in the home. Most natural rubber comes from the rubber tree. When the BARK of the tree is cut, a white juice called *latex* oozes out. The juice is collected and made into rubber. Today, most natural rubber comes from Malaysia and Indonesia.

Scientists found ways of making synthetic rubber during World War I. Synthetic rubber is made from oil and coal. More synthetic rubber is now made each year than natural rubber.

Rubber trees grow on plantations. Rubber is collected by cutting the bark. The milky liquid drips into a cup.

291

RUGBY FOOTBALL

Rugby football is a game played between two teams with an oval ball. The ball may be kicked or handled. To score a *try* in rugby, the ball must be taken over the other team's goal line and touched down on the ground. To score a goal, the ball must be kicked over the crossbar of the H-shaped goal.

In *rugby union*, each team has 15 players. *Rugby league* is a variation of the game, with some different rules. Rugby league teams have 13 players. The name rugby comes from Rugby School, in England, where the game began in 1823.

RUSSIA

Russia is the world's largest country, covering 22,402,000 sq km (8,649,460 sq miles). It lies in EUROPE and ASIA. Its proper name is the Union of Soviet Socialist Republics (USSR). Many people still call it Russia, although Russia is really only one of the 15 republics that make up the country. Russia covers three-quarters of the USSR, and the Russian language is the most important of the 60 or so languages spoken. The capital of the USSR is MOSCOW.

Before 1917, Russia was a poor country ruled by *tsars*, or emperors. In 1917, there was a revolution. A communist government took over, led by Vladimir LENIN. Between 1918 and 1920 Russia was nearly destroyed by a civil war between the communists and their enemies. The communists won, and began to turn Russia into a great industrial nation.

The land of Russia is varied. Large parts of it are cold or dry and have few people. More than 70 percent of the 268 million citizens live in the European part of the country, west of the Ural Mountains.

Above: This market is in Tbilisi, the capital of the Georgian Soviet Socialist Republic. This is one of the 15 republics that make up the USSR.

Below: The USSR is the biggest country in the world. It is nearly two and a half times bigger than the United States.

Russian farmers grow many crops, including wheat, rye and barley. They also grow vegetables, fruit, tea and cotton. The farms are owned or run by the government. Most of the farms are very big, and about a quarter of the population works on them.

Russia is rich in MINERALS. It has great deposits of coal, oil and natural gas, and has more iron, chromium, lead and manganese than any other country. Fishing and forestry are also important industries.

At the beginning of the 1900s, Russia was a country of farmers. There were few factories.

These young Russians (below) belong to the Young Pioneers, a group which is given some military training.

Above: Moscow in springtime is a cheerful place. The sun melts the snow, and the streets are full of flowers and ice cream sellers.

Today, Russia is a leading industrial country. The government runs the factories and tells the workers what to make.

Russians are fond of sport, art and reading. The government helps sportsmen and athletes in their training. Many Russians win gold medals at the OLYMPIC GAMES. The Bolshoi ballet company of Moscow is world-famous. Russia also has some of the best CHESS players in the world. Some of the world's most famous writers, such as Tolstoy, have been Russians.

RUST

Rust is a brownish-red crust that forms on ordinary IRON AND STEEL when they are left in damp air. As rust forms, the surface of the metal is eaten away. Rusting is speeded up near the sea, where the air contains salt, or in cities where air POLLUTION is severe.

To prevent rusting, iron and steel may be coated with such metals as tin or zinc. Grease, oil and paint also protect the metal. Stainless steels are alloys made of iron and rust-resistant metals, such as nickel and chromium.

293

SAHARA

The Sahara is the world's largest hot DESERT. It covers about 8·4 million sq km (3·2 million sq miles) in North AFRICA. It extends from the Atlantic Ocean in the west to the Red Sea in the east. In the north, it stretches to the Mediterranean coast in Libya and in Egypt. In the south, it becomes a dry region with a few small plants. Recently, the lands south of the Sahara have had very little rain. Because of this the desert is slowly spreading southwards.

About a third of the Sahara is covered by sand. Other parts are covered by gravel and stones, or by bare rock. The Sahara is the hottest place on Earth. The world's highest air temperature in the shade, 57·7°C (136·4°F), was recorded there.

The people are mostly ARABS or Berbers. Some are NOMADS. They travel between OASES (water holes) with their CAMELS. The people cover their faces with veils to protect them against wind-blown sand and dust. Other people live in villages around the larger oases. The greatest number live in the fertile NILE valley in Egypt. The Sahara has become an important area because it has a lot of OIL and natural gas.

SAINTS

Saints are holy people. Christian saints are people who have been *canonized* (named

The camel is the best form of transport in the Sahara. It can travel for days without water.

as saints) by the ROMAN CATHOLIC CHURCH or the Eastern Orthodox churches. Most saints are canonized long after their deaths.

When someone is being made a saint, the Church looks at the person's life to see if they were very good. The saint must also have taken part in a miracle.

Countries and even trades may have their own saints. These are called patron saints. The patron saint of Ireland is St Patrick, of England, St George, of Scotland, St Andrew, and of Wales, St David. Many people believe that saints perform miracles, such as healing the sick.

SALMON

Salmon are fish which breed in shallow rivers. After the eggs hatch, the young fish move down the river to the sea. They spend their adult life in the sea (about one to three years). Then they return to their birthplace to breed. This may mean a journey of hundreds of kilometres. Most salmon die after laying their eggs.

SALT

The chemical name for the salt we eat is sodium chloride. We need salt to stay healthy. Each of us eats between 6 and 7 kg

(13–15 lb) of salt every year. Salt is also used to preserve foods and it is important in many industries. Much of our salt comes from sea water, but some is mined from deposits in the ground.

Right: Salt can be made by flooding land with sea water. The Sun dries up the water and the salt is left behind.

SATURN (PLANET)

Saturn is the second largest PLANET in the SOLAR SYSTEM after Jupiter. It is about 120,700 km (75,000 miles) across. Saturn is famous for the rings that circle it. These rings are made of billions of icy particles. The rings are more than 273,600 km (170,000 miles) across, but they are very thin. The particles in the rings may be the remains of a moon which drifted too close to Saturn and broke up.

To the naked eye, Saturn looks like a bright star. The planet is actually mostly made up of light gases, and it is less dense than water. But scientists think that it may have a solid core. Saturn has 23 satellites. The largest is Titan. It measures 5120 km (about 3000 miles) across—larger than Mercury. Titan is the only known satellite to have an atmosphere—a layer of gases surrounding it.

This picture shows how Saturn would look if seen from its satellite Titan. The sky is blue because Titan has an atmosphere.

SCIENCE FICTION

Imaginative stories which are set in the future or on other planets are called science fiction. The writers often use new scientific discoveries in their stories. They imagine how these discoveries might change the world in the future. Many of the stories are about space travel and time travel, and meetings between creatures from different planets. Some writers describe life in the future to show how many things they think are wrong in the world today.

Jules Verne (1828–1905) and H. G. Wells (1866–1946) were two of the first great science fiction writers. Recent writers include Isaac Asimov, Ray Bradbury and Arthur C. Clarke.

SCORPIONS

Scorpions are animals related to spiders, with poisonous stings in their tails. Most live in warm, dry places and grow to 15 cm (6 inches) long. They have four pairs of legs, and a pair of large claws. Scorpions

In some science fiction stories, Unidentified Flying Objects (UFOs) bring creatures from outer space to the Earth.

use their sting to stun or kill their prey. The poison can also make people ill, but it very seldom kills them.

SCOTLAND

Scotland is part of the United Kingdom of Great Britain and Northern Ireland. Most Scots live in a narrow belt in the south where most industry is. In this belt are Glasgow, Scotland's largest city, and Edinburgh, the capital. The Highlands of Scotland have very few people and many beautiful mountains and lochs. The highest mountain in Britain is Ben Nevis, 1343 metres (4406 ft) high. There are many islands off the Scottish coast. These include the Hebrides, Orkneys and Shetlands.

Scotland joined with England and Wales in 1707, but the Scots have kept many of their own traditions. Some Scots want their own government.

SCULPTURE

Sculpture is a way of making attractive models, statues and objects as works of ART. They may be carved from stone or wood, or they may be made by casting. In making a cast, the sculptor first makes a model in clay or wax. He uses this model to make a mould. He then pours hot molten metal, such as BRONZE, into the mould. When the metal has cooled and hardened, it is taken out of the mould. The metal 'cast' is the perfect, finished copy of the original model.

Sculpture has been an important form of art since the early history of mankind. Much early sculpture was religious, but sculptors also carved people and animals. In Europe, the best early sculpture was made by the ancient Greeks.

Early Greek statues were models for Renaissance sculptors like MICHELANGELO, who was possibly the finest sculptor ever.

Modern sculptors have moved away from lifelike figures. Great artists like Henry Moore make *abstract* figures and groups. In these the overall shape and feel of the stone or wood is the most important thing.

Right: The Venus de Milo *is a famous marble sculpture from ancient Greece.*

Below: This head was cast in bronze. It comes from Ife, in Nigeria.

Below: The top of a pillar made from polished stone. It was put up by an Indian emperor in the 200s BC.

297

SEA ANEMONE

Sea anemones are soft-bodied, tube-like animals. They are closely related to CORALS, but they do not build a hard cup around themselves as corals do.

Sea anemones cling to rocks. Many live on or near the seashore. They look like flowers. This is because they have one or more rings of petal-like tentacles around their mouths. The tentacles have stinging CELLS, and trap small fish and other tiny animals that float by. The sea anemone then pulls the food into its stomach through its mouth, and digests it.

Below: Sea horses live in shallow waters where they hide in seaweed.

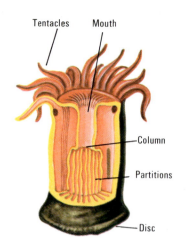

Above: The inside of a sea anemone. Food is digested in the partitions. The disc is used to grip on to rocks.

SEA HORSE

Sea horses are strange fishes with delicate, bony bodies. They are called sea horses because of their horse-shaped heads. Most are between 15 and 25 cm (6 and 10 inches) long.

Sea horses swim by waving their back fin. They often cling to seaweed with their tails. The males look after the eggs. They keep them in a pouch on their bellies until they hatch. Sea horses are found in seas in tropical and warm areas.

SEA LIONS

Sea lions are very like SEALS, but they have small ears on the outside of their heads. They have fur all over their bodies, and the males often have a shaggy mane. There are five different kinds. The Californian sea lion is the smallest. It is about 2 metres (7 feet) long, and is often seen in circuses and zoos. The male does not have a mane. The largest is the Steller's sea lion. The males may weigh over 680 kg (1500 lb). Sea lions feed on fish and squid and spend almost all their time in the water.

Sea lions are mammals. Their 'legs' are flippers, which they use for swimming.

Right: A pup is born with a fine, soft fur coat. Pups grow quickly and soon learn to swim. At first, they feed on their mother's milk, but soon learn to catch and eat fish.

SEALS

Seals are large sea MAMMALS. Many of them live in the icy waters of the far north. They spend most of their time in the sea, but often come ashore to lie in the sun. They also have their young, called pups, on land. Seals have streamlined bodies and legs shaped like flippers for swimming. They can swim as fast as 16 km/hr (10 mph). They also have a thick layer of fat, or *blubber*, under their skin to protect them from the cold. Seals eat fish and other sea creatures, including birds. Some kinds of seal are hunted for their dark, silky and thickly-furred skins.

SEA URCHIN

Sea urchins are small animals that live on the seabed. The urchin's body is inside a hard, round case covered with stiff spines. Between the spines it has tube feet ending in suckers. Its mouth lies under the body and has five teeth that are so sharp they can cut through a steel plate. Urchins eat tiny plants and animals from the seabed.

SEAWEED

Seaweeds are a large group of PLANTS that live in the sea. They grow on rocks along the coast, or on the seabed. Instead of roots, seaweeds have *holdfasts* that glue them to rocks, shells and other objects.

Seaweeds that live near the surface are green. Lower down, they are brown and, in really deep water, red. Like most plants, seaweeds need sunlight to make food. As the Sun's rays do not reach deeper than 180 metres (600 feet), there are no seaweeds below this depth. A jelly made from seaweed is used in many foods and drugs such as ice cream and aspirin. In some countries people eat seaweeds as vegetables.

Some seaweeds, like the bladder wrack and knotted wrack, have little sacs of air. These sacs help them to float in water.

Oarweeds

Bladder wrack

Serrated wrack

Knotted wrack

SEEDS

Seeds are the most important part of a plant; they are the beginnings of new PLANTS. A seed is formed when POLLEN reaches the female part of a FLOWER. The new seed grows inside a FRUIT which protects it. In a grape, for example, the fleshy part is the fruit and the pips are the seeds.

Seeds have to be scattered to find new ground to grow on. Some fruits have wings and are carried by the wind. Others are prickly and stick to the fur of passing animals. Many seeds are carried away by birds. A seed contains the baby plant and a food store. When the seed begins to grow, the baby plant feeds off this store until it has roots and leaves and can make its own food.

Burdock

Dandelion

Ash

Sycamore

Above: Dandelion, ash and sycamore seeds are scattered by the wind. Burdock seeds have spikes that stick to passing animals.

SEVEN WONDERS OF THE WORLD

The Seven Wonders of the World were seven outstanding man-made objects that were built in ancient times. Only one of these Wonders, the PYRAMIDS, exists today. The others have all been destroyed. They were:

The Hanging Gardens of Babylon, which seem to have been built high up on the walls of temples. They were probably a gift from King Nebuchadnezzar II to one of his wives.

1

2

3

4

5

6

7

The Temple of Artemis, at Ephesus (in Turkey). This temple was one of the largest in the ancient world. Some of its marble columns are in the British Museum, in London.

The Statue of Zeus at Olympia, Greece, showed the king of the gods on his throne. It was made of gold and ivory.

The tomb at Halicarnassus (now in Turkey), was a massive tomb built for Mausolus, a ruler in Persia. It became so famous that all large tombs are now called *mausoleums*.

The Colossus of Rhodes in Greece, was a huge, bronze statue of the sun god, Helios. It stood over the harbour entrance.

The Pharos of Alexandria in Egypt, was the first modern lighthouse. It was built in 270 BC on the island of Pharos outside Alexandria harbour. It had a wood fire burning on top.

The Seven Wonders of the Ancient World.
(1) The Pyramids of Egypt. (2) The Pharos of Alexandria. (3) The Tomb of Mausolus at Halicarnassus. (4) The Hanging Gardens of Babylon. (5) The Colossus of Rhodes. (6) The Temple of Artemis at Ephesus. (7) The Statue of Zeus at Olympia.

Right: A navigator uses his sextant to find out the position of his ship.

SEXTANT

The sextant is a scientific instrument used in NAVIGATION. It is used by sailors to find the position of their ship when land is out of sight. A sextant works by measuring the ANGLE of the Sun or, at night, of a star to the horizon to find its *altitude*. By measuring the altitude and direction of the Sun or stars, and by noting the exact time of the observations, the sailor can work out the position of his ship. He uses special mathematical tables to help him do this.

SHAKESPEARE, WILLIAM

William Shakespeare (1564–1616) is England's greatest writer. He is most famous for his plays— about 40 altogether—which include *A Midsummer Night's Dream, Hamlet, Macbeth* and *Romeo and Juliet*.

Very little is known about Shakespeare's life. He was born in Stratford-upon-Avon and was the son of a glovemaker. When he was 18, he married Anne Hathaway, a farmer's daughter, and had three children. Then, at the age of 20, he left Stratford and went to London where he became an actor and playwright. At the end of his life he returned to Stratford. Many of the words and phrases we use today were first used by Shakespeare.

Below: William Shakespeare. His plays are acted all over the world.

SHARK

The shark family includes the world's largest and fiercest fish. Sharks have a wedge-shaped head, long body and a triangular back fin that often sticks out of the water. Their SKELETONS are made of rubbery gristle, not bone. Most sharks live in warm seas. They vary greatly in size. The dogfish, one of the smallest sharks, is only 60 cm (2 feet) long. The largest fish in the oceans, the whale shark, measures over 15 metres (50 feet)—as long as two buses.

The whale shark is harmless to man and other animals as it lives on plankton. But many sharks are cruel killers with rows of razor-sharp teeth. Several are man-eaters. The greediest monster, the great white shark, swallows its prey whole. The remains of big animals, such as horses, seals and other sharks, have been found in its stomach.

Other man-eaters are the blue shark, the tiger shark, and the leopard shark which has leopard-like spots. The smell of blood in water drives sharks crazy so that they attack anything near, even other sharks. Along the beaches of Australia and South Africa, swimmers are protected from sharks by nets, electric barriers and lookouts.

Some kinds of shark lay eggs, but most sharks have live babies.

The thresher shark uses its huge tail to sweep its prey into a group. It can then attack them more easily. The hammerhead shark is named after its odd-shaped head.

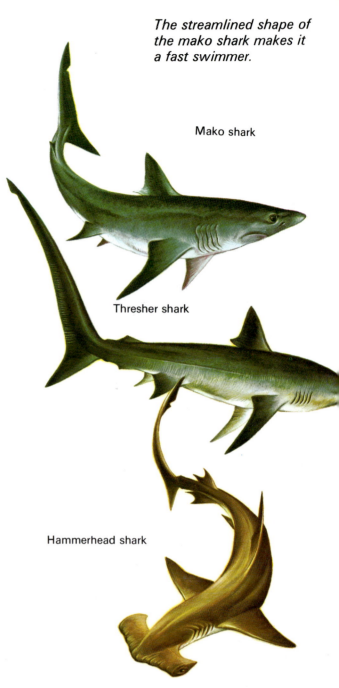

The streamlined shape of the mako shark makes it a fast swimmer.

Mako shark

Thresher shark

Hammerhead shark

SHEEP

Sheep have been part of man's life for thousands of years. At first, sheep were kept for their milk and skins. Milk can be made into cheese and the skins were used for clothing. Then, people discovered that the animals' thick coats could be *sheared* (shaved off) and the wool woven into cloth. Today, sheep are kept mostly for wool and for meat (*mutton* or *lamb*). But, parts of sheep are also used for making glue, and FERTILIZER. The *gut* strings on violins and tennis rackets also come from sheep.

SHELLS AND SHELLFISH

Many animals live inside shells. This is because they have soft bodies that need protection. Shells are usually hard and are all sizes and colours. The shells of some sea snails are no bigger than a grain of sand but the giant clam of the Pacific Ocean has a shell 120 cm (4 feet) across.

Some land animals such as SNAILS and TORTOISES have shells, but most creatures with shells belong in the sea. Shelled sea animals include MOLLUSCS and crustaceans. Some of these, like OYSTERS, scallops, shrimps and LOBSTERS, can be eaten. These are often called shellfish although they are not really fish at all. Shellfish have been an important food for thousands of years. In some places, kitchen dumps of prehistoric people have been found that are just enormous mounds of shells, as high as a three-storey house.

Shells are often used as decorations and for jewellery. Pearly buttons are often made from mussel shells. Big shells can be polished and then turned into paperweights and lamp bases. In former times some shells, especially cowrie shells, were used as money.

Many people collect shells, mostly molluscs, as a hobby. They find shells along the shore, then clean and label them.

Above: Different mollusc shells found on the seashore.

SHIPS

Today, most ships are cargo vessels. They are usually built for a certain type of cargo. *Tankers* carry liquids such as oil or wine. Some oil tankers are so long that the crew can ride bicycles around the deck. *Bulk carriers* take dry cargoes like coal and wheat that can be loaded loose. *Container ships* carry all kinds of goods packed in large boxes called containers. *Refrigerator ships* are for carrying fresh food like fruit and meat.

Planes have replaced most passenger ships, but there are still a few liners such as the *Queen Elizabeth 2* crossing the oceans. And there are many ferries, which take people and cars across smaller stretches of water.

A bottle of champagne is broken across its bows and a new ship glides into the water. After launching, the ship is 'fitted out' or finished inside.

SILICON CHIP

Silicon chips are tiny pieces of the ELEMENT silicon. They can be made to carry very small electrical circuits, called microcircuits. These are used in transistor radios, digital watches, electronic calculators and computers. Because the chips are so small, the objects they are used in can be small too.

SILK

Silk is a natural fibre made from the cocoon of one kind of moth. Silkworms, which are really CATERPILLARS, are kept in special containers and fed on mulberry leaves for about four weeks. At the end of this time they spin their cocoons and start to turn into moths. Then they are killed and each cocoon is unwound as a long thread between 600 and 900 metres long (2000 to 3000 feet).

Silk was first used in Asia centuries ago, especially in China and Japan. Silk WEAVING in Europe began in the 1400s. Silk makes a very fine, soft material. It was used for stockings before NYLON was invented. Silk can be made into other fabrics such as satin and chiffon, and can be dyed in beautiful colours.

Above: Part of a silk dress, made in China 2000 years ago. Rich people wore clothes like this, and sent silk cloth to Europe, where it was made into expensive clothes.
Below left: A picture from ancient China, shows silk being spun into a thread for weaving. Below right: A silkworm's cocoon with the animal inside, changing from a caterpillar into a moth. The animal has to be killed before the silk is unwound.

Cocoon ———

Silkworm in cocoon

SILVER

Silver is a precious METAL. It has been used by people all over the world for thousands of years.

Silver bends very easily, and can be beaten into many shapes and patterns. Like gold, it can be hammered out into thin sheets. It is used to make useful and decorative things, such as spoons and forks, bowls, and jewellery. Sometimes it is used as a coating on cheaper metals such as copper or nickel, to make them look like silver. It can also be mixed with another metal (usually copper), and then it is called *sterling* silver.

Silver used to be made into coins, and is still used in the silver dollar of the United States. Other 'silver' coins are really made of a mixture of copper and nickel. 'Silver' paper is not silver at all, but aluminium.

Silver carries electricity well and is used for this in industry. Some chemicals made from silver react to light and are used in photography. Another chemical, silver nitrate, is painted on the back of glass to make mirrors.

Silver is rare and expensive. It is mined in many parts of the world.

Above: This silver coffin was made for King Psusennes of Egypt about 3000 years ago.

SKELETON

Our skeleton is made up of BONES. If we did not have a skeleton, our bodies would be shapeless blobs. The skeleton protects our vital organs, such as the heart, liver and lungs. It is also an anchor for our MUSCLES.

In humans and other animals with backbones (VERTEBRATES), the skeleton is inside the body, covered by the flesh and skin. In other animals, such as INSECTS and SPIDERS, the skeleton is like a hard crust on the outside of the body. It is called an *exoskeleton*. Some animals, such as the jellyfish and octopus, do not have a skeleton. Their bodies are supported by the water they live in.

There are more than 200 bones in the human skeleton. These include the bones of the spine, skull (which protects the brain), ribs, pelvis, breastbone and limbs. Joints are places where bones meet. Some joints (like those in the skull) do not move. Others, like those in the shoulders and hips, help us to move about. Muscles across the joints tighten, or *contract*, to move the bones.

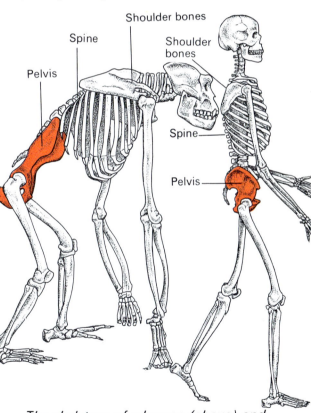

The skeletons of a human (above) and a gorilla (left) show how they walk differently. The shape and position of the pelvis and spine are important. Because it mostly walks on all-fours, the gorilla needs long arm bones

305

SLAVERY

Slavery means owning people to work for you, just as you would own a car. Slaves can be bought and sold. In ancient civilizations, prisoners captured in war were often made into slaves, and poor people sometimes sold their children as slaves.

From the 1500s, the Spanish took people from Africa as slaves for their colonies in America. By the 1770s, British ships were carrying slaves to America. Hundreds were packed tightly into ships. Conditions were terrible, and many slaves died on the way. Slavery was ended in the USA in 1865, after the CIVIL WAR.

SLEEP AND DREAMS

Sleep is a time when we are unconscious and resting. People and other animals need sleep to stay healthy. Without it, people become short-tempered and after a long time they may start having *hallucinations*— seeing things that are not there.

There are four different stages of sleep. At each stage the electrical waves given off by the BRAIN change. When we are deeply asleep, these waves are slow and large. When we are only lightly asleep the waves are faster. This is the time when we—and all mammals—dream.

Different people need different amounts of sleep. Babies need a lot. Adults need between six and nine hours a night.

The sloth is a strange-looking animal with a blunt nose and no tail.

SLOTH

Sloths are a group of MAMMALS that live in South America. They move very slowly, usually at night. Sloths spend most of their lives hanging upside-down in trees. They eat leaves, buds and twigs. Their fur is often covered with masses of tiny green creatures, called algae. This makes the sloth hard to see among the leaves. A sloth's grip is so secure that it can even fall asleep without letting go of the branch it is hanging from.

There are two main kinds of sloth, the two-toed and the three-toed. In prehistoric times there were huge giant sloths that were about 6 metres (20 feet) long.

We call someone 'slothful' when we mean they are lazy and slow.

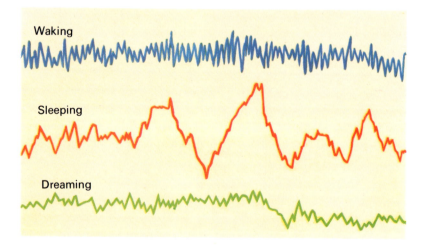

Waking

Sleeping

Dreaming

Left: This chart shows the different wave patterns that our brain makes when we are awake, deeply asleep, and dreaming. Scientists know very little about what happens to us when we are asleep. Studying charts like this helps them to find out more about sleep.

SMALLPOX

Smallpox is a very dangerous disease. It can be spread to other people very easily. It starts like a cold, but soon the body is covered with spots that turn into blisters. These can leave scars if the person gets better, but many people who catch small-pox die from it.

Smallpox can be prevented by vaccination. There have been no new outbreaks of smallpox in the world for several years. It may have been wiped out. Smallpox vaccine was first made in 1796 by JENNER.

SMELL

Smell is an important sense, like sight and hearing. Humans, and other MAMMALS, smell through the nose. We sniff the air, and the scents given off by the things around us are picked up by special cells in the nose. These cells send messages to the BRAIN.

Our sense of smell is useful when we are eating. It helps us to TASTE things. It can also let us know when food is bad. Most other animals have a much better sense of smell than humans. Dogs can use their sense of smell to track down and follow prey. Moths do not have noses, but they can still smell things. Some male moths can smell a female many miles away.

SMOG

There are two kinds of smog. One is a very thick, smelly mixture of smoke and fog. It used to be very common in London. In the winter of 1952, there was a very bad smog and about 4000 people died of chest diseases. Since then, laws have been made to make sure there is less smoke in London and no more smogs.

The other kind of smog is caused by air POLLUTION from car exhausts and other fumes. These are changed by sunlight into a white mist that hangs over cities. Smog of this sort can be dangerous to the people who live in cities. It can hold chemicals that are harmful.

SMUGGLING

Smuggling is the crime of bringing things into a country illegally. For example, many countries have a law which says that if you bring alcohol into that country you must pay a special tax called *duty*. This duty goes to the country's government. Customs inspectors at airports and ports check everything that comes in to make sure the duty is paid. People who do not pay duty are smuggling. Other things that are smuggled are illegal drugs, weapons, animals, and even people.

SNAILS

Snails are MOLLUSCS with a coiled shell on their back. There are more than 80,000 kinds in the world. Some live on land, some in fresh water and some in the sea. They are eaten by fishes and birds, and some kinds are used as food for humans.

Most snails are only a few millimetres long. But one of the largest, the giant land snail, is about 20 cm (8 inches) long.

Smoke like this, from factory chimneys, can cause smog when it mixes with fog. Sunlight shining on smoke makes a different kind of smog.

SNAKES

Snakes are REPTILES. They are long and thin and have no arms or legs. They move along by wriggling their bodies.

Snakes have a dry, smooth skin. Most live in warm places. Those that live in colder climates spend the winter in HIBERNATION.

A few snakes have poison glands. They inject this poison into animals that they bite. The rattlesnake and the cobra are both poisonous snakes.

Most snakes hatch from eggs. A female snake can lay up to ten eggs at a time. Others give birth to live young. The largest snakes are pythons and anacondas. These can grow to 10 metres (30 feet) long.

SNOW

Snow is made up of ice CRYSTALS, which form when the water droplets in a CLOUD freeze. Snow falls when the weather is very cold. Only about one third of the Earth's surface ever has snow. It falls all the year round in the Polar regions at the far north and south of the world, and in winter in places near them. It also falls on the peaks of high mountains.

Snow crystals are always six sided, though each crystal is different from all others. If snow falls in large amounts it can cause problems by blocking roads, railways and airports. But there are plenty of people who like snow, especially if they enjoy winter sports such as skiing and TOBOGGANING. In some countries snow is useful because it protects planted crops.

SOAP

Soap is used for cleaning things. It is made by mixing FAT or vegetable oil with a chemical such as caustic soda. It loosens dirt in clothes and carries it away. Today, chemical cleaners called DETERGENTS are often used instead.

SOLAR ENERGY

Solar energy is energy from the SUN. It reaches the Earth as light and heat. Without these things there could be no life on Earth.

Only about 15 percent of the Sun's energy that reaches the Earth is absorbed by the Earth's surface. Much of it bounces off the Earth and back into space. Solar energy can be collected and used to make electricity.

Snow can cover a landscape very quickly, and though it looks very pretty it can make getting about very difficult. Snow flakes are made up of tiny six-sided ice crystals, like the ones in the picture.

SOLAR SYSTEM

The Solar System is made up of the SUN and the PLANETS travelling around it. Mercury is the planet nearest the Sun. Next come Venus, Earth, Mars, Jupiter, Saturn, Uranus, Neptune and Pluto.

Until the 1500s, most people thought that the Earth was the centre of the Universe, and that the Sun and planets travelled around it. In 1543, a Polish astronomer, Nicolaus COPERNICUS, discovered that in fact, the Earth moved around the Sun.

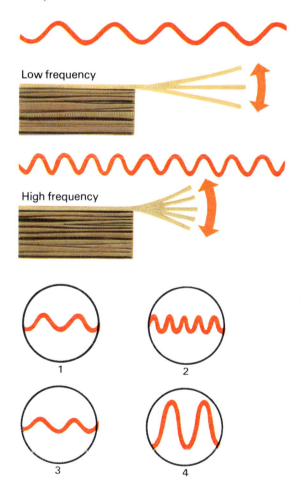

SOUND

Sound is made by vibrating objects, which send sound waves through the air. When these vibrations reach our EARS, we hear them as sounds.

Sound travels through air at about 334 metres (1100 feet) a second. This is slow enough for us to see something happen (if it is far enough away) before we hear it, as the sound takes some time to reach us.

The speed of the vibrations makes a difference to the kind of sound we hear. If the vibrations are very fast, they are said to be 'high frequency' and the sound we hear is high-pitched. If they are slow, the sound is said to be 'low frequency' and the sound we hear is low-pitched.

Left, top: Sound is made by vibrations, or waves in the air. The slower the vibrations, the lower the sound. Left: If sound waves go through a microphone they are turned into electrical waves. These can be seen on a screen like a television. The four sound wave pictures here show (1) a low sound, (2) a high sound, (3) a soft sound and (4) a loud sound.

SOUTH AFRICA

South Africa is a country in southern AFRICA. Most of the country is tableland, a high region of flat-topped hills. Around the coast is a narrow plain. The climate is hot and dry.

South Africa is a rich country. Factories make a wide range of goods. Mines produce gold, ▷

A map of southern Africa, showing South Africa and its neighbours.

diamonds, uranium, copper, iron and other minerals. Farms grow big crops of maize, wheat and fruit. Millions of sheep graze on the grasslands in the centre of the country.

Just over 30 million people live in South Africa. Almost three quarters of them are Black Africans. There are fewer than 5 million Whites. The Whites, who mainly come from Dutch and British settlers, control the country's government and money. Since the 1940s, south Africa has had a policy of *apartheid* or 'apartness'. This means that Whites and non-Whites live separately.

The country has two capitals. Parliament is in Cape Town on the coast. Government offices are in Pretoria on the tableland.

Above: Men working in a South African gold mine. South Africa produces more gold and diamonds than any other country in the world.

SOUTH AMERICA

South America is the world's fourth largest continent. Lying between the Atlantic and Pacific Oceans, it stretches from the EQUATOR in the north to the ANTARCTIC in the south, from the Andes mountains in the west, to the wide AMAZON delta in the east.

The Andes are the longest mountain range in the world. They run along the Pacific coast for 8000 km (5000 miles). They are also the starting point of one of the world's greatest rivers, the Amazon. This huge waterway travels 6437 km (4000 miles) across South America and empties 118 million litres (26 million gallons) of water into the ocean every second. The huge area drained by the Amazon is thick with jungle.

Two other great rivers are the Orinoco, in the north, and the Plate in the south. The land south of the Amazon jungle has swamps, lakes, grasslands and, near the continent's tip, the Patagonian desert.

In most of South America, the climate is warm and sunny. It is very hot and wet in Amazonia and icy cold in the high Andes.

There are 13 countries in South America. The largest, BRAZIL, takes up half the continent. Most South Americans speak Spanish. But in Brazil they speak Portuguese, in Guyana they speak English, in French Guiana, French, and in Surinam, Dutch. These different languages are the

leftovers of history. South America was explored by the Spanish and Portuguese in the 1500s. Then Spain, Portugal and other European countries set up colonies. In the 1800s, most of these colonies won their independence.

The first people of South America were Indians. Most of them, including the INCAS were killed by the conquerors. Later, the Europeans brought in African slaves. Today, most South Americans come from European and African ancestors. There are still some Indians in the Andes and Amazonia. South America is very rich. The rocks of the Andes are full of minerals.

Barranquilla • • Maracaibo • Caracas

Orinoco

VENEZUELA

• Medellin   **Llanos**

■ Bogotá

COLOMBIA

• Cali

Georgetown ■

Paramaribo ■

• Cayenne

GUYANA

SURINAM

FRENCH GUIANA

Equator

• Quito

ECUADOR

Guayaquil •

• Belém

Amazon

• Manáus

Selvas

BRAZIL

• Fortaleza

Chiclayo •

PERU

Trujillo •

• Recife

São Francisco

Callão ■ ■ Lima

• Cuzco

A N D E S   M O U N T A I N S

BOLIVIA

• La Paz

• Cochabamba

Oruro •

■ Sucre

• Salvador

■ Brasília

Brazilian Highlands

PACIFIC OCEAN

Atacama Desert

CHILE

Paraná

PARAGUAY

Gran Chaco

■ Asunción

Rio de Janeiro •

São Paulo •

• Pôrto Alegre

• Córdoba

▲ **Mt Aconcagua**

Valparaíso •

Rosario •

Santiago ■

Buenos Aires ■

ARGENTINA

URUGUAY

• Montevideo

La Plata ■

P a m p a s

Colorado

• Bahía Blanca

ATLANTIC OCEAN

Chubut

SOUTH AMERICA

0   500   1000 miles

0   500   1000   1500 kilometres

■ Capital Cities

Patagonia

Falkland Is

Tierra del Fuego

Cape Horn

There is silver in Peru, tin in BOLIVIA and copper in Chile. There are also huge amounts of oil in VENEZUELA in the north. The open grasslands of ARGENTINA, URUGUAY and Paraguay provide food for millions of sheep and cattle.

Brazil's farmers produce a third of the coffee in the world. Peru's fishermen catch a fifth of the world's fish. So far this wealth has not been used properly. Most South Americans are poor. Many people still scrape a living from the land. They grow potatoes and oats in mountain areas and rice and bananas in the low regions.

The biggest city in South America is Buenos Aires in Argentina. Nearly nine million people live there.

SOYA BEANS

The soya bean is one of man's oldest crops. It comes from China, where it has been grown for over 5000 years. During the 1900s, the soya bean spread to other places. It is now an important crop in many countries, especially the USA, Russia and Brazil.

Most soya beans are grown for oil and meal. The oil is used for salads, cooking and to make margarine. Soya meal is full of PROTEIN and is a nourishing food for animals and people. Both oil and meal are also used to make paint, ink and soap.

SPACE EXPLORATION

People have always gazed in wonder at the Sun, Moon and the stars. Yet for thousands of years, they had no means of studying the heavens above. Then, in the 1600s, TELE-SCOPES were invented and man was able to take a closer look at the universe. More recently, scientists have been able to discover a lot more about space. We are living in the Space Age.

The Space Age began in 1957 when the Russians sent the world's first man-made SATELLITE, *Sputnik I* into ORBIT round the Earth. Only a month later, they launched

Sputnik II with a passenger, a dog called Laika. Instruments connected to Laika collected information about the animal's reactions to space travel. A year later, in 1958, the Americans launched their first satellite.

Since then, Russia and the USA have taken giant steps forward into space. After the first satellites came the first probes. These probes were unmanned spacecraft sent to explore the Moon. In 1961, the Russians sent the first man into space. Yuri Gagarin flew around Earth once in his spacecraft, *Vostok I*.

During the next few years, Russia and the USA continued to launch satellites, manned spacecraft and probes. Some of the probes went to the Moon; others explored Mars and Venus. Then, in 1969, man reached the Moon. Two American ASTRO-

This photo of Jupiter was taken in 1974 by the US probe Pioneer 11. *The Red Spot, near the centre, is probably a storm.*

NAUTS, Neil Armstrong and Edwin Aldrin, landed in their *Apollo* spacecraft.

In the 1970s, space exploration continued with more Moon trips, more probes to other planets, and space stations. Both Russia and the USA launched experimental space stations. Space stations are designed to stay in orbit for many years. Scientists will use them as laboratories and astronauts will use them as bases for space travel.

Above: in 1976, after a year-long journey of 800 million km, an American probe, Viking 1, landed on Mars. This photo, taken by the probe, shows the rocky surface of Mars.

SPAIN

Spain lies in south-west EUROPE, beyond the Pyrenees. Most of the country is covered by high plains and mountains, with a low plain around the coast. The highland has hot·summers, cold winters and little rain. The coast is milder and wetter, especially in the north.

Half the people work on farms, growing potatoes, wheat, wine, grapes, olives and fruits. Wine, olive oil and oranges are exported. Many Spaniards who live on the coast are fishermen. They catch sardines and anchovies. Others work in the tourist trade. Each year, millions of tourists visit Spain to enjoy its sunny beaches. The two main industrial areas are around Bilbao in the north and Barcelona in the north-east. MADRID is the capital and largest city.

Many castles in Spain were built a thousand years ago when the Moors occupied the land.

Above: Spain and Portugal make up the Iberian peninsula.

313

SPHINX

The sphinx is a strange, imaginary beast with a human head and a lion's body. It belongs to the legends of ancient Egypt and Greece. In Egypt, the sphinx represented the power of the king, the PHARAOH. Sphinx statues often had a pharaoh's head.

Greek legends say the sphinx was a woman. She lived near the city of Thebes and asked passers-by a difficult riddle. When they could not answer it, she ate them. But one day, King Oedipus solved the riddle. The sphinx was so angry she killed herself.

Right: Napoleon standing before the Great Sphinx at Giza in Egypt. In 1798, Napoleon's army invaded Egypt. He had some experts with him who studied the ancient monument. The Great Sphinx was carved out of solid rock over 4500 years ago. This giant statue is 73 metres (80 yds) long and 19 metres (22 yds) high.

Nutmeg   Cinnamon

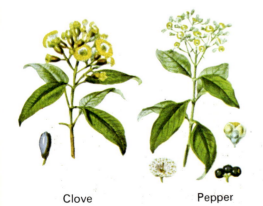

Clove   Pepper

SPICES

Spices have a strong taste and smell and are used to flavour foods and drinks. They are made from the dried parts of plants, usually ground into a powder. Most spice plants grow in hot countries, such as Africa, India and Indonesia. Pepper, ginger, cloves, cinnamon and nutmeg are common spices.

Left: Spices come from different parts of plants. Nutmeg is a seed, cinnamon is bark, cloves are flower buds, and pepper is a berry.

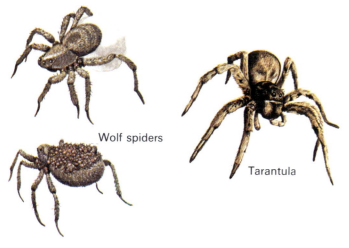
Wolf spiders

Tarantula

Above: Like many other spiders, wolf spiders lay their eggs in silk cocoons. Female wolf spiders carry their cocoons with them. When the babies hatch they ride on their mother's back until they can look after themselves. Tarantulas are among the world's largest spiders.

Above: Baby spiders spread out from their cocoon. Many of them spin a long silk thread and float away on it. Below: Very few spiders are harmful to man, but lots of people find them very frightening.

SPIDERS

Spiders are small animals. Although they look like insects, they are not. Insects have six legs, spiders have eight. Insects have feelers and wings, spiders do not. Insect bodies have three parts, spiders' bodies have two.

All spiders spin silk threads. Many of them use the threads to make a sticky web for catching insects. Not all spiders trap their food in webs. Some are hunters and chase their prey; others lie in wait, then pounce. When a spider catches something, it stuns or kills it with a poisonous bite. All spiders have poison, but in most cases it does not hurt people.

There are about 30,000 kinds of spider. They are all sizes. The comb-footed spider is no bigger than a pinhead, but some bird-eating spiders can be 25 cm (10 inches) across. They have different life stories. Some live for only a year, others for 20 years. Some mate in winter, others in spring. Tiny spiders lay a few eggs, perhaps just one, but the largest lay up to 2000.

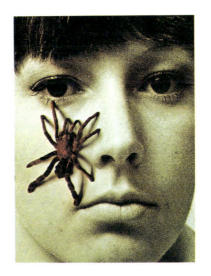

Right: The trapdoor spider lives in a burrow with a lid or trapdoor. When an insect goes by, the spider shoots out of its door, poisons its victim and drags it inside.

SQUID

Squid are MOLLUSCS related to the OCTOPUS. Many live deep in the sea by day but rise to feed at night. A squid uses its 10 tentacles to catch fish and feed them into its beak-like mouth. Some squid are no bigger than a thumb. But the giant squid can grow to 12 metres (40 feet) long.

SQUIRRELS

Most people think of squirrels as a kind of RODENT that is good at climbing trees. Tree squirrels are exactly that. They have sharp claws for climbing and a long, bushy tail that helps them to steer and keep their balance. Tree squirrels can leap 3 metres (10 feet) to reach one tree from another.

Flying squirrels jump 10 times farther than that. These little creatures have flaps of skin between their front and back legs. The flaps form a parachute when a flying squirrel jumps and spreads its limbs. Tree squirrels and flying squirrels feed on leaves, twigs or seeds.

Ground squirrels live in burrows under the ground. They include the chipmunks, prairie dogs and woodchucks.

Above: Each of the squid's 10 arms has rows of sucking discs. These are used to seize and hold on to prey.

Below: The red squirrel builds a nest called a drey, for its young. It is made of twigs and lined with fur.

316

Passengers who sat on the hard seats on the outside of a stagecoach had little protection from the weather.

SRI LANKA

Sri Lanka is an island country off the southern tip of INDIA. Until recently, Sri Lanka was called Ceylon. The island is near the Equator, and so the climate is tropical. Most of the tropical trees and shrubs have been cleared away to make room for crops, but there are still bamboo and palm trees. Animals such as elephants, leopards, monkeys, snakes and colourful birds live in the wilder areas. Sri Lanka's crops include tea, rubber and coconuts.

Over half of the 15,537,000 people of Sri Lanka are Sinhalese. They originally came from India. Colombo, the capital, is also the largest city in Sri Lanka.

STAGECOACH

Before RAILWAYS were invented, many people travelled in stagecoaches. A stagecoach was rather like a big box on wheels. Up to eight passengers climbed in through doors and sat on two rows of facing seats, like the seats in the compartment of a modern railway carriage. The seats were often hard. Travelling became easier when stagecoaches were given springs and cushions.

The driver of the stagecoach sat on an open seat outside to drive the team of horses that pulled the coach. Often there were hard seats on the outside for extra passengers. As many as six horses were used to pull a stagecoach. Every 32 km (20 miles) or so, the driver had to stop to get fresh horses. Even a fresh team took an hour to cover 16 km (10 miles).

STAINED GLASS

Stained glass is a coloured sheet of glass. Pieces of glass of different colours are put together to build a picture. In the MIDDLE AGES craftsmen made stained glass windows for churches. The windows showed scenes from Bible stories. When sunlight shines in through stained glass windows the pictures glow with rich colours—especially red, blue and green.

Craftsmen still make stained glass. They colour it by adding chemicals to the molten (melted) GLASS as it is being made. Artists also use enamel paint to paint details on the glass. The glass is then baked so that the enamel melts into the surface of the glass. Then the pieces of glass are fitted together to make the picture. Strips of lead hold all the pieces in place.

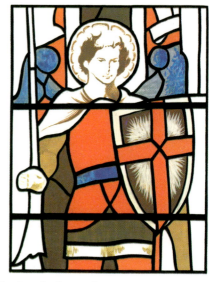

Stained glass pictures are put together like the pieces of a jigsaw.

STALACTITES AND STALAGMITES

Stalactites look like icicles made of stone. Most hang down from the roofs of caves hollowed out of LIMESTONE rock. Stalagmites are similar to stalactites. But they grow upward from the floors of caves.

Stalactites and stalagmites get their names from Greek words that mean 'dripping'. Both are made by water dripping from the ceilings of caves. The water may hold tiny particles of a MINERAL called calcite. As the water dries up, it leaves a little calcite behind. After a long time, this grows into stalactites and stalagmites.

Left: Stalactites and stalagmites are common in limestone caves. Beautiful 'fairy grottoes' like this one are often the result.

STALIN, JOSEPH

Joseph Stalin (1879–1953) ruled RUSSIA from 1929 to 1953. After LENIN died, Stalin made Russia one of the two most powerful nations in the world. He killed or imprisoned millions of Russians who disliked him or disagreed with his kind of COMMUNISM. The name Stalin is Russian for 'man of steel'.

STAMPS

A stamp can be a special mark, or a piece of printed paper with a sticky back. A PASSPORT and many other kinds of document must bear the correct government stamp. Postage stamps are stuck on letters and parcels to be carried by the POST OFFICE. Each nation has its own postage stamps. Millions of people collect postage stamps. Some kinds are scarce and valuable. A very rare stamp can cost more than a row of houses.

Right: Two US postage stamps and (top, right) the Penny Black of 1840, the first postage stamp with a sticky back.

Bread

Potatoes

Rice

Pasta

STARCHES

Starches are a group of white powders produced by green plants. Each plant makes its own type of starch. But all starch is made of carbon, oxygen and hydrogen, the same ingredients found in SUGAR. Starches and sugars are foods called *carbohydrates*. Carbohydrates give plants energy for growth. Plants store energy as starch in their leaves, stems or roots.

CEREALS and POTATOES are rich in starch. If we eat these foods, their starches change to sugars that give our bodies energy.

Left: All of the foods shown here have starch in them. When we eat them the starch changes to sugar during digestion.

STARFISH

Starfish are creatures that live on the seabed. Most have five arms that stick out like the spokes of a wheel. Starfish do not have backbones. But they have a SKELETON made up of bony plates. They creep about on tiny tube feet arranged along the underside of their arms. ▷

Left: Many starfish have tiny spines on their upper sides, which they use to protect themselves. If one arm of a starfish is cut off, the creature can grow a new one to replace it.

319

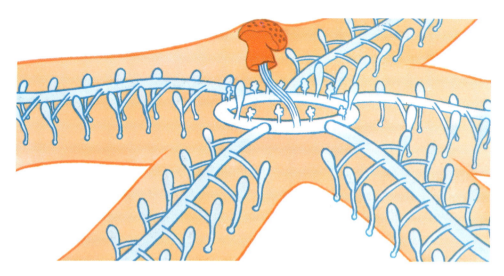

A starfish can open and eat a cockle. It uses its tube feet to grip both halves of the cockle's shell. Then it pulls the shell open. The starfish pushes part of its stomach out of its mouth, which is under the middle of its body. The stomach slips inside the cockle shell and digests the cockle's soft body.

STARS

The stars we can see from Earth are just a few of the many millions scattered through space. Stars look small because they are so far away. But most are huge, fiery balls of gas like our SUN.

Stars begin as clouds of gas. GRAVITY pulls the gas particles in toward the middle of each cloud. There the particles collide and grow hot, and other particles press in.

HYDROGEN atoms change into helium atoms by a process called nuclear fusion. That process give off NUCLEAR ENERGY. This is what makes stars glow so brightly.

Stars swell as they use their hydrogen. Astronomers call such stars *red giants*. Red giants later shrink into tiny white-hot stars called *white dwarfs*. In time, these cool and fade into the darkness of space.

Right: Some of the stars in the Pleiades, a star cluster in the constellation Taurus. Though only a few stars can be seen with the naked eye, there are actually over 100 stars in the cluster.

Above: The five arms of a starfish grip and walk with tiny tube feet. Sea water that enters the starfish's body is squeezed down into these tubes. As the water is sucked back up into the body, the tips of the feet form suckers that will cling to solid objects.

320

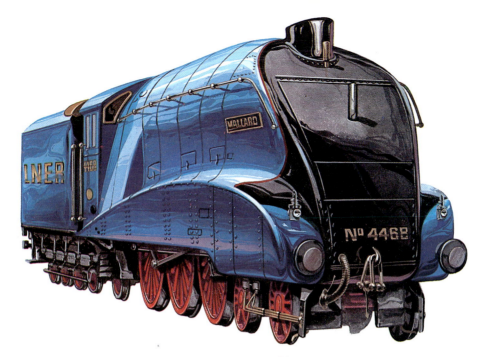

STEAM ENGINES

Boiling water turns into steam. Steam will fill 1700 times more space than the water that it came from. So if you squash steam into a small container it presses hard against the sides. If one side is free to move, the steam pressure will push it outward.

In the 1700s British inventors began to use this fact to build ENGINES powered by steam. Early steam engines worked with a simple to-and-fro motion. In Thomas Newcomen's engine a furnace heated water in a boiler. The water gave off steam that pushed a piston up inside a cylinder. When the steam cooled and turned back to water, air pressed the piston down again. Newcomen's engine was used to pump water from flooded mines.

James Watt built a more powerful engine where steam pushed the piston first one way and then the other. Rods from the piston spun a wheel. By the early 1800s, such engines were moving heavy loads faster than men or horses could. Yet unlike men and horses, steam engines never tired.

Steam engines powered factory machines that made the INDUSTRIAL REVOLUTION possible. They also powered LOCOMOTIVES and steamships. For the first time, people travelled faster than horses or the wind.

The INTERNAL COMBUSTION ENGINE has largely taken the place of steam engines. But many ship's propellers, and power station generators are worked by steam which spins wheels called TURBINES.

Above: In 1938, the British steam locomotive Mallard reached a speed of 202 km/hr (126 mph). This is still a record speed for steam locomotives.

STOCK EXCHANGE

A stock exchange is a place where people called stockbrokers buy and sell *stocks* and *shares*. These are pieces of paper that show that someone owns a share in a business company. A company's stock tends to cost more if the company does well, and gets cheaper if it does badly. People buy stock hoping to sell it at a higher price later. Meanwhile they expect to get *dividends*—shares of the money the company makes.

As business grew after the MIDDLE AGES, people needed a market place for buying and selling stock. In 1531 Antwerp opened Europe's first stock exchange. Now, many cities have stock exchanges. Millions of stocks change hands each day in the exchanges of London, New York and Tokyo.

STOMACH

Your stomach is a muscular bag open at both ends and shaped like a fat letter J. It plays an important part in the DIGESTION of food.

When you eat a meal, food travels down your throat to your stomach. This can store a large meal. Juices produced in the stomach kill GERMS in food. They also moisten and start digesting the food. Stomach muscles churn the mixture, then force it out into the small intestine.

STONE AGE

The Stone Age was the great span of time before men learned how to make metal tools. Stone Age people used stone, wood and bone instead of metal. The Stone Age probably began more than three million years ago. It ended in Iraq and Egypt when the Bronze Age began there about 5000 years ago. But some Australian ABORIGINES and forest tribes in New Guinea still live largely Stone Age lives.

The Stone Age had three parts: Old, Middle and New. The Old Stone Age lasted until 10,000 years ago in the Middle East. When it began hunters could scarcely chip a pebble well enough to sharpen it. When the Old Stone Age ended, people had learnt to chip FLINT into delicate spearheads, knives and scrapers.

In the Middle Stone Age, hunters used tiny flakes of flint in arrows and harpoons.

The New Stone Age began in the Middle East about 9000 years ago. New Stone Age peoples made smooth axe heads of ground stone. Farming replaced hunting in the New Stone Age.

322

Above: An Old Stone Age tool made from a deer's antler and decorated with a carving of a bison's head.

Left: A thumb-sized carving of a woman's head, made from mammoth ivory over 20,000 years ago.

STONEHENGE

Stonehenge is a huge prehistoric temple on Salisbury Plain in southern England. The main part is a great circle of standing stones. Each is more than twice as tall as a man and weighs nearly 30 tonnes. Flat stones were laid across the tops of the standing stones to form a ring. Inside the ring stood smaller stones, and a great block that may have been an altar. The big stones were raised 3500 years ago. Other parts are older.

Right: Stonehenge. These huge stones were dragged on rollers from a site 250 miles away. It must have taken years.

STORKS

These big birds have long beaks and legs. They can wade in swamps and capture fish and frogs. But some kinds prefer feeding on dead animals. More than a dozen kinds of stork live in warm parts of the world.

The white stork is the best known kind. In summer, white storks nest in Europe and central Asia. In autumn, they fly south. Flapping their wings soon makes storks tired. They prefer to soar and glide.

STUARTS

The House of Stuart was a royal family that ruled Scotland from 1371 to 1603 and England and Scotland from 1603 until 1715.

In the 1000s AD the family lived in France. But by the middle of the 1100s a member of the family had become the King of Scotland's steward (the man who ran the royal household). From then on, the family always provided the Scottish king with a steward. Because of this, the family name became Stewart, which later changed to Stuart.

As royal rulers, the Stuarts were unlucky. Out of 14 who were crowned, 6 were killed, and 7 became king or queen before they were old enough to rule for themselves.

MARY, QUEEN OF SCOTS was put to death by ELIZABETH I, who feared that Mary might replace her as the Queen of England. Mary's grandfather had been married to the daughter of an English king. So when Elizabeth died without leaving a child to inherit her throne, the crown went to Mary's son James. He ruled as JAMES I of England and as James VI of Scotland.

The Stuart kings of England claimed so much power that they became unpopular. CHARLES I was executed in the English CIVIL WAR, and CHARLES II's son JAMES II was forced to leave the country. The throne went to his sister Mary and her husband WILLIAM OF ORANGE, then to James's sister Anne. Under Anne, England and Scotland were united as Great Britain. Anne was the last Stuart ruler. She died in 1715.

Stuart supporters called Jacobites led two revolts to win back the throne for James's descendants. In 1715 they fought for his son, James Edward. In 1745 they fought for Charles Edward, James Edward's son 'Bonnie Prince Charlie'. Both revolts failed.

323

STURGEON

Sturgeon are big fish whose eggs are eaten as a costly delicacy called caviar. The fish have a long, slim body protected by rows of bony plates. Most kinds live in seas and swim up rivers to lay their eggs.

The largest sturgeon is the beluga, found in Russian waters. Belugas can grow four times longer than a man and weigh a tonne. Sometimes they eat young seals.

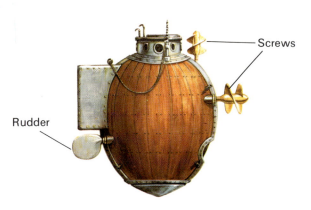

SUBMARINES

Submarines are boats that can travel under water. To dive, the crew of a submarine make it heavier than the amount of water needed to fill the space taken up by the submarine. To rise, the crew make the submarine lighter than that amount of water. When water and submarine both weigh the same, the boat stays at the same level under the surface.

In 1620 someone rowed a wood and leather submarine down England's Thames river. But the first submarine that worked well was not built until the 1770s. Both these early submarines were worked by hand. They were slow and underpowered.

In the 1870s an English clergyman invented a submarine powered by a steam engine. But each time it dived the crew had to pull down its chimney and put out the fire that heated water to produce steam.

By 1900 the American inventor John P. Holland had produced a much better under-

Above: Built in 1775, the Turtle *was an American submarine that held one man. To dive he let in water. To rise, he pumped it out. He moved along by turning screws. A rudder helped him steer the tiny craft.*

water boat. Petrol engines drove it on the surface. But petrol needs air to burn. Under water the boat ran on battery-driven motors that did not need air.

In 1955 came the first nuclear-powered submarine. Such boats can travel around the world without having to come up for air. Nuclear-powered submarines are warships. Today, people use the BATHYSCAPHE and other underwater craft to explore the seabed. Small underwater boats called *submersibles* are used to work on underwater pipes that carry oil.

Below: This cutaway view shows a nuclear submarine. Heat from its nuclear reactor turns water into steam. This spins turbine blades that drive the propeller.

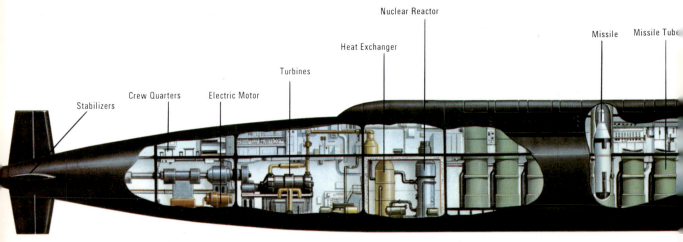

SUDAN

This is the largest nation in AFRICA. It is more than four times the size of France, which is the biggest country in western Europe.

Sudan is a hot country in north-east Africa. Desert sprawls across the north. There are flat grasslands in the middle. The south has forests and a huge swamp.

Sudanese people include Arabs and Negroes. Most live near the NILE, which flows north across the country. The Sudanese raise cattle, grow crops like sugar cane, or work in cities. Khartoum is the capital city.

SUEZ CANAL

The Suez Canal crosses Egypt between Port Said on the Mediterranean Sea and Suez on the Red Sea. It is the world's longest CANAL that can be used by big ships. It measures 160 km (100 miles) from end to end and 60 metres (197 feet) across its bed. Ships use it as a short cut on voyages between Europe and Asia. This saves them sailing 9650 km (6000 miles) around southern Africa.

The canal was begun in 1859 by a French company run by the engineer Ferdinand de

Egypt seen from a spacecraft. The Suez Canal crosses the narrow gap between the Mediterranean (top left) and the long thin Gulf of Suez, part of the Red Sea.

Lesseps. More than 8000 men and hundreds of camels worked on it for 10 years. France and England operated the canal until Egypt took it over in 1956.

Sunken ships blocked the canal for eight years after Egypt's war with Israel in 1967. But dredging has now made it much wider and deeper than it was a century ago.

SUGAR

Sugar is a sweet-tasting food. We eat it as an ingredient in ice cream, jellies, sweets and soft drinks. We use sugar crystals to sweeten cereals, coffee and tea.

Sugar gives your body energy more quickly than any other kind of food. But

Periscopes, Radio and Radar Antennae

Conning Tower

Hydroplanes

Navigation Room

Missile Control Room

Wardroom

Torpedo Room

325

eating too many sugary things can make you fat and cause your teeth to decay.

All sugar contains carbon, hydrogen and oxygen. Different groupings of these ATOMS produce different kinds of sugars. The kind we eat most of is known as *sucrose*.

Every green PLANT produces sugar. But most of the sugar that we eat comes from two kinds of plant. One is sugar cane, a type of giant grass. The other is sugar beet, a plant with a thick root rich in sugar.

Left: When sugar beet is harvested it is sliced and soaked in water to make a syrup. This is boiled and dried to make pure sugar. About one tonne of sugar in every three comes from sugar beet. Most grows in the parts of Europe and North America that are too cold for sugar cane.

Below: The Sun shown as if cut open like an apple. The core holds helium, produced by nuclear reactions that send energy through the outer layers into space. The bright surface layer is the photosphere.

SUN

The Sun is just one of many million STARS in the MILKY WAY. But it is also the centre of the SOLAR SYSTEM. The PLANETS and their moons all whirl around it. The heat and light given out by the Sun make it possible for plants and animals to live here, on the planet that we call the EARTH. ▷

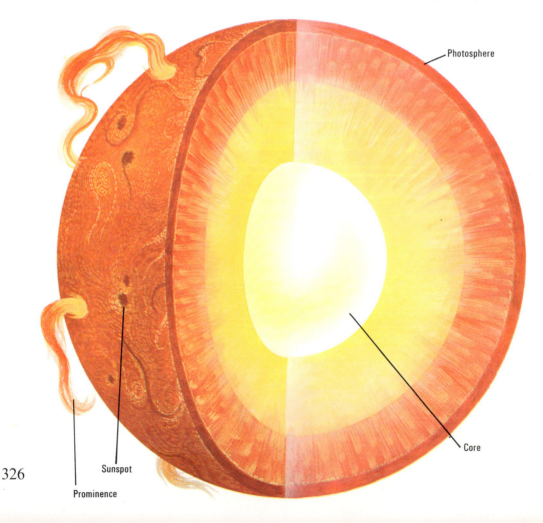

Photosphere

Sunspot

Prominence

Core

The Sun seems small because it is so far away. A spacecraft that took an hour to zoom around the Earth would need five months to reach the Sun. In fact, the Sun is so big that you could fit a million Earths inside it with room to spare. A bucketful of the Sun's substance would weigh far less than a bucketful of rock from the Earth. But the whole Sun would weigh over 750 times more than all the planets whirling around it.

The Sun is a great glowing ball of gases. In the middle of the Sun a process called nuclear fusion turns HYDROGEN gas into helium gas. This change releases huge amounts of NUCLEAR ENERGY. The Sun beams out its energy in all directions as *electromagnetic waves*. Some of these waves give us HEAT and LIGHT. But there are also radio waves, ultraviolet rays, X-rays and others.

The Sun was formed from a mass of gas and dust 5000 million years ago. It contains enough hydrogen fuel to keep it glowing brightly for another 5000 million years.

SUNSPOTS

Sunspots are dark patches that appear on the surface of the SUN from time to time. They look like ink blots, and are places that are cooler than the rest of the surface. But a sunspot is still about 4000° Centigrade— 40 times as hot as boiling water.

Sunspots come in many shapes and sizes. A small sunspot could fit inside Belgium. But a big group may measure five times as far across as the distance around the Earth. Such groups often have two spots larger than the rest. A big group may last for months, but a small group may vanish within hours. Both sorts occur near the Sun's EQUATOR.

Astronomers have found that the Sun's gases whirl up and down where sunspots form. No one quite knows what causes sunspots. But they often happen at the same time as solar flares. These are dazzlingly bright bursts of light sent out by the Sun.

Sunspots are plentiful in some years, but scarce in others. A gap of 11 years separates each main burst of sunspot activity.

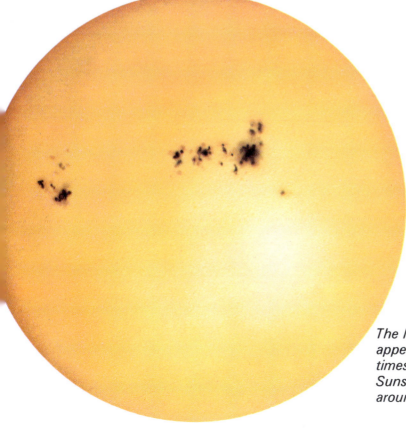

The largest sunspot ever seen appeared in 1947. It covered an area 30 times as large as the Earth's surface. Sunspots form where 'cool' gases swirl around on a part of the Sun's surface.

327

SURGERY

Surgery is cutting someone open to remove or mend a damaged part of the body. Surgery is performed by a specially trained doctor called a surgeon. He works in a hospital, in a specially equipped room called an operating theatre. X-RAY and other tests may help to show the surgeon how best to operate. Before an operation, a patient is given an anaesthetic so that he sleeps and feels no pain.

The surgeon cuts the patient open with a sharp knife called a scalpel. Other tools help him prevent bleeding and hold back flaps of skin. After operating he closes the wound by sewing its edges together.

SURVEYING

Surveying means using measuring instruments and working out certain sums to find out the exact positions of places on the Earth's surface. This kind of information makes it possible for people to make maps and charts and to build bridges, roads, and so on.

Above: A surveyor using an instrument that measures distances by timing radio signals sent from one place to another. Surveyors using it can work quickly, and even measure distances in fog.

Below: A patient undergoing surgery. To protect him from germs, the surgeon and his team wear gloves and masks, and use sterilized instruments and dressings.

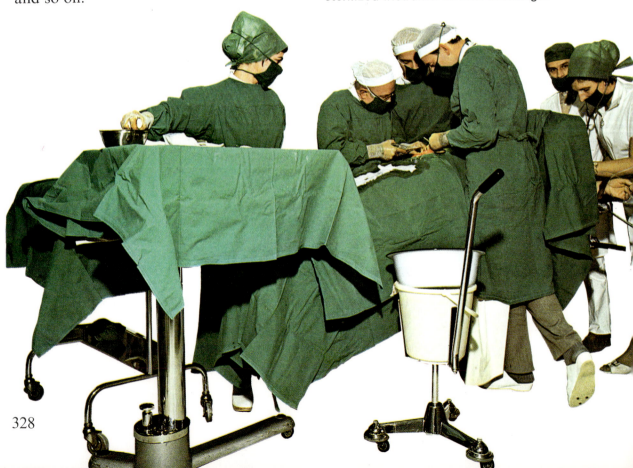

SWANS

These big, graceful waterbirds are among the heaviest birds able to fly. To take off, they need a long, clear stretch of water.

Swans swim with webbed feet, lowering their necks to feed on underwater plants. They build bulky nests by pools or rivers. Their young are known as cygnets.

Some kinds of swan fly south in spring and autumn. They fly in V-shaped flocks.

Right: The handsome black swan lives in Australia and Tasmania. Only two kinds of swan live south of the equator.

SWEDEN

Sweden is the fourth-largest nation in EUROPE. The country lies in the north, between Norway and the Baltic Sea. Mountains cover most of the west, and forests take up more than half of the land. Their CONIFER trees yield much of the world's softwood. Most of Sweden's electricity comes from rivers flowing down the mountains. Farmers produce milk, meat, grains and sugar beet on farmlands near the coast. The north is too cold for farming, but it has rich iron mines.

Most of the eight million Swedes live in the south. The capital, Stockholm is there.

Above: A swan on her nest. Nearby swim her fluffy brown cygnets

SWIFT, JONATHAN

Jonathan Swift (1667–1745) was an English writer, famous for books that poked fun at the silly and cruel behaviour of people and governments. Most children enjoy stories from *Gulliver's Travels*. This tells of three voyages to very strange lands.

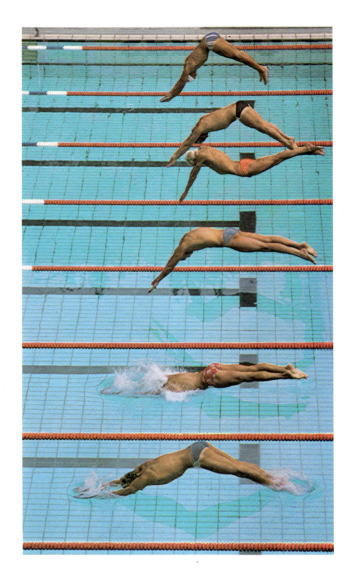

Left: Six divers show different kinds of racing dive. The way a swimmer dives into a swimming pool to start a race can make a big difference to his chance of winning.

Above: Tracy Wickham of Australia won two freestyle titles in the 1978 World Championships. She is using the crawl stroke (see below).

SWIMMING

Swimming is the skill or sport of staying afloat and moving through water. Swimming is healthy exercise, and being able to swim may save your life if you fall into water by accident. Many animals know how to swim from birth. But people have to learn, usually with help from a trained instructor.

Learners often start in a pool or at the edge of the sea. First they should float or glide. Then they can try kicking. Arm movements come last. Beginners must learn to fit in breathing with arm movements.

Swimmers usually use one or more of five main kinds of stroke. These are called breast-stroke, butterfly stroke, backstroke, sidestroke, and crawl.

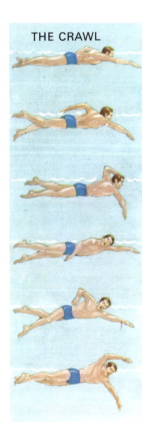

THE CRAWL

SWITZERLAND

This small, mountainous country lies in the central southern part of EUROPE. The sharp, snowy peaks of the ALPS and their steep-sided valleys fill most of southern Switzerland. In summer, tourists pick wild flowers and watch dairy cattle grazing on the mountain meadows. Winter visitors to the many resorts ski down the snowy alpine slopes.

The forests of the Jura Mountains form the country's western rim. Between the Jura and the Alps stands the Swiss Plateau. Big lakes lie where the mountains meet this lower land. Here, where the weather is mainly moist and mild, most of the country's crops are grown. Here, too, stand most of Switzerland's cities, including Bern, the capital. Swiss factories make chemicals, machinery, watches and chocolates.

Most of the six and a half million Swiss speak German, French or Italian. The Swiss people are among the most prosperous in the world.

Above: A skier twists and turns to control his speed as he glides down a snowy mountainside. In summer the melting snow from the mountains helps to fill Swiss rivers and lakes. Power stations use this water to produce electric current.

SYDNEY

Sydney is the largest city in AUSTRALIA, and the capital of New South Wales. More than three million people live in Sydney. It stands on a fine natural harbour (Port Jackson) crossed by a famous steel-arch bridge. Sydney makes chemicals, machinery and ships and is an important port. It was founded in 1788 as a settlement for convicts sent out from England.

Left, top: A view of Sydney. Below: Sydney Opera House, built on the harbour to look like a group of giant yacht sails.

SYRIA

This Arab country lies just east of the Mediterranean Sea. Much of Syria is covered by dry plains that are hot in summer and chilly in winter. There are nearly eight million people. NOMADS drive flocks of sheep and goats over the dry lands. Farmers grow grains, grapes and apricots, where rivers or rain provide water.

Most Syrian towns grew up on the roads used by merchants long ago to bring goods from the East.

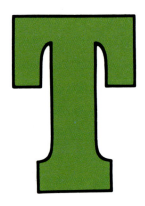

More than 20,000 men took 22 years to build the Taj Mahal. It is made of white marble and surrounded by beautiful gardens of cypress trees and lily pools.

TAJ MAHAL

This is the world's most beautiful tomb. It stands on the Jumna river at Agra, north India. The emperor, Shah Jahan, built it for his favourite wife, Mumtaz Mahal, who died in 1631. The Shah planned to build an exact copy in black marble for himself on the other side of the river. His son prevented this and so when the Shah died he was buried with his wife in her tomb.

TAPESTRY

Tapestries are designs or pictures woven in cloth. It is a very old craft. The Egyptians made tapestries about 1700 years ago.

Tapestries are made by WEAVING coloured silk thread across closely packed rows of strong linen or wool threads, held in a frame. Sometimes real gold or silver threads are used.

The design for the tapestry is drawn onto the linen threads with ink. The weaver works from the back of the tapestry. A mirror placed in front of the work shows how the design is going.

An old Egyptian tapestry woven in the 300s.

TARTAN

This is a woollen cloth, which is woven in different sorts of square pattern. It was invented by the Highlanders of Scotland. They lived in large family groups called clans. Each clan had its own tartan pattern. Some had two: a dull coloured one for hunting and a bright coloured one for special occasions.

At first the tartan cloth was worn in one long piece. Part of it was wrapped around the body to make a skirt and the rest was worn over the shoulder. At night, it could be taken off and used as a blanket. The separate, pleated kilt was not worn until the 1880s.

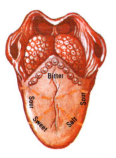

Above: Each patch of taste buds picks up one sort of taste. Bitter tastes are picked up on the back of the tongue, sour tastes at the side, and sweet and salt at the front.

Sinus

Nerve
Fibres

Sinus

Hard
Palate

Soft
Palate

Tongue

Muscle

Epiglottis

Windpipe   Oesophagus

TASTE

We can taste food because we have taste buds on our tongues. Your TONGUE is covered in tiny bumps. The taste buds are buried in the sides of these bumps. There are clusters of buds on the back, tip and sides of the tongue. NERVES, running from the buds to the brain, tell you whether the food you are eating is sweet, sour, bitter or salty.

Taste is not the same as flavour. Flavour is a mixture of the taste and the SMELL of food. If you have a bad cold and your nose is blocked, food hardly tastes of anything. The most comfortable way to take bad tasting medicine is to hold your nose while you swallow.

A cutaway drawing showing the inside of a head, where smells and tastes are picked up. A clump of nerve fibres high in the nose picks up smells from outside. Some smell from food in the mouth can get into the nose past the soft palate. The taste buds cluster in groups around the edges and back of the tongue.

333

TEA

Tea is a refreshing drink that is made by pouring boiling water on the dried, chopped leaves of the tea plant.

Tea was first grown in China. It was brought to Europe by the Dutch in the 1660s. Today, most tea is grown in northern India, Pakistan and Sri Lanka.

TEETH

Teeth are made to cut, tear or crush food so that it can be swallowed. Cutting teeth are called incisors; tearing teeth are called canines; and crushing teeth are called molars. Meat eating animals have large canines for tearing up flesh. Plant eaters have sharp incisors and large molars for snapping off and grinding up stringy stalks. Humans have all three kinds of teeth because we eat all kinds of food.

There are two parts to a tooth. The root, which has one, two or three prongs, is fixed in the jawbone. The crown is the part you can see. Tooth decay happens when bacteria mix with sugar. Together, they dissolve tooth enamel, making holes that let infection get inside the tooth.

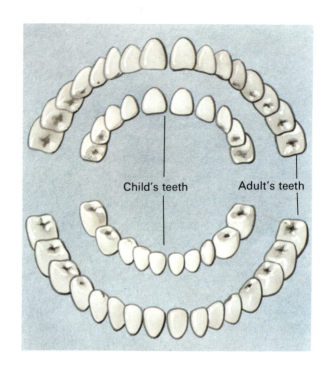

Above: Your first set of teeth are called milk teeth. There are ten on the top and ten on the bottom. Each row has four incisors at the front, with one canine each side of them, followed by two molars. As you grow, these teeth fall out and are replaced by an adult set. These are the same as milk teeth but there are 16 molars (four on each side top and bottom).

Below: The dentist drills away the decaying part of the tooth before filling the hole.

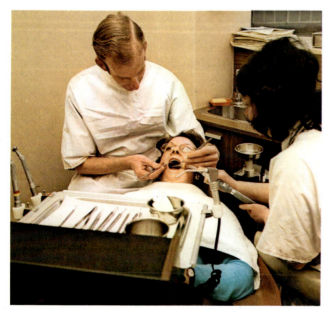

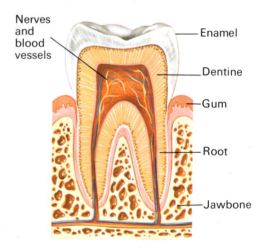

Above: There are three layers to a tooth. Inside is a cavity full of nerves and blood vessels. It is surrounded by a bony wall of dentine. This is covered in hard, shiny enamel.

TELEPHONES

Telephones let you speak to someone far away. When you pick up a telephone receiver a weak electric current is switched on. When you speak into the mouthpiece, you speak into a microphone.

Waves of SOUND from your voice hit a metal disc inside the microphone and make it vibrate. These vibrations travel along the telephone wires as electrical waves. When they reach the other end, they hit another metal disc in the earpiece. This changes the vibrations back into sound waves, which the person you are calling hears as your voice.

The first electric telephone was made by Alexander BELL in 1876. This produced only a very weak sound over long distances, but many other types of telephones soon followed. Today, telephone networks use a world-wide system of cables and communications satellites.

Above right: In 1892, Ericsson designed the magneto telephone. It looked much more like the modern telephone we know than Alexander Bell's first telephone.

Below: A copy of the reflecting telescope made by Sir Isaac Newton in the early 1600s. At one end is a large mirror. The other end is open and there is a tiny mirror set just inside. Light is reflected from the big mirror to the small mirror. And this reflects the light to the eyepiece set in the side of the telescope.

Ericsson's magneto phone, 1892

TELESCOPES

Telescopes make things that are far away look nearer. They work by gathering the LIGHT from an object and bending it to make a tiny picture called an image. The image is then made larger.

There are two kinds of telescope. The LENS or refractor telescope uses two lenses fixed in a tube to keep out unwanted light. A large lens at one end of the tube collects the light. It is called the object lens. A smaller lens, called the eyepiece, makes the image larger.

The image you see through this kind of telescope is upside down. If you want to turn the image the right way round, a third lens is needed. Binoculars are two lens telescopes fixed together.

The other sort of telescope is called a reflecting telescope. Instead of a lens it has a curved mirror to collect light.

The idea of the lens telescope was discovered by accident in 1608 by Hans Lippershey, a Dutch spectacle maker. While holding up two lenses he noticed that the church weathervane looked much closer through them.

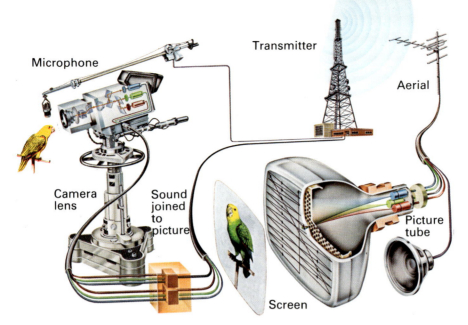

Microphone

Transmitter

Aerial

Camera
lens

Sound
joined
to
picture

Picture
tube

Screen

TELEVISION

Television is a way of sending sounds and pictures through the air by ELECTRICITY. Scientists have been interested in the idea of television since the 1880s. Although John Logie Baird was the first to show how television worked, his success was based on work by many other scientists from all over the world. Baird showed his set in 1926. The first television service opened in 1936 in Britain. Colour television began in the United States in 1956.

At first, all television was black and white. Few people owned television sets as they were very expensive. Now nearly every home has one. In America and Britain there is one television set for every three

Above: The television set you have at home is only part of the television system. In the studio, the camera and microphone pick up the pictures and sound and change them into electric signals. The transmitter sends the signals out as radio waves. Your TV aerial is specially shaped to catch these waves, and change them back into electric signals. Inside the TV set, the signals are turned back into pictures and sounds.

Below and right: Inside a colour TV camera, mirrors and filters split up the scene in front of the lens into three colours, red, blue and green. Each colour goes into a separate tube. Inside each tube, the waves are changed into electric signals. Signals from all three tubes join up outside the camera and are fed into a transmitter.

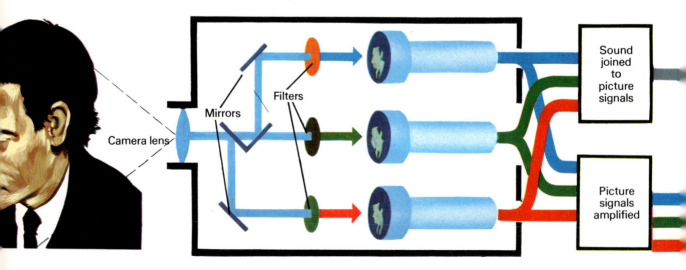

Camera lens

Mirrors

Filters

Sound
joined
to
picture
signals

Picture
signals
amplified

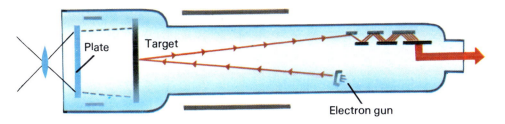

Electron gun

Below: When the electron gun scans the screen, it fires a beam of electrons from left to right. It misses out every other line, then whizzes back to the top to pick up the missed lines. This happens very quickly. The gun scans 25 complete pictures every second.

Above: Inside each colour tube of the camera the light waves hit a special plate. The plate changes them into electrical signals, which pass on to a target screen. Behind the screen is an electron gun. This scans the screen, firing a beam of electrons at it. The beam bounces off, carrying the signals out of the camera.

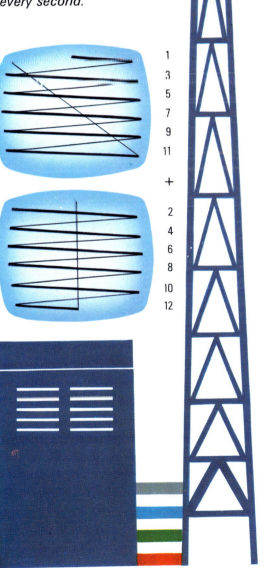

people. In Britain, over half the sets are for colour.

Television works by changing LIGHT waves into electric signals. This happens inside the TV camera. A picture of what is happening in front of the camera forms on a special screen behind the LENS. Behind the screen is an electron gun. This *scans* the screen. It moves from left to right to cover each part of the picture. Each part is turned into an electric signal which is made stronger then sent to the transmitter. All the signals are broadcast by the transmitter as RADIO waves. They are picked up by home TV aerials and changed back into electric signals. These pass into the TV set.

Inside the set is a large glass tube called the cathode ray tube. The screen that you look at is the front of this tube. The screen is covered with tiny chemical dots. In a colour set, these are arranged in groups of three: one red, one blue, one green. At the back of the tube is another electron gun. This fires a beam of electrons to scan the screen just as the camera gun does. As each electron hits the screen, it lights up a dot. These tiny flashes of colour build up the picture on your screen. You do not see lines of coloured flashing lights, because the electron gun moves too fast for the eye to follow. What you see is a picture of what is happening in the television studio.

Live television programmes show you what is happening as it happens. Most programmes are recorded on film or VIDEO-TAPE and sent out later.

TEMPERATURE

Temperature is the measurement of heat. It is measured on a scale marked on a THERMOMETER. Most people today use the Celsius or Centigrade scale. A Fahrenheit scale is also used, for example, to measure body temperature.

Some animals, such as mammals like man, are warm-blooded. Their temperature stays much the same. Humans can stand quite a wide range of body temperatures. When a man is healthy, his normal body temperature is 37°C (98·6°F). When he is ill, his temperature might go up to 41°C (106°F) or more, and he could still survive.

Other animals, such as snakes, lizards and frogs, are cold-blooded. Their body temperature goes up and down with the temperature of their surroundings. Many cold-blooded animals can survive until their body temperature drops almost to freezing point.

Below: The normal human temperature is 37°C (98·6°F). The human body has many ways of dealing with different temperatures. But when it gets too hot or cold the body may find it hard to adjust.

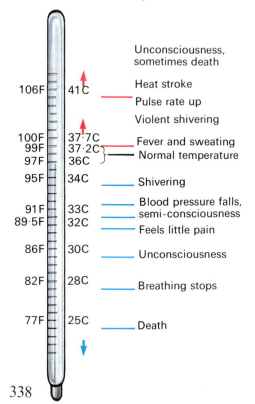

		Unconsciousness, sometimes death
106F	41C	Heat stroke
		Pulse rate up
		Violent shivering
100F	37·7C	Fever and sweating
99F	37·2C	Normal temperature
97F	36C	
95F	34C	Shivering
91F	33C	Blood pressure falls, semi-consciousness
89·5F	32C	Feels little pain
86F	30C	Unconsciousness
82F	28C	Breathing stops
77F	25C	Death

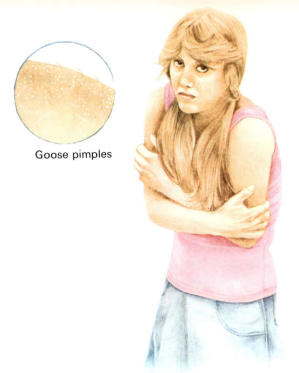

Goose pimples

Above: Shivering helps to keep you warm. Tiny muscle movements warm the body up. Goose pimples happen when the body hairs stand on end to trap warm air in between them.

TENNIS

A game for two or four people played on a specially marked court, which is divided in half by a net 90 cm (3 feet) high in the centre. If two people play it is called a singles match. If four people play it is called a doubles match.

Tennis balls must be about 2 inches (50 mm) in diameter and weigh about 2 ounces (56·7 grams). They must bounce between 53 inches (1·35 metres) and 58 inches (1·47 metres) when dropped from a height of 100 inches (2·5 metres) onto concrete. A tennis racket can be any size.

A tennis match is divided into sets. Usually women play three sets and men play five. Each set has at least six games. To win a game, one player must score at least four points. Modern tennis is a simple version of an old French game called real tennis or royal tennis.

TEXTILES

A textile is any cloth made by WEAVING. Before the INDUSTRIAL REVOLUTION, all cloth was made by hand from natural fibres of wool, silk, cotton or linen. Since then, scientists have developed many kinds of man-made fibre. Rayon is made from wood. Nylon comes from oil. There are even some fibres made from glass. Man-made fibres are cheaper and often easier to wash and look after. Sometimes they are mixed with natural fibres to get the best of both materials.

Weaving is one of the world's main industries. In this Australian factory, a many-coloured cloth is being woven by machine.

THAILAND

Thailand is a country in south-east ASIA. It sits in the middle of Burma, Laos and Kampuchea. The south coast opens onto the Gulf of Thailand, which is part of the South China Sea. Bangkok, the capital city, is on the coast. In the south-west corner a long, thin PENINSULA stretches down to Malaysia. One part of it is only 16 km (10 miles) across.

Thailand is nearly twice the size of Great Britain, but only 49 million people live there. Most of them live in the middle. Many rivers flow through this part of the country, making it very fertile. Most people are farmers. Rice is the most important crop. They also grow cotton, tobacco, maize, coconuts and bananas. Some farmers raise pigs, and buffalo to plough the rice fields. In the north, across the border with Burma, there are large forests of teak, which is an important export. The peninsula is covered in mountains and jungles. It is very rich in minerals, especially tin.

Thailand used to be called Siam. In 1939, the name was changed. Thai means 'free', so Thailand means the land of the free. During WORLD WAR II, the Japanese took over and ruled Thailand, but now it is independent. There is a king, but the country is ruled by an elected government.

THAMES, RIVER

The river Thames is the longest and most important river in ENGLAND. It begins in the Cotswold Hills and flows eastward, growing wider and wider, until it reaches the North Sea. The Thames flows through the middle of London, which was once the most important port in Europe. Now the docks that once stretched 56 km (35 miles) along the riverside, are closed and ships stop lower down the river.

Not very long ago, the Thames around London was one of the dirtiest rivers in the world, full of SEWAGE and chemical waste. Now it has been cleaned so thoroughly that fish are coming back to live in it.

THANKSGIVING DAY

Thanksgiving Day was first celebrated in America by the Pilgrim Fathers. They were PROTESTANTS who sailed to North America in 1620 so that they could follow their religious beliefs in peace. After their first year there, they held a feast to give thanks to God because they had survived. Today, Americans celebrate Thanksgiving Day on the fourth Thursday of November.

THEATRE

A theatre is a place where plays are performed by actors and watched by an audience. A theatre may be just a patch of ground, or a large, expensive building.

The earliest theatres we know about were in Greece. They were simply flattened patches of ground on a hillside. The audience sat in rows on the hill above so that they could all see the 'stage'. When the Greeks built their theatres they followed this plan. They cut a half-moon or horseshoe shape in the hillside and lined it with rows of stone seats, looking down on a round, flat stage.

The Romans copied the Greek pattern, but they built most of their theatres on flat ground. The rows of seats were held up by a wall. The Romans built a theatre in nearly every large town in the ROMAN EMPIRE.

In Britain, there were no theatre buildings before the 1500s. Troops of actors went around the country performing plays outside churches or in market places. They used their travelling carts as stages. Later, they began to do plays in the great halls of rich people's houses. They also put on shows in the courtyards of inns. The first theatres to be built were made of wood, and looked very much like inns. The stage jutted out into a large yard. Galleries of seats ran all around the sides. There were even seats on the stage, but only for rich people. These theatres had no roofs. When it rained, the *groundlings*, people who stood in the yard around the stage, got wet. SHAKESPEARE's plays were performed in theatres like this.

Later on, theatres had proper roofs. The stage was moved back and the audience sat in straight rows directly in front of it.

THERMOMETERS

A thermometer is an instrument which measures TEMPERATURE. It is usually a glass tube marked with a scale. Inside is another, thinner glass tube, which ends in a bulb containing liquid MERCURY. When the temperature goes up, the mercury gets warm and expands (grows bigger). It rises up the tube. When it stops, you can read the temperature on the marked scale. When it gets cold, the mercury contracts (grows smaller) and sinks down the tube. Most thermometers measure temperatures between the boiling and freezing points of water. This is between 0° and 100° on the Centigrade scale or 32° and 212° on the Fahrenheit scale.

Medical thermometers, which are small enough to go in your mouth, measure your blood heat. This is usually 37°C (98·6°F). Household thermometers tell you how warm or cold the air around your house is.

A household thermometer can be used to keep a record of weather conditions.

TIBET

Tibet is a country in central ASIA. It is the highest country in the world. The flat part of Tibet, which is in the middle, is as high as the peaks of the Alps. Enormous mountain ranges surround this high plain. In the south lie the HIMALAYAS, the home of Mount EVEREST.

Tibet used to be ruled by Buddhist monks called *lamas*. In 1959, the country was taken over by China.

TIDAL WAVES

Tidal waves have nothing to do with TIDES. They are nearly always caused by an EARTH-QUAKE under the sea. Sometimes they can be caused by very strong winds. Tidal waves can travel very fast — up to 800 km/hr (500 mph)—and can easily destroy whole towns. One of the worst tidal waves happened in 1883. A VOLCANO on the island of Krakatoa in the East Indies exploded. The tidal wave caused by the explosion killed more than 20,000 people.

One strange thing about tidal waves is that people at sea may never notice them. This is because the patch of sea that is suddenly raised or lowered is so large, and the ships on it so small in comparison, the people on board do not feel the movement.

Another name for tidal wave is *tsunami*.

Above: This Japanese town was hit by a tidal wave that had been caused by an earthquake in Chile, half a world away. Most tidal waves happen in and around the Pacific Ocean. The Japanese have built special hills to help protect their towns.

Below: In 1755, an earthquake struck the port of Lisbon in Portugal. Many buildings crashed into the sea. At the time, people thought it was a tidal wave. Artists drew it to look like one. But, although it was a great disaster, it was not really a tidal wave.

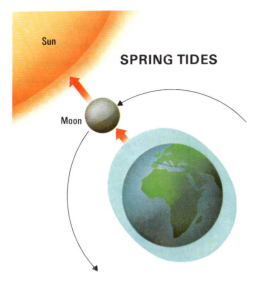

SPRING TIDES

TIDES

Tides are regular movements of the OCEANS. They are mainly caused by the MOON. The Moon is like a giant magnet. It tugs the oceans towards it as it loops around the Earth. The Earth is spinning at the same time, so most places get two high tides and two low tides in roughly each 24 hours.

High tide happens when the water flows as far inland as it can. Low tide happens when it flows out as far as it can.

Left: When the Sun and Moon pull together at the oceans, there is a very high, or spring, tide. When the Sun and Moon pull against each other, there is a very low, or neap, tide.

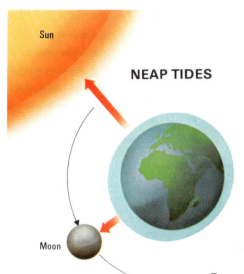

NEAP TIDES

TIGERS

Tigers are the biggest members of the cat family. They live in the forests of Asia and Indonesia, and hunt deer or large cattle. Tigers are very strong. One tiger can pull a dead buffalo, that is so heavy a group of men would find it difficult to move.

Until the 1800s, thousands of tigers roamed through the forests of Asia. Then men began to shoot them. Now they are very rare.

Tigers are rarely seen on open ground. They prefer the cool shade of forests. If it gets too hot they like to go swimming.

TIN

Tin is one of the oldest METALS known to man. Man was mining tin before IRON was discovered. Tin was mixed with copper to make BRONZE.

Tin was mined in Cornwall in England, long before the birth of Christ. An ancient people called the Phoenicians sailed from the Mediterranean to trade cloth and precious stones for it. Tin mining went on in Cornwall until 1928. Then large amounts of tin were discovered in Malaysia and other countries. Today, tin is so valuable that the mines in Cornwall may open again.

Tin cans are made from sheets of steel that have been coated with tin. Tin does not rust.

Above: Tin is found in the rich mud of river beds in Malaysia.

TOADS

Toads are AMPHIBIANS. They look very much like FROGS. Toads have no teeth, a rough and warty skin and are usually fatter and clumsier than frogs. They spend less time in the water than frogs, but most of them mate and lay their eggs in water, and spend the first part of their lives as tadpoles.

Toads eat slugs, snails, caterpillars, insects and other small animals. They flick out their long sticky tongues to catch food. Toad's tongues move so fast that you cannot see them. They can catch insects as they fly. If attacked, toads can produce poison from the two bumps behind their eyes. This poison covers their skin, and makes the toads harmful to most of their animal enemies.

The female Surinam Toad carries her eggs in special pockets on her back. Here they grow into tiny toads before hatching.

TOBACCO

Tobacco is the dried leaves of the plant *Nicotiana*, which belongs to the same family as POTATOES. It was first found in America, but is now grown all over the world. The Spanish traveller Francisco Hernandez brought it to Europe in 1599.

Tobacco leaves can be rolled together to make cigars, or shredded up to be smoked in pipes or cigarettes.

TOBOGGANING

Tobogganing is a winter sport in which toboggans, or sleds, are ridden down snow-covered slopes. The North American Indians first made and used toboggans to bring home their winter catch.

Most toboggans are used for fun. On the famous Cresta Run in Switzerland, big toboggans are ridden by teams of men and can go as fast as 145 km/hr (90 mph).

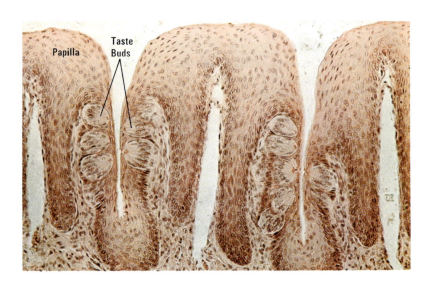

Humans and other mammals have tongues covered in tiny bumps. These are called papilla. You can just about see them if you look at your tongue in a mirror. Inside the papilla, around the edge of the tongue, are taste buds and nerve endings. These make the tongue sensitive to taste, heat, pain and pressure. The tip of the tongue is the most sensitive spot in the body.

Papilla

Taste Buds

TONGUE

The tongue is a muscly, flexible flap fixed inside the mouth. Only VERTEBRATES have tongues. Our own tongues help us to TASTE and eat food, and to talk. The letters T and D for instance, cannot be said without using the tongue in a special way.

In toads, the tongue is fixed to the front of the mouth. Snakes have forked or split tongues which can 'smell' the air. Cat's tongues are covered in tiny hooks of flesh. Cats can use their tongues like combs to clean their fur.

TONSILS

Tonsils are two small lumps at the back of the throat. There is one on each side. They help to protect the body from GERMS coming in through the mouth.

Children have very large tonsils. These gradually shrink as they grow older. Sometimes, tonsils can become infected. They swell up and are very painful. This illness is called tonsillitis. The tonsils may have to be taken out by doctors in a hospital. Having our tonsils taken out does not seem to harm our bodies in any way.

TORNADO

Tornadoes are violent, whirling windstorms. Most of them happen in America, but they can occur anywhere in the world.

Hurricanes are strong winds that build up over the sea. Tornadoes build up over land. They happen when large masses of cloud meet. The clouds begin to whirl around each other. Gradually, these whirling clouds join together to make a gigantic, twisting funnel. When this touches the ground, it sucks up anything in its path— trees, houses, animals, trains or people.

Tornadoes can cause a great deal of damage. In 1925, a tornado in the USA lasted for three hours and killed 684 people.

TORTOISE

Giant tortoises live in the Galapagos Islands and islands in the Indian Ocean. They can weigh up to 225 kg (496 lb) and be 1·8 metres (6 feet) long. Some large tortoises live for over 150 years.

Tortoises are slow-moving REPTILES. They can walk only about 4·5 metres (15 feet) in a minute. When frightened, they pull their heads and legs inside their domed shells. The 40 or so kinds of tortoise live on land in warm parts of the world. They are similar to TURTLES and terrapins, but these reptiles live in water.

TRADE UNIONS

Trade unions are groups formed by workers. Their main aim is to get better wages for their members. They also ask for shorter hours and better working conditions. Some unions look after their members and their families in times of trouble. If a trade union has a serious disagreement with an employer, it may stop its members from working. This is called a *strike*.

Modern trade unions were formed in the early days of the INDUSTRIAL REVOLUTION. They were first made legal in Britain in the 1870s. Since then, unions have gradually increased their power. Today, trade unions play an important part in the affairs of many countries.

TRAGEDY

A tragedy is a kind of play. It usually shows a person who tries to struggle against difficulties that stand in his way. These may be caused by people around him, by himself or by accidents of fate. In a tragedy, the hero is usually unsuccessful and dies at the end. Tragedies make us feel sorry for the hero and for the other people who are caught up in the story.

The ancient Greeks wrote the first tragedies. Their heroes were doomed by fate. SHAKESPEARE wrote great tragedies, such as *Macbeth* and *King Lear*. Modern tragedies are often about ordinary people.

TRANSISTORS

Transistors are small ELECTRONIC devices. They are usually made to *amplify* (strengthen) signals in electronic equipment, such as radio and television sets, computers and satellites. They have largely replaced other devices, called *valves*, which were once used for the same purpose.

Today, circuits containing thousands of transistors can be put in SILICON CHIPS only a few millimetres square. Transistors were invented in the 1940s and millions are now made every year.

TRAWLING

Trawling is a way of FISHING in the oceans. It is carried out by boats called *trawlers*. Most modern trawlers are between 31 and 52 metres (100–170 feet) long. They often carry special equipment to process and freeze the fish on board.

Trawlers often use large, cone-shaped nets, called *trawls*. Boards and buoys (small floats) keep the nets open. Weights on the underside of the net keep it at the bottom. Trawls are dragged over the seabed. Other trawlers use *purse seines*. These are huge nets. They are pulled together around a shoal of fish.

Trawlers drag large, bag-shaped nets over the seabed. They trap fish that live near the bottom.

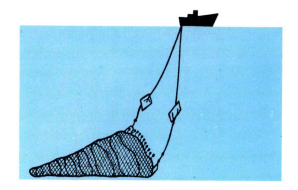

Beech   Common oak   Aspen   Yew   Larch   Sweet chestnut

Black poplar   Sycamore   Ash   Walnut   Whitebeam   Holly

Horse chestnut   London plane   White willow   Lime   Alder   Field maple

TREES

Trees are the largest of all PLANTS. They are woody plants with a thick central stem, or trunk. Most trees grow to more than 7·6 metres (25 feet) high. The biggest tree is a type of sequoia. These giants can grow to over 100 metres (360 feet) high, and can be 25 metres (80 feet) around. Trees can also live a long time. One bristle-cone pine in California is nearly 5000 years old.

Above the ground is the *crown* of the tree. This is made up of the trunk, branches, twigs and leaves. The *roots* are below the ground. They are the fastest growing part of the tree. They support the crown like a giant anchor. The roots take in water from the soil. The water is drawn up through the trunk to the leaves. A fully grown apple tree takes in about 360 litres (79 gallons) of water a day.

There are two main kinds of trees. CONIFERS are trees with needle-like leaves, such as PINES and spruces. In place of

Above: These drawings of 24 common trees will help you to identify them. Points to look for are the shapes formed by the branches, the shapes of the leaves and the appearance of the seeds.

Below: When a tree trunk is cut, you can see the annual rings. Each ring shows the new wood grown in the trunk in one year. If you count up all the rings, you will find the age of the tree.

Elm

Bird cherry

Silver birch

Lombardy poplar

Scots pine

Wych elm

Above: This Greek vase shows scenes from the Trojan War. A warrior is about to kill the Trojan king, who is on the ground. The goddess Aphrodite bars the way of Menelaus, who wants to kill Helen, his former wife.

flowers, they produce their seeds in cones. Most conifers are evergreens. This means they do not lose their leaves in autumn. Conifers grow in cold or dry regions.

The other kind of tree is the flowering, or broadleaved tree. Many of them, such as ELMS and OAKS, are *deciduous*, that is, they lose their leaves in autumn. But some broad-leaved trees, such as HOLLY and many tropical forest trees, are evergreen. Broad-leaved trees have flowers which develop into FRUITS that completely surround the seeds. These trees are often called hardwoods, because of their tough, hard wood. It is harder than that of the softwood conifers.

TRIANGLE

A triangle is a shape with three straight sides. Triangles are important in GEOMETRY. If we know some ANGLES and sides in a triangle, we can work out the others by using MATHEMATICS.

TROJAN WAR

The Trojan War was fought in about 1200 BC between the Trojans of Troy and the Greeks. It lasted for 10 years. The poet Homer, in his poem the *Iliad*, tells the story of only a few days of the war. We know the rest of the story from other writings.

Paris was a prince of Troy. He fell in love with Helen, the wife of King Menelaus of Sparta in Greece. Paris took Helen to Troy, and Menelaus with other Greek kings and soldiers went to get her back. They beseiged Troy for years. In the end they won by tricking the Trojans with a huge wooden horse, filled with Greek soldiers. No one knows, now, if the story was true.

TROPICAL FISH

Tropical fish are among the prettiest fish in the world. They live in the warm seas of tropical regions, often along the edges of CORAL reefs.

Many small, brightly-coloured freshwater tropical fish are popular aquarium pets. Marine fish can also be kept, but they are more expensive and difficult to look after. They have to have salt water containing just the right amount of salt to live in. Many kinds of marine tropical fish can be seen in public aquariums.

Tropical fish live in warm water. Most tanks have a heater to keep the water at around 24°C (75°F). The exact temperature depends on the type of fish. A cover on the tank holds the heat in and stops the water evaporating (drying up). Electric light bulbs in the cover light the tank and also heat the water. Most aquariums have air pumps that add OXYGEN to the water and filter it to keep it clear. Water plants also provide oxygen. Food for tropical fish can be bought at pet shops.

The most common tropical freshwater fish is the guppy. Its young are born alive, though they are often eaten by their parents. Other common kinds of tropical fish are angelfish, barbs and neon tetras.

TUDORS

The House of Tudor was an English royal family which ruled England from 1485 to 1603. The first Tudor King was HENRY VII. He was a grandson of a Welsh squire, Owen Tudor, who had married Henry V's widow. Henry VII came to the throne after defeating Richard III at the Battle of Bosworth. This ended the Wars of the Roses (1455–1485) between the houses of Lancaster and York. To join the houses, Henry VII, who belonged to a branch of Lancaster, married Elizabeth of York.

Henry VII was succeeded by his son, HENRY VIII. During the reign of Henry VIII the arts flourished in England. The King used PARLIAMENT to pass laws which broke all ties between England and the Roman Catholic Church.

Henry VIII was succeeded first by his son, EDWARD VI, then by his daughters, Mary I and ELIZABETH I. When Elizabeth died in 1603, the crown went to King James VI of Scotland, the first of the Stuart kings.

The Tudors were strong rulers. During their time, England became richer and more powerful, especially at sea. The voyages of England's daring seamen led to more trade and new colonies. SHAKESPEARE wrote his plays during the reign of Elizabeth I.

TUNA

The tuna, also called tunny, is a large fish, whose firm flesh is rich in PROTEINS and VITAMINS. Most tuna live in warm seas, but they may swim into northern waters in summer. Different kinds of tuna include the blue fin, which may be 3 metres (10 feet) long, and the albacore. Tuna are the only fish whose body temperature is higher than that of the water around them.

The tuna's body is streamlined and it can reach speeds of 48 km/hr (30 mph). Tuna live in big shoals and feed on other fish.

TUNISIA

Tunisia is a sunny country in North AFRICA. Its beaches attract many tourists from Europe. The north is rugged. It has the most rain. The south is part of the dry SAHARA. Farming is the main industry in this small nation. But oil and phosphates are important exports.

There are about 5,700,000 people, most of whom are Moslems. Near the capital, also called Tunis, are the ruins of Carthage. Carthage was a great Mediterranean Sea power until it was destroyed by the ROMAN EMPIRE in 146 BC.

TUNNELS

Tunnelling is important in MINING, transport and water supply. The Romans built tunnels to carry water. And, today, a water tunnel that brings water to New York City is the world's longest tunnel. It is 169 km (105 miles) long.

The most familiar tunnels are for roads and railways. Road tunnels must have a supply of fresh air, because car fumes are poisonous. But road tunnels can be used in all weathers, whereas roads that wind over mountains may be blocked by snow. Railway tunnels also run under mountains. And many large cities have underground railways.

Different methods are used to build tunnels. In hard rock, the tunnel is blasted out with explosives. Cutting machines, like those used to drill oil wells, are used in softer rock. In the softest rocks, *tunnel shields* are used. These are giant steel tubes, the same size as the intended tunnel. The front edge of the shield is sharp and is pushed into the earth. The earth is dug out and the tunnel behind the shield is lined to stop it caving in.

Some tunnels under rivers are built by lowering sections of tunnel into the river. Divers join them together. When the tunnel is complete, the water is pumped out. Underground railway tunnels can be built in deep trenches. When they are finished, the tunnel is covered over.

TURBINE

A turbine is a machine, in which a wheel, drum or screw is turned around by fast-flowing water, or by steam or gas. Water wheels and windmills are simple turbines.

Water turbines are used at hydroelectric power stations. These stations are next to dams or waterfalls. The force of water carried through a pipe in a dam turns the turbine. The turbine does not produce electricity. But as the turbine spins it drives a generator, which produces the elec-

Below: This cutting machine is being used to tunnel out an extension to London's large system of underground railways.

tricity. Some turbines are wheels or drums, with blades or cup-shaped buckets round their edges. Others are shaped like screws or propellers.

Steam turbines are operated by jets of steam. They have many uses. They are used to produce electricity, to propel ships and to operate pumps. Gas turbines are turned by fast-moving jets of gas. The gases are produced by burning fuels such as oil. Gas turbines are used to turn the propellers of aircraft.

TURKEY

Turkey is a country which is partly in EUROPE and partly in ASIA. The small European part covers three percent of the land. It lies west of the waterway which links the Black Sea to the Mediterranean Sea. This part includes the largest city, Istanbul, which was once called Constantinople. The Asian part, which is sometimes called Anatolia or Asia Minor, includes the capital, Ankara. ▷

349

Turkish women harvest wheat. Wheat, sugar beet and barley are Turkey's chief crops.

Most of Turkey's 47 million people follow the religion of ISLAM. Much of the land is mountainous and large areas are covered by dry plateaus (tablelands). But the coastal plains are fertile and farming is the main industry. Turkey also produces chromium.

Turkey was once part of the Byzantine empire, which was the eastern part of the ROMAN EMPIRE. But after Constantinople fell in 1453, the Moslem Ottoman conquerors built up a huge empire. At its height, it stretched from southern Russia to Morocco, and from the Danube river to the Persian Gulf. But it slowly declined after 1600 and collapsed in Word War I. After that war, Turkey's president, Kemal Atatürk (1881–1938) modernized the nation. Atatürk means 'Father of the Nation'.

TURKEYS

Turkeys are large game birds. They are related to pheasants. Wild turkeys live in small flocks in the forests of North and Central America. Today, turkeys are reared in many parts of the world for their meat. They were probably first domesticated in Mexico around AD 900 by the AZTECS. Spaniards first brought turkeys to Europe in the early 1500s.

Turkey meat is popular on special holidays, such as Christmas, in several countries, and Thanksgiving Day in North America.

TURTLES

Some people give the name 'turtle' to all shelled REPTILES, including TORTOISES. But generally, the name is just used for those that live in water. The shells of turtles are similar to those of tortoises. These are both made of bony 'plates' which are covered by large horny scales. But most turtles have flatter shells than tortoises, and are more streamlined. Small turtles that live in fresh water, rather than sea water, are called terrapins.

Marine, or sea, turtles spend most of their lives in warm seas. They swim great distances to find food, and many of them have webbed toes, or flipper-like legs, to help them swim well. They eat water plants, such as seaweed, and some small sea animals. Turtles often swim under water, but they come up to the surface to gulp air into their lungs.

Turtles go ashore to lay their eggs. They are very fast moving and graceful in water, but on land they are slow and clumsy. They usually bury their eggs in sand, or hide them among weeds. Both of these places help to keep the eggs warm, and safe from animals that would eat them.

The baby turtles hatch out on their own. When they have hatched, they dig themselves out of their nest and head for the sea. This journey is very dangerous, because their shells have not yet hardened. Crabs, snakes and birds are waiting to snap them up, before they reach the water.

There are several kinds of marine turtle. The largest kind is called the leatherback turtle. It can weigh over 725 kg (1600 lb) and be up to 1·8 metres (6 feet) long. It has a smooth, leathery skin instead of scales. The green turtle is used for turtle soup, and its eggs are eaten in Asian countries. Because of this, it is becoming rare. The hawksbill turtle almost became extinct. Its shell was used to make 'tortoiseshell' ornaments and jewellery.

TYPEWRITER

Typewriters are hand-operated writing machines. They produce letters and figures, which look like lines of type in a book. When you strike a key on a typewriter keyboard, it moves a metal bar. A raised letter on the end of this bar is pressed against an inked ribbon. This marks an inked image of the letter onto a sheet of paper which is held around a roller.

The first practical typewriter was invented in 1867 by an American, Christopher Latham Sholes (1819–1890).

Above: This early typewriter was designed by two Americans, C. L. Sholes and C. Glidden, in 1876. It wrote capital letters only.

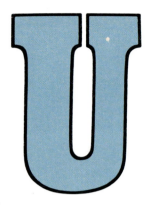

UFO

Unidentified Flying Objects are more often called UFOs. They are unknown objects that people see in the sky. Reports of UFOs go back thousands of years. Some may be METEORS or air BALLOONS. Others could be tricks of light, and some are probably just jokes or mistakes.

But some reports of UFOs seen by several people or tracked by radar have never been explained. Some people think that these may be alien spacecraft. They are often called 'flying saucers', because some are supposed to look like upturned saucers. No one really knows if they exist.

UGANDA

Uganda is a small republic in the middle of East AFRICA. It was ruled by Britain until 1962, when it became independent. General Idi Amin seized power in 1971. He was a brutal dictator and many people were murdered under his rule. But in 1979, Ugandans and Tanzanian soldiers took over Uganda and Amin fled.

Part of Africa's largest lake, Lake Victoria, lies in Uganda. Most of the 14 million people are farmers. The most important crops are coffee, tea and cotton. Uganda's capital is Kampala.

ULTRA-VIOLET LIGHT

If LIGHT from the Sun shines through a prism it splits up into a rainbow of colours, called a spectrum. Red is at one end of the spectrum and violet at the other. Ultra-violet light lies just beyond the violet end of the spectrum. We cannot see it, but it will blacken photographic film and make some chemicals glow. Most ultra-violet light from the Sun is lost in the atmosphere. But enough rays reach Earth to give us sun tans. If more rays reached us, they would be very harmful.

ULYSSES

Ulysses is the Roman name for a brave and cunning Greek hero, called Odysseus. His famous adventures are told in HOMER's poem the *Odyssey*. It tells how Ulysses took ten years to return home after the TROJAN WAR.

On his journey he was captured by a cyclops, a one-eyed, man-eating giant. A witch called Circe, changed his men into pigs. And sirens (sea maidens) lured his men to their deaths. When he finally reached home, his wife, Penelope, was surrounded by suitors. She had agreed to marry any man who could shoot an arrow from Ulysses' bow through 12 rings. Ulysses, in disguise, was the only man to do this. He then killed all the suitors.

This Greek vase shows the hero Ulysses and one of his men driving a stake into the eye of their captor, a one-eyed giant.

UNDERGROUND RAILWAYS

Each day millions of people use underground railways. Underground electric trains can carry passengers across cities much faster than buses, driving slowly through the busy streets above. Most underground RAILWAYS run through TUNNELS driven through the rock beneath a city. Lifts and escalators carry passengers from the surface to the stations deep underground.

Below: A cutaway view of escalators, tunnels and platforms in an underground railway system. Modern systems often have machines to issue tickets, open and close doors, and even drive the trains.

The first underground railway opened in London in 1863. Today the world has over 60 underground systems. Some of these are vast. London's system employs enough workers to people a town. Its 480 trains run on 400 km (250 miles) of track. New York City's track is almost as long. This is the busiest underground of all. About 1000 million people travel on it every year.

New York has almost 500 stations. But the largest underground stations are in Moscow. Their huge platforms were also built to serve as giant air raid shelters.

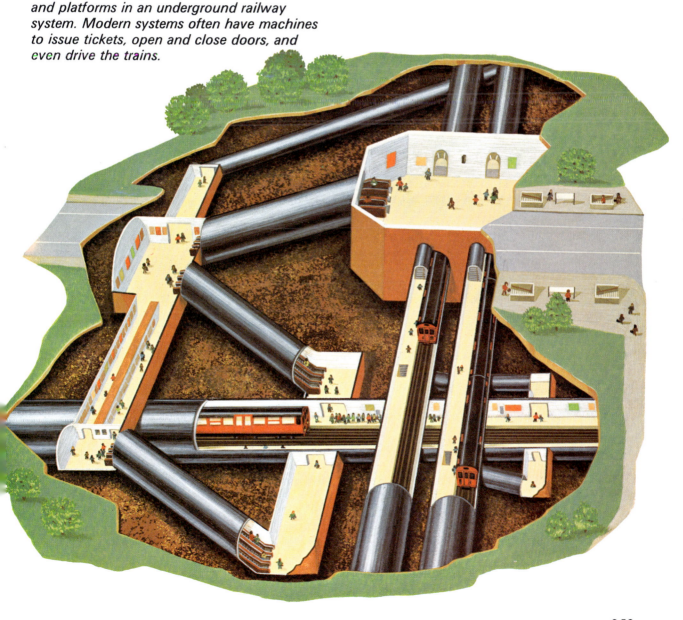

Unicorns are often shown rearing up on hind legs. These creatures appeared in the royal Scottish coat of arms.

UNICORN

Unicorn means 'one horn'. In old legends the unicorn was a creature like a horse except that out of its forehead jutted a long, straight horn with a spiral twist.

The first picture of a unicorn was carved on stone more than 2500 years ago. Later, tales of the unicorn were told in lands as far apart as China and Italy. A Greek writer who lived about 2400 years ago thought that a unicorn was white with a purple head and a red, white and black horn. He wrote that drinking from the horn could save people from poison.

In the Middle Ages, rich people who were afraid of being poisoned used to drink from what they thought were unicorn horns. In fact, these were really rhinoceros horns.

UNITED NATIONS

Most of the countries of the world belong to the United Nations. The United Nations is an association that works to keep peace and to help the people of the world.

Each member country sends delegates to regular meetings at the United Nations' General Assembly Building in New York City. The General Assembly suggests how countries should behave. It cannot make them take its advice. But the United Nation's Security Council can ask member countries for troops to help stop nations fighting.

The United Nations works largely through 14 groups. The Food and Agriculture Organization helps countries to grow more food. The World Health Organization fights disease. The International Monetary Fund lends countries money.

The United Nations has managed to prevent some wars and has helped millions of people in different countries.

Above: The United States is North America's second largest nation. It includes Alaska in the far north and Hawaii in the Pacific.

Combine harvesters gather wheat. Today vast wheat fields cover the plains where prairie grasses used to grow.

UNITED STATES OF AMERICA

The United States of America is the world's fourth largest nation. Russia, Canada and China are bigger in area, and more people live in China, India and Russia. There are 50 states in the United States. Forty-eight are in the same part of NORTH AMERICA. The other two are Alaska in the north, and the Pacific island of Hawaii in the south.

The mainland United States stretches from the Pacific to the Atlantic. Long mountain ranges run down the Pacific coast. Inland are flat-topped mountains

and basins. In this region is Death Valley, the lowest place in the Americas. Here too, is the Grand Canyon, a huge gorge cut by the Colorado River. Farther east lie the tall peaks of the Rocky Mountains that run from Canada to Mexico. Beyond these stretch the Central Plains where the mighty Mississippi River flows. Another mountain range, the Appalachians, runs down the eastern side of the United States.

The United States is a young country. In 1976 it was just 200 years old. The original 13 colonies declared their independence from England in 1776. George WASHINGTON was elected first president in 1789. By the mid 1800s the United States looked much ▷

These clocks show that the Sun rises in the eastern USA three hours before it rises in the west. The country is so wide, the Americans have had to divide it into four time zones.

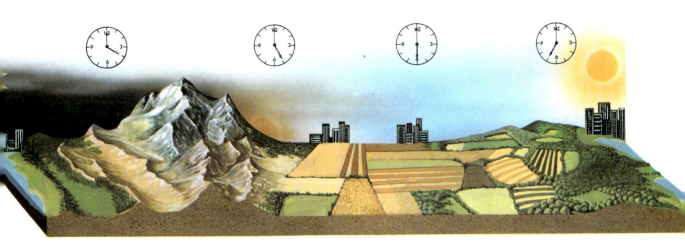

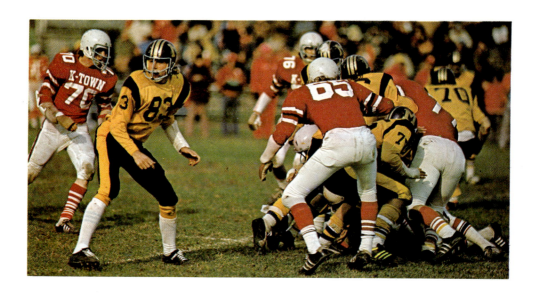

as it does today. Explorers had added new land to the original colonies, and the country stretched as far west as the Pacific. From 1861 to 1865 a CIVIL WAR was fought between the south, which believed in SLAVERY, and the north, which wanted every man to be free. The northern states won and slavery was abolished. Between 1870 and 1900 thousands of Europeans came and settled in the United States. They were seeking land and a new life. By 1900 the country's population had doubled.

The 226 million citizens of the United States include Eskimos, Indians, and people whose ancestors came from Europe or Africa. Americans speak English. Seventy in every 100 Americans live in cities. Washington D.C. is the capital but New York is the largest city. Los Angeles and Chicago each have over two million inhabitants.

The United States is one of the world's richest countries. Its farms produce huge wheat crops, and more oranges, meat, eggs and cheese than any other country. American miners mine more coal, copper, lead and uranium. The United States is the world's largest manufacturer of cars and chemicals.

Until recently the United States produced enough coal, oil and gas of its own to run its farms, factories and homes. But now it has to buy oil from abroad.

Above: American football players wear helmets and thick pads under their clothes to protect them.

Below: Disneyland in Los Angeles is a playground for both young and old.

Above: American schoolchildren start the day by saluting the flag. Left: Mickey Mouse is a favourite Disneyland character. Below: American dollar bills. There are 100 cents in a dollar. Basketball began in America over 80 years ago.

UNIVERSE

The universe is made up of all the STARS, PLANETS, MOONS and other bodies scattered through the emptiness of space. The EARTH is just a tiny part of the SOLAR SYSTEM, in a great group of stars known as the MILKY WAY. Beyond our GALAXY lie possibly 10,000 million other galaxies. Some are so far away that the light from them takes thousands of millions of years to reach us.

Scientists think that all matter in the universe was once squashed together as a fireball that exploded, shooting matter out in all directions.

Below: African students in local dress outside Ibadan University in Nigeria.

UNIVERSITIES

Some people who leave school at 18 go on to university. At school people are taught a little about several subjects. But at university a student often learns about just one or two subjects. He goes to talks called *lectures*, and smaller study groups known as *tutorials* or *seminars*. He has to write essays and maybe carry out experiments in a LABORATORY. University students use libraries to find out much of what they need to know from books.

After three years or so students take their final examinations. If they pass they are given a degree, usually a Bachelor of Arts or a Bachelor of Science. If they continue their studies they can earn higher degrees. A Master's degree takes a further one or two years and a DOCTOR's degree can take as long as seven years. A university degree often helps people find better jobs. Nearly all doctors, lawyers and teachers have studied for a degree.

Arab peoples had universities more than 1000 years ago. Europe's first university grew up in the 1000s at Bologna in Italy.

URANIUM

This metal is one of the heaviest of all known ELEMENTS. It was named after the planet Uranus. Uranium gives off RADIOACTIVITY. As it loses atomic particles it decays, and ends up, after millions of years, as LEAD. People working with uranium often need protective clothing to shield their bodies from radiation damage.

Uranium is the fuel used to make ATOMIC ENERGY in atomic bombs and nuclear power stations. It is mined in many countries. Most of the western world's uranium comes from the United States and Canada.

Right: If a uranium atom is split up, the pieces can bump into other uranium atoms and split them up. This goes on and on in a chain reaction that gives out a lot of energy.

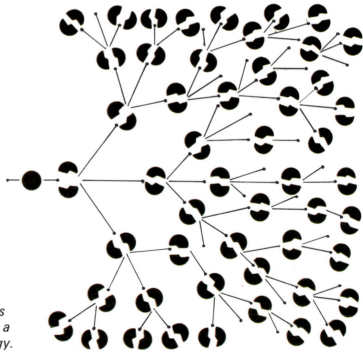

URANUS

The PLANET Uranus is 19 times farther away from the Sun than the Earth is. We cannot see Uranus just with our eyes. It was the first planet discovered with the help of a TELESCOPE. Uranus looks like a greenish-yellow disc, with faint markings that may be clouds.

Uranus is unlike our Earth in many ways. For one thing, it is much larger. You could fit 52 planets the size of the Earth inside Uranus. The distance through the middle of Uranus is nearly four times the distance through the middle of the Earth.

Unlike our planet, Uranus is mainly made up of gases. Its whole surface is far colder than the coldest place on Earth.

Uranus spins at a speed that makes one of its days about the same length as an Earth day. But Uranus takes so long to ORBIT the Sun that one of its years lasts 84 of ours. Five small moons travel around Uranus. Astronomers have also found that the planet is circled by five thin rings.

Below left: Uranus and the Earth. Uranus is much larger than the Earth. Below: A cutaway view of Uranus might show the kinds of layers pictured here.

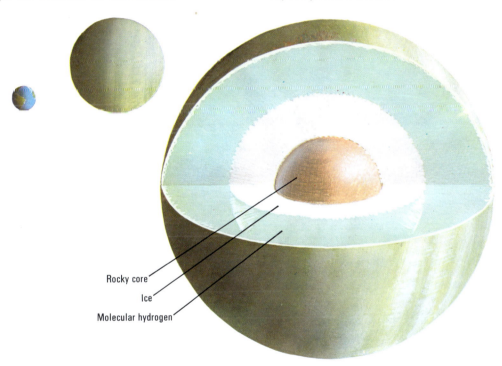

Rocky core
Ice
Molecular hydrogen

URUGUAY

Uruguay is one of the smallest countries in SOUTH AMERICA. But it is wealthier than most of the others. It lies in the south-east, between the Atlantic Ocean and its two big neighbours, Argentina and Brazil.

Low, grassy hills and lowlands cover most of Uruguay. Many rivers flow into the big Uruguay river or into the wide river mouth called the River Plate. Uruguay has mild winters and warm summers.

About three million people live in Uruguay. Most of them are descended from Spanish or Italian settlers. Uruguayans speak Spanish. More than one in three of them live in the capital Montevideo. Its factories make clothing, furniture and other goods. But most Uruguayans work in meat-packing plants, wool warehouses or on country ranches. Millions of sheep and cattle graze on these ranches.

Uruguay sells large amounts of meat, leather and wool to other countries.

V

VACUUM

A vacuum is a space with nothing in it. It gets its name from *vacuus*, the Latin word for empty. In fact there are no complete vacuums. When you try to empty a container by pumping out the air, some air always stays behind. This partly empty space is called a partial vacuum. New air always rushes in to fill the space. This is how your LUNGS work. When you breathe out, you make a partial vacuum in your lungs. Air rushes to fill the space, making you breathe in.

You can see partial vacuums at work in many ways. The space does not always fill up with air. When you suck air from a straw dipped in lemonade, it is the lemonade that rushes to fill the vacuum and so into your mouth.

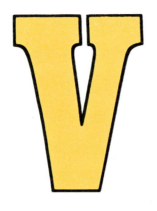

Above: St Peter's Basilica is in Vatican City. The great church stands over a tomb, which is believed to hold St Peter's body. St Peter was the first Pope. Michelangelo helped to design the church. It was begun in 1506 and took about 150 years to complete. It is the largest Christian church in the world.

VATICAN CITY

The Vatican City is the home of the Pope and the headquarters of the ROMAN CATHOLIC CHURCH. It stands on Vatican Hill in north-west Rome, and is the smallest independent country in the world. It is only the size of a small farm and about 1000 people live in it. Yet it has its own flag, radio station and railway. It also issues its own stamps.

The Vatican City is surrounded by walls and contains many famous buildings. These include the Vatican Palace, which has more than 1000 rooms; the Sistine Chapel, decorated by MICHELANGELO; and St Peter's Basilica.

VEGETABLES

Vegetables are plants with parts that we can eat. They taste less sweet than the plant foods we call FRUIT. Some vegetables, such as lettuce and spinach, are eaten for their leaves. Others are eaten for their roots or stems. Carrots and parsnips are roots. Celery and asparagus are plant stems. Tomatoes and marrows are the fruits of their plants. Peas, beans and sweet corn are seeds.

Vegetables are very good foods. Peas and beans are rich in body-building PROTEINS. Leafy and root vegetables provide VITAMINS, minerals and fibres that help to keep our DIGESTION working properly. Potatoes contain STARCHES, which the body can burn up to make energy.

VEINS

Veins are narrow tubes that carry used BLOOD from all parts of your body back to the HEART. Blood flowing through the ARTERIES is pushed along by the pumping of the heart. Blood in the veins has nothing to push it along. So many veins have flaps inside them which close the tube if the blood begins to flow backwards.

VENEZUELA

Venezuela is a large country on the north coast of SOUTH AMERICA. Most of southern Venezuela is covered by flat-topped mountains. Here stands Angel Falls, the highest waterfall in the world. A grassy plain stretches across the middle of the country on either side of the Orinoco river.

Venezuela grows coffee, cotton and cocoa. But its minerals, especially oil, make it the richest country in the continent. Venezuela's capital is Caracas.

Below: Seven popular sorts of vegetable. They are lettuce (1), peas in a pod (2), cauliflower (3), a runner bean (4), onion (5), carrot (6) and beetroot (7).

Above: A 'forest' of drilling rigs in Lake Maracaibo. Much of Venezuela's oil comes from this large shallow lake.

VENUS (PLANET)

The PLANET Venus is named after the Roman goddess of beauty and love. Venus is the brightest planet in the SOLAR SYSTEM. We see it as the morning star or the evening star, depending on where it is on its journey round the Sun.

Venus takes only 225 days to go round the Sun. So more than three years pass on Venus for every two on Earth. But Venus itself spins so slowly that one day on Venus lasts for 243 days on Earth. It is the only planet to spin in the opposite way to the direction of its ORBIT.

Venus is about the same size as Earth, but weighs a little less. It is also much hotter, because it is much closer to the Sun. The surface of Venus is hidden under a dazzling white cloak of cloud. This may be made of tiny drops of sulphuric acid. The atmosphere on Venus is mainly CARBON DIOXIDE. This acts rather like a greenhouse roof, trapping the Sun's heat. The rocks on Venus are hotter than boiling water.

Above: This picture shows how Russian space capsules parachuted down to Venus.

Left: This photograph of Venus was taken by an American spacecraft 720,000 km (450,000 miles) from the planet. The picture shows the cloud that hides the planet's surface.

VENUS (GODDESS)

Venus was the Roman goddess of love, grace and beauty. The Greeks had a similar goddess called Aphrodite. Many of the stories about Venus began as tales about Aphrodite.

Most stories say that Venus was born in the sea foam near the Greek island of Cythera. Although she was the most beautiful goddess, she married the ugliest god. He was Vulcan, the god of fire. But Venus also fell in love with other gods and with men. Venus and the war god, Mars, had a son called Cupid, the god of love. She also loved a Greek king called Anchises, and they had a son called Aeneas. The Romans believed that Aeneas helped to start the city of Rome.

Venus liked to help lovers. She started the TROJAN WAR, by making HELEN OF TROY fall in love with Paris.

Left: Venus, the goddess of love, appears in the middle of this scene. It comes from a painting called Primavera *(Spring). It was painted 500 years ago by the Italian artist Sandro Botticelli.*

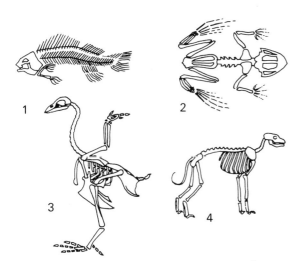

Above: These four kinds of vertebrates have bony skeletons. They are fish (1), amphibians (2), birds (3) and mammals (4). Mammals and birds are the most advanced vertebrates.

VERBS

Verbs are 'doing' or 'being' words, such as *go, hit, choose, have, be.* Verbs tell you what people or things are doing, or what is happening to them.

We know who or what a verb describes by its place in a sentence. When you say 'the dog *bit* the man', you know that the dog is doing the biting, not the man. The way a verb is spelled is also a clue to what or who is being described. To describe ourselves, we say 'I *go*', but when we are talking about someone else we say 'he *goes*'.

We also add different endings to verbs to show when something is happening. Sometimes, the verb is changed completely. For instance, we say 'I *go*' (meaning now), 'I *shall go*' (meaning in the future) and 'I *went*', (meaning in the past).

VERTEBRATES

Vertebrates are animals with a backbone or spine. The backbone is made up of short bones called *vertebrae*. This name comes from a Latin word that means 'to turn'. Most vertebrates can bend and straighten their backbones by slightly turning their vertebrae.

Many things make vertebrates different from other animals. Most have a bony case to protect their BRAIN, a set of ribs to protect their HEART, LUNGS and other delicate parts, and one or two pairs of limbs. And most vertebrates have a SKELETON made of bone.

There are seven main kinds of vertebrate. They are grouped according to how well developed they are. The simplest kind are the lamprey group. Lampreys are eel-like fish with no jaw. They have a spine but no skeleton. Next come sharks and skates, which have a skeleton of cartilage. All other vertebrates have bones. They are the bony FISH, AMPHIBIANS, REPTILES, BIRDS and MAMMALS.

VESUVIUS

Vesuvius is one of the world's most famous VOLCANOES. The mountain rises over the Bay of Naples in southern Italy. It is about 1200 metres (4000 feet) high, but gets shorter every time it erupts.

The first eruption we know about happened in AD 79. Vesuvius threw out ash and lava that between them buried the Roman cities of POMPEII and Herculaneum. There have been nine bad eruptions in the last 200 years.

Below: Plaster casts, made from shapes left by bodies buried in lava at Pompeii when Vesuvius erupted. About 2000 people died.

VICTORIA, QUEEN

Queen Victoria (1819–1901) ruled GREAT BRITAIN for 64 years, longer than any other British monarch. During her reign, the nation grew richer and its empire larger than ever before. She was the queen of many countries, including Australia, New Zealand, Canada and South Africa, and the empress of India.

Victoria was the daughter of Edward, Duke of Kent. GEORGE III was her grandfather. She was just 18 when she inherited the throne from her uncle, William IV. Two years later, she married her German cousin, Prince Albert. They had four sons and five daughters. Prince Albert died of typhoid fever in 1861. His death left the Queen deeply unhappy. For many years she wore only black clothes to show her grief. She also stopped going to public ceremonies. She took a dislike to London and spent most of her time in her big country houses. She had a castle at Balmoral in Scotland and a house called Osborne on the Isle of Wight.

Victoria was very popular with her people.

VIETNAM

Vietnam is a country in south-east ASIA. It is just a bit smaller than England and only 55 km (40 miles) wide in some parts. Vietnam is a hot damp country.

Vietnam used to be divided into two countries, North Vietnam and South Vietnam. Hanoi was the main city in the north and Saigon (now called Ho Chi Minh City) in the south. From the 1950s until 1975, the two countries were at war. South Vietnam was supported by the United States. North Vietnam was communist. Now the whole country is communist.

VIKINGS

The Vikings were a fierce people who lived in Norway, Sweden and Denmark. Between 800 and 1100, a great number of Vikings left their homes to raid villages and build settlements in northern Europe. They settled in England, Ireland and France. Vikings also travelled to Russia, and even to the great city of Constantinople. Many settled in Iceland, and from there, some went to Greenland.

The Vikings sailed in long ships, which were faster than any others at that time. Ships were very important to the Vikings. They sometimes buried their kings and chiefs in large ships. These 'tombs' were then buried or burned.

The Vikings were the first European people to discover North America. They sailed there from Greenland, but they did not settle there.

Viking warriors were fearsome raiders. In their swift ships they would appear without any warning.

VINEGAR

Vinegar is an ACID liquid. It is made when alcohol is left uncovered. The alcohol mixes with oxygen in the air and goes sour. Vinegar can be made from wine, cider or malt.

Vinegar is used to season and flavour food. People use it to make sauces and salad dressings. Food can be preserved (to stop it going bad) by keeping it in vinegar. This is called pickling. Onions and beetroot are often pickled in vinegar.

Violins are usually made of maple at the back and pine wood at the front.

VIOLIN

The violin is a MUSICAL INSTRUMENT. It belongs to the string family. It is usually the smallest string instrument in an ORCHESTRA.

A violin is a curved wooden box, shaped rather like a figure eight. A long neck is fixed to one end of the box. Four strings, made of gut or nylon, are stretched from the top of the neck to the bottom end of the box.

The violin is played with a bow made from horsehair. When this is drawn across the strings they vibrate to make sounds. The strings can also be plucked with the fingers.

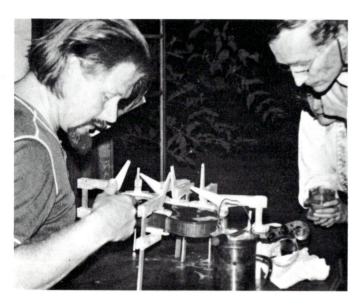

Making a violin needs skill and patience. The most famous maker was the Italian Stradivarius (1644–1737). About 600 of his violins still remain.

VIRUSES

Viruses are very small living things that cause diseases in plants and animals. They are smaller than bacteria and can only be seen with a very powerful MICROSCOPE.

You can be infected with viruses by swallowing them or breathing them in. Some insects carry viruses, which they pass on when they bite you. Once inside the body, a virus travels around in the bloodstream. It gets inside a living CELL where it produces more viruses. Sometimes the cell is entirely destroyed by the virus.

Diseases caused by viruses include measles, chicken pox, mumps, influenza and colds. Viruses are very hard to kill. INOCULATION helps to prevent these diseases.

Poliomyelitis (polio) viruses seen through a very strong microscope. Polio attacks the brain and spinal cord. Polio vaccine, which helps to prevent the disease, was developed 25 years ago.

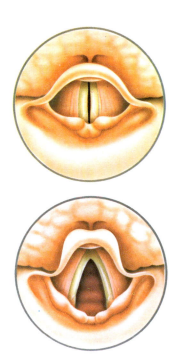

VOICE

We use our voices to speak and sing. The noise is made by air forced up from the LUNGS, through the windpipe in the throat, and past the vocal cords. The vocal cords stretch across the top of the windpipe. Muscles in the windpipe open and close the cords. When air from the lungs hits the cords they vibrate to make a noise. If the cords are stretched tightly, they produce a high noise.

The noise is shaped by our mouth, TONGUE and lips to make words and sounds.

Left: The vocal cords stretch across the windpipe. If the space between them is narrow we make a high sound. If it is wide, the sound is low. Women and children usually have higher voices than men.

VITAMINS

Vitamins are chemicals that our bodies need to stay healthy. They are found in different kinds of food. There are six kinds of vitamin. Scientists call them A, B, C, D, E and K. Vitamin B is really a group of vitamins.

The first people to realize that certain kinds of food were important to health were sailors. On long voyages they got a disease called *scurvy* if they could not eat fresh fruit and vegetables. These contain vitamin C. From the 1700s, English sailors were given limes to eat to prevent scurvy. This is why they were nicknamed 'limeys' by the Americans.

No one food has all the vitamins we need. That is why it is important to eat a mixture of things. Some people take their vitamins in pills. No-one really needs pills if they eat well. Very old people, young babies and women expecting babies all need more vitamins than usual. But too much of some kinds of vitamin, such as vitamin A, can be bad for you.

VOLCANOES

A volcano is an opening in the surface of the Earth. Burning gas, boiling rocks and ash escape from this opening. Sometimes they trickle out, sometimes they explode. If they explode, it is called an *eruption*.

In ancient Greek stories, volcanoes were the chimneys of the underground forge of the fire god. The Roman name for this god was Vulcan. Volcanoes are named after him.

Some volcanoes are gently sloping mountains with cracks, or *fissures*, in them. Hot liquid rock called *lava* flows out through the fissures. Other volcanoes are steep-sided mountains with a large hole at the top. These are called cone volcanoes. They are the kind that explode.

Erupting volcanoes can do a lot of damage. The city of POMPEII was destroyed by Vesuvius in AD 79. In 1883 Krakatoa, a volcano in Indonesia, erupted causing a TIDAL WAVE that killed 36,000 people. Volcanoes can also make new land. An island called Surtsey, south of Iceland, was made by a volcano erupting under the sea in 1963. ▷

The map shows the parts of the world where volcanoes are found. They make a pattern of long chains. These chains mark the edges of the huge 'plates' that form the surface of the Earth. They are the weakest part of the Earth's crust. One chain goes right round the Pacific Ocean. It is called 'the ring of fire'. Earthquakes, geysers and hot springs are all found in the same areas as the chains of volcanoes.

Below: Low volcanoes (1) are made of liquid lava. This spreads out a long way before it hardens, so there are no violent eruptions. Cone volcanoes (2) are made from thick lava. This may spill out in many small eruptions. Sometimes it turns into a solid plug. Pressure builds up inside the volcano and the plug blows out in a violent explosion (3).

Below: A cutaway picture of a volcano. The mountain (1) is made of layers of cold ash and lava sandwiched together. Hot lava and melted rock (2) spouts up through a central crack (3).

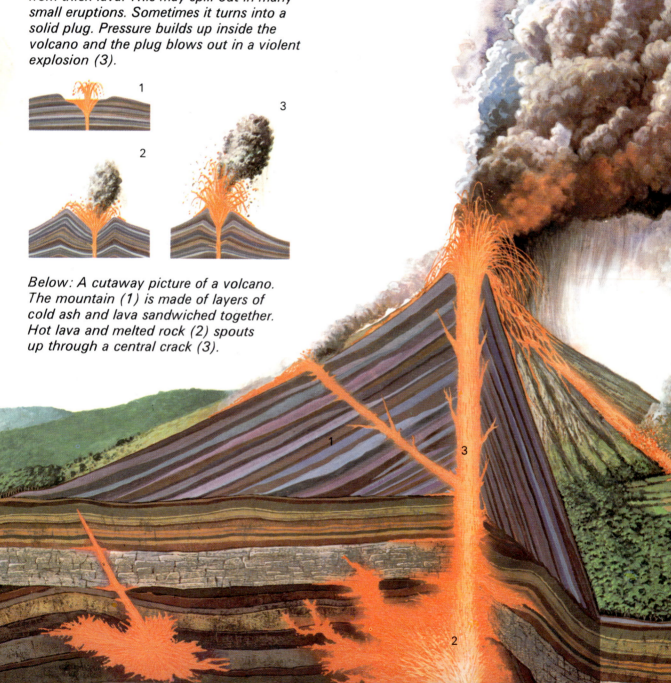

VOLUME

The volume of an object is the amount of space it takes up. You can find out the volume of something by measuring its height, width and depth and multiplying the figures together. So a brick with equal sides, each 10 cm (4 inches) long, has a volume of 1000 cubic cm (64 cubic inches) that is 10 cm × 10 cm × 10 cm.

It is easy to find out the volume of boxes or bricks or anything with straight edges. Measuring the volume of something with irregular sides is more difficult. A very simple method was discovered by ARCHIMEDES, the Greek scientist. A story told about him says that he was getting into his bath, which was full to the brim, and water spilled over the side. He suddenly realized that the volume of water that spilled over was exactly the same as the volume of his body. This means that any irregularly shaped object can be measured by plunging it into water and measuring the rise of the water level.

Vultures live in large flocks. Although each bird searches for its own food, they soon see if another one of the flock drops to the ground. Then they all join in the feast.

VOWELS

Vowels are the letters A, E, I, O and U. Sometimes the letters Y and W are used as vowels. Vowels are pronounced with the mouth open. What they sound like depends on the position of your TONGUE in your mouth. The shape your lips make is also important. If they are pushed forward, as if you are whistling, you make an *oo* sound. If they are pulled right back, you make an *ee* sound.

Because the tongue and the lips can shape themselves in hundreds of different ways, there are hundreds of different vowel sounds. Sometimes two or three vowel sounds are run together to make a new sound. The vowel sounds in one language are often very difficult for speakers of another language to learn.

VULTURES

Vultures are large birds of prey. They live in the hot, dry parts of the world. The largest land bird in North America is a type of vulture. This is the California condor. When its wings are spread out, they measure up to 3 metres (10 feet).

Vultures do not hunt for their food. They live on carrion, the rotting bodies of dead animals. Sometimes, vultures have to wait for their dinner until a large hunter such as a lion has made a kill. When the lion has eaten its fill, wild dogs and hyenas gorge on the remains. Then it is the vulture's turn.

Most vultures have bald heads and necks. This stops their feathers getting messy when they plunge their heads into large carcases. They have very good eyesight and can spot dead or dying animals from far away. They also have a keen sense of smell.

Vultures spend most of their lives in large flocks, circling lazily over the land looking for food. Vultures do not make nests. The female lays two or three eggs directly on the ground, inside a cave or under a cliff.

A Welsh woman spinning wool, and the seal
of Owen Glendower who led the Welsh
against the English in the early 1400s.

WAGES

Wages are the money people earn for their
work. Wages used to be paid according to
the amount of work done—the weight of
coal dug, or the number of shirts made.
Today, most wages are paid for the length
of time people spend working. Overtime,
or time worked in addition to normal
hours, is paid at a much higher rate. TRADE
UNIONS were formed to see that their
members were paid fair wages and given
reasonable working conditions.

WAGTAIL

Wagtails are small birds with sharp beaks
and long tails. They eat flies and other
insects and are often found near water.
As they run along the ground in search of
food their heads bob fast and their tails
wag up and down. There are yellow wagtails
and pied wagtails.

WALES

Wales is part of the kingdom of GREAT
BRITAIN and Northern Ireland. It lies to
the west of England and is a country of low
mountains and green valleys. The highest
mountain is Snowdon, and Cardiff is the
capital city.

*The Welsh often rebelled against English
rule. Edward I built strong castles along the
Welsh border to check these uprisings.*

The Welsh are descended from the CELTS.
English is their main language today, but
about a quarter of the people still speak
Welsh. Many Welsh people are fighting
passionately to keep their language alive.

South Wales is one of Britain's biggest
coalfields. Most of the people live in the
coal-mining areas, or in industrial towns
like Swansea and Cardiff. Steel is another
important industry. In the mountains of
north and mid-Wales many people are
sheepfarmers. Wool is one of Wales' main
exports.

WALRUS

The walrus belongs to the SEAL family. Its enormous canine teeth look like two tusks. These tusks can be up to a metre long. The walrus uses them to scrape up the clams and shellfish it eats. It also uses its tusks to fight, and even polar bears keep away from fully grown walruses.

The Atlantic and the Pacific walrus both live in the cold ARCTIC. They are big animals. The male Atlantic walrus measures up to 4 metres (13 feet) and weighs as much as 1800 kg (3970 lb).

In the 1930s walruses almost disappeared through being hunted for their tusks and skins.

Walruses live in large families on beaches and ice floes. Because so many of them live together they are very easy to catch and kill. Some were killed just for their tusks, and the rest of the body was thrown away. The females are usually smaller than the males and have one pup a year.

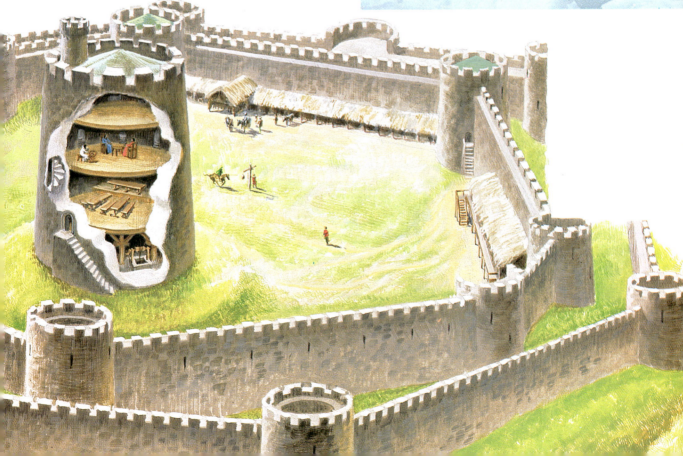

WASHINGTON, GEORGE

George Washington (1732–1799) was the first PRESIDENT of the United States of America. America had been owned by Britain, but in 1775 the War of Independence broke out. It was fought between British troops and the American settlers. Washington was in command of the American army. The Americans won the war and the United States became an independent country. George Washington became President in 1789.

WASPS

There are many different kinds, or *species* of this insect. Some wasps are called social insects because they live together in large groups. These wasps have different jobs to do for the group. A few of them are queens, and lay eggs. Others are workers. They build the nests and collect the food. But most wasps are solitary insects. They live alone, build their own nests, lay their own eggs and collect their own food.

Above: The density, or 'thickness', of water can be increased by adding salt to it. Fresh eggs sink in ordinary water, but if enough salt is added they will float.

Below: Water is made from two gases, hydrogen and oxygen. When two parts of hydrogen are put with one part of oxygen, liquid water is formed.

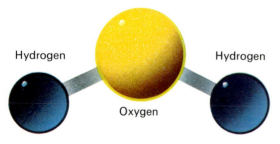

Hydrogen

Hydrogen

Oxygen

WATER

Water is the most common substance on Earth. Seven-tenths of the world's surface is covered by water. If this were spread evenly across the world it would be over 3 km (almost 2 miles) deep. Water is also the most important substance on Earth. Without it life would be impossible. Life first started in water, and the bodies of all living things are mostly water.

There is no such thing as 'pure' water. Water contains many MINERALS, which it has picked up and dissolved from the surrounding earth and rocks. Some dissolved minerals give water a pleasant taste.

Water exists in three forms. At 0° Centigrade it freezes into solid ice. At 100° Centigrade it boils into steam. Normal air takes up water easily, and CLOUDS are enormous collections of water *vapour*. At any time, clouds contain millions of tonnes of water, which falls back to Earth as RAIN. This adds water to the lakes and rivers on land, which flow back to the sea.

WEATHER

The weather—sunshine, fog, RAIN, CLOUD, WIND, heat, cold—is always changing in most parts of the world. Today may be hot and dry, tomorrow cool and wet. These changes are caused by what happens in the atmosphere, the layer of air above the Earth.

The atmosphere is always moving, driven by the Sun's heat. Near the EQUATOR the Sun's strong rays heat the air. At the North and South Poles the Sun's rays are weaker

Below: Four home-made weather instruments. The anemometer *shows wind speed. Its paper cups are fixed to a cork disc tha. spins on a nail. The* weathervane *shows wind direction. It swings round a nail set in a board marked with compass points. The* rain gauge, *made from a funnel, glass jar and tin can, measures rainfall. The* barometer *shows differences in air pressure. A tube stands in a bowl of water. The tube has water sucked part-way up it and is then sealed. As air pressure rises and falls, the water in the tube goes up and down.*

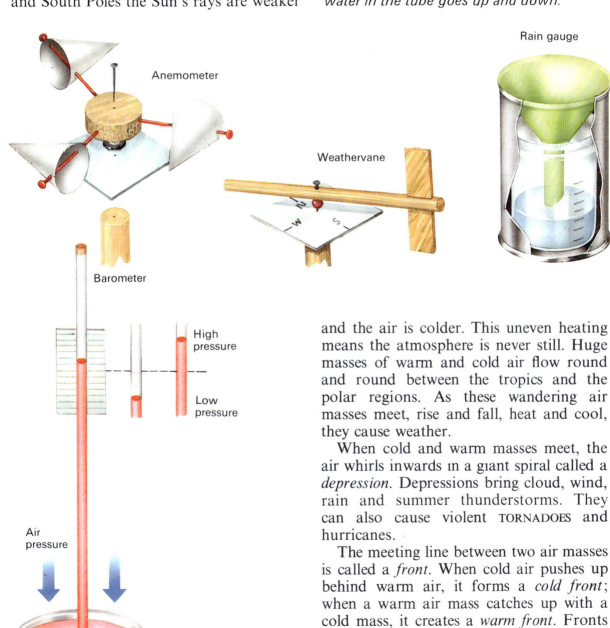

Anemometer

Weathervane

Rain gauge

Barometer

High pressure

Low pressure

Air pressure

and the air is colder. This uneven heating means the atmosphere is never still. Huge masses of warm and cold air flow round and round between the tropics and the polar regions. As these wandering air masses meet, rise and fall, heat and cool, they cause weather.

When cold and warm masses meet, the air whirls inwards in a giant spiral called a *depression*. Depressions bring cloud, wind, rain and summer thunderstorms. They can also cause violent TORNADOES and hurricanes.

The meeting line between two air masses is called a *front*. When cold air pushes up behind warm air, it forms a *cold front*; when a warm air mass catches up with a cold mass, it creates a *warm front*. Fronts usually bring changes in the weather.

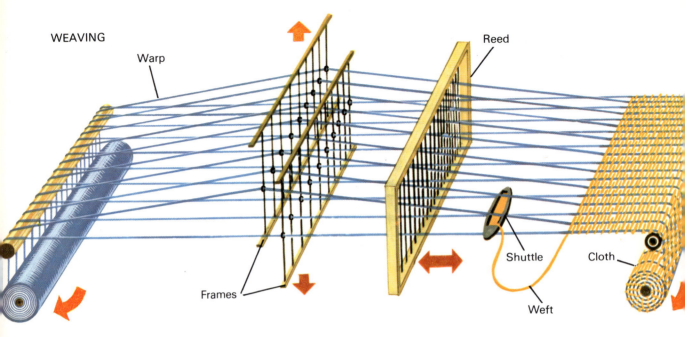

WEAVING

Warp

Reed

Frames

Shuttle

Cloth

Weft

Above: How a loom works. The warp is a set of threads running the length of the cloth. The weft is another thread that goes across the cloth. A shuttle laces the weft over and under the warp threads from one side of the loom to the other. To help the shuttle pass through more easily, special frames raise some warp threads and lower others. The reed is pulled up to the cloth to tighten the weave.

WEAVING

Curtains and carpets, shirts and sheets, towels and trousers are just some of the many useful articles made by weaving. In weaving, threads are joined together in a criss-cross pattern to make cloth.

People have been weaving cloth to make clothes since the New STONE AGE. The oldest fabric we know of was woven nearly 8000 years ago in what is now Turkey. These first weavers learned to make LINEN from FLAX. By 2000 BC the Chinese were weaving cloth from SILK. In India, people learned to use fibres from the COTTON plant. Meanwhile NOMADS from the deserts and mountains of Asia discovered how to weave WOOL.

For thousands of years, making cloth

was slow work. First, the fibres were drawn out and twisted into a long thread. This process is known as spinning. Then, rows of threads were stretched lengthwise, side by side, on a frame called a *loom*. These threads made up the *warp*. A crosswise thread, the *weft*, was then passed through from one side of the loom to the other, going over and under the warp threads. A *shuttle*, like a large needle, was used to feed the weft through the warp.

Spinning wheels and looms were worked by hand until the 1700s. Then, machines were invented for spinning and weaving. As these machines worked far faster than hand looms, cloth became cheap and plentiful. Today, most woven fabrics are made by machine.

Fumitory

Petty spurge

Germander speedwell

Goosegrass (Cleavers)

Chickweed

WEEDS

A weed is any PLANT that grows where it is not wanted. On farms and in gardens, weeds damage crops and flowers by taking a large share of water, minerals and sunlight. In places where weeds grow thickly, cultivated plants do not develop properly; they may produce only a few flowers, small seeds, unhealthy leaves or weak roots.

There are several ways of controlling weeds. In gardens, people break up the soil with a hoe. This disturbs the weed roots and stops growth. They also pull the weeds out of the ground: this is called weeding. On farms, the soil is broken up by ploughing and harrowing. Farmers also spray their fields with weedkiller. Weedkillers are chemicals that destroy weeds. Most of them are *selective*. This means the chemicals only affect certain plants: they destroy weeds without harming crops. Sometimes farmers set fire to fields or even flood them to destroy weeds.

Weeds are only a nuisance when they interfere with cultivated plants. In woods and fields, away from gardens and farms, weeds are useful plants. Weeds are food for many insects, birds and MAMMALS.

Eight common weeds. All weeds grow and spread quickly and soon choke cultivated plants. The black berries of the nightshade are very poisonous, especially after a hot summer.

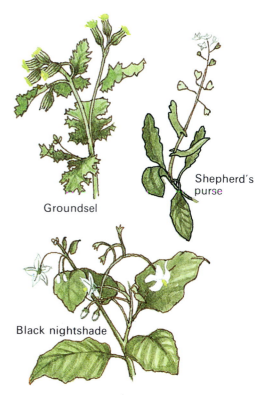

Groundsel

Shepherd's purse

Black nightshade

WEIGHT-LIFTING

Weight-lifting is one of the sports included in the OLYMPIC GAMES. In a weight-lifting contest, the competitors lift very heavy weights from the floor to above their heads. Weight-lifters, like boxers, are divided into classes according to their own body weight. Champion weight-lifters can lift over 250 kg (550 lb).

Many other sportsmen, such as swimmers and footballers, do weight-lifting as an exercise to strengthen their muscles and improve their breathing.

Right: Most weight-lifters lift bar bells, a bar with heavy discs at each end.

Below: Early measuring systems were often based on parts of the body. In ancient Egypt a span (across the hand) and a cubit (from fingertip to elbow) were used to measure length.

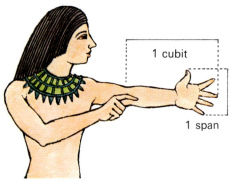

WEIGHTS AND MEASURES

Weights and measures are used to work out the size of things. The two main kinds of measurement are weight and length. They answer the questions 'How heavy?' and 'How long?'. Length is also used to find area and volume. There are several systems of weights and measures. The most common is the METRIC SYSTEM.

WELDING

Welding is a way of joining metals by heating. The edges of two pieces of metal are heated until they melt together. When they cool they form just one piece of metal. A join made by welding is extremely strong.

Welders work with gas or electricity. In gas welding a very hot flame from a gas torch melts the metal. In electric welding, an electric CURRENT jumps from an electric welding rod to the metals and melts them.

In this welding machine, electric current melts the metals and joins them together.

WELLINGTON, DUKE OF

Arthur Wellesley, the Duke of Wellington (1769–1852), was a famous British soldier and statesman. In 1803 he led the troops whose victories put India firmly under British rule. In 1808 he began to drive NAPOLEON's French troops out of Portugal and Spain. In 1815 his British troops helped to defeat Napoleon at the great Battle of Waterloo in Belgium.

Wellington later held important jobs in the British government. He was made commander in chief of the army in 1827.

WEST INDIES

This chain of tropical islands stretches from Florida in the United States to Venezuela in South America. On one side lies the Caribbean Sea, on the other stretches the Atlantic Ocean. The islands are really the tops of a drowned range of mountains. Palm trees and tropical grasses grow here, where it is almost always warm. But fierce autumn hurricanes often destroy trees and houses.

The thousands of islands are divided into more than 20 countries. CUBA, JAMAICA, Haiti, and the Dominican Republic are among the largest. Most West Indians are dark skinned. Many are at least partly descended from Negro slaves who were taken there long ago from Africa. Other West Indians have ancestors who lived in India or Europe. Most West Indians speak English, Spanish or French.

People grow bananas, cotton, sugar cane and other tropical crops. Some work in hotels beside the warm blue sea. Tourists from many lands come here to swim and sunbathe.

The West Indies were discovered in 1492 by Christopher COLUMBUS.

Above: A portrait of the 'Iron Duke', as the Duke of Wellington was often called. As a boy, he did so badly at school that he was sent into the army. His disappointed parents little guessed that the failed scholar would become a brilliant soldier.

Left: Sun, sea, sand and palm trees bring rich tourists to West Indian beaches. But many people living in these lovely islands (shown in the map above) are poor and lead hard lives.

WHALES

Whales are big sea MAMMALS well built for living in the water. A thick layer of fat called blubber keeps out the cold. A whale's body is shaped for easy swimming. Its front limbs are shaped as flippers. It also has a broad tail flattened from top to bottom, not from side to side like a fish tail.

Unlike fishes, whales must swim to the surface to breathe. They take in air through a *blowhole*, or two slits, on top of the head. Baby whales are born in water. As soon as they are born they swim up to take a breath.

There are two groups of whales. Toothed whales like the DOLPHIN mostly catch fish. But killer whales are toothed whales that attack seals, penguins and other whales.

Baleen whales are the other main group of whales. Baleen whales include the blue whale, the largest mammal that has ever lived. Each baleen whale catches tiny shrimplike creatures with a special sieve. This is made of a horny substance called baleen or whalebone. When the whale opens its mouth, long baleen plates hang from its upper jaw like the teeth of a giant comb. Hunting by man has made the biggest whales very scarce.

Killer whale
12 metres (40 feet)

Above: The sperm whale is the largest toothed whale. It can measure 20 metres (65 feet) and weigh over 40 tonnes.

*Left: Beluga or white whales are toothed whales twice as long as a man. They are born grey, but turn white as they grow older.
Top left: Packs of killer whales will attack and kill the biggest whales.*

WHEAT

Wheat is a valuable food crop. Grains of wheat are seeds produced by a certain kind of grass. Mills grind the seeds into flour for making bread, breakfast cereals, cakes, pies, noodles and spaghetti. Such foods are good for us because each grain of wheat is mostly made of energy-giving STARCHES. It also contains plenty of body-building PROTEIN, as well as FATS, MINERALS and bran.

Wheat grows best in dry, mild climates. Farmers sow the seed in winter or spring. They harvest it when the grain is dry and hard. Most wheat comes from Russia, the United States, China and India. The world grows more wheat than any other kind of grain.

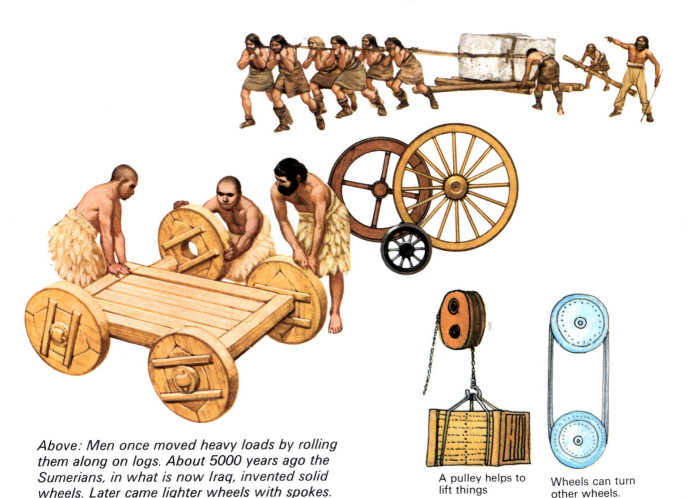

Above: Men once moved heavy loads by rolling them along on logs. About 5000 years ago the Sumerians, in what is now Iraq, invented solid wheels. Later came lighter wheels with spokes.

A pulley helps to lift things

Wheels can turn other wheels.

WHEELS

Wheels are one of man's most useful inventions. This is because a wheel turning on an axle is a very good way to move loads. It is easier to move a heavy load with wheels than it is to lift the load or drag it on the ground.

STONE AGE people may have learnt to roll loads along on logs. But Bronze Age people first invented the wheel about 5000 years ago. The oldest known wheels looked like slices cut across a log. But each solid disc was made of three parts.

Later, people learnt that a wheel with spokes was just as strong as a solid wheel, but much lighter. Today the wheels of cars and planes have hollow rubber tyres filled with air to make them springy.

Ball bearings keep wheel hubs turning easily on their axles. Wheels with notched edges turn one another in the gears that help to work all kinds of machinery.

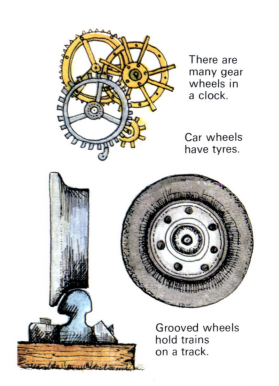

There are many gear wheels in a clock.

Car wheels have tyres.

Grooved wheels hold trains on a track.

WIGWAMS AND TEPEES

Wigwams were huts built by AMERICAN INDIANS living in wooded countryside in eastern North America. Some wigwams were shaped like an upside-down bowl. Others had upright sides and a sloping roof like that of a house. They were built of a framework of poles, covered with bark or mats made of reeds.

Many people think that tents, like the one shown on the left, are called wigwams. But these tents with round floors and pointed tops are tepees. Tepees were made by American Indians who lived on the grassy plains. They arranged poles into a cone. Then they stretched buffalo hide over the poles. Smoke from the fire inside escaped from a hole at the top. The plains Indians were nomads, who moved from place to place following the herds of buffalo. Their tepees could be easily taken down and carried with them.

WILLIAM THE CONQUEROR

William the Conqueror (1027–1087) was William I of England, and England's first Norman king. Before that he was Duke of Normandy in northern France. (Normandy was named after the Normans or Northmen, also called VIKINGS).

When William visited England in 1050, his relative EDWARD the Confessor may have promised him the throne of England. In 1064 William forced Edward's brother-in-law HAROLD to agree to help to make William king. But when Edward died in 1066, Harold had himself crowned as the next king of England.

William quickly set about invading England to seize it for himself. His Norman army sailed across the English Channel in open boats. There were about 7000 troops, including knights who brought their war horses. William defeated Harold's ANGLO-SAXON army at the Battle of HASTINGS, fought in Sussex near where the town of Battle stands today.

William spent three years winning all England. To do this he built many castles, from which his knights rode out to crush their Anglo-Saxon enemies.

By 1069 the Normans had conquered one-third of England, and William had become the most powerful king in western Europe. He claimed all the land as his, but he lent some to his Norman nobles. In return, the nobles supplied soldiers for William's army. William's descendants ruled England for many years.

WILLIAM II

William II (about 1056–1100) became king of England when his father WILLIAM THE CONQUEROR died in 1087. William II was called William Rufus because of his red complexion (Rufus means red).

William II was a very harsh and cruel king. He was hated by many of his subjects.

WILLIAM OF ORANGE

William of Orange (1650–1702) was a PROTESTANT ruler of the Netherlands, who became King William III of England, Scotland and Ireland.

In 1677 he married his Protestant cousin Mary. In 1688 the English invited William and Mary to rule them in place of Mary's unpopular father, the Catholic James II. James fled when William landed with his army. No-one died in this so-called 'Glorious Revolution', and William defeated James in Ireland in 1690.

William III ruled from 1689 to 1701, but Mary died in 1694. Since their time all British rulers have been Protestant Christians.

WIND

Wind is moving air. Slow winds are gentle breezes. Fast winds are gales. You can see the speed of the wind by its effect on trees and buildings.

Wind blows because some air masses become warmer than others. In warm air, the tiny particles of air spread out. So a mass of warm air is lighter than a mass of cold air that fills the same amount of space. Because warm air is light it rises. As warm air rises, cool air flows in to take its place. This causes the steady trade winds that blow over tropical oceans. CLIMATE and WEATHER largely depend on the wind.

A scale of wind speeds was worked out in 1805 by Admiral Sir Francis Beaufort. It is called the Beaufort Scale. In it the force of the wind is shown by numbers from 0 to 12. The number 0 shows that there is a calm in which smoke rises straight up. At 1 smoke drifts slowly. By the time we get to 4 we have a breeze in which small branches are moving and flags flap. At force 7 whole trees are moving and it is difficult to walk against the wind. Force 12 is something few of us will ever see. It is a full hurricane, with terrible damage to ships at sea and houses on land.

Below: A map of the Earth's main winds. They are set off by the Sun's heat, which warms some parts of the Earth more than others. Most winds are named after the place or direction from which they blow.

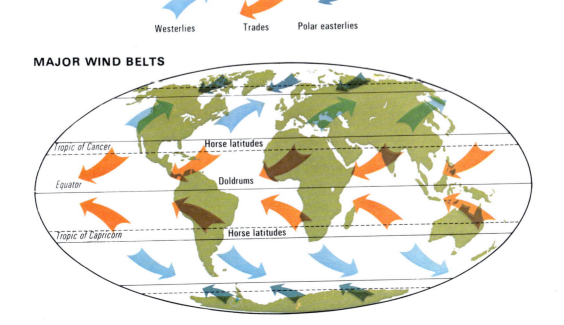

Westerlies   Trades   Polar easterlies

MAJOR WIND BELTS

Tropic of Cancer
Horse latitudes
Equator
Doldrums
Tropic of Capricorn
Horse latitudes

WINE

Wine is a drink made from plant juice, containing alcohol produced by fermentation.

Most wine is made from grapes. But you can make wine from other fruits as well. First the fruit is crushed. Then the juice is fermented in containers called vats. The wine is stored in casks until it is ready to drink. Sweet wines are rich in sugar. In dry wines most sugar has become alcohol.

WOLVES

These CARNIVORES include the red wolf of South America, and the grey wolf of the world's northern forests. Grey wolves have thick fur, long legs, and powerful jaws. A pack of wolves can chase and kill a sick or injured deer much larger than themselves. When grey wolves are hunting, they howl to signal to each other where they are. Each spring a she-wolf has four to six pups.

WOOD

Wood is one of the most valuable materials that people use. It can be sawed, carved and worked into almost any shape.

Thick timber is used for buildings and ships, while roughly cut logs and boughs are used as fuel for fires. Planks are made into furniture, barrels and boxes. Seasoned pieces can be shaped into musical instruments and delicate ornaments. Wood is important for houses. Most house frames are wooden, and doors, floors, stairs and wallpaper are generally made from wood too.

The wood we use is the tough inner material of trees and shrubs. It is protected by a thin layer of BARK. It is very strong, and can support many times its own weight. The wood of a tree is made up of thick fibres that give it strength, and tubes that carry food and water from the roots to all parts of the tree.

Softwood, from pines and firs, is used mostly as pulp to make paper. Hardwood, from broadleaf trees, is used to make furniture and for building.

Below: Grey wolves may hunt on open ground outside the forests. They eat any bird or mammal they can kill.

WOODPECKERS

There are about 200 kinds of woodpecker. They are found in many parts of the world, but most live in America and Asia.

Woodpeckers have sharp, powerful bills with which they drill holes through the bark of trees. They reach in with their long tongues to fish out the insects that live there.

Most woodpeckers have bright colours and markings, especially on their heads.

Above: The recorder is one of the easiest woodwind instruments to play.

WOODWIND

Woodwinds are a family of MUSICAL INSTRUMENTS, played by blowing through a mouthpiece and into a hollow tube. Different notes are made by opening and closing holes in the instrument. Recorders, flutes, oboes, clarinets, horns and bassoons are all woodwind instruments.

WOOL

Wool comes from the fleece of SHEEP. It is a very long and thick kind of hair and can easily be turned into yarn. The yarn may be woven into blankets, carpets and clothing, or it can be knitted. Woollen cloth is heavy and warm.

Wool has been spun and woven since STONE AGE times. Modern wool, however, comes from specially bred sheep that have good, fine wool. The best wool comes from Merino sheep. Most wool is produced in Australia, New Zealand, Argentina and America.

The spinning wheel was used to draw out the wool and twist it into yarn. This wheel had a foot treadle to make it turn.

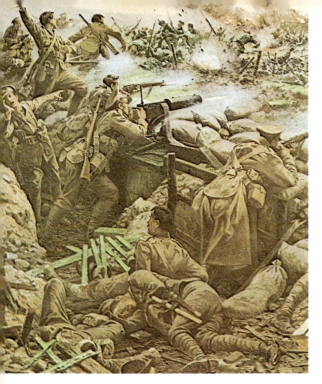

WORLD WAR I

Between 1914 and 1918 Europe, America and much of the Middle East were locked in the first struggle that could rightly be called a world war. On one side were Germany, Austria-Hungary and Turkey and on the other were France, the British Empire, America and Russia.

The battle soon became a stalemate in the west. The two great armies spent four long years in trenches in northern France fighting over the same bloody patch of ground. In the east, however, Germany had better luck. She attacked Russia so strongly that by 1917 Russia withdrew from the war.

After America joined the war in 1917, the Allied armies slowly pushed the Germans back. In November 1918 peace was declared.

Above: A scene of bitter fighting at Ypres in 1915. German soldiers are being mown down during an attack on Canadian troops. Below: Some of the weapons first used in World War I.

Italian Cerrano 75 mm Auto Cannone

Barbed wire

German mask and helmet

British Mk IV Male 2324 tank

French version of Hotchkiss 8 mm machine gun

French Renault ambulance

Above: Germany used blitzkrieg *tactics to smash through enemy lines with dive bombers, tanks and heavy armour. Trucks and infantry then poured through the hole. Right: In the weeks after D-Day on June 6, 1944, the Allies poured hundreds of thousands of men into France.*

WORLD WAR II

With the invasion of Poland in the autumn of 1939, Germany, Italy and then Japan entered into a six-year war with most of the major nations of Europe, Asia, Africa and America. The battles raged from the Pacific Ocean, China and Southeast Asia to Africa, Europe and the North Atlantic.

Germany's early attacks were hugely successful. Her armies swept through Europe and on into Russia and north Africa. However, the tide turned after 1941 with the entry of America into the war. By June 1944, Allied forces had landed in France and by May the next year Germany surrendered.

In the east, Japan's armies rolled through China, Malaya and Indonesia and captured many Pacific islands. In the end, Japan fell too, but not until two atomic bombs had been dropped on her cities by the Americans.

WORMS

There are hundreds of different animals with soft flat bodies that are commonly called worms. Some are very simple creatures, such as roundworms or flatworms. Others, such as earthworms, leeches and the larva of some INSECTS, are more complicated animals. Their bodies are divided into several segments.

Most of the simple worms are small. They usually live as parasites inside the bodies of animals or plants. Liver flukes and tapeworms are two such creatures.

Above: Earthworms 'eat' their way through earth. They feed on tiny bits of plants found in the soil. The rest passes through them and comes out as small coils called casts.

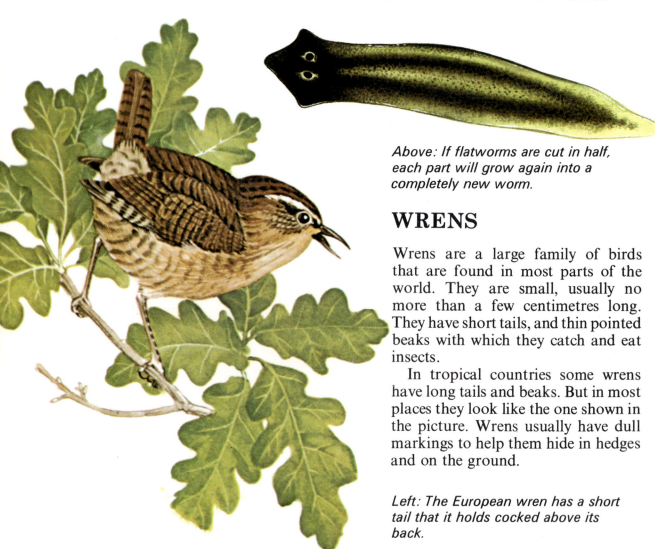

Above: If flatworms are cut in half, each part will grow again into a completely new worm.

WRENS

Wrens are a large family of birds that are found in most parts of the world. They are small, usually no more than a few centimetres long. They have short tails, and thin pointed beaks with which they catch and eat insects.

In tropical countries some wrens have long tails and beaks. But in most places they look like the one shown in the picture. Wrens usually have dull markings to help them hide in hedges and on the ground.

Left: The European wren has a short tail that it holds cocked above its back.

WRIGHT BROTHERS

Wilbur and Orville Wright were two American bicycle engineers who built and flew the first AIRCRAFT. Their successful machine was made after years of studying small models.

The first actual flight took place at Kitty Hawk in North Carolina, in December 1903. Their simple petrol-engined craft flew for 59 seconds. Five years later, they flew an improved model for 75 minutes.

Above: Orville Wright was the first man ever to pilot a heavier-than-air machine on a controlled flight.

WRITING

The earliest forms of writing were just simple picture messages, or notches on sticks that were used for counting. Gradually, pictures that were used time and again became simplified until they were just symbols. These symbols meant certain objects, like 'man' or 'house'. Egyptian HIEROGLYPHICS were used in this way.

In time, the symbols came to stand for sounds. These sounds could be written together to make up words. Later still, ALPHABETS of these sounds came into being. But VOWELS did not appear until the times of the ancient Greeks and Romans. Their alphabets were much the same as the one we use today.

Left: The clay tablet (top) is from the Middle East. It is Sumerian and about 5000 years old. The writing on it still looks like pictures. The other tablets (below) are in a style called cuneiform. Here the symbols no longer look like pictures. They stand for sounds instead.

X-RAYS

X-rays are waves of energy like RADIO or LIGHT waves. They can pass through or into most living things. They are also able to leave an image on a photographic plate, making a picture of the body or thing they have passed through. Doctors can use them to take 'photographs' of the insides of people. This helps them to find out if the person has anything wrong with them.

Wilhelm Röntgen, a German scientist, discovered X-rays by accident in 1895, while he was passing electricity through a gas.

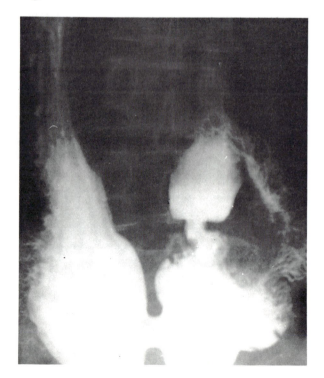

XEROGRAPHY

This is a way of copying writing or printing by using a machine called a *photocopier*.

The page to be copied is laid face down on a glass panel on the machine. Whatever is on the page is focused through a moving LENS onto an electrically charged metal plate, coated with black powder. When a clean sheet of paper, also electrically charged, passes over the plate, the powder clings to it, making an exact copy of the original. When the paper is heated, the powder 'sets' so that the copy is permanent.

Above: Xylophones are played with two wooden mallets with curved ball-shaped heads.

XYLOPHONE

The xylophone is an odd-looking MUSICAL INSTRUMENT that produces a crisp, bell-like sound when played.

A xylophone has rows of solid wooden or metal bars fixed to a frame. Each bar is a different length and produces a different sound when struck. An electric version of the xylophone, called a *vibraphone*, is sometimes used.

Left: An X-ray photograph of a person's stomach.

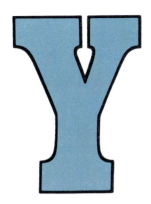

YAK

The yak is a large, shaggy kind of ox with a set of long, thick horns. Yaks live in Tibet, China and northern Asia. Wild yaks may be as tall as a man, but tame yaks are about the size of a European cow.

In spite of their size, yaks are very sure-footed and are used as pack animals. They also provide meat, milk and wool.

YANGTZE

The Yangtze is the longest, most important river in CHINA. From its beginnings, high in the mountains of Tibet, it flows 5470 km (3400 miles) across the centre of China, pouring into the Yellow Sea near Shanghai.

The river takes its name from the ancient kingdom of the Yang, which grew up along its banks 3000 years ago. Today, the Yangtze is still one of the main trade routes in China. Big ships can sail up it as

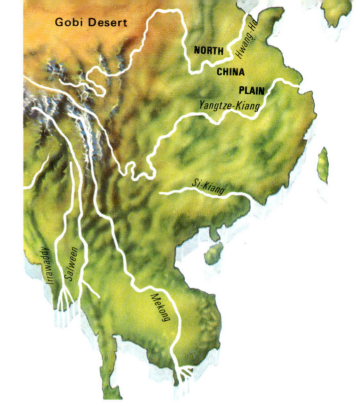

Above: The Yangtze and the Hwang-Ho are the two great rivers that cross China.

far as Hankow, nearly 1125 km (700 miles) inland. Smaller boats can reach as far as I'Chang, which is 1600 km (1000 miles) from the sea.

Millions of people live and work on the Yangtze. Some live on the river itself in wooden sailing boats called *junks*.

YEAR

A year is the amount of time it takes for the Earth to travel once around the SUN. It takes $365\frac{1}{4}$ days. A CALENDAR year is only 365 days long. Every four years, the extra quarter days are lumped together to make a 'leap' year of 366 days.

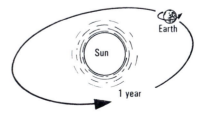

Above: The Earth takes one year to spin around the Sun in a huge circle.

YEAST

Yeast is a kind of FUNGUS. It is very useful to man because it turns sugar into alcohol and carbon dioxide gas. This process is called *fermentation*. Today, yeast is grown in huge vats. It is then pressed into cakes or small pellets, ready to be sold.

There are over 150 different kinds of yeast. The most important are brewer's yeast and baker's yeast, which are used to make beer and bread.

In wine and beer-making, yeast turns the sugar in grapes or malted barley into alcohol, while most of the gas bubbles away. In bread-making, the carbon dioxide gas forms bubbles, which makes the bread dough rise.

Above: A frothy scum covers the tops of huge vats of fermenting beer in a brewery. The froth is caused by the action of the yeast on the malt in the liquid.

YIDDISH

Yiddish is a language of the JEWS. It was first spoken in the Middle Ages. It was used as an everyday language by Jewish people all over central Europe. Yiddish is an amazing mixture of German, Hebrew, Polish and Russian, with a few French and Italian words thrown in for good measure.

At first, Yiddish was only a spoken language. Then in 1593, a Yiddish dictionary was printed in Cracow, Poland. From then on, Yiddish quickly became a written language as well. In Israel, modern Hebrew is the national language.

YOGA

Yoga is a very important part of the religion of the HINDUS. Yoga is an ancient word that means 'union'. People who follow yoga believe that their soul can be united with a World Soul. To get ready for this meeting they must train their bodies and their minds. They do special exercises to get their bodies fit. They also do 'mind' exercises, called *meditation*.

Yoga body exercises are very popular with people who are not especially interested in the religious side of yoga. The exercises help to keep you fit.

YUGOSLAVIA

Yugoslavia is a country in south-east EUROPE. Most of it lies in the BALKANS. It is a rugged, mountainous country. In the west, the mountains sweep down to the Adriatic Sea. Inland, the country is mostly scrubby and poor. Around the river Danube in the north, the land is fertile. Most of the country's farming goes on around here. Farmers grow wheat, barley, plums, olives and grapes, and keep a lot of cattle.

Yugoslavia's 22 million people come from different nations and speak many different languages. Most of them are Serbs, but there are also Croats, Slovenes and Macedonians. They also follow different religions. Some are Roman Catholic, some are Moslem and some belong to the Greek Orthodox Church. The capital city is Belgrade.

ZAIRE

Zaire is a huge country that sprawls across the heart of AFRICA. It includes most of the vast Zaire river. The Zaire, once called the Congo, flows 4320 km (2700 miles) from its source to the Atlantic Ocean.

Zaire is a hot, rainy country. Much of it is covered in thick jungle. There are lakes and highlands in the east and south. Copper, cobalt and diamonds are mined here. These minerals make Zaire a wealthy country. But most of the people are farmers. They grow tea, coffee, cocoa and cotton.

Nearly 30 million people live in Zaire. The capital is Kinshasa. Zaire once belonged to Belgium. It became the Republic of Zaire in 1971.

ZAMBIA

Zambia is a country in southern AFRICA. It is entirely surrounded by land. Zaire, Tanzania, Malawi, Mozambique, Botswana, Zimbabwe (Rhodesia) and Angola all share borders with Zambia. The capital is Lusaka.

The name Zambia comes from the Zambezi river. This runs across the western end of the country, and along the border with Zimbabwe.

Much of the country is rolling, highland plains. Most Zambians are poor farmers. Nearly all of the country's wealth comes from its copper mines. Almost a quarter of the world's copper is mined here.

Zebras share a waterhole with a herd of eland in the dry grasslands of Africa.

ZEBRA

Zebras belong to the horse family. They live in the open grasslands of Africa to the south of the Sahara Desert. Zebras have creamy white coats covered with black or dark brown stripes. Each animal has its own special pattern of stripes.

Zebras live in herds. They feed on grass and are often found roaming the grasslands with herds of antelope. Although zebras can run very fast, they are often hunted by lions, leopards and hyenas. People also used to hunt them for their attractive skins and tasty meat.

Most Zambians live in small villages like this one. They earn their living farming on small plots of land.

ZIMBABWE

Zimbabwe is a ruined city in southern Africa. The name Zimbabwe comes from an African word meaning 'home of a chief' and it is possible that the city was once the capital of a great African empire.

Explorers first found the ruins in 1868, but archaeologists did not begin to dig there until the 1940s. They discovered temples, towers and massive walls all built of huge stone slabs mostly fitted together without mortar. The most spectacular ruin is the Elliptical Building. It has curving walls over 250 metres (275 yards) long and as high as a house. A long eerie passage separates these outer walls from similar inner walls. Inside the building stands a tall, tapering tower.

Finds at Zimbabwe show that people were living there 1700 years ago. They were probably farmers. But it seems that the city was later abandoned. People returned to live in Zimbabwe about AD 1000 and the oldest stone ruins date from this time. From then, until the early 1800s, Zimbabwe appears to have been a busy city and was perhaps the centre of an important gold trade. Nobody yet knows how and why the city of Zimbabwe came to an end.

Below: The ruined walls and towers of Zimbabwe. Many of the ruins have been damaged by treasure hunters. But so far, no treasure has been found.

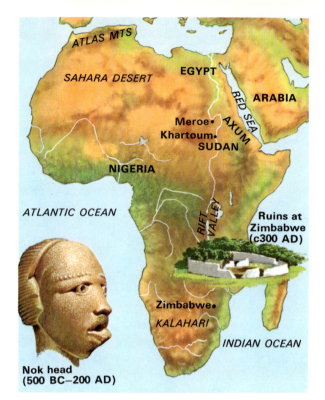

Zimbabwe was probably the home of a great African civilization. Another ancient civilization, the Nok, lived in Nigeria.

ZIMBABWE (COUNTRY)

Zimbabwe used to be called Rhodesia. It is a small country in southern AFRICA, and lies inland, about 240 km (150 miles) from the Indian Ocean. Only 7,800,000 people live in the country. About 97 out of every 100 are Black Africans; the others are mostly English-speaking Whites. The capital is Harare.

Zimbabwe is bordered by the Zambezi river in the north. The Zambezi is famous for the VICTORIA FALLS and the Kariba Dam. The Kariba Dam is a great hydro-electric scheme that supplies power to both Zimbabwe and its neighbour Zambia.

Until 1965, Zimbabwe-Rhodesia was a British colony. In that year, it declared itself independent. Britain, however, did not recognize the new nation's existence. During the next 15 years, growing unrest and guerrilla warfare finally forced Zimbabwe to turn to Britain again to help solve its troubles. In 1980 the country became independent.

ZINC

Zinc is a hard, blue-white metal ELEMENT. It has been mined since ancient times and has been used in making BRASS for over 2000 years. Brass is an alloy of zinc and copper.

A large share of the world's zinc comes from Canada, Australia and the Soviet Union. Zinc mines usually contain other metals such as copper, gold, lead and silver.

Most zinc is used to *galvanize* steel. Galvanizing is putting a thin coat of zinc on steel to protect it. Zinc is also used to make cells in electric BATTERIES. As well as brass, zinc forms part of many other alloys including nickel and bronze.

Right: Zinc-mining in Canada. The miner uses a powerful drill to cut into the rock.

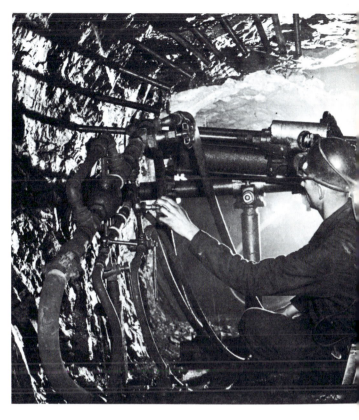

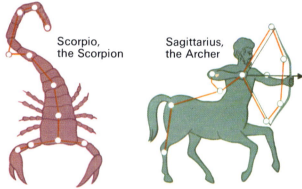

Scorpio, the Scorpion

Sagittarius, the Archer

ZODIAC

The Zodiac is the name given to the part of the sky in which the Sun, Moon and planets move. The first people to study the Zodiac, over 4000 years ago, were the astronomers of ancient Babylon. They divided it into 12 sections, with a group of stars in each section. The sections get their names, called *signs*, from the shapes of the star groups. The 12 signs of the Zodiac are Aries (Ram), Taurus (Bull), Gemini (Twins), Cancer (Crab), Leo (Lion), Virgo (Virgin), Libra (Scales), Scorpio (Scorpion), Sagittarius (Archer), Capricornus (Goat), Aquarius (Water-carrier) and Pisces (Fish). Each Zodiac sign is linked to part of the year. Pisces, for example, covers the period February 19 to March 20. Astrologers use the Zodiac signs to discover people's characters and foretell their futures.

Left: Each Zodiac sign has its own symbol. The ones shown here (top) are for Sagittarius and Scorpio. The astronomical clock shows the Zodiac signs.

393

ZOO

Zoos are places where wild animals are kept. They are cared for, bred, studied and sometimes saved from dying out. There are now more than 330 zoos in the world.

The first zoos were in ancient Egypt. Queen Hatshepsut kept a zoo in 1500 BC. More than 3000 years ago, the emperors of China kept animals, birds and fish in natural gardens where they would feel at home. In the Middle Ages in Europe, kings gave each other presents of apes, peacocks and lions. Private collections of animals were called *menageries*. Travelling menageries used to tour through the towns of Europe in the 1800s.

Since the 1700s, scientists have been interested in the study of animals. They began to sort animals into groups and give them Latin names so that the same animal would have the same name wherever it lived in the world. Their work led directly to the building of the first public zoos. These were first called zoological gardens, then shortened to zoo. The very first one was London Zoo, built in 1829. Today it is home to more than 1.100 different kinds of animal.

Above: Nowadays, instead of bars and cages, animals and visitors are kept apart by moats and walls.

Early zoos seem very cruel to us today. The animals were crammed into small cages. Modern zoos have natural settings for their animals. Moats, ditches and hedges separate the animals from the visitors, instead of iron bars. This means that the animals have room to walk about and can stay indoors or go out, according to the weather.

Zoos are also important for the care and breeding of rare or endangered kinds of animals. For instance, the Hawaiian goose and Père David's deer would not exist today if zoos had not saved them.

Left: Feeding times are always a popular sight to watch at zoos. Here, a flock of penguins are fed by hand by their keeper. Many animals grow so used to humans that they are not afraid to be handled by them.

INDEX

Page numbers in *italics* refer to pictures.

Subject Index

All the entries in the encyclopedia are divided up by subject in this index. The entries are in alphabetical order. Some entries appear in more than once place. The subject headings are: Animals, Art and Music, Astronomy and Space, Your Body, Countries, Our Earth, History, Machines, People and Government, Plants, Religions, Science, Sports, and Transport.

Animals

Aardvark
Albatross
Alligators
Amphibians
Anteaters
Antelopes
Ants
Apes
Armadillo
Baboon
Badgers
Bats
Bears
Beavers
Bees
Beetles
Birds
Brontosaurus
Butterflies
Camels
Carnivores
Cat
Caterpillars
Chimpanzee
Crabs
Crocodiles
Cuckoo
Deer
Dinosaurs
Dodo
Dogs
Dolphins
Dragonflies
Ducks
Eagles
Ecology
Eels
Egg
Elephants
Falcons
Finches
Fish
Fleas
Fly
Fossils
Fox
Frogs
Giraffe
Goose
Gorilla
Hibernation
Hippopotamus
Horse
Hummingbird
Iguana
Insects
Jackal
Jaguar
Jellyfish
Kangaroo
Kingfisher
Kiwi
Koala
Ladybird
Lizards

Llamas
Lobsters
Locusts
Mammals
Migration
Molluscs
Monkeys
Mosquitoes
Moths
Mouse
Nails and claws
Octopus
Opossum
Orang-utan
Ostrich
Otters
Owls
Oxen
Oysters
Peacock
Pelicans
Penguins
Pigeons and doves
Pigs
Prehistoric animals
Prehistoric man
Puffins
Pythons
Rabbits
Raccoons
Rats
Rattlesnakes
Reindeer
Reptiles
Rhinoceros
Salmon
Scorpions
Sea anemone
Sea horse
Sea lions
Seals
Sea urchins
Shark
Sheep
Shells and shellfish
Sloth
Snails
Snakes
Spiders
Squid
Squirrel
Starfish
Storks
Sturgeon
Swans
Tigers
Toads
Tortoise
Tropical fish
Tuna
Turkeys
Vertebrates
Vultures
Wagtail
Walrus
Wasps
Whales

Wolves
Woodpeckers
Worms
Wrens
Yak
Zebra

Art and Music

Architecture
Art
Ballet
Books
Building
Cartoons
Castles
Cinema
Crete
Dance
Furniture
Handel, George Frederic
Harp
Harpsichord
Houses
Ivory
Jazz
Leonardo da Vinci
Michelangelo
Mime
Mozart, Wolfgang Amadeus
Music
Musical instruments
Opera
Painting
Picasso, Pablo
Pottery
Sculpture
Seven Wonders of the World
Tapestry
Theatre
Violin
Weaving
Xylophone

Astronomy and Space

Astronomy
Comets
Earth, the
Eclipse
Galaxy
Jupiter
Mars
Mercury
Meteors
Milky Way
Moon
Orbit
Planets
Pluto
Radio astronomy
Rockets
Saturn
Solar system

Space exploration
Stars
Sun
Sunspots
Telescopes
Universe
Uranus
Venus

Your Body

Arm
Blood
Bones
Brain
Breathing
Cell
Digestion
Drugs
Ear
Eye
Fat
Fleming, Alexander
Germs
Hair
Hand
Harvey, William
Heart
Inoculation
Jenner, Edward
Kidneys
Lister, Joseph
Liver
Lungs
Milk
Muscles
Nerves
Nursing
Poison
Skeleton
Sleep and dreams
Smallpox
Smell
Stomach
Surgery
Taste
Teeth
Temperature
Tongue
Tonsils
Veins
Viruses
Vitamins
Voice
X-rays

Countries

Africa
Albania
America
Argentina
Australia
Austria
Belgium
Bolivia

Brazil
Bulgaria
Burma
Canada
China
Commonwealth
Congo
Cuba
Cyprus
Czechoslovakia
Denmark
Egypt
England
Finland
Flags
France
Germany
Ghana
Gibraltar
Great Britain
Greece
Holland
Hong Kong
Hungary
Iceland
India
Indonesia
Iran
Iraq
Ireland
Israel
Italy
Jamaica
Japan
Kenya
Korea
Libya
Malaysia
Malta
Mexico
Mongolia
Morocco
New Guinea
New Zealand
Nigeria
Norway
Pakistan
Palestine
Peru
Poland
Portugal
Romania
Russia
Scotland
South Africa
Spain
Sweden
Syria
Thailand
Tibet
Tunisia
Turkey
Uganda
Uruguay
Venezuela
Vietnam
Wales
West Indies
Yugoslavia
Zaire
Zambia
Zimbabwe

Our Earth

Air
Amazon, river
Antarctic

Arctic
Asia
Balkans
British Isles
Canals
Climate
Clouds
Coal
Continents
Continental shelf
Copper
Coral
Cyclones
Dams
Desert
Diamonds
Earth, the
Earthquake
Ecology
Elements
Equator
Europe
Everest
Explorers
Farming
Fertilizer
Fiord
Forest
Geography
Geology
Geysers
Glacier
Gold
Gravity
Great Lakes
Himalayas
Humidity
Ice Ages
Iron and steel
Island
Lakes
Latitude and longitude
Lead
Limestone
Mediterranean Sea
Metals
Minerals
Mining
Mountains
Niagara Falls
Nile, river
North America
North Sea
Oasis
Oceans
Oil
Oxygen
Pacific Ocean
Panama canal
Quarry
Radium
Rain
Rainbows
Rivers
Sahara
Salt
Seaweed
Silver
Snow
Stone Age
Suez canal
Thames, river
Tides
Tornado
Vesuvius
Volcanoes
Water
Weather
Wind
Wood

History

Alexander the Great
Alfred the Great
Archaeology
Armada
Boer War
Caesar, Julius
Castles
Cavemen
Celts
Charlemagne
Charles I
Charles II
Churchill, Winston
Civil War
Civil War, American
Columbus, Christopher
Cook, James
Cortés, Hernando
Crete
Crimean War
Cromwell, Oliver
Crusades
Drake, Francis
Edward (kings)
Egypt
Elizabeth I
Elizabeth II
Fawkes, Guy
French Revolution
Gama, Vasco da
Genghis Khan
George (kings)
Hannibal
Harold, King
Hastings, battle of
Helen of Troy
Henry (kings)
History
Hitler, Adolph
Industrial Revolution
Ivan the Terrible
James I
Joan of Arc
Lenin, Vladimir
Lincoln, Abraham
Marco Polo
Mary Queen of Scots
Mussolini, Benito
Napoleon Bonaparte
Nelson, Horatio
Pompeii
Prehistoric animals
Prehistoric man
Raleigh, Walter
Richard I
Roman Empire
Slavery
Stone Age
Stonehenge
Stuarts
Trojan War
Victoria, Queen
Wars of the Roses
Waterloo, battle of
Wellington, Duke of
William the Conqueror
William II
William of Orange
World War I
World War II
Zimbabwe

Machines

Abacus
Aircraft

Archimedes
Canals
Clocks
Computers
Diesel engines
Engineering
Ford, Henry
Helicopter
Hydrofoil
Internal combustion engine
Jet engines
Locomotives .
Machinery
Motor car
Pulley
Railways
Turbine
Typewriter
Xerography

People and Government

Aborigines
American Indians
Anglo-Saxons
Arabs
Aztecs
Bushmen
Celts
Communism
Democracy
Electrons
Eskimos
Gipsies
Houses of Parliament
Incas
Jews
Lapps
Maya
Nomads
Presidents of the United
    States
Prime Minister
Pygmies
Trade Unions
United Nations
Universities
Vikings
Wages
Writing

Plants

Bamboo
Banana
Bark
Bulb
Cabbage
Cactus
Cereals
Chestnut
Chlorophyll
Cocoa
Coconut
Conifers
Cotton
Elms
Figs
Fir trees
Flowers
Forest
Fossils
Fruit
Fungus
Grass
Herbs

Leaf
Lemons
Lichens
Mosses
Mushrooms and toadstools
Nuts
Oak trees
Olive
Oranges
Orchids
Palm trees
Pineapples
Pine trees
Plants
Pollen
Potatoes
Rice
Rubber tree
Seaweed
Seeds
Soya beans
Spices
Sugar
Tea
Tobacco
Trees
Vegetables
Weeds
Wheat

Religions

Abbey
Bethlehem
Bible
Buddha
Christianity
Churches

Crusades
Easter
Francis of Assisi
Islam
Jerusalem
Jesus
Koran
Mohammed
Mormons
Popes
Presbyterians
Protestants
Quakers
Roman Catholic Church
Saints
Vatican City
Yiddish

Science

Archimedes
Astronomy
Atomic energy
Atoms
Chemistry
Colour
Computers
Copernicus
Crystals
Curie, Marie and Pierre
Darwin, Charles
Echo
Edison, Thomas
Einstein, Albert
Electricity
Electronics
Energy
Faraday, Michael

Franklin, Benjamin
Friction
Fuse
Gravity
Gyroscope
Heat
Lasers
Light
Marconi, Guglielmo
Mendel, Gregor
Microscope
Newton, Isaac
Nuclear energy
Radio
Radioactivity
Radium
Recording
Rockets
Silicon chip
Solar energy
Sound
Telephone
Telescopes
Television
Transistors
Ultra-violet light
Uranium

Sports

Bicycle
Cricket
Discus
Diving
Football
Gymnastics
Horse
Javelin throw

Olympic Games
Rugby football
Swimming
Tennis
Tobogganing
Weightlifting

Transport

Aircraft
Balloons and airships
Blériot, Louis
Bridges
Canals
Clipper ships
Diesel engines
Ford, Henry
Galleon
Helicopter
Horse
Hovercraft
Hydrofoil
Internal combustion engine
Jet engines
Lindbergh, Charles
Locomotives
Motor car
Railways
Roads
Rockets
Ships
Stagecoach
Steam engines
Submarines
Tunnels
Underground railways
Wheels
Wright brothers